Richard Eyre

Richard Eyre worked for ten years in regional theatre in Leicester, Edinburgh and Nottingham (where he commissioned and directed Trevor Griffiths's *Comedians*, which later transferred to London and Broadway). In London his work includes his adaptations of Jennifer Dawson's novel *The Ha Ha*, Sartre's *Les Mains Sales* and Ibsen's *Hedda Gabler*; and *Hamlet, Edmond, The Shawl* and *Kafka's Dick* at the Royal Court. He was Artistic Director of the National Theatre from 1988 to 1997, directing twenty-seven productions including *Guys and Dolls, The Beggar's Opera, Hamlet, Racing Demon, Richard III, Night of the Iguana, Sweet Bird of Youth, Skylight, La Grande Magia, White Chameleon, The Prince's Play, John Gabriel Borkman, King Lear* and *The Invention of Love*. His theatre and opera work since includes *Amy's View, The Crucible* and *Mary Poppins* on Broadway, *La Traviata* at the Royal Opera House, *Le Nozze di Figaro* in Aix-en-Provence, *Vincent in Brixton, The Reporter* and *The Observer* at the National Theatre, and *The Last Cigarette* in Chichester and the West End. His film and television work includes *Comedians, Country, The Insurance Man, Tumbledown, Suddenly Last Summer, The Ploughman's Lunch, Iris, Stage Beauty, Notes on a Scandal, The Other Man* and *Changing Stages*, a six-part look at twentieth-century theatre which he wrote and presented for the BBC. He has published three books, including *National Service*, a journal of his time at the National Theatre, which won the Theatre Book Prize. He has received many awards for theatre, TV and film, and was knighted in 1997.

Richard Eyre

TALKING THEATRE

Interviews with Theatre People

NICK HERN BOOKS
London
www.nickhernbooks.co.uk

A Nick Hern Book

TALKING THEATRE

First published in Great Britain in 2009
by Nick Hern Books Limited
14 Larden Road, London W3 7ST
by arrangement with BBC Worldwide Limited

First paperback edition published in 2011

Cover designed by Peter Bennett

Typeset by Nick Hern Books, London
Printed and bound in Great Britain by
Ashford Colour Press, Gosport, Hampshire

A CIP catalogue record for this book
is available from the British Library

ISBN 978 1 84842 138 7

For Suze and Lucy

If a person were to try stripping the disguises from actors while they play a scene upon stage, showing to the audience their real looks and the faces they were born with, would not such a one spoil the whole play? And would not the spectators think he deserved to be driven out of the theatre with brickbats, as a drunken disturber? Now what else is the whole life of mortals but a sort of comedy, in which the various actors, disguised by various costumes and masks, walk on and play each one his part, until the manager waves them off the stage? Moreover, this manager frequently bids the same actor to go back in a different costume, so that he who has but lately played the king in scarlet now acts the flunkey in patched clothes. Thus all things are presented by shadows.

Erasmus, *The Praise of Folly*

I personally would like to bring a tortoise onto the stage, turn it into a racehorse, then into a hat, a song, a dragoon and a fountain of water. One can dare anything in the theatre and it is the place where one dares the least.

Eugène Ionesco, *Notes and Counter Notes*

From the start it has been the theatre's business to entertain people… it needs no other passport than fun.

Bertolt Brecht, *A Short Organum for the Theatre*

Contents

CONTENTS

Introduction

I started going to the theatre when I was eighteen, in the early sixties. The start of my theatregoing coincided with a period of extraordinary theatrical energy and invention. I saw the work of Joan Littlewood at Stratford East, the Royal Court in its most fertile years, the newly formed Royal Shakespeare Company under Peter Hall in Stratford, and the newly formed National Theatre under Laurence Olivier at the Old Vic; *Oh! What a Lovely War* and *The Wars of the Roses*; Scofield's Lear and Olivier's Othello; the young Maggie Smith, the young Albert Finney, the young Vanessa Redgrave, the young Judi Dench, the young Ian Holm, the young Ian McKellen, the even younger Michael Gambon; the older Richardson, Gielgud, Guinness, Ashcroft, even Edith Evans and Sybil Thorndike; the plays of Harold Pinter, John Osborne, Peter Shaffer, Arnold Wesker, Edward Bond, David Storey, Peter Nichols, Charles Wood and Tom Stoppard—with Kenneth Tynan presiding over it all as a mercurial judge and godfather.

What I liked about the theatre then and what I like about it now is its 'theatreness', the properties that make it distinct from any other medium—its use of time, of space, of light, of speech, of music, of movement, of storytelling. Theatre is intrinsically poetic, it thrives on metaphor—a room becomes a world and a group of characters becomes a whole society. It conscripts the imagination of the audience to transform the obvious unreality of costumed actors standing on a stage saying things they've said to each other many times into something that is both real and truthful. Theatre insists on the present tense—there's a sense of occasion and of being part of a community in any theatre performance. We go into a theatre as individuals and we emerge as an audience. Above all, theatre can never dissolve its reliance on the scale of the human figure and the sound of the human voice.

In 1997, shortly before I left the directorship of the National Theatre, I was asked by Andrea Miller (the producer) and Mark Thompson (then Controller of BBC 2) to write and present a six-part television series for the BBC and PBS on the history of twentieth-century British theatre. The series was christened *Changing Stages*. I knew little of how these sorts of programmes are put together but enough to know that my contribution couldn't be improvised—I needed to do deep research and hard thinking before I could speak with any authority on the subject. In short, I had to write the book of the series before the series existed. I knew that I couldn't do this job alone so I asked Nicholas Wright, who had been an indispensable associate director at the National Theatre during my directorship, if he would join me in writing the book during the year before filming started.

Making television programmes about the theatre is a virtuous folly. You'll never be able to describe a memorable moment in the theatre accurately, because the essential element of context—real time and real space—will never be there in the description. It's like putting ventriloquism on the radio. But perhaps because I came from a generation which happily listened week after week to a radio programme called *Educating Archie* in which a ventriloquist did sketches with an invisible dummy, I leant towards believing that the effort was worthwhile.

Changing Stages was broadcast as part of the BBC's 'Millennium Project' in 2000. The programmes were composed of archive footage, pieces to camera, documentary film and, most importantly, interviews with people who had played a significant part in making and influencing the theatre of the previous half-century in Britain, with occasional glimpses across the Irish Sea and the Atlantic beyond. If there were omissions it wasn't because there was a host of people who refused to be interviewed: almost all the people we asked agreed to talk to me on camera. The most notable refusal was from Marlon Brando, who sang down the phone from Los Angeles to the Glaswegian producer, Andrea Miller:

> *Just a wee deoch an doris, just a wee drop, that's all.*
> *Just a wee deoch an doris afore ye gang awa.*
> *There's a wee wifie waitin' in a wee but an ben.*
> *If you can say, 'It's a braw bricht moonlicht nicht',*
> *Then yer a'richt, ye ken.*

While he was enthusiastic to sing and discuss the work of Harry Lauder and the plight of the American Indian, he told her that he would rather do anything in the world than talk about acting.

The interviews in this book are a selection from the sixty or so that we recorded almost ten years ago. I can't claim that they give an encyclopaedic account of the British theatre at the end of the twentieth century, but they do give an authentic if partisan description of it. Reading these interviews is like looking through the wrong end of time's telescope, but the contours of the theatrical landscape that appear are still present today. Sadly many of the people who shaped the landscape are not: John Gielgud, Arthur Miller, Jason Robards, August Wilson, Percy Harris, Jocelyn Herbert, Frith Banbury, John Bury, John McGrath and Harold Pinter. It's a doleful roll call of great talents, some of whom were also friends of mine.

The interviews were filmed on theatre stages and in auditoriums, dressing rooms, homes and hotels. The questions that I put to the interviewees were related to the topics of the six programmes:

• *Shakespeare: the DNA of our theatre. Changing styles of production and acting throughout the century.*

• *Ireland: the dependence of the English theatre on Irish playwrights for nearly three centuries.*

• *America: the Broadway musical and the plays of Eugene O'Neill, Arthur Miller and Tennessee Williams. The American Dream and the American Nightmare— aspiration and desperation.*

• *1956: Before—Coward, Rattigan, Ackland, Lawrence, the repertory movement and censorship by the Lord Chamberlain. After—Look Back in Anger, the Royal Court and Joan Littlewood.*

• *Brecht and Beckett: godfathers to a post-war generation. Their influence on the writers, directors and designers of the sixties and seventies.*

• *The future of theatre: the challenge of mass entertainment in film and television and the reassertion of the properties of theatre.*

All the interviews have been—often radically—edited and distilled from the transcripts. I've tried to retain all of the meaning and most of the idiosyncrasies of the speakers while removing what Janet Malcolm once referred to as 'Tape-recordese—the bizarre syntax, the hesitations, the circumlocutions, the repetitions, the contradictions, the lacunae in almost every non-sentence we speak.'

In addition to the interviews with the theatre artists, I have added, in an Appendix, one interview which seemed anomalous in the main body of the book. It was with Lieutenant-Colonel John Johnston, who worked for the Lord Chamberlain and was the official censor of the nation's theatre until his role was abolished in 1967. Until then, censorship lowered like a grey cloud over the British theatre and its presence affected many of the people I interviewed. My own experience of the censor was limited to applying to the Lord Chamberlain in 1966 to stage the first performance outside a club theatre of John McGrath's *Events While Guarding the Bofors Gun*—a play about national servicemen on guard in West Germany during the Cold War. I received a letter from the Lord Chamberlain which read something like this:

The following words are to be eliminated from the text:
> *fuck*
> *bugger*
> *prick*
> *bugger*
> *bloody*
> *go for a piss*
> *bloody bastard*
> *the late King George VI…*

And so on.

The order in which these interviews are presented broadly follows the thematic sequence (Shakespeare, Ireland, America, and so on) of the questions I asked in each of them.

I am grateful to Nick Hern, who has helped me to discriminate between what is interesting to me and what is interesting to the general reader. Above all, though, I am grateful to all the people who generously gave up their time to be interviewed.

A friend of mine once rashly invited Paul Scofield to give a lecture on acting. He wrote this in response:

> *I have found that an actor's work has life and interest only in its execution. It seems to wither away in discussion, and become emptily theoretical and insubstantial. It has no rules (except perhaps audibility). With every play and every playwright the actor starts from scratch, as if he or she knows nothing and proceeds to learn afresh every time—growing with the relationships of the characters and the insights of the writer. When the play has finished its run he's empty until the next time. And it's the emptiness which is, I find, apparent in any discussion of theatre work.*

I hope this collection proves him wrong.

Richard Eyre
2009

Interviews

John Gielgud

1 9 0 4—2 0 0 0

Actor and director. John Gielgud performed all the major Shakespeare roles, and was instrumental in introducing Chekhov to English audiences. In later life he acted in plays by Alan Bennett, Charles Wood, David Storey and Harold Pinter. I interviewed him on the stage of the Theatre Royal, Haymarket, well before the start of filming the rest of the interviews—'in case I drop off the twig,' as he put it. He seemed then—the summer of 1998—to be eternal. He warned me that he was 'just an actor' who'd never had an idea in his head, which was typically self-deprecating. No one could have mistaken Gielgud for an intellectual, but although his conversation was showered with actorly anecdotes, it was impossible to discount his mercurial intelligence and his extraordinary recall of theatre history, even if life outside the theatre had passed him by.

When he died, there was a move by well-meaning friends to organise a gala and memorial service. He hated all such occasions and, modest to the last, his will expressly forbade staging one. If there had been a celebration of his life it should have taken the form of a mass gathering of actors vying with each other to tell anecdotes about him in his all-too-imitable voice. This—from Judi Dench—is a favourite of mine. She was in the canteen of the BBC rehearsal room at Acton with the cast of her sitcom. She waved to Gielgud, who was rehearsing for another show, to join their table. He came over and sat down. The group became silent, awed by his presence. The silence was broken by Gielgud: 'Has anyone had any obscene phone calls recently?'

1

What was the theatre like that you encountered as a child?

Well, it was very much a theatre of stars. Actor-managers were beginning to die out, but I looked for the big names on the marquee, so I got to know the theatre very well because I stood in the pit and gallery and went whenever I could; my parents were very long suffering. They both went to the theatre quite a lot, but they were never in the theatre, although my mother had strong links with all her Terry relations. I was fearfully lucky because from the very beginning I got my first jobs through personal introductions and so I never had to sort of stand in the queue to get work. I was earning seven or eight pounds a week from quite early times, and I got scholarships at two dramatic schools, so I didn't have to pay fees, I didn't cost my parents anything, and I lived at home. I really had a very easy time those first ten or twelve years, and I learned a bit of hard work.

What did you think of what you saw in the theatre in those days?

I didn't think then what acting really was like. I loved spectacle and I was immediately taken in by colour and groupings, and the childhood drama of the curtain going up and the lights going down, which would vanish from the scene in years to come. I think that it was spectacle and romance and love scenes and people waving capes and looking out over balconies and things that appealed to me so much.

And the stars.

Oh yes. I didn't see Forbes-Robertson as he'd already retired, but I saw Irene Vanbrugh, whom I admired very much, and her sister Violet. They were big stars. And there was Gerald du Maurier, who I saw in a good many plays: he was wonderful. But when I came to meet him I was very disappointed because he rather snubbed me. I think he felt that we were trying to destroy him.

He was regarded as something of a revolutionary in his day.

Well, he was terribly modern; he invented the throwaway technique, which Noël Coward, afterwards of course, developed tremendously.

So before that, people just plonked lines, did they? Was it a rather histrionic style?

It was. There was a great deal of romantic acting still going on.

When you say romantic, do you mean extravagant gestures?

Yes, and costumes and heavy make-up, and knowing how to take the stage, and entrances and exits, and big rounds of applause when the actors came on and when they went off. And very romantic lighting.

Would the star always be at the centre of the stage?

Pretty well. But I didn't feel that actors did anything technically clever. They said the lines, and I knew exactly the ones I admired and the ones I didn't admire.

And you admired them because they were natural?

Well, they seemed to hold your attention the moment they got on the stage, and they lived up to their reputations. But very often they were disappointing too.

What about Sarah Bernhardt and Eleanora Duse?

I saw Bernhardt when she was an old lady in the Coliseum. My father took me. I was terribly impressed by her vocal power, and the fact that she still looked quite young, although she had only one leg. I was impressed by that. And Duse also I saw, standing at the back of the circle. I didn't understand because it was in Italian, but her presence was tremendous. The public were worked up even before she made her entrance. And she knew to a T exactly how to hold a big house.

And did they act in an operatic style?

I don't think Duse did. She was very repressed, she wore no make-up and she was very quiet. But she had an extraordinary power.

Wilde thought that Duse was a great actress.

Yes and Bernard Shaw did too.

Were Wilde's plays performed then?

I saw a very bad revival of *The Importance [of Being Earnest]*. And I did see *An Ideal Husband*, but that was with Robert Donat right at the beginning of the Second War. I don't know whether there were any more revivals in between.

When you were growing up did you have any sense of Wilde as a great revolutionary?

Oh, I was mad about the fairy tales, and *Salomé* I read, of course, and thought it was very improper and exciting. And all the erotic side of the theatre was very much suppressed, of course, with the censor.

What was the social mix in the audience?

It was very much divided.

Upper-middle-class?

Very much. I mean, the stalls and dress circle were the middle-class and aristocratic public, and then there was the upper circle and the pit and gallery, which were the cheap parts, which hissed and booed or applauded on the first night and were very important for the commercial success. And there were enormous commercial successes: plays that ran a year. And things like *Chu Chin Chow* that ran three and four years.

Did you see Chu Chin Chow?

Yes, I never stopped seeing it.

The theatre at that time wasn't was all light comedy, was it? It was also the age of Ibsen and Shaw.

Yes. I was in great difficulty because all my life I've been so stupid and flippant. I never cared to think of what was going on in the world or in the two wars, which I in a way lived through. But I had such a childlike adoration of the theatre and of actors and actresses and the ones I met in my parents' house. My own relations were all very exciting to me and they lived this make-believe world. But when it came to Ibsen and Shaw I rather jibbed; I hadn't got the appetite for dialogue and I found them very talky. I never got over that. I never have got over it. I've never really liked plays that are entirely talk.

I think the unsung genius of twentieth-century British theatre is—

Barker.

—Granville Barker, yes. You knew him very well.

Well, I knew him—I have a whole bunch of wonderful letters he wrote me having seen various productions I did. The two times I worked for him he came for a few days only and then retreated into his Paris grandeur where he gave lectures and things. And his second wife who loathed the theatre: she would drag him away the moment he got very interested. The few hours he was on the stage with me I was so impressed by him, but I never got to know him intimately at all. When I did *Lear* at the Old Vic [which Barker helped direct, though it was never publicly announced] at the beginning of the war, the Second War, he never took me out to lunch; but he came once to my house, on the night that peace was declared, and was already not well and tired and dejected somehow. But he made an extraordinary impression on me. He seemed to know exactly what he wanted and how much to give and how much not to give.

What was he like?

He was like a surgeon.

Very reticent?

Very, and very, very terrified of getting involved again in anything to do with the theatre. But a number of actors who had been with him earlier—when he had a company and had three Shakespearean productions at the Savoy—said he was a sort of young genius and wore sandals and ate nuts.

But you didn't meet him until probably ten years later?

No, we did some Spanish plays which his wife had translated. She would pop in and drag him off to lunch the moment he started working. I thought the moment he stepped onto the stage he was an absolute genius to me; he was like a wonderful conductor of an orchestra; he knew exactly what not to bother with. When we did *Hamlet* just before the Second War he was in London and came to a rehearsal which I arranged specially for him to see. I went the next morning to the Ritz, where he was staying, and he kept Mrs Barker out of the room for about two hours while he gave me notes. I wrote and wrote and wrote and rushed off to rehearsal and put all the things in that he told me. He would say such cogent, simple things, you know: 'The King is a cat and you play him like a dog,' or words like that.

Is it apocryphal, the story that he told you after a run-through of Lear, *that you were an ash and what was required was an oak?*

He did. He did. He wrote me these wonderful letters about what I should do if I went into management during the war and whether I should join up or whether I shouldn't and all that. He was marvellously helpful. But this lady was always in the background egging him on, and she didn't want any talk about the theatre at all. When I tried to arrange a memorial service in London she forbade it, wouldn't allow any notice to be taken.

Were you aware of him as a writer?

No, I wasn't. I never saw *The Voysey Inheritance*. I saw *The Madras House* in a production he did himself at the Ambassadors, which was very good. I remember the first act, which has the whole family on the stage together, and the way he moved the people and the grouping and the placing on the stage were so marvellously good. I think Peter Brook has the same extraordinary quality: he knows where to put the actors. When I became a so-called stage director, I was always worrying how the groupings should be and where people should cross, and the blocking. It worried me always the night before, so I would make plans and plottings and use models and things.

Granville Barker is alleged to have written on an actor's dressing-room mirror: 'Be swift, be swift, be not poetical.' Do you think that's good advice?

Yes, I'm sure it is. I suffered so dreadfully for many years from being told I had a beautiful voice, so I imagined that I had and rather made use of it as much as I could. It wasn't until after I worked with Olivier, who was very scathing about my voice—very resentful that the public and the critics didn't like him better when he played Romeo—he thought I sang all my parts, and I'm sure he was quite right.

You and Olivier must have been fiercely competitive at that age.

I was by then just becoming a leading man; my name was bigger than his, and without knowing it—we were very friendly, always, we got on extremely well—I had a feeling that he rather thought I was showing off, which indeed I was.

Well, he probably was as well.

Yes, but his showing-off was always so dazzling. [*chuckles*] My showing off was more technical and was more soft and, oh... effeminate, I suppose.

I'm surprised you say that because I would have characterised it the other way round, that his showing-off always seemed to me to be ahead of his interest in playing the truth of a character.

Well, I think his great performances were mostly comedy. I was never so impressed by his Oedipus or the Othello, which were two of his greatest successes. But I was enormously impressed by *The Dance of Death* and by Hotspur and Shallow and Puff [in Sheridan's *The Critic*], and Richard III of course. And I loved working with him, the little that I did. But I always thought he went behind my back and directed the actors his way. When he played Malvolio for me at Stratford with Vivien [Leigh] as Viola, I was certain that he'd gone away and told her how he thought it ought to be played and that she was torn between the two characters trying to work with her.

Did you feel hurt when the National Theatre started and Olivier didn't bring you into the company initially—and then only asked you to do Oedipus *with Peter Brook?*

Yes, I was a bit hurt, but I always had so many other sorts of offers. I'm not, funnily enough, very jealous, I never have been. I had great ambitions but I was never jealous. And I was always surprised to find that some actors were very jealous.

When the new National Theatre started, Peter Hall took you into the company.

Yes, but he gave me a very flat year—Julius Caesar and that old part in *Volpone*—so I really had no fun at all. I hated the National Theatre building: I hated that feeling of being in a sort of airport. And the Royal Shakespeare Theatre's like a nursing home. [*laughs*]

Would you say the real father—or mother—of the National Theatre and the Royal Shakespeare Company is Lilian Baylis?

Well, I think she didn't know her arse from her elbow. She was an extraordinary old woman, really. And I never knew anybody who knew her really well. The books are quite good about her, but except for her eccentricities there's nothing about her professional appreciation of Shakespeare. She had this faith which led her to the people she needed.

Did she choose the actors?

I don't think so.

She chose the directors.

Yes, she had a very difficult time with them. There was Robert Atkins, who was a real tough old pub-drinking monster, that she put up with, but she was able to cross swords with somebody like him without being afraid. She had no fear, that was remarkable about her, I think.

And with Robert Atkins she did all thirty-seven plays of Shakespeare.

Yes, I think she did.

Which is something that no management would dare attempt in London now.

And she went through bombings, and the theatre being destroyed, and moving, and opening Sadler's Wells, the most adventurous things. Sadler's Wells was absolute hell—we hated it—but we all went because she was there, and we all obeyed her. But she never had a definite effect, and yet she must have had a sort of spiritual effect, I suppose.

You became an actor-manager with a season in '37/'38, when you did Richard II, The School for Scandal, Three Sisters *and* The Merchant of Venice.

That's right.

It's almost identical to a season that the National Theatre or the RSC might put on without any embarrassment, so in some way is it fair to see your company as the precursor?

Well, I suppose I had a sort of matinée-idol public.

But was it regarded as an adventurous repertoire?

It was considered rather daring, because we engaged the people for forty-three weeks or something like that, and we had a permanent company of about fifteen, twenty people.

7

Did you enjoy the business of being the management?

Oh, I did, yes very much. Because—

You were the director as well.

—particularly as I hadn't got to pay for it. And I had a nice flat and a great deal of attention paid to me. And I had a lot of friends in the company.

It's hard for us to believe that there was ever a time when Shakespeare wasn't very popular, in the same way it's hard to imagine there was a time when Mozart wasn't very popular.

It wasn't till John Barrymore came from America and did *Hamlet* with a complete English cast—except for two characters, I think—that suddenly it was box-office.

You talk often about how you love the frivolousness of theatre and the make-believe of it. It's true that that's partly what's attractive about it, but this century has seen a number of people constantly turning the frivolity of the theatre to seriousness. Whatever you say about yourself, you've made the theatre seem serious. And one of the ways you've done that is by your championship of Chekhov, most of whose plays you've performed in or directed. When did you first encounter Chekhov?

Well, I did *The Cherry Orchard* at Oxford, and we all thought it was very mad; we were told that at the first Stage Society performance a lot of people had walked out. We rehearsed a little longer than usual, more than two weeks, I think. We all thought it was going to be a terrific flop. And then the Oxford papers gave it good notices and some of the London critics came down and saw it, and we moved to the West End and ran all through the summer. We were so surprised because it was the first time Chekhov had ever been given for a run, I think.

Do you have any thoughts about why Chekhov has taken such an extraordinary hold on the English imagination?

Well, I think that people suddenly realised how very, very English or rather Irish, Russian writers are. And of course the books were so much more read in cheap editions: people began to read them much more. Everybody had to read *War and Peace*.

Chekhov is the *modern writer, in the sense that he cast the die for the shape of modern writing, but the other writer who's done a similar thing is Brecht.*

I never understood Brecht or Beckett, and I've never understood why everybody says that *Godot* was such a great play. The only one I ever thought I would like is *Happy Days*, which I've never seen, but I read it with great pleasure. I also heard on the radio a one-act play by Beckett about somebody catching a train, which I thought was wonderful [*All That Fall*]. They tried twice to persuade me to play *Endgame*, but I said I can't act without my eyes and I have to be [*chuckles*] blind on the stage and I couldn't do that.

Your first West End appearance was in The Vortex, *when you took over from Noël Coward. Did it seem to you a revolutionary play?*

Oh, it was considered very improper, and it was very much in the feeling of the bright young things: I went to night clubs and the Gargoyle Club and all that, and led a sort of semi-Francis Bacon existence for a short time. But I always had an enormous zest for everything to do with the theatre. And I was anxious to learn the new style of production.

Did it have the effect in its day that Look Back in Anger *had in 1956?*

Well, I suppose it did. I loved *Look Back in Anger*, and I remember Olivier suddenly going to see it a second time and being very impressed with it. I met Osborne, who was always rather nice for some obscure reason, and I always rather hoped to do something of his.

Was there a long period between The Vortex *and* Look Back in Anger *when theatre didn't seem very challenging?*

I don't know. I've worked all my life so hard, been so busy and so anxious to get on with the next play and try this play and that play, and a few films as well, and quite a lot of broadcasting… I was so occupied, and have always been until this last year or two. And I find it very odd not to be, not to have my diary full of engagements.

I'm sure you would if you could.

Well, I don't know. Now they won't insure me because I'm too old.

Did you feel that the Royal Court era—that whole volcanic eruption of talent—passed you by?

I did and I thought I was going to have to go to Hollywood and play sort of… as Cedric [Hardwicke] had so sadly done.

Play the Pharaoh?

Play old gentlemen and kings and things. I was fortunate not to have to do that. I always rather cocked a snook at the cinema.

You did the film of Julius Caesar *directed by Joe Mankiewicz, which I admire enormously. Do you regard that as a successful translation of Shakespeare to the screen?*

I think it's one of the best. I saw it again after many years. It isn't bad at all, except for the last part of the battle, which was done for tuppence in the last two to three days. But the main part of the film I enjoyed very much, and they were all very sweet to me. I got on excellently with Brando and with Mankiewicz, and the girls were very charming, and it was very exciting to be in Hollywood and see all the stars and I made quite a lot of money, and it was a new experience altogether.

Did you help Brando with his performance?

One day I did. He only had one scene in which I appeared with him. We worked on that one day, and he said: 'What did you think of my performance?' And I said: 'I don't want to discuss it.' And he said: 'Oh.' 'Let me think about it,' I said. The next week I wasn't working, and they came to me and said Brando had just done the speech over Caesar's body and 'It's so wonderful you must come and see the rushes.' So I went and saw them, and I didn't like what I saw at all, but I naturally didn't say so. But he then said, would I help him with the speeches in the scene we had together. And so I did. I didn't know he was really listening, but the next morning he'd put in all the things that I'd suggested to him immediately. He was bright as a button. But I would have loved to have worked with him over some of the rest of it. They were all so pleased with him, but naturally I didn't interfere. I didn't want them to think I was teaching them how to speak Shakespeare.

I've always liked the liveness of theatre, so I've never been keen on recorded versions of theatre performances.

When it's on tape or screen, it's depressing when one's old: you can't believe you did things so badly. But I'm sorry there aren't certain records of certain things. I'm sure there were some things I'm proud of having done. And there were certain parts I would like to have had immortalised. I wonder if I'd done a complete version of *Hamlet*... I didn't care for Olivier's *Hamlet* film at all. And the Orson Welles films were fascinating but never satisfactory.

I love your performance in Chimes at Midnight.

Welles was awfully interesting, and I loved working with him. He was a real theatre man. And impossible conditions, always in debt, always in trouble with women, always out of sync with everything. But he was wonderful company.

What saved you from playing pharaohs in Hollywood? Was it Oedipus *with Peter Brook at the National? It was a very daring production. How did Peter work with you?*

Well, we never knew what was going to happen. He wouldn't tell us what we were going to wear, the scenery was all done twice, and it cost a fortune. Larry was very angry because it was letting them in for huge expense. We rehearsed in this horrible sort of drill hall down in Waterloo Road. Brook brought records for us and made us do improvisations and we did Tai Chi every morning. It was a nightmare, like being in the army or something. But I trusted him and did whatever he told me.

A lot of actors have resented the rise of the director, and with ample justification probably, because there's always a reason for resenting the rise of a bad director. But you've always regarded it as a partnership.

Yes. Both the actors in the company and people I'm acting with. I mean, the only people I've ever had violent quarrels with are two or three actors who I worked with, who wouldn't play my game at all. I've said: 'I can't play this scene if you won't speak up,' and they just, you know, gabbled through the cues. I've found that coordination between actors and actresses is so important that if you don't find it it absolutely baffles you: you don't know where you are. And you never want to work with them again. Just three or four that I could mention because they let me down so much.

But do you think that comes from the actors not wanting to communicate with an audience?

I think a lot of actors think that it's rather cheap to deliver too definitely to the audience.

Alan Bennett's play Forty Years On *brought you back into working with young writers.*

And it also made me feel that I'd learned a lot in the war, to have played to the troops and, you know, gags and doing numbers and all sorts of strange things I'd never done, with a spot of Shakespeare now and again: that widened my scope very much.

And during the fifties you did a play of Tennessee Williams at a time when he wasn't established.

The Glass Menagerie.

What attracted you to Tennessee Williams's work?

I met him in America several times, and I met him at the time of *Streetcar*. I saw a rehearsal of *Streetcar* with the original cast, with Jessica Tandy and Marlon Brando. Kazan [the director] invited me to come to see a rehearsal with no costumes and a big cabin-trunk on the stage. I was always rather fascinated by Tennessee, but awfully put out by the fact that he was so drunken and tiresome, you know; after ten minutes you began to be bored with him, because he'd tell you the same story about the lobotomy of his sister and all this stuff.

But there was a vigour in his writing that wasn't in a lot of English writing at the same time.

Yes, but I thought it was so overwritten. I always longed for him to cut and pull together. He used all his mannerisms to such an extent it was like a terrible box of show-off fireworks.

And would he not cut?

I don't think so. I think he rewrote everything. Wrote it five times, you know, and wanted to rewrite the whole thing again. All his plays were done again and again with different backgrounds and different companies.

And were you interested in Arthur Miller's work?

I found him awfully sticky. I've never seen *The Crucible*. I did see *All My Sons*.

'Sticky' meaning melodramatic?

I found him awfully sort of stodgy.

Moralistic?

Like Shaw.

You don't like people who try and teach you.

No, I don't really, I don't. It just makes me feel very ignorant, which I am.

You worked with Harold Pinter and David Storey.

That was a miracle. I loved *Home*, which I almost turned down because I didn't think Bill Gaskill liked me. And it was Lindsay Anderson and David Storey himself who kind of… I was frightened of Lindsay.

Who wasn't?

I'd met him on two occasions, and he'd snubbed me terribly, so when I heard he was going to direct it, I thought he won't want me. But when we did *Home* and it came off so well, I was of course mad to do something else. Then came *No Man's Land*, which I read in forty minutes and just jumped on it.

What's always struck me about the way you speak Shakespeare is that you always let the meaning lead.

You've got to be awfully sure of your material. I've found a great deal of Shakespeare very hard to follow and very difficult to act. But if a part appealed to me pictorially then I immediately grabbed it and that was all. I've never lost my very childish attitude towards the theatre, which is so-called make-believe romance, or pretending to be somebody else and having people round me who were also in the same kind of dream world.

You had an instinct for Shakespeare even if you didn't fully understand him.

I think I always saw everything in theatrical terms—entrances and exits and applause, sensational groupings and colour and light. And I was always fascinated by all the attributes that made me want to be a director, because I wanted to govern the look of the thing, which mattered so much to me.

You seem to be able to play Shakespeare as fast as he thinks and very, very few actors can do this.

I never thought of it. I only know that when I played *Midsummer Night's Dream* again at the end of the war—I was tired and getting old and I played Oberon, which I'd played on my head at the Old Vic years before—that I was very bad, and by that time I was beginning to repeat a lot of tricks which at intervals I've always done. I've always tried to listen to people who said: 'Don't use your mannerisms and your kind of stage tricks and your long vowels and sensational climaxes and things: try to be real.' Edith Evans was the great example of sorting the sheep from the goats, so to speak. She would hold back on all emotion until she wanted to show it; then she would show it to you for a minute and then she would slam the shutters. She did it as Rosalind when she was fifty and she gave an extraordinary performance that I'll never forget. I admired her beyond words, although in many ways she was rather a limited sort of woman. Very encouraging but at the same time very strong, and rather lacking in the kind of—

Not very generous.

She was very good to act with but on the other hand I never felt very warm acting with her. I don't think she allowed you to.

At the age of twenty-five you did your first Old Vic season, and you played—am I right?—you played Romeo, Orlando, Mark Antony, Hamlet and Macbeth?

Yes, right.

In the same season.

We only had three weeks' rehearsal, and of course we only gave about nine or ten performances. We had the ballet one night and the opera had another night, so we didn't play every night, which was a help. But the company was not very first-rate.

And the second season you played a twenty-six-year-old Prospero, Antony, Richard II, Benedick and Lear—but not Hamlet.

Well, I suppose I'd had enough of Hamlet by that time. I'd played a complete version and a cut version, and we'd moved to the West End, and I'd quarrelled with old [Donald] Wolfit, who played the King and was very jealous and very stupid, and I didn't admire him at all, although I thought he had great power. He was rather a sore thumb in my company.

Because he belonged to a Victorian tradition.

He did the old thing of shaking the curtain before he would come on for his solo call and things like that. I didn't realise how much he resented me. I was of course rather conceited and vain and he probably had every right to resent me, but he did it rather unpleasantly. So he was rather a thorn in my flesh during the *Hamlet* times. But he was very good as the King.

That was the first Hamlet, but your 1934/5 Hamlet—that was the great Hamlet. It defined the part for the twentieth century, certainly until the early sixties.

Well, that was my own production, which was very daring. For many years I enjoyed directing just as much and was very proud of the few things that I thought I brought off as a director. But the critics never gave me much credit for directing, and I thought that was rather a compliment in a way, because the direction wasn't too apparent.

Wasn't too obtrusive?

I didn't think it was. On the other hand, it wasn't very creative. In some ways I think I was better in America. I did it in New York in '36 and worked with an almost entirely American company, only two English actors besides myself in the cast. It was such a challenge that I really enjoyed it enormously, although I stayed up too late at nights and got frightfully tired and all that. And then I came back to England and had rather a bad time for about ten years, I think.

You were a powerful reason for getting me interested in the theatre. I think I must have been thirteen when I heard you on the Third Programme doing Prospero. I must've read a Shakespeare play and I couldn't make head or tail of it, but you made me understand it perfectly. I wondered if you could retrieve my childhood for me by doing Prospero's last speech.

Which one?

'This rough magic I here abjure…'

[*pause*]

No, I don't think I can do it.

No?

[*pause*]

I'm terrified now that if I tried to act a part I would dry up immediately. I began to make mistakes and dry up in the last play I did and it terrified me and since then if I pick up Shakespeare and try and do a speech even from *Hamlet*, I find I make mistakes and miss words and miss phrases. And I tried to do a Prospero speech in a pulpit in a small church at some do two or three years ago and dried up in the middle and I was so horrified. And I suppose that kind of memory does leave you.

[*pause*]

—It's very alarming.

Peter Brook

1 9 2 5—

Director. Peter Brook's productions include Measure for Measure, Titus
Andronicus, King Lear, the Marat/Sade, A Midsummer Night's Dream,
Oedipus, The Ik, The Mahabharata *and* The Man Who. *I interviewed him
in January 2000 in Paris at his own theatre, the Bouffes du Nord. It's the most
congenial theatre I know: perfect acoustics, a sense of the past, like worn stone steps
in a church, layer on layer of human presence, a touch of oriental in the tracery above
the proscenium, beautifully distressed walls, plasterwork like medieval frescoes. Peter
Brook has stimulated British theatre for fifty years—first, in his twenties, in the
West End, then with the Royal Shakespeare Company, and for the last twenty-five
years from outside the country. He disclaims any desire to escape from the insularity
of British theatre, but his self-exile appears to have inoculated him against the
infection of self-doubt, the vagaries of fashion, the attrition of parochial sniping, the
weariness of careerism, and the mid-life crisis that affects most theatre directors (not
always in midlife), which comes from repetition, from constant barter and
compromise. But, he always stresses, nothing is achieved in the theatre that doesn't
come from the practical rather than the theoretical. He was wearing a tangerine
sweater with an indigo shirt, and, sitting in the circle of his theatre against the
terracotta walls, he glowed with well-being and undiminished enthusiasm. All his
sentences had a shape; he spoke with no hesitations—no 'ums', 'ers', or 'wells'—
by turns grave, impish and passionate.*

Is it our marvellous luck in the English theatre to have had Shakespeare?

Oh, I'm sure. Absolutely sure. Although one sees that the plays are still powerful in other languages and are done all over the world, they can never be as powerful as they are in the English language. And because of this it's become part of the English nature and the English temperament. All theatres all over the world, all good theatres have their hero figures, their pivotal figures, and we're lucky in having the best.

What's his particular genius?

The genius is that everything comes together. He's not a product of Elizabethan times, but he was totally influenced by all that was around him. It was a time of enormous social change, intellectual change, artistic experiment—a period of such dynamic force that he was open to all the different levels of life. He was open to all that was going on in the streets, he was open to all the conflicting religious and political wars of the time, and spiritually he was deeply involved in the vast questions that were there for all mankind at a time when the dogmas, the Church dogmas, were exploding. When there was a spirit of inquiry. And all his plays, which is what makes them so remarkable, correspond to the ancient Indian definition of good theatre, which is that plays appeal simultaneously to the people who want entertainment, people who want excitement, people who want to understand psychology and social reality better, and people who really wish to open themselves to the metaphysical secrets of the universe. Now, that he can do that, not only within one play and within one scene but within one line, is what makes Shakespeare remarkable and corresponds to something hidden in the English character. Of course, foreign views of England are always stereotyped, but from the inside one knows that the cold English are the most emotional people. The English who scoff at anything that's in any way supernatural are in fact deeply inquiring poetically and philosophically, and are extraordinarily concerned about true ethics, about the truth, reality, and practicality of social structures. And the fact that Shakespeare contains all those questions makes him very English.

What you've said suggests that the English should be particularly drawn to theatre as a medium.

All the richness of the English inner life is something that so embarrasses the English that they can't give light of day in everyday social behaviour to either philosophy, poetry or metaphysical inquiry. So the theatre is the only area where the hidden Englishness can reveal itself respectably.

Yet for three hundred years the Irish dominated the English theatre.

You could almost say the English as a whole daren't let their inner richness appear in public, and do everything to hide this behind all sorts of facades, which have been heavily implemented by the whole class structure of England over hundreds of years. The Irish are the opposite. The Irish allow their deep natural poetry and imagination to come out, all the time. If you go into an English pub you may meet some enjoyable companions, but you're not going to hear any sudden bursts of lyricism in the conversation. It's hard to avoid them in Ireland. Anyone you meet there has at his disposal and on the tip of his tongue all the richness of his natural imagination. And that goes very naturally into Irish writing. Synge famously says that, to capture the extraordinary colourful dialogue that the theatre needs, you've only to lie on the floor in an attic and listen to what's being said in the room below. That is the reason that what is rather condescendingly called the 'gift of the gab' is part of the natural healthy exuberance and ebullience of their essentially tragic experience. I'd compare it to what I've seen in South Africa. Within a deeply tragic human experience, a people have maintained their capacity to survive joyfully in tragedy, and to turn even the worst experience into something that can be shared with humour, with joy and with vividness. Those are essential theatrical qualities.

What about the most celebrated Irish playwright of the twenieth century? When were you first aware of Beckett?

I was first aware of Beckett when I was sent a play called *Waiting for Godot*. I read it and thought: 'Oh, this is a charming, whimsical play, but I don't know that it's particularly interesting to anyone.' A few weeks later a very young director called Peter Hall did a production. I went to see it and said: 'My God, this is something much more remarkable than I thought when I read it.' And then quite soon I got to know Beckett and was enormously taken by him as a friend, and by the fact that he wasn't at all this austere pessimist that the world thought he was, but was an engaging and fascinating and delightful human being, who loved all aspects of life and living. I proposed to him that we do a workshop in which we'd try to evolve a play together. He was very excited by the idea until it became real the following year, and then he invented an illness. It was a pure invention to get out of it, because the idea of actually sitting there and writing in front of other people sounded good but was so against his secretive nature that in a way it was impossible. The great Beckett experience for me was seeing Beckett performed by Irish actors: I saw Pat Magee and Jack MacGowran playing *Endgame* at the Aldwych. This was Beckett as I've never seen it done again anywhere. Although one can do Beckett in many ways, to me the essential Beckett is when he's played by the Irish.

Why doesn't one feel depressed when one sees Beckett's plays?

Well, it's very simple: it's the whole basis of Greek tragedy. The impression you have at the end of *King Lear* and when you see a play of Beckett is that you are brought uncompromisingly in front of the naked truth—and I say uncompromisingly, without that secret pleasure which can come from enjoying the fact that it's bad or rotten. You're beyond that feeling. You're there in front of the bones of an experience, the white bones of experience. Truth never pushes towards death, it reveals life, and life always emerges from a strong confrontation with truth. If you'd asked Beckett, 'Are you optimistic?' he would've hated it, and he would've said: 'Oh sure, I'm very pessimistic and I'm very nihilistic.' And in a sense, in the effort of conceiving and writing, which he couldn't help doing, he touched something deeply painful all the time in himself. I once said to him: 'Why do you write?' And he said: 'Well, I feel that like a snail, I want to leave my trace of slime as I leave this world.' But that is not true. You can't love and struggle all your life for perfection and actually be totally destructive, self-destructive and nihilistic, because with that attitude you genuinely abandon everything and commit suicide. But Beckett wasn't in that post-war existential despair, even though at first sight he seemed to be, because of the passion and love that he put into creating perfect works of art.

If Beckett wasn't a pessimist, was Brecht a wilful optimist?

Personally I believe that both attitudes, optimism and pessimism are completely false. There's only one attitude possible, which is realism, and that's much more difficult to maintain because you have to accept so many opposites. I think that Brecht was full of contradictions. Whatever you say about Brecht you can find the opposite. Any good thing you can say about Brecht, you'll find something bad; anything bad you say about him, you can compensate it with something good. 'Wilful optimist' is absolutely right. I don't think that he could have truly believed in simplifications such as that everything must be sacrificed, brutally, violently, ruthlessly, because there is this Communist dream-world just round the corner, and that we're just one revolution away. Just push down the last wall and there will be this marvellous utopia. I don't think he could have believed that. And yet again and again he closed his eyes to the things he knew about Stalinist Russia. Not only did he not disclose them, but he wilfully wrote poems of praise even though he was under no pressure to do so because he wasn't living under the threat of a Stalinist regime. Yes, he was an optimist for mysterious reasons because he wanted to be.

But did he do all that because he wanted his own theatre and a subsidy for it?

Oh yes, but from the start of his career he was playing ball with utopian ideas which he couldn't have believed in completely. He was a marvellous politician and manipulator and played his cards very well all his life. The way that he got out of his troubles with the Un-American Committee showed how well he could play his cards. And of course he wanted his theatre. He was very aware of the fact that he was a magnificent director; he didn't want to stay liked in America merely as a writer and a theorist. He knew that to do the directing that he wanted to do, he had to have all the elements. He had to have his actors, his theatre, in his own social surroundings. So of course he did everything, against great difficulty, to have this theatre, and, at the same time, he very shrewdly kept a certain distance so that he wasn't officially the person who could be attacked. But he was attacked and had great difficulty all the time.

What's his influence been as a director?

I saw the great, great productions. And what struck me was the absolute magnificence, I mean the rich magnificence, of his work on the stage. The use of scenery was quite simply of tremendous quality and beauty and imagination, as was his use of music, his use of stage craft, of revolving stages, of entrances and exits, of crowds. And above all the way his actors played—because there wasn't a single actor in his company who played 'Brechtian' in the sense of giving what he himself would describe as being just illustrations, caricatures. None of them worked in that way at all: they did everything he wanted and they filled it in with tremendous personal and rich inner life. And so the work was truly of an ensemble of unique richness with an absolute perfection of living stage craft. For me, Brecht was and still is much more fascinating as a great theatre director than as a playwright.

So was his theory simply thinking out loud?

I think that, with all theatre theory, it's a process of reaction against what's gone before. And that's very healthy. Perhaps the theatre, more than any other part of society, can very rapidly respond when yesterday's form goes out of date. Brecht came into a big, solid German bourgeois theatre. Very successful for a certain class of people. Deeply based on well-established nineteenth-century ideas. But Brecht said: this is dreadful, everything about this must be broken, the audience are treated in the wrong way, the values are wrong. So he swung to the opposite extreme. In terms of his work he got it absolutely right, but in his writing he simplified it. He wrote, for instance, about the need to break illusion. What he really meant was that we need to clear the stage of a lot of shit, get all the rubbish out and let something purer, simpler, appear. He said: let's get rid of dark, murky, atmospheric lighting and let's put bright light onto the stage. This is absolutely marvellous. But the reason for putting bright light on the stage is because an actor in a brilliant light is more alive and more expressive. But to say that you can take illusion out of the theatre is a deep naivety; it's like saying: let's pass a decree to take illusion out of life.

The creation of the Royal Shakespeare Company was something of a revolution. What was it like at Stratford before the RSC?

You know, with all love and respect for everyone in the RSC, it wasn't the RSC that was the revolution. The Shakespeare Memorial Theatre at Stratford had become old-fashioned, stereotyped, in the hands of a small number of very conventional people who did Shakespeare in the most boring way imaginable, really castrating the works or—no, that's even too vivid a metaphor—just letting the life drain out of the works so it was bad, uninteresting, provincial theatre which bored everybody and put them off Shakespeare for life. Then this marvellous old gentleman, Sir Barry Jackson, at the age of well over seventy, was asked to take the theatre over. I was with him that first day when he went from Birmingham [where he was running the Birmingham Repertory Theatre] to look round the theatre in Stratford. He looked round it and very quietly said: 'Everything here must be changed.' And in his first season he changed everything. Plays had been put on with hardly any rehearsal—the most famous Russian director Komisarjevsky did a *King Lear* there with five days' rehearsal; plays were revived with perhaps two days' rehearsal; all the new productions, seven or eight new productions, were done in the first week, and then they were just played mechanically for the rest of a very short season. Sir Barry said: 'Each of these great plays has to be properly rehearsed; it must have its own team, its own director, its own designer.' He decreed four full weeks of rehearsal, an enormous time for those days. There mustn't be one design pattern imposed for the whole season: each designer must be free to go his own way, and the season must go on much longer because of this. And we must bring back to Stratford actors from London who certainly wouldn't have dreamed of playing in that boring, old-fashioned festival. He did all that. He was an elderly gentleman, very reserved, very polite. In making a change he got the whole town against him. He got the governors largely against him. After two seasons with their ups and downs he was politely asked to go. And when the next generations came—first of all Anthony Quayle taking over from him, and then Peter Hall—the groundwork was done. Peter came with tremendous energy and vision. The first thing he said was: 'Well, we don't want this place to be a memorial so it won't be called a memorial theatre any more; it's the Royal Shakespeare Theatre.' Then he said: 'To get good actors, we must have much more work, we must have a theatre in London.' All those things came out of a preparation that had been done by Sir Barry Jackson. That was the big revolution.

For my generation The Wars of the Roses *and your production of* King Lear *were catalytic moments. In particular your* Lear, *which made me see, as I'd never seen before, that, as Jan Kott said, Shakespeare was our contemporary. What was the genesis of that production?*

Well, of course I can't really look at it in that way because already at Stratford I'd done *Love's Labour's Lost* and then *Romeo and Juliet*, which caused a scandal in its time because we did it with very young people and had very violent fights. And there were screams of horror: 'Where's the poetry gone?' And *Measure for Measure* with John Gielgud, which was a play that was unknown at the time. That and *Titus* were suddenly seen as new and vivid plays for contemporary audiences. So that the progress towards *Lear* was a very natural one. I'd always wanted to do *Lear*, but I'd waited and waited until there was an actor. I'd worked then I think already ten or eleven times with Paul Scofield. The real decision to do a big Shakespeare play is that you have to believe in the actor. And there was Scofield at forty-something, full height of his powers, absolutely right and ready to play this much older man needing all the vitality and skills of a mature actor. I read Jan Kott, knew him well, was very impressed by all his writing, and it was said that our *Lear* was based on that. I don't think that was the case. I think that what was quite clear was that *Lear* had suffered like all the other plays from tradition, and where tradition in some cases is a good thing, in the case of Shakespeare, tradition is not a good thing. Because we hadn't got a true Elizabethan tradition: we had at that time a very, very bad Victorian tradition that took you far away from the plays. It had put a wrong pictorial stamp on the plays and a wrong moral stamp, because the Victorian tradition told you very strongly who were the good and who were the bad people. And in re-examining *King Lear* we found that this was completely wrong. That *King Lear* is not about a poor, dear, old man and two monstrous vipers who are his daughters, but is a very complex play. Shakespeare often wrote rambling imperfect constructions, but if he did happen to make two perfect constructions, where really you can't take away anything, one is *Midsummer Night's Dream*, where all the different levels fit together, like in Mozart, and the other is *Lear*.

Granville Barker talked about the dream of presenting Shakespeare brightly lit within a white space.

Really? I never knew that.

And you realised his dream in your Dream.

Oh, I'm delighted.

How did you arrive at that staging of the Dream?

Two key events. I was convinced that the *Dream* was not about trees and fairies, but that it was a complex play about love, about all the different shades of meaning that that single word covers, expressing itself in an extraordinarily free and theatrical way by endless changing forms and gears and levels. I had two experiences that were very powerful. One was seeing Chinese acrobats. Looking at them I thought: ah, now this is the nearest image I can imagine to what it means when you say 'fairy'. 'Fairy' means something lighter than life—the body soaring in the air, transparent. And when I saw these Chinese acrobats, who in white clothes were completely unlike our heavy muscular acrobats, they were just figures of energy, leaping and dancing around the stage and doing incredibly difficult things as though it was no problem at all. And I thought: ah, that's what fairies should be. And then the other experience, equally powerful, was that I went to see a ballet of Jerry Robbins called *Dances at a Gathering*. Here was a ballet played to the same sort of nostalgic Chopin music as *Swan Lake*, yet suddenly instead of the images of night and a moon and a lake and white tutu—the same conventional, nineteenth-century, poetic, Victorian romantic imagery which always I'd seen related to *Midsummer Night's Dream*, or *Swan Lake*—here was a young group of very cool, very laid-back dancers on chairs, somebody playing Chopin on the piano. And I remember a man getting up, one of the male dancers who had cowboy boots, and he started suggesting classical ballet through the body and the approach of a Jerry Robbins, Broadway jazz dancer. It was overwhelming to see how the whole of the feeling of Chopin in the nineteenth century could be used without entering into that whole heavy, dated imagery. And it's with these that I began to think: first of all, the fairies mustn't look like fairies. 'Fairyness' must be dexterity, agility and doing brilliantly and easily things that seem impossible—that's a fairy. And the other side of it was that night in the forest must be conjured up lightly and amusingly, so the image of darkness must be swept out. I talked to Sally Jacobs [the designer] and we said: 'Well, the first thing is a white box, in which the imagination is free for the words which say "It's night" to ring through the audience and the audience sees night. And yet at the same time there is a lightness because it's all in light.'

This was where we took a risk that today I can't imagine could have been possible—I said to Trevor Nunn: 'Do you think that you can find a group of actors who can in five weeks' rehearsal learn to do what takes the Chinese twenty, thirty years—and it's been in the family for hundreds of years?' And he said 'Yes.' We got this company who, with such enthusiasm, managed to do these incredible things—like Alan Howard doing difficult speeches with a perfect Shakespearean understanding of words, while doing this tricky thing of making a plate spin on a stick and throwing it and catching it with Puck. I could never believe this was possible, but the actors managed to do it. The aim was to appeal to the imagination through a lively humorous contact between stage and audience, and for that, light was essential.

Several years before the Dream, *in the early sixties, there was much talk of social and sexual liberation, of R.D. Laing and the sanity of the mad, and you started a period of research under the title the Theatre of Cruelty, taken from Artaud. To what extent did your research on Artaud come out of the spirit of the times?*

I think everything comes, not totally but very largely, from the spirit of the times. And one is within that climate. Artaud was valuable when we started the Theatre of Cruelty, and I said from the start: it's not because we want to do a sadistic theatre showing cruel events. It's not snuff movies. Artaud's idea with cruelty was a pitiless rejection of conventional forms. Very good basis for research: that the sweeping away of existing forms should be extreme. This goal of extremism is a very valuable spur when you're working. When we did the experiments of the Theatre of Cruelty, we opened up all sorts of directions, and felt that now we needed a subject that makes demands that a conventional play doesn't need. There's no reason, with a conventional, three-act, naturalistic play, to have developed all these particular means and techniques. So we said we would apply them to Genet's *The Screens*, and in fact we did—in the Donmar Workshop—a half of *The Screens* as the next stage of the work of a research group. Then suddenly out of the blue came this play, *Marat/Sade*, from Germany, and I thought: well, this is an extraordinary coincidence. But there are no coincidences: just at the moment when this group has developed to a point it needed that challenge, here's a play. But the play was on a scale beyond what our little eight-men-and-women research group could handle. So we had to bring this extreme research into the mainstream of the Royal Shakespeare Company. But it was possible, because the other actors—Ian Richardson, Pat Magee, all the other actors who were concerned with it—weren't part of our experimental group. This is where experiment is useful, because you prepare something, and then other people who are open to it can very rapidly assimilate. So in a short time this big company began to work in exactly the same way as we'd worked.

You talk about Artaud, and about Brecht, but I think it's very, very important to remember that there is someone who was before them, and more important than any of them, more important than Artaud, more important than Brecht, more important than Meyerhold, more important than Stanislavsky, in the sense that he was at the origin of it all, which was [Edward Gordon] Craig. Craig has never been truly honoured in his own country, and died in exile feeling himself deeply wronged and neglected, although he never lost his humour. But right at the beginning of the century Craig was the person who swept scenery off the stage. Craig was the person who went right back to the origin of the theatre, described—before Artaud—how theatre had its roots in the temples, described vividly how that happened, and who wrote marvellous, humorous but incisive pieces like his *Advice to a Young Director*, where he said if you want to put on *Hamlet* the first thing that you have to recognise is that there is a ghost and there is the supernatural. If you're not prepared to accept the supernatural in Shakespeare, go home. Don't touch this author because you won't understand anything about it. Many of Craig's writings are out of print and many of them are neglected, but when one sees what Craig was saying, there is nothing more important as an influence penetrating the whole of the twentieth-century theatre. Deeply influencing people like Brecht, who perhaps didn't know about it, but Brecht's approach to scenery was entirely in the direction of what Craig was looking for. I would say that the true influence, which we all carry today whether we know it or not, comes from Gordon Craig.

Like Craig, Artaud realised very little work, but he was a brilliant theorist. One of the things he said was that he craved a theatre whose origins were in the dance, that the means of expression employed in the dance are equally the natural means of expression for acting, the difference being merely one of range.

I think that Artaud's great qualities go beyond being a poetic theoretician—'poetic' meaning that a poet has these deep intuitions. Theorists rarely have any intuitions at all. But he turned into theory what he sensed poetically. And although, in practice, he didn't know how to implement them in the theatre, intuitively he sensed that there is something that could appear in performance in the theatre that comes from deep, deep, hidden springs in the human organism that express themselves equally through movements of the body, through the capacity of a voice to make strange sounds. And that ideally every word is charged with the full capacity of the whole organism. I think that Artaud is tremendously valuable to everyone in the theatre if you follow him on that intuitive level. If you follow him on the superficial level of an angry man saying this is all appalling, this is hateful—furiously saying: you mustn't do this, but you must go out and yell and scream—then you can very, very easily lead young people into very poor quality excesses, because they have Artaud in their hand, and Artaud says one must be excessive, without realising that the true excess he means is the height of creativity.

And above all, spontaneity.

And spontaneity, but then spontaneity is, in all of human life, the most difficult state to reach.

And achieved how?

Spontaneity—it's like simplicity. You don't start with it. We've found this in improvisations. You take a group of people who haven't improvised much together, and you ask them all to be spontaneous. If that can go on for thirty seconds you're very lucky, after which, even though people think that they're doing something freely, they're just repeating their own stereotypes. And stereotype is meeting stereotype and blending into a super-stereotype. To free yourself of that is exactly the same as in football, as in boxing, as in any sport. It's an enormously long process before you get to the World Cup state, when you have that absolute freedom of improvisation—that's where you see spontaneity. You see spontaneity in the World Cup. And what a process.

What about the 'revolution' of 1956 at the Royal Court?

Oh, that was a real revolution. And the revolution can be called social in the sense that there was a very stratified class system in place. Something was emerging in the name of a lower class that was freeing itself from an intermediate class and refused to have anything to do with the establishment. And also freeing itself from what was rigid in the working-class ideology of the time. So this free-moving class, rising up in the social scale, wished to be heard, and in wishing to be heard it naturally wanted to be heard with a different language, with a different dynamic, in a different way from the established theatre. And as the established theatre hadn't much going for it, there was every good reason to break all the conventions. When I did *Romeo and Juliet*, which was before that time, I had a very young actor playing Romeo very well. I wanted somebody very young, and during rehearsal he told me about his life, he talked about his origins: poor, working-class boy, who spoke with a regional or cockney accent. He talked about how hard he had struggled at drama school to learn to speak correctly so that he could go one day to Stratford and play a part like Romeo. And this seemed normal and natural because it was quite clear that he would be thrown out of the first audition if he came in and read Romeo with a regional or cockney accent. The big revolution starting with Albert Finney—an actor affirming his right to play the prince without sacrificing his own individuality, his own colour, his own personality, and saying: 'The hell with it—if I've been born talking like this, I'm going to bloody well go on talking like this.' And this was a big revolution in England.

So with Look Back in Anger *what was shocking was the tone of voice and the accent rather than the form?*

I think everything. It's bewildering today to watch the gradual movement from the day when it was daring to say 'bloody', to the fact that today, if you don't say 'fuck' every third line, your play most likely won't be accepted. It was just about that time that 'fuck' was said for the first time on an English stage.

But you were constantly at war with the Lord Chamberlain?

Oh yes. I think that I was part of those who managed to get rid of him. And we got rid of him—after a long series of head-on attacks which got us nowhere—by ridicule. In the end we found different ways of making him not only a complete anachronism but a *ridiculous* anachronism. One day when I visited the Lord Chamberlain, he received me—because he was going on to a reception at the Palace—in full Palace uniform: we were sitting there discussing a play of Genet's and whether or not these words would be suitable, and the anachronism was complete. But everything was interconnected: when there's a gradual change it has its influence everywhere. And then there're the landmarks: *Look Back in Anger* just was that shock landmark which dramatised the whole process of change that was going on all through the artistic life of the country and of the theatre.

At the same time, there was theatre at least as interesting in Stratford East with Joan Littlewood.

Oh yes, but is that forgotten today?

Yes.

Oh, that is very terrible, because, as I was saying, there was a climate, because the forces of change were underway, and of course many different things were sprouting. *Look Back in Anger*, because of the phrase 'the angry young men', has become vastly well known. But somebody of tremendous talent and fired with the same feeling of protest and refusal—an impossible character, which made her even stronger—was Joan Littlewood. Joan Littlewood made her little band of people around her—and all the work that went on in her theatre—as revolutionary, as dynamic and as exciting as any other aspect of those times.

There have been three—well, four if you include Craig—great theatre artists this century who have become exiles or self-exiles: Granville Barker, Joan Littlewood and yourself have all left Britain and British theatre, and come to France—obviously for different reasons. But is there a common strain?

Absolutely not. Absolutely not. I knew from Barry Jackson why Granville Barker left. He left because of a woman: his second wife. They got a house in France and she was very possessive. Barry Jackson told me the tale of how he would come to see Granville Barker, they'd have lunch together, and then he'd say: Granville, come for a walk in the garden, because he wanted to persuade him to come back and do a production in England. And the wife would never leave them alone for a second, because she knew that this was in the air, and she didn't want to let her husband go. That was one reason. Joan: nobody understands why. There were personal things—I think almost entirely personal things. When Gerry Raffles died it was a tremendous shock and blow to her. She was dissatisfied for various reasons. She came temporarily to France. She was disillusioned with a lot of things, but on a psychological level what really happened with Joan is a mystery that none of us really can penetrate. The reason that I came to France has got nothing to do with either a woman or secret psychological reasons. I didn't get up and leave the English theatre from any sense of frustration or disapproval. I came here having, over ten years, enjoyed the difference of working in England and France, and continually working here and going back again, and I came here in the end because in '68 I did in France the first experiment with an international group—the International Workshop—when everyone was doing workshops and I'd started doing them in England. I made this experiment of what happens if people who normally have nothing in common but are actors and theatre workers come and work together on a common project. We worked together in the middle of the events of '68, and it was so rewarding that when that ended I said: 'We've got to pick it up again.' And there it was—something very, very specific. England has every strength and every advantage except that today it cannot believe itself part of the world, and it won't go easily into Europe—and it was even more so in those days. The bringing together of an international group was natural in Paris. We were at once supported and understood. The government didn't give us money at first, but they at once gave us a place to work in. It was in the tradition of Paris, that has been a turning point for artists, although the French have their own xenophobia which can be considerable on other levels, but not artistically. Artists from Picasso, Modigliani and others, artists from all parts of the world, are welcomed to Paris and even more so if they settle and work in Paris. I'm sure, looking back, that if I had tried for the last twenty-five years in England to make a basis for something truly international and racially mixed in the way that we've been doing here, I don't think we would have had the same support, because it wouldn't have had the same natural resonance.

In Britain, I don't know if it's true in France, there's a gulf between people who feel that the theatre is for them and people who feel excluded from it. Do you have any idea of how we can dissolve that division?

I think that these are local issues. They can't be solved nationally or by decree; they can only be solved event by event if the people are concerned by that. Here it's been a question that we feel very strongly about, to which the answers are very simple. From the start we tried as best we could within our budget to keep our prices extremely low. And from the start we had the lowest prices in all Paris. When we did *Carmen*, you could see *Carmen* for thirty francs. That's 3p—an incredibly small sum. And every production we do here, we do one or two free performances for the whole of the *quartier*, who are invited. We put up little notices: people from around are welcome to come. We've worked a lot with African and the North African people, around the theatre there's an enormous African and North African population. We have done a great deal in the past. We've gone and played improvisations in hostels round here, and at the end of these things we've said: 'This is theatre, you're welcome, come to the theatre.' And hardly ever have we succeeded in this way, although we've made very good relationships on the spot. None of the people we've invited come; that's why it's very good to raise the problem and one always comes back to it. The theatre worldwide has established this reputation that if you go through these doors you're expected to behave in a certain way. That's totally untrue. I think that in Covent Garden they're now trying to make it appear that you don't have to put on a black tie. Whether this will help to make it more accessible or not, I've no idea. I think the best answer is low seat prices, and recognising that the theatre has to pay for its sins. It's no use saying: 'Ah, but the same young people who you're giving seats to at this very low price will go and buy a pair of shoes for three times the price.' Because shoes haven't let anyone down over the centuries and the theatre has.

Margaret 'Percy' Harris

1 9 0 4—2 0 0 0

Designer. Margaret Harris, always known as Percy, was one of the three-woman design firm, Motley, whose other members were the sisters Sophie (who was married to George Devine) and Elizabeth Montgomery. They dominated British theatre design for many years. Percy was a very sprightly ninety-five and, like all lively old people, was very moving. I interviewed her in her terrace house in Barnes.

You introduced an approach to design in which meaning took precedence over decoration?

We were reacting against fuss; everything was so complicated, and it looked so complicated, and I don't know where they did their research, I suppose from paintings. But you get different views of paintings according to what type of life you are in, what time, what date you are working from.

Were there large lumps of scenery on stage?

Well, no, because it was all painted, there was really very little built; nothing was built until you come to Gordon Craig. Everything had been painted up until then.

So Craig was your strongest influence?

He was, yes. He still is a great influence, I think, on everybody. He was the beginning of the modern theatre.

What was it that Craig brought to theatre?

He brought the fact that it was the *play* that was the important thing. He brought the fact that you didn't need to put everything on the stage, you could select. He brought the fact that simplicity was better than elaboration, and he brought a sort of individuality of his own to the theatre. He was a sort of god to all the young designers of our time.

It's very difficult to imagine a designer with that influence whose work was never realised.

He wrote a lot of course and he illustrated a lot. I don't know where we picked up what he did, but his whole attitude to the theatre seemed to be much more sensible than what they had been doing before.

Did you know him?

No, I never met him, but George [Devine] used to go and see him a lot in France.

You worked very, very closely with actors and with directors. Was this a departure from a previous way of working?

I suppose it was. When we first worked with Gielgud he was at the Albery Theatre [1932–37], and he used to come over after the show and we would work on the next show. He would put his great hands into the model and smash everything. He's very, very clumsy: it's funny.

What was it about Gielgud that attracted you to him?

It was the kind of work he did and the kind of generosity of his personality, because he never claimed anything for his own; he always acknowledged who had done the work and who had helped him. But he had the most amazing visual sense, because of course as a boy he used to design a lot. He had a model theatre and he used to do all sorts of things for himself. He contributed tremendously to our first work, you know.

If you were looking at the visual arts of the time, were you and Gielgud aware of what was going on in painting? Were you aware of modernism?

Not at all. We never went to modern exhibitions, as far as I remember. We used to spend a lot of time in the National Gallery looking at medieval paintings and things like that, and sometimes the Pre-Raphaelites, but we were very unintellectual about anything. We just did what seemed to us to be attractive and suitable, and Gielgud very much agreed with that. He was wonderful in the way that he would accept what we wanted to do. When we were going to do *Richard of Bordeaux* [1932], he said he thought it would be wonderful to use primary colours. And we said: 'Oh no, we don't want to use primary colours, we want to use hardly any colour.' And he said: 'Okay, if you want to do it that way, try it out and we will see.'

What were the fabrics you used?

For the men's clothes we used almost entirely woollen material as cloth, which was quite cheap.

But was this to introduce a sense of texture, of costumes being lived in?

It was because it hung in the right sort of way, and it had body and didn't look phoney: it looked real.

Did you disapprove of what was going on in the West End theatre?

We thought it was nonsense. I mean, lacking in any kind of belief in anything, just froth. That's what we thought, but whether it was, I don't know, but that was what we felt. There were no plays which really taxed one's intellect at all. I mean, there was practically nothing which we approved of except John. At the Old Vic, for instance, the actors used to go to the wardrobe to pick out their costumes. There was an old gentleman who ran the wardrobe called Orlando, who used to say: 'Would you like to have a nice clean pair of tights? Well, you can't have them.' So they used to fight as to who could get to the wardrobe first and get the few good costumes that were there.

You introduced to the Old Vic the idea that what you put on stage was decided by the designer?

I think that is so and that was what Lilian [Baylis, who ran the Old Vic from 1912 to 1937] found so very, very trying about us, because it was expensive. She had a wardrobe where they used to repair things, and the wardrobe then took on making things that we designed. She thought that we didn't design them to last. In *The Merchant* we had an organdie dress for Peggy [Ashcroft] in a very pale colour, and Lilian was absolutely furious about that. She said it was hopeless, and that if we must go on working in that way, we must think of the future.

You knew Lilian Baylis well.

Oh, very, very well. She used to sit in the stage box during performances, with her dogs and with her cooking stove, and cook herself sausages and bacon, and the smell used to permeate the theatre. She paid us practically nothing: she was absolutely in charge and practically lived in the theatre. I don't think she slept there, but she had a room there with her dogs. When we were doing *Macbeth* [1937] she died during the production week, and that made things rather difficult.

What did she sound like?

She was very, very cockney. It wasn't a shrill voice—it was quite a decent voice—but she had a very strong accent.

You designed the Romeo and Juliet *[1935] in which Gielgud and Olivier alternated Romeo and Mercutio. How did that work?*

It was extraordinary. Larry, I am afraid, was more right in both the parts, but he got absolutely slated for the Romeo because of the way he had treated the verse. They were used to John's beautiful interpretation of the verse, and Larry brought it up to date and made it like just talking: they practically slaughtered him. After the first night, after the papers came out, he said he wasn't going to do it any more. However, John persuaded him to, and everybody who wasn't a critic told him how wonderful he was. He *was* wonderful—he was young and vital and sulky and all the things that Romeo should be. Then he took over Mercutio and was very, very good in that too. John was in a different category altogether—he was beautiful in it, and Larry was real in it.

How was working with Olivier as opposed to working with Gielgud?

We did a *Romeo and Juliet* in America with Larry, and he liked to have his own way about the scenery. He cared about his costumes and Vivien [Leigh]'s costumes, but he didn't really take very much interest in the others.

You designed Dance of Death *[1967] for him at the National, didn't you?*

That was almost the last thing he did, wasn't it? Glen [Byam Shaw] and I went to Sweden where we found a wonderful picture in the archives of a person we thought looked exactly as the Captain should look. We brought it back and showed it to Larry, and he said: 'Oh no, no, not at all.' And then he went away and made up and came out looking exactly like the picture. He couldn't accept that anybody had suggested it except himself. Larry was always tremendously vital but entirely selfish. Part of John's difficulties was that he was so unselfish: he would never push himself in, he would never take the stage when he didn't need to take the stage. He's the most generous character, I think, in the world.

And generous too in his vision of the theatre that companies needed to be formed.

Everything was influenced by him, and he's never taken the credit for any of that, I don't think.

You were involved very closely with George [Devine] and the Royal Court.

I was very much sort of part of it, because we had prepared the theatre when George was going in. We painted it all. We hung about on ladders tending to the top of the pros[cenium arch] and things like that. George was so sure of what he believed without being in any way a conceited man. He was less conceited than anybody I can think of, but he wanted so much to change what he thought was wrong in the theatre.

You were present at two revolutions. The first time, when you started working with John, you felt that you were sweeping away what?

Fuss and rabbit fur.

And the second time with George. What was he bringing in?

I think it was partly his up-to-dateness, his modern-ness, and partly the people he collected round him. There was Tony Richardson who went on to be an enormous influence, and there was the way George found plays and the company, the actors. I think he chose all the most interesting young actors—as indeed John did in his time. His choice of actors was amazing. There is nobody who became successful who wasn't found by either John or George as far as I can remember. I suppose to some extent that we were just sweeping away anything that wasn't to do with what was going on in the world at the time, with modern life, with the life people were leading.

Were you influenced at all by Brecht?

I did go to Berlin and see one of the plays there—*Mother Courage*—but they used to sit for a long time while he changed the scenery.

What you were interested in was a fluency of playing?

Tremendously important. Also to have a permanent structure to which one could attach things rather than having to change everything.

You've always believed in minimalism, but not as a dogma. You did a celebrated production of The Importance of Being Earnest [1939] *that was highly realistic?*

Oh yes. That was very enjoyable. I mean, we cast aside our minimalism for that and put everything in—you know all the detail of the things they had in that period. John took a very direct view of it. We went to the Caledonian Market and bought all Edith [Evans]'s clothes: she insisted on having all the underclothes that were correct in the period, although you never saw them, so one had to search around for the right things for her.

That production was real in the sense it was trying to be absolutely true to its period?

Yes, so it was. The exterior set was based on a house in Holland Park which John knew about and sent us to see, and the interiors were very, very real and detailed.

I find now that the students are not able to understand anything of that kind; most of them don't understand the realism of Edwardian plays.

Do they not understand, or are they not curious about it?

They don't know about it, so it doesn't mean anything much to them, and they don't seem to be able to do it. Perhaps because they don't want to.

You were interested in trying to introduce reality to a world which was smothered in escapism.

Yes.

Do you think it's possible now that people are wanting escapism and that there is too much reality?

Perhaps. Perhaps. You see, I think they are rather stuck because they can do modernism with the scenery, abstract scenery, but you can't make an actor abstract, he's got to be himself. And if you try to dress him abstract, it simply doesn't work, and he can't move. So you have to accept that you are in two halves, that the scenery is abstract and the actor is not abstract.

Peter Hall

1 9 3 0—

Director. Founder of the Royal Shakespeare Company in 1961, and director of the National Theatre from 1976 to 1987. I interviewed Peter Hall at the Old Vic, a house of spirits, haunted by the ghosts of actors and audiences, where he'd been before relocating the National Theatre to the South Bank and also for three years in the nineties with his own repertory company. He talked with such warm enthusiasm about his early years that I couldn't help feeling that nothing could match or did match the frenzied thrill of helping to reinvent the British theatre in the early sixties. I told him that by the time I'd finished the TV series for which we were conducting this interview and written (with Nicholas Wright) the book of the series, I wouldn't have directed anything new for nearly two years. He looked really concerned. 'I'd go mad,' he said.

What makes theatre so special?

It's the only art form in which a group of people meet together in order to play a game of imagination with the actor, who invites them to imagine things, and that union makes them more intelligent than they are individually. Collectively they're sharper, they're more alive. The experience is more incandescent than if they were reading a book or a poem or listening to a piece of music by themselves. The desire to imagine something which isn't there is stronger in the theatre than in any other media. If we go and stand on the stage, which is a completely bare black box, and we speak with some clarity a piece of *Julius Caesar*, if we're any good at all, the audience will believe it's Rome. They'll say:

35

yes, those two guys are in Rome. If we bring a camera into the auditorium and film the two of us doing exactly the same thing in the same circumstances and we then show that piece of film, the audience will say: well, that's not Rome, that's a black void in a black box—where's Rome? In other words their imagination is not stimulated by any visual imagery, which after all is the basis and strength and extraordinariness of film. I think what's really been interesting about the theatre in the last fifty years is that the increased visual media and, in a sense, the increased literalness of our age has freed the theatre to be more imaginative.

Or to try to be as imaginative as Shakespeare?

The theatre's strength comes out of its limitations to some extent. Shakespeare initially played in daylight: it's much more eloquent because it's imaginative for Lady Macbeth to come on with a candle in daylight and say the night is black, than actually for us to walk onto a modern stage where we can create blackness and yet we can't see. And then we can't hear her telling us about the nature of blackness and of evil. Shakespeare was there in daylight in a large space with two or three thousand people with a permanent stage which could become anything or anywhere he wanted it to become. Or nowhere if he didn't want to tell us where it was. One of the problems with doing Shakespeare today is that we think it has to be *somewhere*. Why did Shakespeare happen? It's the—it's the genetic pack of cards. Genius makes its own rules. Shakespeare inherited a very formal method of writing with the iambic pentameter and broke all the rules, and therefore made it sound human and flexible and extraordinary.

There's his humanity, there's his use of language and his coinage of language, but what is it that's so singular that survives translation into foreign languages and to other media? We could watch Prokofiev's ballet and still think in some way it's Shakespearean.

If Shakespeare is in another language and in another medium, you've already lost a lot, but what you haven't lost is Shakespeare's extraordinary sense of ambiguity—the ability to say: this is so, but then that is also so. I think that's what is finally eternal about Shakespeare and makes him transcend any barriers of culture and nationhood or anything else. It's significant, isn't it, that Shakespeare becomes something different to every age? He has this negative capability of becoming anything and anybody. It depends which angle you look at him. You can say that's because he's comprehensive or broad-minded, he's conservative, he's radical, he's revolutionary, he's reactionary, and he's progressive. Any label you choose to set on Shakespeare will in some sense be valid. That's partly because he is so extraordinarily comprehensive in his sympathies and understandings, but mostly because he revels in contradiction.

He has a rather sceptical view of authority. Perhaps it came out of being an actor, living in a little society that mocks the greater society.

A little kingdom. A good theatre is a metaphor for what society ought to be, what a family ought to be, what any tribe ought to be. I think a lot of that stems from the maverick boy from Stratford-upon-Avon who finds a home and a place and a status within a community of actors. Although we know very little about Shakespeare, we also know a lot. There are fifty recorded notes of him in the Public Record Office, because he was a very litigious man. I find the whole thing that this working-class boy from Stratford couldn't possibly have written these plays because he didn't have sufficient education, he didn't have sufficient background, he didn't have sufficient travel, all rubbish. Genius is genius. I think his sceptical attitude to authority is a given throughout—people are dressed in a little brief authority and for that reason need to be questioned. I think that's the centre of Shakespeare, in that sense he remains a revolutionary.

Do you think he was a Catholic?

I think he was a heretical Catholic, a sceptical Catholic, an emotional Catholic. I think he was born thus, brought up thus and lived in a Catholic society. But I think he would have been the first to criticise the Pope and the papacy.

Do you think it's a marvellous piece of luck to have had Shakespeare as our theatrical DNA or is it a burden?

Some people take the view that Shakespeare is a dead weight, a kind of albatross round the neck of the British theatre. I don't believe that's true. Strangely enough, unlike the French classicists, he's entirely questing and revolutionary. He questions form all the time, whether it be the form of his own blank verse line or whether it be the form of the play. Whatever it be he's writing about, his historical sense changes and develops. Everything is questioned. But it's a sobering thought that in two or three hundred years we shan't understand Shakespeare because the language is now changing at an accelerating rate, and Shakespeare will be like Chaucer: he'll need to be modernised.

If the ability to speak verse is dying out now, how can it be rectified?

I believe in the traditions of William Poel, who was the great Shakespearean revolutionary at the end of the nineteenth century. He was anti-Irving, anti the gaslit or electric-lit theatre-with-scenery: he wanted to put Shakespeare on a bare stage, speak the speech trippingly and make it witty and lean and quick. He said that that went back to Betterton, to the Restoration, and in that sense went back perhaps through the Civil War to Shakespeare himself. He taught Harley Granville Barker, who I think is still the only great Shakespearean scholar who understands Shakespeare as a dramatist. He taught Edith Evans when she was seventeen, and one of the first people I worked with in the theatre was Edith Evans; I made her sit down for a whole period night after night and teach me what Poel taught her.

What were you taught?

What I was taught primarily was that Shakespeare wrote lines not words. That the iambic pentameter, which is like the system underneath a piece of jazz, has a strong rhythm and needs marking as a line, and that great Shakespearean playing is exactly, as we would say now, like great jazz playing. You keep the beat, you preserve the line, but it's how you nearly break the line which enables you to express the emotion and enables you to actually say what it feels. Now those are actors' choices. Shakespeare does not tell the actor what to feel. He does say, however, this is where you pause; this is where you come in on cue; this is where you go fast; this is where you go slow; these are the words you accent; and you must find the human reason that enables you to do so. So it's much like an opera singer studying a piece of music, and it's the other way round to the way that we're normally taught drama, which is: what is my character, what is my conflict, what is my action, what am I feeling, now what do I say? In Shakespeare, you start with: what do I say? You don't breathe in the middle of the line, you breathe at the end. You try and keep your lungs full so you can control the whole line. But mostly it's the sense. That is the central tradition, and people like Gielgud, Ashcroft, Evans, even Olivier, were marinated in it as young actors and did it almost without thinking, almost without knowing. Now our actors today do much less Shakespeare. Sometimes they don't even do it at drama school. So young actors come to the RSC and come to the National Theatre without knowing anything about how to speak Shakespeare at all. They get themselves in total knots, they can't get their tongues round it, they can't breathe in the right place and they end up losing their voices and being incomprehensible. So now we have to teach. It's not a mystique and it's not hard: it takes approximately a fortnight to learn it and to do it. It's like riding a bicycle.

Is there a reluctance on the part of today's actors to play what is written?

I think there are two points to make. Most actors now when they pick up a script are dealing with something not very good, with shit. By dealing with it they have to invest it with some personal idiosyncrasy, some personal style. The average television script is unspeakable, so they have to disguise that fact. So you can't blame the actor for not trusting the text because most of the texts that they're given today are not worth trusting. There's a bigger problem in the theatre: while I find that *actors* will respect the text, and do understand that if Pinter chooses a certain word or Beckett a certain phrase, there is a reason for it and it's not for them to say 'I'm better or I know better than these geniuses', it is the *directors* on the whole who are deconstructionist and don't rate the text. Young actor after young actor says to me: I want to know how to speak Shakespeare, I want to know where to breathe, I believe in the verse. I understand that, but the young directors don't. They say: I know all about verse, don't worry about that. But you have to worry about that. It's easy, but it has to be taken into account. I believe that it's important that knowledge is handed on. In my view there are about half-a-dozen directors and about fifty actors left in England who actually know how to do Shakespeare, and there are not more. That's enough to pass it on; it will swing back again. It always comes and goes. There are actions and reactions, and the theatre, as you well know, is always dying.

You worked with many of the leading actors of an earlier generation—Gielgud, Olivier, Redgrave, Evans, Richardson, Ashcroft—who were all steeped in a classical tradition.

They were all Shakespeareans. They all believed in text. And however good any of them were, and some of them were very, very good on the screen, their real strength was their verbal dexterity on the stage, their telling quality, in the sense of what they told an audience. They all had fine voices, and they all had wit. Now what do I mean by wit? To me, it's an attempt to define something which is complex and paradoxical by paradoxical comparisons. 'If music be the food of love'—well, music is not food, but once you've made it into food what do you do with it? You play on. That to me is not a soupy, lyrical line, it's a witty line. I can hear Peggy Ashcroft—although she never played Orsino for obvious reasons—saying a line like that with wit, with humour: minting it, making it happen. So I worshipped all those people. I grew up watching them on the stage, and then I actually started to work with them. I worked with Olivier in '59 on *Coriolanus*, and I found him the most immaculate verse speaker, which of course he hadn't been in the thirties when the critics trounced him for trying to chop up the verse. But by '59 he had accepted the form and had made it his own. He was a wonderful person to work with. Very exhausting. People would say to me—I was twenty-eight—how do you tell Laurence Olivier what to do? And the answer, of course, then as now with a great actor is that a director doesn't 'tell the actor what to do'. He encourages the actor maybe to go into areas that the actor didn't know he possesses or has not been into often; he edits what the actor provides so that the actor has to trust him as a kind of mirror. And he then uses what the actor creates in order to select for the interpretation of the play.

The two people I found the most difficult to direct of that great bunch were Edith Evans and Ralph Richardson. Because I think both of them had a fundamental distrust of directors, although Ralph was like a father to me finally and accepted me. But the difficulty of directing them was that most actors when they rehearse have an attitude of: 'When I do it, which is not now, it will be something like this. Of course, when I actually do it I will be doing ten or fifteen per cent more, but this is the sort of way.' Ralph and Edith pressed a button in themselves and did it completely from a standing start: they would take a few lines and go straight up into complete creation. And it was always therefore magical.

Paul does that.

Paul Scofield does that, exactly the same. No, but he has exactly the same quality. Different generation though. So they would come off it and then say: well, that wasn't very good, was it? And you'd say it was wonderful. And you didn't know which to choose because they had so many things they could do. I think that's a kind of genius, and I would say Evans had it, Richardson had it and Scofield has it.

What about Gielgud?

Gielgud is a wonderful improviser. Witty, fast. Fast like quicksilver. I think the spell he exerts on an audience has always been that his mind and his tongue are so agile that they run after him, saying: no no no no, please wait for us, please give us more; and he's gone. He's like that. Of course the difficulty with John is that he is so endlessly inventive that he will throw stuff away and say: well, I think that's rather boring, I don't think we want to do that, we'll do this instead; and he's off. He's like a kind of wild horse, you have to rein him in. All these people, as you know, are terribly easy to direct because they want to do it. It's the second-class citizens who are somewhat difficult to direct, the ones who believe they should be first. That's the difficult area for a director.

When I tentatively started to direct Wendy Hiller, she said to me, 'You must just tell me, dear, I do want to be good.'

Well, that's it. They're voracious. They're not going to allow you to sit around saying, 'Aren't I lucky, I've got a lovely cast here?' They'll get on and do it. I think that whole, great generation gathered round Gielgud or gathered round Olivier. Those were the two polarities. And they weren't as different—Gielgud and Olivier—as each would like to think. [*chuckles*] Olivier was more animalic and more instinctive and a more glowering kind of sexy being. But Gielgud had extraordinary sexuality and vulnerability on the stage of a quite different kind, but nonetheless just as attractive. The idea of Gielgud the walking head and Olivier the great sexy body I don't quite subscribe to; I think they were much closer. And they were united in believing in the word and in the classical virtues. Ferociously classical, they all were. Which to some extent still exists, doesn't it? Scofield is still with us, Dench is there, Gambon is there, McKellen is there.

What were you trying to achieve when you started the RSC?

Stratford had a renaissance immediately after the war. It seemed to come at the same moment: the beginning of subsidising the arts, the coming of the Third

Programme, the new Education Act, our post-war hopes. And there was a huge boom in Shakespeare. Barry Jackson, who ran Birmingham Rep, took over Stratford and made it a rather glittering and glamorous place. He got the great stars to come. He got Diana Wynyard, he got the young Paul Scofield, he got the young Peter Brook. And he also built an infrastructure of rehearsal rooms and workshops which actually took the theatre seriously for the first time. I mean, there'd been a theatre at Stratford since the late nineteenth century, though it had burnt down in 1931 and the new Art Deco, rather cinema-like building went up, which wasn't very easy to play in. That was the main problem that Barry Jackson had and then Tony Quayle had and then Glen Byam Shaw had. But they actually put Stratford on the map. Suddenly Shakespeare was hot. I went there first in 1956, when I was twenty-five, to direct a play, and I directed a play each year from then on. The season ran from March until October: it was a star-led company. There were always two or three really big West End stars. And there were a lot of young actors who would do one, two or three years there gradually coming up through the ranks. Some of them became stars in their own right, like Dorothy Tutin, Geraldine McEwan and people like that.

In 1958 Glen Byam Shaw said he was going to retire, so he asked me if I would be interested in taking over. I was twenty-seven. My ambition as a young man had been to do Shakespeare, which is why I did what I did and why I went to Cambridge and why I followed the path that I tried to follow. Even more shamingly, I suppose—because it's like Harold Wilson standing outside the door of Number Ten—I wanted to run Stratford. So it was an extraordinary moment for a twenty-seven-year-old man. I can't imagine how I had the nerve to do it looking back, but I said: I don't want to run a Shakespeare Festival from March until October; I don't want to be a runner of an ad-hoc festival; I want to try and make an ensemble; I want to give the actors three-year contracts, I want us all to speak Shakespeare in the same way, I want us all to approach Shakespeare in the same way. So therefore I want a team of directors and a team of designers and most of all I want to do modern plays and other classics as well as Shakespeare. Because I believe a classical company that is not alive to the present has absolutely no prospect of making the past live. Therefore I want a London theatre because I want it to be a year-round operation. The idea was that a company, a family, would achieve more than an ad-hoc group. The chairman of the theatre's board, Sir Fordham Flower—of the Flowers brewers who had been the patrons and the starters and the supporters of Stratford from the previous century—was terribly interested in all this, but he was an arch-diplomat and extremely clever. He said: 'I think this is all very good, but I don't know whether it'll get through. We've got a hundred and seventy-five thousand pounds in the bank, which is savings from our Australian and American tours from the past, but those are our total resources.' And I said to him: 'There is a political reason why you've got to do this: within the next five or six years the National Theatre will come, and if the

National Theatre comes, Stratford will become a very provincial repertory stuck out in the country, visited only by tourists.' And he said: 'Well, we can't have two national theatres.' And I said, for the first time, and I've gone on saying it all my life: 'We must have two theatres.' I think the fact that France had the Théâtre National Populaire of Vilar, as well as the Comédie Française, gave some hope for young actors and young writers and for the future. That artistic competition is absolutely essential. So I said there must be two national theatres and we must be the first.

Anyway, to cut a long story short, the board was very, very hostile to it, particularly Binkie Beaumont, who was the doyen of West End theatres and a great manager and a great producer. He took me out to lunch and he said: 'If you do this, you will ruin the West End theatre. Once an actor is allowed to play less than eight times a week, he will never want to play eight times a week.' And I said: 'Well, he shouldn't play eight times a week; that's nineteenth century and dreadful.' And he said: 'All the playwrights will give you plays because you'll be able to nurse them in repertory, and they won't be instant flops or successes, and you will ruin the commercial theatre, and I'm not having it. If you succeed in getting this, I will resign.' And I said: 'That's fine.' He was a friend, I'd worked with him and I'd work with him again. And he said: 'I will resign, and I will resign quietly and without fuss or without bother, but I will go.' Ultimately he did.

Anyway, the Stratford company went to Russia in November, December 1958. I was director designate at that time and a rather worried director designate because I wasn't sure whether what I wanted was going to happen. And I wasn't therefore sure whether I was actually going to take the job, although I already had it. In Leningrad—as it was then, now again St Petersburg—in one of those vast Edwardian hotels, Fordy Flower sat up all one night with me and said: 'Now let's get to the bottom of this: tell me the whole thing again.' And I went over it all in painful detail until about four in the morning over several quantities of drink. And at the end of it Fordy said to me: 'You are absolutely mad, but I think you've got something. I will back you, and here's my hand: through thick and thin I will back you.' And he did. The board practically resigned but didn't. Then it started to be a success. It wasn't an instant success; it took two years before we became internationally famous. Then everybody said: oh, how wonderful. But looking back on it, the interesting thing to me is that it is absolutely inconceivable that such a thing could happen now. This is not an old man being nostalgic. I mean, now there would have to be money from the Lottery, and there would have to be a feasibility study, and the feasibility study would certainly say we don't need to do this, we don't need any more classical theatre in London, and this shouldn't happen.

Was it The Wars of the Roses [*1963*] *that was the first big success?*

The Wars of the Roses was the first absolute, extraordinary success. Before that, in the first year [1961], we had a very successful season—the Peter O'Toole *Merchant of Venice*, Dorothy Tutin's *Twelfth Night*, the sandpit *Troilus and Cressida*. The first year was very successful, then we opened the Aldwych and that went very well initially. The second year was a bit of a dip and the third year was the crown.

What did you bring to The Wars of the Roses?

John Barton and I worked on it together. He and I were at university together, and he was with me in those early years of the RSC. He's still at the RSC forty years later. We woke up in 1963 to find ourselves internationally famous for having done this *Wars of the Roses* cycle: we were told that we were post-Brechtian and Socialist, we were examining the routes of power, we were da da da. As far as we were concerned, certainly as far as I was concerned, the primary building block of the RSC was the verse and the text, speaking it trippingly on the tongue, speaking it wittily, not singing it, not being pompous, meaning what you said, and therefore exposing the dialectic of the scene. And if you expose the dialectic of the scene, you expose the political truth of the scene and you expose Shakespeare's scepticism about the nature of power. I wanted to do the *Henry VIs* simply because I've always been fascinated by politics, by the hypocrisy of politics—the fact that politicians seemed to me even to deceive themselves, and they still do. In Shakespeare, baron after baron says: I don't want power, I would not wish to be king, of course not. And every night on television you can see a politician saying: oh, I have no ambitions to be leader of the party, but of course it would be my duty if I was called. That level of hypocrisy fascinates me; it seems to be almost a necessary source to being political. Now *The Wars of the Roses* were different—I can see this now looking back—because we treated kings as people. We treated kings as people who were motivated by the same sort of desires—self-preservation, success, hanging on to power—as any other person. There was in the air in the early sixties the beginnings of a scepticism about politics and politicians, which I'm happy to say still exists and is very healthy and very fruitful.

Was this borrowed in any way from the Cold War?

Certainly the Cold War and the nature of politics in Eastern Europe informed part of our understanding of the power politics of the Histories. You couldn't avoid it. And obviously Brecht had been an enormous influence on us all. His company came to London in 1956 just after his death, and that changed everything. Though I had been to the Berliner Ensemble in '54 in East Berlin for a short period and watched them work and tried to understand.

What had you learned from watching Brecht's company?

I hadn't learned alienation because I think English actors are naturally the most alienated in the world anyway—they distrust emotion and they're sceptical. The whole Brecht theory of alienation only makes sense if you look at what German acting was like in the forties and fifties: over-the-top, sentimental, terribly slow and very self-indulgent. What I learned from Brecht was clarity: if you achieve clarity on the stage you actually make an audience understand the sexiness of argument, the sexiness of political argument, and that dialectic is actually theatrical. Now that was not thought about before the early sixties. Certainly the great cycle of history plays that Tony Quayle did in 1951 at Stratford—where he did *Richard II*, the two *Henry IV*s and *Henry V* with the young Richard Burton— that was about England as an emergent nation, and very fine too. And that of course is partly what the plays are about anyway. But a critique of *Realpolitik* it wasn't—we didn't think that way then. That's what we brought to it in the sixties. Did we know we were doing it? I don't think we did. I really distrust any form of theatre where you walk into the rehearsal room saying: good morning, now we're going to show how hypocritical politicians are and what a shitty business politics is. That should come from the work not from a pre-emptive strike, which is not creative. So we went on a journey at a particular moment in time, and the time was good for the plays we were doing, and that's why *The Wars of the Roses* happened. I do believe very strongly in the organic nature of theatre. I don't believe that we can be conscious of what we're doing: we can only be instinctive. I have a daughter doing A-level Theatre Studies, a directing course, and she said to me the other day: 'We were told that when we choose a play we must decide what style we're to do it in—Brechtian or Stanislavsky or Beckett or modern.' And I said: that is absolutely appalling, that's not what theatre is about. Theatre is about going on a journey with a group of actors and a dramatist and finding out your style from the way that you do it.

But that's what teaching theory is about.

Yes, absolutely.

To what extent do you think there was a revolution—or an alleged revolution—detonated by Look Back in Anger *at the Royal Court in 1956?*

I'm deeply sceptical—I'm not being wise after the event: I was deeply sceptical at the time. To me, *Look Back in Anger* was a bit like *Hernani* [by Victor Hugo]— you know, a famous play which changed the course of history, but when you go back and actually look at the play you say: well, how did it do that? Where is the play? Because it isn't there. What *Look Back in Anger* did do was to convince a whole generation of young writers that writing for the theatre was as vital and progressive and attention-getting as writing your first novel or your slim book of poems. It unquestionably made writers think about theatre. We all read into *Look Back in Anger* a kind of Socialist cry for new freedoms and breaking down of class barriers and moving into the future. Looking at the play now, you wonder where it is, you wonder how we saw that. But we saw it because we needed to see it. The success of *Look Back in Anger* was a journalistic success of its day; I think the play now is a somewhat creaky period piece.

But Joan Littlewood's work at Stratford East seems to me to be genuinely revolutionary.

It was.

And has informed a whole theatre ever since. In 1956 the Berliner Ensemble visited and— equally significantly—it was the first performance in London of Waiting for Godot, *which you directed.*

1955. One year earlier. What Brecht brought to us was passionate advocacy of the fact that what you put on the stage has to be necessary. It begins with the fact that you can't ask people to spend two hours of their lives, three hours of their lives, without considering carefully what you're doing. Brecht made us understand that to put an object on the stage there had to be a reason for it to be there, that decoration was actually irrelevant and misleading. He made us understand that argument could be sexy, that politics could be sexy and passionate, and above all, just in technical terms, he made us understand that texture on the stage, whether it be human or scenic, was all important. And that with new lighting we could now put a brick wall on the stage and turn it into a thing of beauty: we didn't need to paint a brick wall because it would never be as beautiful as the bricks. I mean, all those things were in the air, and they certainly were in all of us when we were creating the Royal Shakespeare Company. As far as Joan Littlewood is concerned, she made that flesh—all that I've been saying. It was popular in the best sense, and she had a passion about her work, which wasn't dry and wasn't teutonic. And there was humour. I would agree with you: I think she was the greatest revolutionary in the British theatre.

More significant than the Royal Court?

What George [Devine] did by bringing the writer back into the theatre, I don't think we should diminish that. Because of Osborne and because of the respect given to the writer, writers' theatre happened again. Now whether that was more important than Joan or not, I would find difficult to say. Where the juice is, where the passion is, where the emotion is, where the entertainment is, is where Joan Littlewood is. There's no question. I spent many, many, many dismal evenings at the Royal Court during the late fifties and sixties watching plays that didn't tell very good stories but which were socially committed and weren't very entertaining. On the other hand I also spent some good evenings there. So, I'll vote for Joan Littlewood, but I don't want George Devine to be knocked off the list.

Is it the case that Devine and the Royal Court have been lauded because the texts survive, whereas Joan Littlewood's work was wholly theatrical and therefore wholly ephemeral?

It doesn't exist, does it? And that's the sadness of the theatre. People learn about Joan Littlewood in Theatre Studies, but they can't know about her as they can know about Osborne or Bond or Wesker or all the other Royal Court dramatists. It's typically British that we come back to text, because we love being able to define things in literary terms which is one of the problems that our theatre always has.

You did Godot *in '55. Nothing was known about Beckett in this country. What was the response?*

I was running the Arts Theatre in Great Newport Street. I was twenty-four, and I was in the middle of dress-rehearsing *Mourning Becomes Electra*, which I'd always wanted to direct. I went into my little cupboard office and found a script which said *'Waiting for Godot* by Samuel Beckett', and a letter from Donald Albery, who was a West End impresario. It said: 'I don't know whether you know this play: it's on in Paris in a seventy-five-seat theatre, and it's been on for some time; it's very highly regarded. No one will do it in the West End, no director will touch it, and every actor has turned it down. I've seen some of your work at the Arts Theatre, and I liked it, so I wonder whether you'd like to do it.' So with a sense that I was certainly at the end of the queue, I looked at it. I'd vaguely heard of Beckett; I hadn't read a word of him; I hadn't seen the play in Paris, but I'd heard of it. And I read it. I won't say that I said to myself: this is the major play of the mid-century and it's a turning point in drama, but I did find it startlingly original. First of all that it turned waiting into something dramatic. Second, that waiting became a metaphor for living. What are we actually living for, what are we waiting for, will something come, will Godot come, will something come to explain why we're here and what we're doing. And I found it terribly funny, and I also found it genuine, poetic drama. We'd just lived through the time of T.S. Eliot and the time of Christopher Fry and the time of W.H. Auden, where poetic drama—which was usually done in tiny theatres in Notting Hill Gate—was trying to put poetry back into theatre by sticking it onto ordinary dialogue like sequins. It was very false and very artificial. And here was somebody who had an extraordinary ear, an extraordinary rhythm for writing, which was both clear and eloquent and full of character and very funny. Of course I knew it was Irish: that's very important, because you know out of O'Casey comes Beckett. No question. No question. Out of Joyce comes Beckett, no question. But it was an individual voice, and I thought: well, what have we got to lose, let's do it. So I went off on holiday leaving *Mourning Becomes Electra* running, armed with all the volumes of Proust which I'd never read. I was a very serious-minded youth.

Translation from the French?

Oh, translated; no, no, not in French, alas. And I settled down on the beach to read all these, and I think I got to volume eight or nine and a telegram arrived saying: '*Mourning Electra* failing return at once for *Godot.*' Which I did, and I've never finished Proust which seems to me an eloquent moral to the whole tale and I did *Godot*. Very hard to cast it, nobody wanted to do it: they all thought it was mad, they all thought it made no sense. I could never understand why people didn't understand what was going on, what was happening, but they didn't. We ended up with a cast of Peter Woodthorpe, Paul Daneman, Peter Bull and Timothy Bateson, and in a hot summer we started rehearsing it. Peter Bull practically died as Pozzo carrying all those bags and whips. Gradually the cast began to understand it and began to feel it. I have to say I felt from the very beginning terribly comfortable in the rhythms. I didn't know whether I was doing the right thing, but I had that wonderful feeling that a director can have when he's happy: that there's only one thing to do and that's what you do. So you don't say to yourself: what *ought* I to do? I felt completely at ease. The play opened in late August or September 1955. The first night was full of cheers and counter cheers. When Estragon said: 'Nothing happens, nobody comes, nobody goes, it's awful,' an English voice said: 'Hear, hear!' There was a good deal of that going on, and audible sighs and yawns, and at the end there were cheers and boos. My new agent, who was terribly grand, met me backstage pink with rage and said: 'Everything is just beginning for you as a director, you've got a West End play, you're going on Broadway and then you go and do a thing like this.'

So people were shocked?

They were absolutely baffled, a lot of them. But half the people said: this is it, this is what we've been waiting for. And the press reaction was equally divided. Philip Hope-Wallace in the *Guardian* said: 'This is the sort of thing that we saw in basements in the twenties in Berlin, and it really won't do.' And there was quite a lot of patronising and joke-making, because it was an easy target. I was very dubious after the daily press whether it would run. The owner of the Arts called me the day after it opened and said: I don't think we can keep this on. I said: just wait for the Sundays, please. I'd sent a copy of *Watt* [Samuel Beckett's novel] to Harold Hobson [drama critic of the *Sunday Times*] just saying: this might interest you as background to the play. And he had a complete Pauline conversion to Beckett. And he went on writing about it for the next six weeks. Tynan [in the *Observer*] was enthusiastic but less so than Hobson, though he became very enthusiastic as the *Godot* bandwagon rolled. And it did roll. It's extraordinary now to think of—we were more one nation then. We didn't have so much press, we didn't have so many television channels, we didn't have so many radio channels. But it was everywhere. There were cartoons about *Godot*. I was on *Panorama* interviewed about what was the meaning of it, was it the Cold War? It went on, on and on and on and on, and it ran for over a year. It really got me started, it got me to Stratford. Because of that I met Leslie Caron, who became my first wife and I directed her. Tennessee Williams gave me his plays to direct in London. It completely transformed my life. On the level of what it brought to theatre, I think it nailed the colours again to the old mast of theatre: that theatre is a place of imagination and of metaphor and of contradiction. It's the Shakespearean mast to me. It also says that there is no active theatre without the tension between the form of the writing, the form of the creation, and the emotion that the actor is trying to express. Whether it's Shakespeare's iambic pentameters or whether it's Beckett's very precise, beautiful cadenced prose, it has a rhythm and an actuality.

And it frees you from feeling that theatre has inevitably to be about social subjects?

I would advance the theory that *Godot* is the masterpiece of the mid-century, certainly way, way, way more important than *Look Back in Anger*. And it's still there now as a great play and will remain so because it has a metaphorical richness which makes one think of Shakespeare. If you want to think of *Godot* as a play about politics, it's there. If you want to think about *Godot* as a play about relations, intimate relations between man and woman, or man and man, or friend and friend like an early version of *Who's Afraid of Virginia Woolf?*, it's there. Those two tramps quarrel like man and wife, they need each other like man and wife, they can't split up like man and wife. I said they're tramps. Well, Beckett doesn't say they're tramps, Beckett just says they're Estragon and Vladimir. I made them into tramps without thinking about it: they seemed to me to be tramps. And they've gone round the world as tramps because of me and I'm very embarrassed about that, so I wish to record they're not necessarily tramps.

But they are in Beckett's own production.

More or less, yes, more or less. But that was after mine. I mean. [*laughs*]

In your view did he emancipate a whole generation from naturalism?

I don't think that Harold [Pinter]—or Tom [Stoppard]—would have written the way they did write—or at all, had it not been for Beckett.

Harold's is a voice that is entirely singular, as with all great writers.

Harold Pinter's voice is rooted in cockney and in Jewish cockney. And that's what it is. And even when he moves out of it, it's still there as a point of reference in some strange and peculiar sense. The basis of Harold's drama isn't anything to do with Beckett: it's piss-taking, the cockney phrase. 'Piss-taking' is me mocking you. The essential thing about piss-taking is that, as I mock you, you should not be sure that I am mocking you, because if you can see I'm mocking you then I have lost. The whole of Harold's drama is based on that in one form or another. And the piss-take actually hides violent emotions. Underneath every Pinter play there is a very strong melodrama, very basic and full of hate and hostility. When I'm directing Pinter I often rehearse with all the inner feelings made overt, and the actors all scream at each other. Then they know what it is they're bottling, what they're hiding, what they're containing. I get the feeling always in Harold's work that somewhere or another there is this outsider, this maverick, this boy from Hackney Grammar School who's threatened by all sorts of impossible people who have power over him. That's become more and more clear: it's a kind of surrealistic image.

Talking of power, let's talk about the National Theatre.

Power, [*chuckles*] yes.

The genesis of the National Theatre was a long one.

Well, the genesis of the National Theatre was a hundred and fifty years or so. The RSC was actually started in '59, the National Theatre opened in '63. I mean, I—these dates are on my mind because I've always been told that I made the RSC in order to try and stop the National Theatre. I made the RSC because I wanted to be sure the RSC could go on in spite of there being a national theatre.

If the RSC came out of artistic desire, what was the motivation for the foundation of the National Theatre?

Olivier and Richardson ran the Old Vic at the New Theatre at the end of the war, and those great seasons certainly had an enormous effect on me, because I saw all the work. There was a kind nostalgia for a repertory theatre and a company, which I think was enshrined in Olivier, and a feeling that the long march of the theatre had become respectable through Irving and then Olivier and all the knighthoods and all the rest, you know. The theatre needed that kind of recognition. Granville Barker's idea of the National Theatre was as a great lending library with some thirty-five plays on the shelf ready to be performed. I've personally never believed in that because I don't think you can maintain more than three or four plays at a time at the right level. But everybody subscribed to it. Olivier saw it as his crowning achievement, his life work. Probably, without wishing to be rude about him, I think it was that more than any aesthetic desire—a feeling that the theatre and he must meet in order to crown the whole thing. There were enormous attempts to stop the RSC, because it was thought that we couldn't have two national theatres. Indeed in 1959 Larry asked me to join him at the National to be his number two, and I said: I'm going to Stratford to be my own number one. We had many little, slightly irritable fights during those early years. There was quite a lot of tension at times, although we remained friends.

But the friendship was broken when you were appointed?

When he was starting the National Theatre there came the moment when his health went and he really wasn't in a state where he could go on running the theatre. And I deeply sympathise with the tragic nature of this: he wanted to stay one day and he wanted to go the next. I was approached to succeed him and I said: I really can't consider it until he knows. Because he's got to be talked to. So nothing happened for months and months and months and months, and then finally the board said to Larry—this was Lord Goodman and Lord Rayne—Lord Goodman was Chairman of the Arts Council: 'You know, you can't go on and we want to approach Peter Hall.' At that point I had a telegram from Larry which was pages long and was in very purple prose, which he was very addicted to, saying: 'Dear heart, I never dreamed that I could be so lucky as to have you come and succeed me, I feel the future is in safe hands.' And it went on and on and on and on. And I thought, well, that's all right. 'Do come round and see me.' And I went round and saw him, and we had a wonderful chat at his apartment, and I thought all was well. The next day or the day after—I'm not quite sure which—he called a meeting of the entire company and all the staff, with Ken Tynan, who was the *éminence grise* of Larry's political self, and Larry said: 'They've appointed a man from the opposition, the RSC, and I'm very upset about it, and I wasn't consulted.' And that's what I came into. I had a very difficult time trying to make Larry stay, trying to get him to open the South Bank, trying to help him through a succession of dreadful illnesses. And I really felt it was his National Theatre and it was his building: he should've opened it, and he didn't. It was one of the nastiest periods of my life: the friendship went because I was the next generation—I was the future. And I understand it all: none of us likes giving up. And Larry wasn't just the king, he was the emperor of the theatre.

You were on the building committee of the National Theatre with Olivier and John Dexter, Michel Saint-Denis, Ken Tynan, Peter Brook, George Devine, Jocelyn Herbert and others.

We were all firmly of the opinion that the National Theatre should be two auditoria. One that was, as far as we could manage it, a state-of-the-art theatre from the moment that we were building it, and one a studio space which was completely flexible. Larry said: 'Where will I be able to invite the Comédie Française? We must have a proscenium theatre.' And Tynan said: 'If a proscenium theatre is good enough for Brecht, it must be good enough for the National Theatre; we must have one.' So the unloved object, the Lyttelton Theatre, was created. I think it still looks unloved. It doesn't have any real dynamic: it looks as if it's there because everybody thought we'd better have it but no one really wanted it. So we made a minority report, Michel, Peter, George and I, saying we don't want this. But it was overruled because Larry was the boss man, and that was it. So the National Theatre was built with three diverse auditoria, and I don't have to tell you the aesthetic of the three spaces is entirely different. Added to which it has a remit to do the best of world drama from Aeschylus to David Hare and beyond. So how can you actually run the National Theatre—you've done it, I've done it—except as a kind of Harrods? You can't run the National Theatre with a view, with an aesthetic. It's impossible. That's the weakness of the situation. The National Theatre is too big, and the RSC is too big. Both organisations—and I should know because I grew up with both of them—became bigger and bigger by the year because only by overproductivity could they justify their subsidy and only by getting the subsidy could they have proper working conditions. What we really wanted was one theatre, one company and a repertory of four or five plays a year subsidised at a level which the English would never accept.

Called the Old Vic Theatre.

Called the Old Vic Theatre, yes, in some measure. Yes, of course. One of the hideous problems I had in opening the South Bank was that an organisation which had done four or five productions a year in the Old Vic and had a company of some thirty or thirty-five actors was suddenly doing twenty or twenty-one productions a year in three theatres. We didn't just expand, we exploded.

So is the National Theatre's artistic vision defined by its building?

The good thing about it is that the English don't like artists, but they like institutions. And they love institutions that have buildings, because if you have a building you have to fill it.

Looking at the theatre of the past century—company after company, artistic movement after artistic movement—it seems it's impossible to sustain creative momentum for more than seven years.

Yes, I would agree: seven to ten years. What saddens me now is that the RSC is no longer a company. But that is partly because they engage actors on a seasonal basis and partly because Equity doesn't allow long contracts any more, whereas I made the RSC with three-year contracts, and some people stayed for seven years. The National Theatre doesn't have a company because you can't have a company that serves three theatres and that amount of work. I don't believe that a theatre ever changes anything except by being a company. Where have been the revolutionary moments? You speak of Joan Littlewood: there was a company. You speak of Brecht: he had a company. One of the problems of the Court and of George Devine was that there wasn't a company: there was a loose group of actors and writers, but there wasn't a company. On my gravestone I want: 'Created the Royal Shakespeare Company.' You can then put a footnote: 'He opened the South Bank.'

Ian McKellen

1 9 3 9—

Actor. Ian McKellen's performances include Edward II, Richard II, Hamlet, Faustus, Romeo, Macbeth, Salieri, Coriolanus, Lopakhin, Iago, Richard III, Vanya, Lear and Widow Twankey. He has been a very active campaigner for gay rights. I interviewed him at the Old Vic, and he mused about the wisdom of exchanging this theatre for the one on the South Bank. As he uttered this heresy, there was a huge thunderclap and torrential rain. Water started spewing over the stage from the flies and gushed out of an imperfect downpipe near huge electrical junction boxes. He said ruefully: 'Well, I suppose that's our answer.'

Shakespeare is fascinated by the process of acting, isn't he?

Shakespeare wasn't the last actor to become a playwright. Harold Pinter, John Osborne, David Garrick, Noël Coward, Alan Bennett, many others. It seems to us theatre people, sentimentalists that we are, that Shakespeare is one of us. He's not an outsider. That's why we resist so strongly the idea that he could have been Francis Bacon or the Earl of Oxford or Queen Elizabeth or anybody else who's a candidate for having written the plays. They were clearly written by a man steeped in the theatre, who found in the theatre an inspiration. The metaphor so often used to express a character's dilemma will be taken from the theatre: the idea that Richard III is playing a part, that Iago too is disguising in a way that an actor disguises his intentions, and the idea that all the world's a stage and all the men and women merely players. That notion rings through all the plays, and it's a very potent image for actors: my goodness, Shakespeare thinks that if you can understand acting you can understand human nature better. Certainly we're the only animal to act.

Does 'acting' mean 'pretend to be someone you're not'?

That's right. Lions don't, you know, a lion is a lion. A leopard might change his spots, but he's still a leopard. And you look at a dog on screen or on stage or in your living room, whatever it does, whatever position you put it into, whether it's sleeping, walking, farting, it's a dog and has its own dogginess. Human beings are forever changing. Very good at lying, human beings.

Is it possible to apply a system to acting? A method? Or 'The Method'?

I'm the wrong person to ask about the Actors Studio or any acting discipline because whenever I pick up a book on acting I agree with it. I think where I find the Stanislavsky system true—which was revealed to the Americans through Lee Strasberg and the Method school of acting—is that I can't be believable in a part unless I've absorbed the character's experience somehow into my own experience, found some equivalent in my own life, probably emotional, which will help me identify with the character's emotional situation. And that's at odds with that sort of 'well-darling-we-just-learn-the-lines-and-we-don't-bump-into-the-furniture' acting. Of course you can act like that and the play may work because the playwright's intention and message is so strong, but it's likely to work better, more effectively, more satisfyingly if the actor is committed through their own experience.

But at the same time as the actor is doing everything you say, you're standing outside yourself at the same time as being within the character.

Well, yes, yes, you're right. I part company with any actor who says: 'Oh, please don't make me rehearse.' I've heard actors say this about film, for example: 'I don't want to say the lines until the camera's rolling, otherwise they won't be truthful, they won't be me.' Well, I do believe in preparation, and I do believe in recollecting the lessons learned during the rehearsal period. I also know that on stage particularly—but also in the intensity of the moment in which you film— you are the character as much as you can be, but you are also inevitably ninety-nine per cent yourself and aware of what you're doing. You have to hope that you're not *entirely* aware of what you're doing, and that the experience of the rehearsals and the support of the rest of the cast and the magic of the words you're saying will support you in daring to jump off the top of the diving board, not entirely certain that there's enough water underneath. Or maybe you'll fly just as you reach the surface of the water. That aspect of acting is terribly important and is probably what marks out the great performers from the lesser.

Shakespeare loves playing with the idea of people pretending to be something that they aren't and then revealing themselves to the audience. That's something like the process of acting itself, isn't it?

I would argue that though all human beings are adept at disguise and that acting is part of human experience, some of us are better at it than others. [*laughs*] And Richard III and Iago are supreme. When Richard III tells the audience that he's going to get a wife and proceeds to woo the widow of the man that he himself has killed in battle, you have to admire him.

Because it's a great piece of acting?

It is a great piece of acting, but where does it come from? It comes from his sympathy with Lady Anne's predicament. Knowing what she wants to hear— which is better than just lying because it implies an understanding. What does the widow want more than anything else? A return to the massive security of money and social position and so on, which Richard himself can now offer her as a substitute for her dead husband. Being alert to that possibility makes his lies very specific and makes the audience admire it.

That's exactly like acting, isn't it? You have to sympathise with the character, but you don't actually become the character, is that right?

Well, these are sort of imponderables. I don't think I've ever been impersonating a character or acting on a stage or in front of a camera when Ian McKellen has ceased to exist and the character has become me. However, there have been moments in the rehearsal room of intense concentration when I have, apparently spontaneously, done—and seen other actors do—things that could not have been planned or arrived at by talking about them: the director and the actor know that in that moment of inspiration—you have to call it that—you've landed on a truth about the character which you hadn't known before. And from that truth, and from the memory of that moment when you did feel to be less yourself than normal and more the character, you can build the rest of the character and the rest of the performance.

Shakespeare constantly moves between private scenes and public scenes and examines people's responsibility to society and their individual responsibilities. This is something that theatre, it seems to me, does uniquely well, because you put a group of people on a stage and you have a whole society.

I think the nature of Shakespeare that most appeals to me is the theatricality of the presentation of the stories. For other people it might be the philosophy, it might be the beauty of the verse and so on, or the variety of his characters. For me it is that every story he tells is told theatrically.

What exactly do you mean by 'theatrical'?

The audience is within sight and sound of the person telling the story. The fascinating thing about the discovery of the remains of the Rose Theatre—a theatre which predates the Globe—is that the Rose was very small. It might have held two thousand people just, packed in very tightly like a crowd at a football match, but they would all of them have been very close to the stage. When King Lear said: 'Pray you undo this button,' the button would be visible to the audience. And there would be a degree of naturalism and reality there which is at odds with the notion of Elizabethan actors being rather bombastic and unnatural in their presentation. The contact between the actor and the audience through the airwaves and the voice—generated from the diaphragm muscle and intimately going through the larynx and the cheeks and the lips and the tongue— travelling across the space and landing on your eardrum… it's a very intimate process going on.

These days there doesn't seem to be a tolerance of what you might call 'heroic acting'—the acting of Olivier and Gielgud. It's not considered fashionable or acceptable. We want our Shakespeare in small spaces—like your Macbeth at The Other Place [with Judi Dench, directed by Trevor Nunn, 1976].

Shakespeare's popularity seems to change as the centuries go by. In the eighteenth century the nobility of the characters was much remarked upon, and the Victorians too were interested in the heroics of Shakespeare. Today we are at least as interested in the minor characters, who are much closer to our own lives. But I think some critics talk about the actors of the past as if they were somehow incompetent, and that their high-flown, Victorian style of acting—which suited the large theatres in which they worked—was crude and detrimental to Shakespeare. Those actors—and actors before Henry Irving, right back to Richard Burbage and all the rest of them—have all been renowned in their time for being real, being true, being natural and introducing those qualities to Shakespeare's plays. When Burbage died someone said: Burbage, he can't be dead, I saw him die before, as Othello. In other words, Burbage's death scene had been so real that a member of the audience was prepared to believe that the actor had died. Today we're post-Freud: we're very interested in what goes on behind the eyes; we want to be close to the actors; we want to *guess* at what's going on and not have it thrown in our face. We don't look at Coriolanus and say: what a magnificent creature of the jungle he is, determined to get his own way. We say: well, what's his relationship with his mother? This man's got a psychological problem.

You said to me once that you went into the theatre for the boys. To what extent was the theatre a world of coded homosexuality?

It seems to me that people who want to become professional actors are one of two types: either their ego is so well developed that they can't find satisfaction unless they stand up on a stage or in front of a camera, or they are like the rest of us, who are more tentative, unsure of our place in the world, seeking the security of learning lines and standing up on stage knowing that nothing's going to go wrong on the whole because life—at least for the two hours' traffic of our stage—is organised. Then the real world imposes itself. If you're a gay man you might well be in either category. I was in the latter, living in a country where sex with my own gender was illegal and hoping in the theatre to be able to be open as a gay man. I'd heard that there were other homosexuals flourishing in the theatre, and indeed it proved to be the case and I became one of them. But I might have been that sort of flamboyant homosexual who can't get enough attention. The world that I was trying to join, of course, was dominated in the fifties by famous men, famous homosexuals, none of whom said that they were in public.

Coward?

Noël Coward, yes, Terence Rattigan—playwrights. And John Gielgud, prime actor. All of them working with H.M. Tennent, the West End management that was run by Binkie Beaumont—another closeted gay man.

But do Coward's plays contain coded gay signals within them?

Coward seems to have been proudest of his 'talent to amuse', which he exercised supremely for a very specific audience—whether it was the audience of middle-class holidaymakers in Las Vegas or the high society of London's West End or of Broadway. He gave them the sort of fare that they would like, much of it ironic and satirical. He would poke fun, but I don't think he was the sort of playwright or performer who was in the business of self-revelation—'understand me and you will understand the world'—rather he was commenting on the world that he moved in. His homosexuality crept in every so often: he certainly wrote plays in his youth and his old age about homosexual characters, but they don't dominate his major work. I think he and Rattigan accepted the status quo in which they were allowed to flourish as highly paid entertainers adored by their public: why should they have wanted to rock the boat by declaring that there was something about them that their public mightn't have liked?

Judi Dench

1 9 3 4—

Actor. Judi Dench has been at her considerable best in theatre, film and TV since her debut as Juliet in Franco Zeffirelli's production at the Old Vic in 1960. When I interviewed her she was recovering from appendicitis but still climbed four storeys to a dressing room at the Theatre Royal, Haymarket, without complaint. At one point in the interview, as we were talking about Shakespeare, she gave an effortless demonstration of verse-speaking with some lines of Cleopatra—rhythm, sense and sound in perfect sync:

> *'His face was as the heavens, and therein stuck*
> *A sun and moon which kept their course and lighted*
> *The little O, the earth.'*

Is Shakespeare all-inclusive?

He tackles things like love, jealousy, envy, greed, meanness of spirit—there's no end to that list, in fact. And he tackles them in such a complete way, in a kind of contemporary way. I defy any young person who goes to see a really good performance of *Romeo and Juliet* not to have those feelings in their gut when they watch it. 'My bounty is as boundless as the sea' —any young girl who says that can't help but strike chords in people who have been through the gloriousness of falling in love. There's only one play I don't like and that's *The Merchant of Venice*, because I don't think anyone behaves very well in that. Or that anyone comes out very well from it.

Is that part of why Shakespeare's so good, because we talk about this group of people that we don't like very much, as if they existed? After all, that's true in life.

Indeed it is. I know that in life there's perhaps no redemption for us all, but in most of Shakespeare's plays there's a bit of redemption for somebody. In *The Merchant of Venice* there's no redemption for anybody at all. I just find that at the end, the tunnel closes.

So part of his genius is that his characters are as complex and as mysterious as people?

I think that's right. How did he not only understand how men feel, but also how women feel—and not just young women, but much older women, and women of every class?

Can you give me an example of a woman he really understands apart from Juliet?

Hermione in *The Winter's Tale*. That's just such an extraordinary part to play. And then you come to somebody like Mistress Quickly in *Henry V*. There's virtually only the one speech, but in that speech is everything that you need to play that part. Everything you need about her love for Falstaff. And about his death.

Can you remember it?

'For his nose was as sharp as a pen and a babbled of green fields. How now, quoth I, how now Sir John, quoth I. What man, be of good cheer. So he lay, he bade me lay more clothes on his feet…' I've never played Quickly in *The Merry Wives of Windsor*, but if you were to just read that speech first, it would give you an incredible clue as to how to play her when she was younger, with Falstaff behaving very badly all over the place.

Does the fact that Shakespeare effectively grew up in a theatre have a bearing on his work?

Well, he certainly knew what worked in the theatre. And for four hundred years people have been doing him in different ways. There was a wonderful film of *Romeo and Juliet* [directed by Baz Luhrmann, 1996] recently. Everything in me resisted going because I thought it was going to be very much bent in order to make it work, but it wasn't. That whole thing of the guns having 'Sword' written across them meant that when they said 'Put up your swords!' it made complete sense. You can't really mess about with Chekhov or Ibsen or Tennessee Williams, but you can in a way mess about with Shakespeare and very often it's very successful.

Do you think there's something about being an actor that gives you a particular view of the world or just a particular view of theatre?

Actors don't judge people. They're able to stand outside and mock authority and take rather an objective view about things. It's why I resent very much the nickname of 'luvvies'—it's only used by people who don't understand what our job is about. I don't mean to elevate it in any way: I just mean that there's something more compassionate about a group of actors, simply because what they have to learn in their job—and I won't say 'craft' because I do think that sounds a bit grandiose—somehow makes them see things in a more three-dimensional way than a lot of other people do.

It's more or less the definition of a bad performance when you see an actor making a judgement on a character, isn't it?

The thing about acting is: you don't play what's on the page. What you play is like that cake called *mille-feuille*, which is made of thousands of layers of that thin pastry. It's as if the line is the bit of icing on the top. The bit you're playing is the fifty-ninth bit of pastry. So that what you're saying is one thing, what you're meaning is quite another. And that's not to say it's duplicity in any way.

The production of Macbeth [for the RSC] that Trevor [Nunn] directed with you and Ian [McKellen] is really the only successful production of the play in the last thirty years. Why do you think that was so?

Actually, Trevor tried to pull out of it just before we did it. Ian and I stuck rather tenaciously to it because it was the reason we were going back to Stratford. But he said: 'You know, I've done it three times and I'm not sure about it,' but we just absolutely stuck to it. It was at The Other Place. We rehearsed it and rehearsed it, I remember one day, after three weeks rehearsing, walking back towards the theatre with Trevor, I turned to him and said: 'This is not going to work, is it?' And at that minute I fell off the pavement, which is something I'm rather given to. I picked myself up, and we had a bit of a laugh, and I said: 'But it isn't, is it?' And then I did an *enormous* trip. I remember it because of those two incidents. That was at a stage when it looked like it wasn't going to work. The play just wasn't taking off, you know. So Trevor shut all the lights off, then sent Ian up the stairs and me to the bottom and said: now feel your way round, try and do the scene after the murder. And from that minute, something took a kind of turn. I remember saying to Trevor: 'We ought to really do this for schoolchildren who might come to it and think that perhaps they don't even do the murder.' We somehow concentrated the play more. And of course there was really no money for costumes, we all just got our costumes from store and we all dressed together in a tiny room, in a cupboard actually. I was with the three witches, all of whom smoked heavily. The level of childishness in the dressing room before the performance every single night was like I have never experienced in the theatre before.

I've felt in the presence of evil watching that play. Is it true that the theatre had to be exorcised?

I don't know, but a very nice vicar friend of ours saw it many times, and he used to sit there holding this crucifix in front of us.

How much is Shakespeare's language a barrier? How much do you treat it as an ally and how much as an obstacle?

When I first started to work at the Old Vic there wasn't much pressure about language. Nobody talked about it very much. When I played Juliet there for Zeffirelli [1960] nobody talked about it at all. In fact, we got criticised for it, but then I went to Stratford and learned about speaking the verse, which always sounds much more frightening than it actually is. Once you learn the rules you chuck them out of the window.

What are the rules?

The rules are that you obey the punctuation and you obey the line ends. I'm going to sound, you know, analytical to talk of it that way. It ceases to become like that. But all I can say is that once you have learned that, and learned that you must actually mark the line ends and not run the thing on, and that half-lines must be half-lines—Shakespeare tells you where you should pause and where you shouldn't pause. What it teaches you is to be not indulgent about the verse. Because sometimes it's like somebody singing: 'I left my heart in San Fran.' What you also learn about language is to use the line for the emotion. You don't pause and *then* drum up the emotion of what you've just said: the line and the emotion are on the same level. That's what you use. Then you always have that inside you, and it never goes away. I always feel that it's up to us to pass it on, because it's the most wonderful storehouse to draw on and something you should never forget.

Can you give me an example of line endings, of end-stopping the line?

I remember Peter Hall saying that Peggy Ashcroft used to stress the end of the line before. Some people stress the beginning of the next line. It's just a way of marking how it's written. I've always said that if you speak Shakespeare, the two people you can learn the most from are John Gielgud, who presented the entire arc of a speech, and Frank Sinatra. He never indulges any bit of it. You never lose out on the absolutely essential part of it.

Is it difficult to talk about acting?

I don't think we should talk about acting because there's nothing to talk about, really. It's as if we are blank canvases. It's the play and the author and the author's intention that energise the actor. It's only when you're telling the story that you're doing your job; after you've done that there's nothing really to talk about. The glorious thing about live acting is that something changes every night. An audience is never ever the same. And actually I don't think the performance is ever the same. Not that you wilfully change things, but you react in a different way. The audience brings a reaction out of you that elicits another kind of reply or another stress, and that's why it's always moving. It never stands still. And you never actually get it right. You go on night after night after night trying to get it right and sometimes it gets better and sometimes it gets worse. But the actual business of doing it is what is exciting. Orson Welles said that the allure of live theatre is that that this could always be the night that the actor falls off the wire or something goes wrong.

Trevor Nunn

1 9 4 0—

Director. Trevor Nunn was Artistic Director of the Royal Shakespeare Company from 1968 to 1986, and of the National Theatre from 1997 to 2002. He has directed many musicals, including the world's longest-running, Les Misérables. *I interviewed Trevor Nunn at the National Theatre in what had been my office two years earlier. We talked about the difficulty of large theatres. He told me that he'd just had a letter from the architect who designed the National, Denys Lasdun, congratulating him on using the Olivier 'properly' for his production of* Summerfolk. *Trevor said he should have written back saying: 'Thank you. I had to raise the stage by three feet, move it downstage by seventeen feet, and cover most of the walls of the auditorium with black drapes. Apart from that, everything was as you designed it.'*

Do you think it's true to say that Shakespeare is our theatrical DNA?

I wish it were more true. Look, Shakespeare we think of as the great originator: I mean, what is Shakespeare's originality? Well, he invented the theatre as we understand it. Of course, he wasn't original in so many ways: he didn't create his own plots, he didn't create his own characters' names, he didn't do his own historical research and so on, so what is original? He created a theatre of recognition, a theatre wherein we see ourselves, we see human behaviour as we encounter it, as we feel the need to understand it. We can be shamed by him because of that recognition, or we can be elated by him because of that recognition. I don't think his contemporaries were really doing that. When I say

I wish Shakespeare were more identified as our theatrical DNA, I mean the great novelists of the nineteenth century clearly wanted to write like Shakespeare. They were writing in a different form, but they wanted to take on board all the lessons of Shakespeare. By the time we get to the twentieth century, Shaw puts himself in a competition with Shakespeare, and according to Shaw he himself emerges as the clear winner. Actually, our twentieth-century drama has been much more influenced by Ibsen and by Chekhov than by Shakespeare.

Do you not think recently we've seen a sort of leaning back towards a Shakespearean ambition?

I wish there were more of that ambition. I think that sort of Shakespearean ambition happens in a patchy way. Tony Kushner in *Angels in America* has got that exhilarating ambition, and we yearn for more. Of course when it happens, we recognise it as the real thing, but that's partly because we recognise it as a rare thing. Some of that is economic, some of that is because writers grow up in a world where the advice is: don't invent more than five characters because your play will never get on; don't invent too many scenic requirements because you know the main chance you've got is for it to be staged in a room above a pub. Those constraints somehow get into the system, but maybe if a big revolution could occur that stripped away scenic devices and presented texts in greater purity, then more of that ambition would be visible.

Your production of Macbeth *stripped away scenery and presented the text with great purity and intensity in a small space. How did that come about?*

My dear friend and late colleague Buzz Goodbody changed my mind completely about Shakespeare in small theatre spaces when in 1975 she did her formative, groundbreaking production of *Hamlet*. For me there was something definitive about that. It took place in a building called The Other Place. Ironically that building came into being as a small studio for Michel Saint-Denis to be able to train young actors for a brief time at Stratford. By the time that I [as Artistic Director of the RSC] discovered it, it was a scene store, a junkyard for discarded lumps of scenery. I initiated a move to convert it into a small theatre space. After a year of experiment and trial I appointed Buzz Goodbody as the first Artistic Director and gave her a very particular brief. She had a great time challenging it and at times refusing to do it—that's how we love such relationships to be. In her first year she did a small theatre production of *Lear*. What was interesting about that was that, although it had a lot of impact, it was still fundamentally a big theatre production spoken quietly.

What's the difference?

With her *Hamlet* there was a conversational tone; there was the certainty that thought was producing the text, because we were so closely involved we could hear every breath and sort of see into the eyes of each and every character. Therefore we could see the origin of thought, and that in itself banished textual music as a priority completely and totally and overnight. Now the shattering thing is that Buzz Goodbody took her own life just after the dress rehearsal of that production of *Hamlet*. That was something I was left with and continued to work on for the next year: her having made that breakthrough and probably not having realised the full impact of it. She left an extraordinary legacy, and the production that I did of *Macbeth*, which was the following year, was created entirely with the purpose of carrying on that work. I was incredibly fortunate that I had Ian McKellen and Judi Dench: that's something that being attached to a large company can provide. It's a staggering privilege because in most instances small theatre work can't begin to afford the time and the salary of major artists. Of course what we discovered with this radically unprojected piece of work was that we were able to dispense with every element of blasted heath and castle wall and apparitions underlit out of cauldrons and all of the detritus that had kind of barnacled the play over most of the century. What we had instead was an examination of the mental state of two people who were approaching an acknowledged act of evil, and then an investigation of the consequences of that act of evil upon their mental state, and upon their marriage. There was a kind of even-handed stillness and quietness about it. Everything was taking the audience towards the belief that they were in the room with real people, who were thinking those thoughts and who were convincing them that a murder was going on in the building which they were in some way party to, because they could hear the breathing of the other people asleep in the household in the middle of the night where it was taking place.

It seems to me that once this glorious dawn broke it's been impossible to go back. I've rarely seen a large-scale Shakespeare production that satisfied me since.

When you're working with a group of actors on a big theatre production what you have to stress is that they must find every image and they must float it across that huge auditorium: finding it, coining it, using it with energy are part and parcel of how you breathe a pentameter text. I think what we're discovering is that those things *can* happen in a big theatre without going to that other extreme of mouth music, of just singing a text, whereas in the small theatre you're actually asking the actor to do the opposite. You're saying in some way: we have got to convince an audience that this text is not being written down, it's not being learned and therefore there is no question of recitation, it's happening in the moment.

But that seems to me to be the essence of what I'd describe as the 'theatreness' of theatre, living in the moment.

Oh, entirely so, and of course different people will define what 'theatreness' is…

How do you define it?

I guess the best way that I can define it is when I did this huge labyrinthine show of *Nicholas Nickleby*, which was I suppose a kind of maniacal attempt to include every incident of a Dickens novel in one theatrical experience, inviting the audience to lose themselves in it while at the same time acknowledging that they are witnessing a theatre process. We came to film it, and an excited film producer was saying: look, I think I've got enough budget for us to be able to go out in the streets and we can get a real stagecoach and we can get some horses involved and so on. Of course what we had to say was: no, this is a theatre event, it's not at all in competition with those filmed Dickens works which are so splendid. This is theatre and it makes a quite different contract with its audience. The audience must have that sense that at any given moment they are part of what's happened to the point where they could change it, they can interrupt it, they can get more of it, they can extend the moment, they can diminish a moment.

How did you get involved with musicals?

I'm a kind of theatrical Gemini: some people would say a hopeless split personality. I grew up in a working-class community where my first exposure to theatre was musical shows and revues—I myself got involved in revue and a great deal of singing. I was part of a very primitive rock 'n' roll band, and my first jobs in the professional theatre turned out to be musical ones. I did a musical version of *Around the World in Eighty Days*, and my very first appointment at the RSC was to attempt to make a musical out of documentary material concerning the General Strike—*Oh! What A Lovely Strike*, if you see what I mean. I'm bound to say I didn't succeed, but I did several other things at the RSC, including a musical version of *The Comedy of Errors*, which David Merrick wanted to take to Broadway, so I suppose by then my name was on a list of people that commercial producers might be thinking of. And I suppose that was pushed along by the *Nicholas Nickleby* thing—which Andrew Lloyd Webber went to see. The first commercial musical that I did was *Cats*, which I suppose is like winning the lottery when you buy your first ticket, so I don't have a long history of struggle about how to hit the musical-theatre jackpot.

You never felt that there was a war between straight theatre and musical theatre, between 'serious' theatre and popular theatre?

I'm aware of people who most emphatically do, the people who think that there's a Grand Canyon between the two and that it's unbridgeable. I have no problem with it. I've never had any problem with it. I mean, my intention with *Cats* wasn't a small-time intention. I was thinking it would be good if we could invent something of a new theatrical form that would be environmental, that would be participatory, that would be fantastical, that would be a children's show for all generations. Consequently we broke pretty much all the rules that up to that point had applied to musical theatre. It wasn't behind a proscenium, there wasn't an orchestra pit, it wasn't under the constant control of a visible conductor, and so on and so forth. It was a piece of work that happened out in the auditorium: there were performing spaces around the auditorium, the audience was wrapped around three quarters of the stage, and the design was like a huge installation, so the audience had a very unusual level of live contact with the event. And I do believe that grown people felt that they were being induced back towards their childhood and were enjoying the experience. Now I'm really surprised that very, very few things have picked up in that territory. I'm not being pompous, but when I go back to see *Cats* it still feels like something of an experimental show, twenty years later, because most musical theatre since has stayed resolutely behind the proscenium arch.

Hugo's novel Les Misérables *was knowingly written for a mass readership. I think he said: 'I do not know whether it will be read by everyone, but it is meant for everyone.' He anticipated the modern historical novel, didn't he? It's history from the point of view of the scapegoat.*

Something very extraordinary still continues to happen in *Les Mis*, which I've witnessed in this country, in America and in Australia. There's a standing ovation that happens at the end which seems not to do with applauding actors taking a bow, because it happens as the last notes of the show are sung. The last notes of the show are a climactic kind of challenge to the audience: will you join this crusade? And the people who lead that standing ovation, in every audience, seem to be saying: 'I want to bear witness to something that this show is saying. I believe that we live in a profoundly unequal world and in an unjust society and not enough has changed since Victor Hugo wrote this, and I want to stand up and say that in some way.' While a show is continuing to do that with its audience then it seems to me that the show is still fully alive.

Vanessa Redgrave
1 9 3 7—

Actor. Vanessa Redgrave has played leading roles in Shakespeare, Chekhov and Ibsen, and has been a consistent campaigner for human rights. I interviewed her in a dressing room at the Gielgud Theatre, where she was in a Noël Coward play, A Song at Twilight. When she was very young, Coward came to see her in a play and gave her a wonderful compliment. I practically had to pull her fingernails out to get her to tell me what he had said: that she was incapable of being untruthful on stage. 'Not true,' she told me. Her performance as Rosalind in a TV version of Michael Elliott's production of As You Like It *in 1962 was the first Shakespeare performance that took my heart completely.*

In what way does Shakespeare hold a mirror up to the twentieth century?

Because persecution of people, on account of their race or their religion, has been the dreadful, terrible hallmark of the whole of the century, and because it was also the hallmark of the late years of Elizabeth and the early years of James I. And because being a refugee and being sent into exile has also been the hallmark both of our century and of Shakespeare's period. It seems to me that those are the chords that keep knocking and singing, and they certainly didn't sing in the eighteenth century. Or the nineteenth century as far as one can make out. Stalin would never allow *Macbeth* to be performed for one very simple reason: that Mandelstam referred in a poem to the 'Scottish Highlander' and everybody knew he meant Stalin. Of course, I only know at second hand through my East European friends, who lived through and survived into *perestroika*, what

67

it was like performing in the theatre, going to the theatre and translating in your head all the time—which is what I'm sure Shakespeare's audience was doing. You have to look at those artists in the 1930s in Hitler's Germany, Hitler's occupied Europe, Stalin's Russia and, post-Stalin, through to Gorbachev's vague political revolution to be able to get close to Shakespeare, I think.

You embrace Shakespeare's language easily. Did that come naturally to you?

I don't think so, no, I'm sure it didn't.

How did you learn?

Well, I went in for poetry competitions. And found Milton quite hard. And Milton is hard. And Wordsworth's hard too. I think that I learned the most, if we're speaking about Shakespeare, from a recording, a single 78 rpm record that I had of Michael Redgrave and Edith Evans doing Act Three of *As You Like It*. I was working on *As You Like It* with Michael Elliott at the time [1961] and was in very great difficulties. So I did two things. I started reading Elizabethan short stories, and as soon as I started reading those prose short stories everything began to come to life. However, I still needed a discipline. And listening to the recording of Dame Edith, speaking one of those wonderful complicated love scenes that Rosalind has with Orlando, I thought: there's my matrix. Now I'm going to learn how she's phrased all this and then be free and go with what Shakespeare wants—through and on top of and beyond that matrix. So I literally learned that matrix. It was only one scene.

There's something else too, that I discovered when I did the play that Eileen Atkins wrote, *Vita and Virginia* [1994]. Vita wrote to Virginia: 'You are incredible *par excellence*, you always have the *mot juste*.' And Virginia went for her as only Virginia could—and she adored Vita. She said: 'You are absolutely wrong, it's got nothing to do with it. Everything starts with an event, an emotion which produces a sort of a wave and out of the wave words come tumbling.' And when I realised that Virginia Woolf said that—and she, obviously with Shakespeare, are the two great writers of the last four centuries to be born in the UK or whatever we call it, not counting the wonderful Irish writers who are also amongst the geniuses of the world—when I realised that, it put into a sharp context what I had instinctively felt but couldn't formulate: that there is a matrix in verse and prose, and some people can find the way to the emotions and the events that created those words via the discipline, but I personally can't. I have to find the knowledge of the events that invades my body and mind and the emotions produced by those events that then made those words tumble. If I can get near to that then I find the way through. So I don't believe—with the most enormous respect for Peter Hall—I don't believe in the tick-tock pentameter approach to verse.

You started acting when you were very young. Were you seventeen?

First performances on the stage, the real stage, was in the Women's Institute in Frinton-on-Sea [1957]. I was eighteen. No I wasn't, I was twenty.

What did you think of the theatre of the time?

Well, the interesting thing is that I loved everything about the theatre that people like my father and George Devine and Tony Richardson absolutely could not stand. I loved it all. I loved red curtains, and I liked the razzmatazz, the trumpets and the kings and the queens. I was a real old-fashioned girl. And my father got so worried about it he sent me and my brother up to see some Joan Littlewood productions up at the Theatre Royal, Stratford East, and I hated the first performance I saw of Joan Littlewood's.

Which was?

Which was a fantastic production of *Richard II* [1954, with Harry H. Corbett]. I automatically compared it to my father's Richard II, which I'd seen two years before at Stratford. And I was horrified by the fact that there was no scenery, there was no velvet. There was no colour, no pageantry and I came back and, of course, my father was waiting up to hear me. And he said: 'Well, what did you think?' And I spieled off how much I'd hated it, and he got more and more solemn and began to look deadly, deadly disappointed. And then finally I had to stop because I realised something was terribly wrong. He said: 'I never want to hear you talk like that again. You are never, never to talk like that again.' I said: 'Why?' And he said: 'Because when you go and see anything, you must first of all try and understand what are they trying to do and why are they trying to do it. And when you've understood that, then you can say to yourself: have they succeeded in doing what they're trying to do? If you just ram out your own prejudices and preferences, you will understand nothing in the theatre, nothing in life.' And that I think is my lesson for life. Unfortunately I had to learn it a lot of times.

Good advice for critics too.

My father sent me off to watch Joan rehearse and watching her rehearse was fantastic, it was wonderful. It was thrilling. I watched her for a whole month, how she'd improvise and how she'd slam in a very friendly way, in a way that obviously everybody was totally used to, being very free and straightforward with each other. It was a modern dress *Volpone* [1955]—Mosca gets thrown into the grand canal of Venice, so he went along the orchestra pit with a snorkel in his mouth. It was full of all kinds of inventions like that. I was crazy about Joan Littlewood and didn't want to see any of the other old kind of theatre except my great hero Richard Burton.

What about Coward? More often than not he's viewed as somebody who is limitlessly superficial and is a brilliant light comedian, but you see him as somebody altogether more profound.

Yes I do. I feel him that way. I only knew him a little and that little remains my treasure, because of what he said to me when I was a young actress about acting needing to be totally, totally truthful. I always had the feeling that Coward's plays were of a much greater emotional and social depth than was customarily evident in the productions. I was convinced when I saw *The Vortex* at Greenwich for the first time in the early seventies with Vivien Merchant playing the mother: that powerful horror of what that mother and the son do—and especially what she does to him—is a landmark. And I think *A Song at Twilight* has got very, very great depths. He carries within him winds of some of the best writing that was ever produced. I actually rate him far higher than George Bernard Shaw, whom I absolutely loathe except for his first play, *Mrs Warren's Profession*.

You talk about Coward as committed to truthfulness, but it's hard not to see him as a sort of master of concealment.

We all know the court jesters were pretty brilliant, and I suppose Noël Coward's social position was something of the most brilliant court jester that ever lived. But I personally think that when in *A Song of Twilight*, his last play, he has the actress say to this writer: 'You might have been a great writer instead of a merely successful one,' he was talking to himself, relieving himself of whatever pain it caused him. He was a very kind man, and he was very kind to a load of people behind the scenes as well as loving them very much: women and men—because he did love women, and you can feel that in those marvellous parts.

Why does the theatre matter so much to you?

It's unique as a medium because, as far as I can see, it's the only place left in the world where people can stop and listen. I think that is as important as having a home and having food and having water and having health—to be able to sit together communally and listen and reflect and think and share. How many times have I been to the theatre and, though it might be that the production wasn't the most brilliant I'd ever seen in my life, nevertheless somehow the work that was being done, what had been written, a scene, an approach, made me think: 'Yes, life is worth living and we might win'?

Fiona Shaw

1 9 5 8—

Actor. Born in Cork, Fiona Shaw is celebrated for playing many classical roles—
Medea, Electra, Hedda Gabler, even Richard II. Most good actors are highly
intelligent; few are highly articulate. Fiona Shaw's fluency never leads her into
waffle, but as an actor she has often struggled to conceal her intellectual brilliance, like
a great beauty concealing her glamour. I interviewed Fiona Shaw in the living room
of my house in West London. With a film crew squeezed round the sofa where I was
used to sitting watching TV with my family, I felt as if we were playing an ambitious
children's game. Of the future of theatre she said: 'The theatre is a fantastic whore
and could be anything. If a thousand atom bombs drop, somebody will stand up in
the ashes and tell a story.'

Why do all the great Irish writers emigrate?

I suppose until this very decade the whole nation emigrated, I don't think it's
just writers that emigrated. Engineers emigrated, doctors emigrated. It's partially
the tragedy of the famine that the country just bred its nation for export. But
Joyce of course said that it is the sow that eats its own farrow.

Let's take two exiles: Yeats and Shaw. Shaw emigrated when he was twenty.

Shaw emigrated in desperation at the age of twenty. Actually not entirely
emigrated because he was trying to join his mother in London. He came to
London to write books and to make a name for himself, and I suppose, post-
Freudianly one would say, to recover what had been an absolutely tragic

71

childhood. He felt abandoned really by his mother, who was only interested in singing. And abandoned by his father, who was only interested in drinking. He had had a pretty tough time for a boy who was clearly very talented with words. So he came to take the place by storm, really. And he did, and he sort of didn't mind how he did it. As it happened, he wrote four or five novels—all of them unsuccessful—and then he wrote a play called *Widowers' Houses*. He had been very influenced at that time by Ibsen, who he felt was absolutely the coming thing. And he had been very influenced by Wagner and for a while was going to call *Widowers' Houses* '*Rheingold*', but he felt that it was too grand a name for something as modest as *Widowers' Houses*. He was very against the popularity of Shakespeare, because he felt he was popular for the wrong reason. He felt that the language of Shakespeare was being elevated for its poetical and for its philosophical content rather than as the voice of people speaking. So his aim was to write plays that had people speaking on behalf of political matters and social matters. Maybe he hit a moment when England really needed that. And he was shocking: *Mrs Warren's Profession* showed that prostitution was dependent on how you sold yourself, whether you sold your body or your skills.

He chose to write for the theatre at a time when actually there was no place in the theatre for somebody who was writing about politics or poverty or women's issues.

When he wrote *Widowers' Houses* nobody would put it on, so he finally raised the money and sort of put it on himself. And when they were trying to find an actor to play the character of Mr Lickcheese [a rent collector] they couldn't find anyone, so they found a fellow in the pub who was sort of dragged in to do it. Shaw had some sort of fundamental belief that the public statement was the thing that would get people going. He was absolutely prolific in every direction. He wrote, he cycled, he argued, he stayed with the Webbs and they all wrote. I mean, they cycled and argued.

It's one thing to write pamphlets for the Fabian Society, but it's another thing to write plays which you have to get put on when there's no audience for them. When he wrote Mrs Warren's Profession, *he couldn't even get it licensed by the Lord Chamberlain.*

You only had to put the word 'sex' in a stage direction and the Lord Chamberlain would ban it. So, like a lot of writers at the time, he had to be very dexterous to find a way in which he could discuss the subjects and get his plays on. And he had to wait. But he was full of a sort of weird, very Protestant, moral righteousness. You wouldn't get a Catholic writing like that. His moral righteousness was almost something of his own making. I mean, Wilde, who was his contemporary, didn't seem to have that moral righteousness at all. Shaw had a sort of fire or fury—I think anger was a very useful tool for him. He used the theatre because he was a theatrical concoction himself. He said: 'GBS is no truer in reality than a pantomime ostrich.' He was a self-invented fury, although he was rather shy, probably rather a sensitive man. He's a phenomenal contradiction—full of generosity and full of fury, full of public-spiritedness and full of private suffering. The theatre suited him because he could put the debate of two arguments—although many would say to a fault, in that he began merely to use the characters as voices of these arguments, making it terribly difficult to act.

You describe Shaw as self-invented, but Wilde is more or less a definition of self-invented man.

Wilde is a phenomenon. It's so interesting that he 'declared nothing but his own genius'. I think he was stunned by his own genius. I think he couldn't believe it. His ability to take a sentence and make it elegant and barbaric at the same time was really quite unprecedented. He, of course, came to London for slightly different reasons, and he had a different London, a much more privileged London than Shaw's London. They didn't share the same world. Yeats shared both their worlds.

Shaw took Wilde to lunch at the Café Royal to try to persuade him to leave the country during the first trials.

What they both shared, I suppose, is a reaction to a country which could never have contained the size of who they were—apart from anything else.

They both wrote eloquently about Socialism. Was Ireland the crucible of their political thinking?

In Shaw's case one feels it is absolutely, from his early days working in an estate agency that he absolutely loathed, and he was forced, unlike many Protestants in Ireland, for a moment in his life to be up against the banality and the cruelty of low city life, of a kind of business life. And, because he was sort of under-educated, he had to educate himself by going to municipal galleries. He felt very strongly the worth of public institutions. And he had a morality that he had to follow to the nth degree. He took his Fabianism to the end—he wouldn't accept the money that came with the Nobel Prize—which is so indicative of his genuine largesse when he had made enough money, after his genuine terror in early life that he would never be able to make a living.

Do you think that generosity of spirit is sometimes reflected in his characters?

His most popular play is *Pygmalion*, isn't it? I think it shocked him that it was so popular, because he hoped that it was a much more aggressive play. The English have in the end won by turning this rather vibrant man into an armchair matinée idol of Socialism. He was absolutely revolted by the class system, and yet somehow *Pygmalion* went to the heart of England in a way that both charmed the English as well as stunned them. So in *Pygmalion* you get both, don't you? You get the father of—what's her name?

Eliza.

The father of Eliza Doolittle seems to be some sort of rubric for a lot of London, yet Eliza has a kind of *grand esprit*. She seems to live in a way that a lot of his characters don't. Florence Farr, who played some of his early heroines, ended up going to run a school in India. He found that inconceivable. It implied that somehow he hadn't really known who she was at all, that he would sort of make constructs of people.

Do you think it's a fair criticism? Yeats said of him that he wrote like a sewing machine.

That's one of the wittiest things that Yeats said. I would've thought Yeats missed the point. Yeats comes from such a different area of interest and language. Yeats who can write lines like 'I have met them at close of day, / Coming with vivid faces / From counter and desk among grey / Eighteenth-century houses. / I have passed with a nod of the head / Or polite meaningless words.' It is this self-conscious symbolism of language which is not at all what Shaw was doing, is it?

He sometimes created characters which developed a heart in spite of him.

In just my little experience with Shaw you hit a sort of wall. It doesn't rise. You can put in the ingredients, stick it in the oven and somehow it is what it is. That's not to knock it for what it is. Brecht is the other person a bit like that. You can't turn Brecht into Chekhov; it just won't do it.

With Shaw, you have to follow the music of the language, you have to follow the punctuation, you have to follow the rhythm.

He's his worst enemy as people sometimes find with his stage directions. He describes the raised eyebrow of a character—which is just folly, because you can't expect good actors to mimic these particular visual gestures. In *Saint Joan*, of course, he's taken a poetical character and has damned her by insisting that she speak in a sort of peasant manner that he's written a special dialect for, which doesn't ever free her really to go beyond what he's written. And yet, of course, with the force of the argument, despite being trapped in this funny language, she does surmount it. Maybe actually she's a character who can float above him. He was strangely very admiring of actresses, as though somehow he acknowledged that he himself couldn't create the female characters in the end. I mean, he was very fond of Mrs Campbell and indeed Sybil Thorndike.

But his interest in actresses was rather more basic, wasn't it?

He did a lot of wooing, didn't he? He didn't necessarily always conquer. But he was interested in wooing. He used to drive the women mad—he would drop them, and he would get disinterested. He sort of stumbled—he was twenty-nine when he lost his virginity, and ended up being in bed with a friend of his mother's. A woman of fifty when he was twenty-nine. He withdrew from her and then endowed Florence Farr with his affections, and she got fed up walking around Primrose Hill with him as he blathered on about this and that and the other. He also had a tendency to get involved with a sort of *ménage à trois*, in that he would cuckoo-like inveigle his way into a family. He had no reason then to take responsibility for the woman because the husband already was doing that. He was best really conducting his affairs at a distance. He and his wife had, by her declaration, an unconsummated marriage. Maybe he just couldn't bear the drama of passion in that way. And I think in that way the person you read is very much the person who he is.

But at the same time he was a passionate advocate of women's freedom.

It is ironic that he should be the sort of marvellous feminist he was. But that was connected with his Socialism, wasn't it? It's the Socialist feminist, the notion of what is sauce for the goose. And sometimes his actresses complain that the characters are not full enough of contradiction, that they're vessels of morality, vessels of goodness, that they symbolise goodness. Something that I suppose David Hare took up later, that they became an object through which you could argue very complicated points.

They offer an argument against the men's world.

There is a sort of feminine in Shaw that nobody sees because of that big red beard and tweed suits.

Yeats was another self-construct. What was the character that Yeats invented for himself?

Yeats had a very emotionally underprivileged background—actually a bit like Stravinsky, somehow envious of his brothers and therefore needing to get his own back on everyone. So he became a poet and dressed like a poet and talked like a poet. And sadly by the end of his life people would cross the street in Dublin to avoid talking to the poet, because by then it had become ossified into this construction. However, within that he exercised a part of his brain which allowed himself the notion of having visions. That had always been a major part of a poet's life but had begun to go out of fashion as people were getting more social-realistic. But he constructed a kind of language where he could say anything in any way. Fantastic conglomerations of language that don't bear much scrutiny. It's not that they're without a truth, but they're pure language.

As in 'that gong-tormented sea'? He was a mystic and visionary, who at the same time was one of the most successful theatre producers of the twentieth century—responsible for launching Synge and O'Casey.

He wrote about himself that poets should be on their own, but he couldn't resist when he came to London setting up societies for Irish literature. In spite of himself he had this need to communicate with others. And I think also he and Maud Gonne, and maybe a few other lunatics like Countess Markiewicz, had this sort of permanent drawing-room world where they had been incarcerated for years, and suddenly there was a revolution. So it was very attractive to be able to piggyback your poetry or your energy onto a revolution, otherwise maybe the poetry would have died on a sort of stick of beauty. In that way he was very intelligent to map his energies onto something that could have a political and a poetical mystical dimension: that the Irish Revolution would produce a sort of Ireland which was full of leprechauns.

The paradox is that his protégés were Synge and O'Casey, who in neither case were what he and Lady Gregory had dreamed of.

He and Lady Gregory had a vision of Ireland which later turned into 'Irishness', that became a parody of itself. At the time what he was trying to do was recover stories that had been nearly lost. The famine and the penal laws were a catastrophe—this was the dark ages for Ireland. And it was fantastic that there was this man who could put his formidable intelligence into gathering the stories and writing them in his beautiful language. Also, of course, he was very committed to the English language because he himself didn't speak the Irish language. So if he was going to fuse with the culture, he was forced to find a way of making that culture modernise itself to the English language and yet not allow that language to be stolen by England. He had a complicated need to put himself at the centre of it. He and Lady Gregory were very laudable in what they wanted, but inevitably once you start something you can't control it. He couldn't have known what would happen when he encouraged Synge, who was looking for a subject to write about, to go to the Aran Islands: having come from Rathfarnham in Dublin, Synge was dazzled by this foreign language that was on his doorstep. O'Casey, of course, had to work like a blacksmith to create a sort of language about real things using real people.

Was O'Casey doing the equivalent of Synge listening through the floorboards?

I remember asking Donal McCann this, and he said that you could wear O'Casey's language like a coat—that it matched the Dublin that he lived in. He doesn't put air between the language and who he is. He steals from what people are saying and writes it down. He's not pretending it's poetical, and yet it does have of course a fantastic rhythm within it. Partially because those people, even though they are urban themselves, come from a culture that was just by nature musical.

Yeats and Lady Gregory—and Synge—always felt uncomfortable with O'Casey.

I think that went on right into his later life, in his relation to other writers. Yeats was snobbish. He was very fond of Lady Gregory because she was Lady Gregory. He couldn't help that aspect of his personality. I think they're very interesting, these vast contradictions of people who are so unable to shed fundamental sociological terrors, whilst opening landscapes in the soul.

Juno and the Paycock is about poor working-class people, but they're constantly invoking literature...

I think it goes right back to the hedge schools. In West Kerry and in West Cork there are children called Virgil and Ovid. Maybe there was a great comfort in these ancient classics for these people, who were able at least to create a notion of elevation so that they could survive their terribly low self-esteem, which was even worse after the famine. Because strangely, as in all sort of holocaust victims, there was a sense that they were responsible themselves for the famine. However much they blamed the English, there was this terrible fear that if you'd survived the famine, you had survived because somebody, your neighbour, had starved on your behalf. This had affected the psyche of the country and still does.

O'Casey wrote rather sceptically and sometimes scathingly about the Irish Revolution.

Yes, and he was right. But he himself also fell into traps of sentimentality, which is something that has dogged Irish writing, sometimes even to this day—an impossible inability in the end to not feel sorry for oneself, and whilst being in one way very brave about it, absolutely collapsing at the last minute and endowing the ignorant with significance or a need to do that. He was rather tough on the Revolution, and he was right to be. It's terribly hard for any country to monitor its own actions at the time that it's doing it. It always has to appear to be in the right. And no country wants to question on whose side is God.

What about the response at the time both to Synge and O'Casey's plays. Were audiences—or at least male audiences—upset by the women in Synge's and O'Casey's plays?

Maybe in the history of Ireland the men were so held down that they felt emasculated and unable to stand up for themselves, and their only dignity lay in the pub, which brought with it a big sweep, right through the nineteenth century, of puritanism in women. Which became incarcerated into a kind of an idealism about women being silent, forbearing, virtuous in impossible circumstances, creating a sort of obviously sexual terror in their menfolk. In Synge and in O'Casey you meet more earthy, imaginative, self-defining women, and that was very challenging to the growing male middle class in Dublin.

Is all Irish culture underscored by British colonial rule?

I think that temperament is history, and so in that way the Irish temperament has been fundamentally affected by being the baby sister or brother to this big island. The effect of London on Dublin has been enormous. It's the jumping-off ground, isn't it? It's the Ellis Island of Irish culture. Beyond Dublin what made Ireland separate from England is that the Irish had no bourgeoisie. You had an aristocracy and a remarkably kept-down peasantry—in that way, very like Russia: the parallels between Russia and Ireland are enormous. We didn't produce a Chekhov, but we produced an O'Casey. The other big effect of England on Ireland were the penal laws which forbade Irish people to speak Irish and which caused a sort of surrealism in the country, where people couldn't own a horse worth more than five pounds, couldn't own land or hand land over. So the average age of marrying for men in Ireland was fifty. And people attended mass on rocks and in caves and were taught in hedge schools. So the fusion of landscape with the metaphysical, or the fusion of landscape with learning, was not like any other country in the world. Irish English is, on one level, a language forced onto a country that was trying not to speak it, and it then became a sort of tool of revenge: the Irish have attacked the English with their own language. And on the other side you had this rural lost language of people speaking a sort of archaic English forced on them by early settlers, and people struggling with translations from the Gaelic and of course being laughed at by the English for speaking a peculiar English. In Gaelic you say: '*Toin traich megonair*,' which is 'I am after my dinner.' That's still used as the construction for that kind of sentence.

With the exception of Joyce, Irish writers—Congreve, Farquhar, Wilde, Beckett and so on—choose to write for the theatre. Why?

The theatre is immediate: it needs people. It's not like a French literary tradition, which would be about intellectual thought. England is a very odd hybrid because I'd say the centre of the English theatre since the seventeenth century, maybe from Shakespeare, is antithesis, isn't it? The notion that you can declare an argument: 'To be or not to be', and at the end of that you could've concluded something about the world. The Irish theatre is based on hyperbole and contradiction.

If it's possible to talk about any national character with Ireland without resorting to stereotype, is there something about the Irish—I mean the Irish-Irish—that is more given to storytelling and to wearing your heart on your sleeve than the English?

Caesar wrote about going to Hibernia, and he said that they just talked and drank all the time, so I suppose it isn't connected to recent modern history. Perhaps the relationship to alcohol is connected to the climate. There's also great desolation in Ireland, people who don't speak from September to springtime because there's nobody to talk to. Religion is another big part of it.

But is storytelling something to do with having a verbal culture not a written culture?

The culture in cottages that was finally caught by Synge is interesting. Yeats provoked Synge to go to the Aran Islands. Synge went and observed this strange translation of a Gaelic into English and made a sort of heightened self-conscious poetry out of it. But there was a sort of truth in it as well. People were speaking in a language that was self-referential, because they had so little stimulus. I'm not sure that they're using the language for reality. They couldn't use it to negotiate, because there was nothing to negotiate, so they had to use it for the imagination.

Liam Neeson

1 9 5 2—

Actor. Born in Ballymena, Co. Antrim. Liam Neeson was a successful amateur boxer and trainee teacher before he became an actor. He acted on stage at the Lyric Theatre, Belfast, and for two years at the Abbey Theatre, Dublin, before he started his film career. I interviewed Liam Neeson in New York, where he has lived for many years. He was a veteran of a thousand promotional interviews for films, so it was a comparative novelty for him to do an interview where he didn't know the questions and had to consider the answers. Before the interview he talked of his Irishness: 'I remember when I decided to come over and live in England, I was very, very, very conscious of being Irish. I was aware especially when the Queen's cavalry were blown up in Hyde Park. If I was in a shop or something like that, I'd put on this faux English accent.'

Do you recognise the argument that British theatre would be nothing without the Irish theatre?

I emphatically recognise it because I was brought up with it: 'Oh, we taught the English how to speak English.' I recognise it, but I kind of inwardly laugh at it. Ireland produced some extraordinary dramatists, whether or not it was a coincidence I don't know, but Yeats and Lady Gregory and the whole Gaelic movement coincided with the country being fashioned and that produced a great spark of writers and writing.

What were Yeats and Lady Gregory trying to do?

Yeats always had a passion for the spirit life and paganism. And when he discovered these extraordinary Celtic mythological tales, it galvanised him and Lady Gregory into seeing this wealth of extraordinary gold that this nation had, and they felt it had to be used to inspire everyone on this island for the greater good of us all. Out of it came the Gaelic League and the desire to play Irish sports and… just pride in being Irish.

Were you inculcated with that as a child?

I was, at school, because we had a wonderful headmaster, who only allowed us to play Gaelic games. Soccer was not allowed in the school at all. Basketball, sure that was okay, that was the American cousins, but otherwise Gaelic games. He was quite nationalistic. But it was never forced on me. It was only many years later that I started to really read about the history of my country and read about the history of the Abbey Theatre and the growth of the arts and the Gaelic movement.

What about the prohibition of the Irish language?

Well, it wasn't just the language obviously; the populace weren't allowed to practise their religion, or speak their language, or own more than two horses or a horse over five pounds, or more than a third of an acre of land. Maybe that's why Irish to this day is spoken only in certain pockets of the west of Ireland, although I think it's making a resurgence.

What effect did it have on the English of people who spoke Irish as a first language?

I think it enriched the English language. Because the Irish language is very poetic and lyrical, and the phraseology kind of delves into mythology and legend. That carried through into the English language, most noticeably with Synge in *Playboy of the Western World* and *Riders to the Sea*, which was a play I did many, many years ago. It's almost like a verse play.

Synge actually went to the west of Ireland and was listening to people's conversation and transcribing it. He wasn't making it more poetic than it actually was.

Yeats had said to Synge: look, you must go out to the West of Ireland. Because Synge was dulling around Europe, dabbling in this, dabbling in that, wondering what he was going to do with his life. It wasn't quite just a love affair at first sight. I think Synge was quite shocked and stunned by this little enclave of people who were totally independent of the rest of Ireland and, indeed, the rest of Europe. And then the magic of the place kind of hit him. I've a friend once told me I was going to do a film in India, and I said: I don't want to—it's just so far away, and it just seems so alien, and I could go for only two weeks or something. He says: no, no, if you go, you must go for at least five weeks, and after three weeks, he says, then the magic will just seep into you. You'll get a sense of it, do you know? I think the same thing happened to Synge.

I think he went for four years. But I don't think he spent the winters there.

Do we blame him? That horizontal rain and fifty-foot waves.

Did you learn Irish at school?

I didn't learn Irish at school, no. It was taught in this secondary school in my home town of Ballymena, which is a very, very Protestant town. Not that that's important, maybe it's not. But there was an A, B and C stream in my school, and only the A stream could learn the Irish language. Ninety per cent of the class were girls, and we boys were shoved into the woodwork and metalwork room, which was fine for me. But I actually didn't learn the language. However, I did Synge's *Riders to the Sea* as a twelve-year-old, and I learned the language phonetically. And I just remember it being very, very difficult just getting my tongue round it. And partly because I was in a class with this nun, God rest her, who was teaching these other kids. Between teaching the other kids she was putting me through this part. However, when I got on stage and we were doing it day after day, it just filled me, like listening to a great track of Mozart. I'm not saying I spoke it wonderfully, but there was something of the music of it did enter my whole body and persona, and I fell in love with it, and I fell in love with the play too.

Did it seem to you simultaneously beautiful music and absolutely real dialogue?

Yes it did. And these extraordinary things they were talking about, especially in *Playboy* but in *Riders to the Sea* too. It was surrounded by death. As *Riders* opens they're hoping a body is going to be washed up by this Mother Moira who's waiting for her son. She's already lost four boys to the sea. And here's this other son saying: where's that piece of rope I bought in Connemara, because I have to go over to the mainland? And so she's waiting on a body washing up, and there's the son getting ready to go out in these incredible seas—there's this wonderful kind of tragic and exciting fusion of life and death and people living on the edge.

Playboy provoked riots at the time. Why do you think it provoked such an outcry?

I guess a son boasting about not just killing his father but exactly how he did it— with this extraordinary tool that's used for digging turf… For a son to do that to a Catholic father and the community to kind of revel in it… And the sexiness of it: all the girls coming round and wanting to hear it and stuff. It was that kind of devil's brew of death and sex, and the fact that Synge dared to show Catholic Ireland succumbing to this little weasel of a guy. It just kind of messed with everything: they would have been absolutely incensed.

Synge's case is a rare example of a theatre producer actually offering a successful commission— although it was maybe not the result that Yeats had hoped for. He wrote a play set at the heart of the peasantry and the heartland of the Irish dream, and he overturned it. Did he have any sort of political motive?

I don't think it was a deliberate affront to the nation or to the leaders—you know: I'm going to show them something here. I think ultimately he genuinely fell in love with the Aran Islanders' lifestyle, and from the stories he'd gleaned and transcribed, something came together the way these extraordinary playwrights get inspired in some way, and, come hell or high water, they have to write that play. It just kind of poured out of him.

As did O'Casey's plays. When he wrote The Plough and the Stars *and* Juno and the Paycock, *they were white hot. They were almost living newspapers, weren't they?*

Shadow of a Gunman was the first, that's kind of a one-act play. It was the first one done—I want to say 1923—just after the Civil War. And that produced a ruction. *Juno* came next, and then with *The Plough and the Stars*, which was set in 1916, this was 1926, they went ballistic, you know. Because there was a Civil War: you had brother fighting against brother, uncle against cousin. You still have it to a certain extent nowadays. There's still a scab over the wound. O'Casey showed the whole kaleidoscope of Ireland at that time, you know. Nationalist leaders, down-and-outs, good-for-nothings, Republicans, Free Staters, they were all there on the stage. So someone was bound to be annoyed. [*chuckles*] Especially in *The Plough and the Stars*, where you see Jack Clitheroe, who's the anti-hero, suddenly having this nervous breakdown. Because he's witnessing death for the first time. His wife coming out to comfort him, pull him back in. You could imagine these diehard Republicans. And there he is, wearing the green uniform. I would love to have been there, I'd love to have seen that reaction.

The Irish often close the doors on their own. Like Joyce and Beckett in later years. And, after he wrote The Silver Tassie, *O'Casey was rejected.*

Maybe it's something to do with not liking to see you rise above your station. In those days there was a certain amount of that: 'Oh, look at your man, who does he think he is?', you know. Also O'Casey was holding a mirror up, and it wasn't a very pretty image. He was asking audiences to accept a lot: it was very, very hard for an Irish nation, having gone through this war of independence with British troops, and then this unbelievable Civil War.

What would a Martian make of O'Casey's plays?

O'Casey always saw himself as the common man. He more than dabbled in Socialism, and felt at one time that Ireland's freedom lay in Communism, in the Labour movement. Part of why he exiled himself was seeing these national leaders and figureheads scamming a lot of stuff for themselves. That totally disillusioned him and so, in tandem with the reaction to his plays, suddenly he was out. But he was able to laugh at himself, and that comes across in his plays too. I know he said he would never go back there again, but he did.

Have you only played in The Shadow of a Gunman?

I was in the centennial production of *Juno and the Paycock* at the Abbey Theatre. I was the Irregular Mobiliser, who comes in to Johnny Boyle to say: there's a meeting, you're expected to be there. We know the diehard Republicans know that he's probably the informer that killed Mrs Tancred's son. I remember never experiencing nerves like it, because the guy that played my part in the original production was—I forget his name—was in the first row of the audience. He was in the original production of it. And of all the characters it happened to be mine and I had like five lines to say. But this was 1979, 1980. And the Troubles had started in '69/'70. So we were well and truly steeped in it, and obviously there were still atrocities going on in the North and in the South too. It was a strange night because—shall I say so myself?—I thought it was quite wonderful. We had the great Siobhán McKenna giving her Juno, you know.

Did you ever see her in Playboy?

I saw a filmed version of it. I remember being struck by her absolute beauty and majesty, this big wonderful big buxom woman. I kind of fell in love with her. I remember telling her that too, when I had the chance to be in this production with her.

I'm sure she was pleased.

[*laughs*] Anyway, *Juno* was a night of extraordinary celebration, and with what was happening up North sure there was a feeling of the relevance of O'Casey and what he was saying.

I have Irish friends who felt that doing O'Casey's plays around that time was unhelpful in that it made the English feel that it let them off the hook. That by saying 'take away these hearts of stone', it was showing the Irish as eternally fighting and squabbling between themselves, and it made the English feel that it absolved them of blame. Do you think it's a fair criticism?

That wouldn't be putting the plays in their proper context, you know. I did a production in Belfast of *The Plough and the Stars* in 1976, and that was particularly relevant. The Lyric Theatre in Belfast never closed its doors during the worst Troubles in Belfast. Bombs going off right, left and centre: those doors never closed. Occasionally we'd all have to leave the theatre while it was searched for bombs, but we'd all come back in again. And I remember us thinking that maybe it would happen during *The Plough and the Stars*. It actually didn't happen, but playing Jack Clitheroe had a particular relevance for me, knowing that maybe a few streets away there were some like-minded young men or young women about to give their life for Ireland. Just made me question: is it worth it? You know just through playing and saying these words of O'Casey, and just putting these characters under the microscope in what we know was an awful, awful war—the independence war and the Civil War in Ireland—really struck chords with me. And gave all of us that acted in it an extra charge. And we were packed every night too. Absolutely packed.

And nobody from any political movement ever said: this is not helping?

No one stood up in the audience—I wish they had, you know; it would be great to get into that, do you know. But that's part of the Northern Irish character too. You just sit and take it in, and maybe afterwards you might say something. I played the part again in Manchester. 1981, '82 or something like that. It had a totally different feel at the Royal Exchange, we had this wonderful kind of collage of British and Irish working-class actors. And it was an okay production, but I just remember the audience thinking it was quaint, it didn't have a relevance.

You acted in O'Casey's plays and in O'Neill's. Are there similarities?

I would liken him to O'Casey in the playing, in that if you pull back, you're sunk. You've got to go with O'Neill, you've got to absolutely throw yourself into it. Chuck away the safety net. I remember we played it [*Anna Christie*] for like three months at the Roundabout Theatre in New York, and about halfway through I discovered the absolute pessimism of O'Neill. At the very, very end of the play, where I'm sitting there with Anna, this character's been out on this incredible binge because he's found out she's a prostitute. And there's this little Swedish father talking about 'Ah, that old devil sea, it's nothing to do with us, it's all nature's way, and that's the way it is, you know.' And there was just this tableau: we all just froze on stage for this awful wait. And you were left with these sorry people, and you think: how are they ever gonna get out of this? There's a kind of ruthless energy mixed with this unbelievable pessimism, that this is as good as life gets, you know. This is their lot. But the journey in getting there as a performer was extraordinary.

You feel uplifted when you play O'Neill?

In that particular production I certainly did. It was a part that absolutely suited me—as an actor and as a human being, you know. And my own circumstances of having done some of these awful Hollywood films, where I was just climbing up the walls with boredom and stagnation, then to suddenly get this crusty eighty-year-old play that just spoke to me in some way, and was a great physical character. And just to speak this wonderful Irish language. Again like Synge, O'Neill—with my part Matt, this coal stoker—he just captured the West Irish idiom beautifully. I know some actors in the past have said: oh yeah, I played Matt, that language was very antiquated, did you have trouble saying it? I didn't. I had absolutely no trouble saying it at all. In fact, you know, I'm sticking my neck out now: one night I opened my dressing-room door, and there was Gregory Peck. I was in my underwear, getting all the slap off my face and stuff. And there's this big six-foot-four, big majestic, big ex-film star. Fine actor. And he said he played the part when he was like eighteen or something at college and was never able to make it work for him at all. And he said: tonight I saw what O'Neill could do. That was great, you know.

Stephen Rea

1 9 4 6—

Actor. Born in Belfast. He founded Field Day Theatre Company in Derry in 1980 with Tom Paulin, Brian Friel, Seamus Heaney and Seamus Deane, and has acted at the Abbey Theatre, Dublin, as well as the National Theatre in London. I interviewed him in Ryan's Pub in Dublin, an ideal set for Act Two of The Plough and the Stars—*no concessions to the fickleness of pub fashion, even down to the brass cash register. Exasperatingly, he looked no older than when I first met him twenty-five years earlier.*

What did Yeats and Lady Gregory want to achieve with the Abbey Theatre?

They wanted the theatre to be an instrument of Irish nationalism, an expression of an independent Ireland. I'm not sure how comfortable they were with the armed struggle and the actual insurrection, but they did pave the way by having this intense debate about what Ireland was, and how she could develop separately and be distinct from Britain.

So the movement to reclaim an Irish culture and to get rid of the British are linked together?

Inevitably, if all your major writers have been annexed into the British experience. People regarded Wilde then, and even today, as an English writer, but he was a Dublin man, who put on an English accent. He arrived in Oxford, and two days later decided the Dublin accent wouldn't do. If all your great geniuses are being turned into Englishmen, then it needs a radical step to change all that. Yeats changed that very personally.

Have you ever heard that wax recording of Wilde?

Apparently it isn't him, because it was recorded on a machine that wouldn't have existed while he was alive. But, as Trevor Griffiths said to me, if everyone believed it was authentic then it must have sounded like him. It doesn't have to be him, but that's what he must have sounded like. It was a rather high-pitched, drawling sound, you know. It's terrible. Really I'm sure it wasn't him. He does *The Ballad of Reading Gaol*, and it's like a lament—very weird. Totally artificial, I suppose, but then, of course, Wilde *was* totally artificial, because he was being someone else, pretending to be an Englishman.

Didn't he go to an elocution teacher?

Apparently he still had some Irish sounds in his voice, so it is impossible to know for sure, but I don't know if he went to an elocution teacher.

But he was trying, as it were, to pass for white?

That's precisely right, yes, and he was furious with anyone who didn't try and pass for white.

But at the same time Wilde was a subversive—a Socialist who believed in an Irish Republic.

He did when it suited him. When he went to America and lectured there to Irish and America miners and things, he was very, very nationalist. His mother, of course, was one of the nationalist leaders. But it was a period of transition—a lot of people had grown used to the idea that Ireland was part of Britain and would remain so. At the turn of the century everything seemed kind of calm.

So do you think for all Wilde's Socialism and his Republicanism he was actually not a subversive?

His son—Vyvyan Holland—said that he believed the point when the British establishment turned against Wilde was when he wrote *The Soul of Man Under Socialism*, because he was obviously quite serious about it. Previously they had been quite happy to see him as this exotic, humorous creature, but he obviously had some kind of agenda, which was a threat. I'm sure that he was ambivalent about Ireland though, that he wanted to escape from the narrowness of it. And it was narrow. He wanted the world of London and Paris, but he was unquestionably Irish in London.

Have you ever felt obliged to change your own accent?

I've been invited to change my accent. They've all asked me to change my accent. I was told I could do anything I wanted at the National Theatre if I adjusted my accent, but I didn't feel inclined to do so. Then I went to see a production of

Julius Caesar at the National with John Gielgud, and there were three Scottish actors in it. All of them spoke with broad Scottish accents—I couldn't really see why they could do that but that my accent was not quite so acceptable.

Do you think that's a residue of a colonial attitude?

I think it's absolutely a colonial attitude. I mean, the Scots, for all their separateness—and I believe they should be independent if they so choose—have been part of the government of Britain for a long time, haven't they? And the Irish have not quite been absorbed unless they pretend to be something else.

So do you think the English, hearing an Irish accent, will always think: 'inferior person'?

Or 'trouble'. It's a very strange thing because the Irish have entertained the English for years. I did *The Playboy of the Western World* at the National Theatre at the height of the Troubles, when people were deeply nervous about Irish people and their relationship to Ireland, but somehow they didn't seem to mind when they came to see this play. They were absolutely overwhelmed by the power of the play. Maybe we presented it in a way that wasn't threatening or that was some how de-politicised. I remember it being very strange to be stopped by English people in the street having seen *The Playboy* and them saying how wonderful it was. Yet it was a time when you were very nervous to be Irish in London: there was a lot of resentment and there was a lot of intimidation of working-class Irish people.

Do you think the Irish have an extraordinary capacity for storytelling?

Well, it's true that they do. I suppose the Gaelic culture did have a language which was more exotic in ways, and it did have an oral tradition of storytelling, which meant that they were more inclined to be imaginative. When we did *The Shaughraun* [at the National] a woman wrote to me and said how much she loved it. She said: this is what theatre was like before the intellectuals got hold of it. There is a sense of pure entertainment about it, although it is very moving as well. I mean, *The Shaughraun* was basically turning the stage Irishman on its head. He's the smartest guy on the stage, wittier than any of them. So there was a kind of political edge too.

It's an observed truth that the Irish seem to enjoy talking to each other more than the English.

It could have been that the Irish had more time to do it. Irish people do sit around and talk a lot, there's no question about that. Alun Armstrong, the actor, came to Belfast and stayed with me, and we talked all night and then went to bed and then got up and talked all day, and he said: that's what they do here, they talk the whole time. There is still the sort of easy sociability around here that encourages conversation.

So this would mean that the Irish are particularly adept at a medium of speaking which becomes an art form in itself—an artistic medium that encourages public conversation: i.e. theatre?

I can only say 'yes' to that, Richard. [*laughs*]

Why was this whole Irish literary and political revival—Joyce is the sole exception—led by Protestants?

And Joyce was the greatest. If you go back to 1798 and the birth of the Republican movement, of course, that was led mainly by Protestants and every subsequent rebellion—Emmet's rebellion and the Fenian movement—was famously dominated by Protestants. I think that was just because they were more advantaged, they had more time to work out what was wrong and why they were angry, and they made the connections with the French Revolution and the American Revolution. Perhaps, you know, the peasantry didn't have time or access to it. I think that, having come as agents of the Empire, the Protestants embraced the country that they were in—and maybe nobody more so than Synge, who gave expression to a deeply Gaelic culture in the English language.

What were Synge's origins?

He came from a very narrow Protestant background, landowning. He had seen evictions on his own family's land. He realised he was on the side of the people being evicted and that his own family had been responsible for that kind of treatment. He was just an enormously sensitive, unusual creature. I always connect him to Beckett in a way, because Beckett, who had the good fortune to work with him, said the one of all that crowd that he admired was Synge. They are very similar in ways, coming from very narrow Protestant backgrounds in the south of Dublin. They both had their incredibly original view of life—and it's a very tough view.

Synge didn't know he wanted to be a playwright.

He was trying to be a poet, wasn't he? He was in Paris writing strangely derivative bits of poetry, because he wasn't connecting to the roots that were available to him. He was in some kind of limbo of international writing, and then Yeats absolutely rooted him to where he should be, which is an incredibly insightful thing to do.

What happened when Playboy *was first performed at the Abbey?*

Well, the citizens of Dublin couldn't stand it. To a large extent because it was a picture of Ireland that they couldn't accept. You had this rising Catholic nationalist bourgeoisie, who thought that Ireland was pure and Irish women were the purest in Europe, and they didn't like Synge's picture of these kind of quite randy, full-blooded people. They made a lot of fuss about it, but the Trinity students were there as well, and they were shouting back at them because they didn't think that Ireland should be moving towards independence anyway. It's interesting to have a theatre that actually stimulates that kind of debate.

It's something of a paradox, though, that the movement that is wanting to endow Irish national culture turns out to want a very reactionary culture.

They weren't just products of the same thing, you know. The would-be Irish nationalism was developing anyway through the idea of Catholic emancipation and from Daniel O'Connell on. It was very much related to the Catholic Church: we have seen that develop right through the century. Then you would have these hearty Yeats figures who believed in high art, and of course the bourgeoisie will always be at war with high art. And Synge was, of course, a dedicated artist, but while he was interested in Irish independence and an expression of Irish culture, he was interested in something bigger as well, like the truth.

Yeats was a great poet and a very successful theatre producer. How did he operate when he ran the Abbey?

He defied Dublin Castle by putting on Shaw's *The Shewing-Up of Blanco Posnet*, which had been banned in London. He was really quite daring and radical.

Apart from Synge, Yeats's other great discovery was O'Casey. How did that come about?

O'Casey was there writing and submitted his plays to the Abbey. I think Yeats was rather suspicious of him. The relationship between O'Casey and the Abbey ended rather abruptly with Yeats's refusal to put on one of his plays.

But that's after he had done several.

Three massively successful plays, but there was trouble about those plays too. I mean, there were riots at *The Plough and the Stars*.

Because?

Because they seemed to be suggesting that the 1916 revolutionaries were less than heroic because they were running from the gunfire and because they looked down upon the ordinary working people. It was too close to 1916 for that to be acceptable. Nowadays the play's done as a bit of a romp really—we are so far from that period—and even though we've been living through terrible times in terms of the Troubles in Ireland, when you see an O'Casey play you never feel that it is informed by that experience. They always seem to be rather too warm as evenings in the theatre.

Are you saying that this is a betrayal of the writing?

I think that very quickly the plays were turned into pure entertainment. You know *The Plough and the Stars* is about sex and violence. And about poverty.

Is O'Casey's great theme poverty?

I believe that it is, and it's something that's still with us despite our booming economy. We have massive problems of poverty in this country. You know what Brendan Behan's grandmother said about independence for Ireland? She said the only difference is that your eviction notice will have a harp on it instead of a crown—and that must be the feeling that the poor get in Ireland now.

How do productions betray the plays?

Perhaps because they are so entertaining you forget the source of it. I mean, if you look at Rosie Redman and Fluther in the pub scene in the *Plough*. Yes, it is great fun, knockabout fun, but what you actually have there is a nineteen-year-old girl who is having to have sex with an older alcoholic in order to get the rent. In some way you never feel this, you always just feel they're having a bit of knockabout fun. I think that must be in the writing. Maybe the writing isn't sharp enough, but certain productions have never wanted to be as hard-edged as they should be.

Do we all—English and Irish—conspire in presenting a stereotype of the Irish?

The English certainly want to see a stereotype of the Irish which is not threatening, and the Irish are very willing to collaborate on that. It's strange how Irish people like [the John Ford film] *The Quiet Man*, which is not exactly a true representation of Ireland. I believe that a TV series like *Ballykissangel*, for instance, has been promoted to make the English feel comfortable about the Irish—to say they're not threatening, they're not going to bomb you, they're just rather quaint and strange people who live in nice little villages. What's threatening about *The Playboy of the Western World* is that it isn't stereotypical, it's savage and true, and that's what everyone was screaming about at the riots when it opened. They couldn't bear the truth—Irish peasants were often ignorant, savage, passionate, sexual and violent.

You couldn't accuse O'Casey of taking the easy way out: the conclusions of all his plays are extraordinarily bleak and unsentimental.

Yes they are, but somehow they're seen through some kind of fog of sentimentality. If you look at what happens in the *Plough*. Yes, a young consumptive girl dies, a woman miscarries and you sense the whole problem of childbirth and tenement houses, but somehow the end result is, when those

Tommies sit down and pour themselves a cup of tea and sing 'Keep the Home Fires Burning', it's not quite savage enough. That's my view anyway.

Perhaps the problem is something to do with the nature of theatre itself.

It could be that our instincts as practitioners is not to be as critical as we should be: we want to be liked, and we want to have an evening that is fun. And O'Casey, of course, produces so many good lines. And a style of acting O'Casey has grown up, which is based on the original actors no doubt. If these plays are going to be done again, then I think you have to look at how they're performed.

Isn't it that in theatre, as opposed to any other medium, you're faced with real people—albeit they're actors—so aren't you in some way responding just to their enduring humanity?

Of the actors performing this piece?

The characters as well as the actors.

There have been productions with people going around like terrible Brechtian figures—I don't believe you should do that—but if you look at the comic edge of Beckett, for instance, and Synge, that seems to me to be really truthful and really threatening. They have tried to make the *Playboy* easier than it is, but it's a very violent play with very unpleasant people in it and it has to be done like that. And it's impossible to sentimentalise Beckett.

When you're watching a Beckett play do you feel despair?

'I can't go on, I'll go on.' It's just an appalling journey, but it has to be done. I don't think he despairs: he aspires. He was a wonderfully warm and generous man, and it was a wonderful relief to discover that we didn't have to find out what the plays meant. He wasn't interested in meaning and, in fact, said to me: don't think about meaning, think about the rhythm, think about the music. We were rehearsing *Endgame*—Beckett was present at all the rehearsals and Clov, who was my character, has to say to Hamm: 'I leave you,' and he does this very often throughout the play. I pointed to one occasion when he says it, and I asked Beckett: when he says he is leaving here, does this mean he is going to the kitchen or is he leaving for good? And Beckett said: it is always ambiguous. And suddenly I realised what modern acting is: art should be ambiguous, and acting should have more than one meaning. There should be a spectrum of meaning in everything you do, and maybe that's what makes Beckett different as a writer, his writing is very akin to music.

Stephen Sondheim
1 9 3 0—

Composer and lyricist. His shows include A Funny Thing Happened on the Way to the Forum, Company, Follies, A Little Night Music, Sweeney Todd, Sunday in the Park with George, Into the Woods *and* Assassins, *as well as the lyrics for* West Side Story *and* Gypsy. *I interviewed him in a hotel room in New York. He had a show in workshop—*Wise Guys, *later renamed* Road Show—*so he was writing at night and rehearsing by day, but his energy seemed undimmed.*

You met Oscar Hammerstein when you were around thirteen?

I was thirteen exactly. When I was fifteen he took me to the first night of *Carousel* in New Haven. He took me and his son Jimmy, who was a year younger than I, and it was during our spring vacation at school so we were able to do it. I don't even remember when I saw *Oklahoma!*: it certainly wasn't on the first night, and I'm not sure how close I was to the family by the time *Oklahoma!* opened. I was close but not as close as I was in *Carousel*, because I remember that one of the high points of my childhood was being asked for advice on *Carousel*, when he and Rodgers were writing it. They wanted the opening of the second act to be this treasure hunt on the island, and I was into treasure hunts, so I was the treasure hunt consultant.

He'd give you brilliant advice subsequently.

Yes, he—that dreadful word—he critiqued my work. I showed him everything I wrote from the age of fifteen on, and he treated it absolutely on a level with

94

professional work. He never pretended for one second that I was a child: he just treated it seriously, and I learned a great deal very quickly. I've said before: as a result of Oscar I think I probably knew more about writing musicals at the age of nineteen than most people do at the age of ninety.

What was he like?

He was exactly the reverse of the image of his lyrics. He was a very sharp city boy, as opposed to somebody who sat on a porch with a stick of hay in his teeth and looked at the cattle. Which he also did. But he was a very good critic and very sharp-tongued. Not mean but sharp. He was in fact a sophisticated man. I once asked him why he didn't write sophisticated musicals, and he said: you mean musicals that take place in penthouses with people smoking with cigarette holders? I said: well, yes, if you want to put it that way. He said: because it really doesn't interest me. And in fact it didn't: what interested him was quite the reverse of what his life was like. Not that he was a partygoer or anything like that, but he was a sophisticate. He was enormously kind and generous, and a true idealist and a true optimist. What he writes about often in his lyrics, that did fit him: he was an optimist. I won't say he always looked on the lighter side, but he believed in the better part of mankind not in the worse. And he did not die a disillusioned man.

Do you think he's a peculiarly American figure?

No, no, I don't. That generosity that I'm talking about: it's not so much an American generosity as it is a generosity of viewpoints. It would be easy for Oscar to understand a French viewpoint, a German viewpoint, a Russian viewpoint. I think there was something—I can't think what the word is—I don't mean international, but something worldly in the best sense about him.

But if you take Carousel, *for instance, a story about wife beating, it's inconceivable that a European would have ended that story with the—*

But he didn't—

—message: 'You'll never walk alone.'

—no, wait a minute, he didn't think of it as a story about wife beating. He thought of it as a story about love triumphing over death. Now that may not be what Molnár meant [whose play *Liliom* is the basis of *Carousel*], any more than Lynn Riggs, who wrote a bleak Western play called *Green Grow the Lilacs* about homosexuality, intended it to be *Oklahoma!* But Oscar saw it as a story of pioneering—and of the loneliness and the triumph of pioneering. Lynn Riggs saw it as a story of loneliness and what it does to sexual relations. And *Carousel* is the same kind of transformation. Oscar in each case saw something that interested him: which is incidentally why with musicals the best adaptations generally, though *My Fair Lady*'s a great exception, turn out to be the ones that differ most from their originals. *West Side Story* being an example. There's no attempt to poach on Shakespeare: it's merely taking the bare bones of Shakespeare's plot and then transforming it into something else—well, they're both about prejudice, fair enough.

Did the book musical come into being as a result mostly of Oscar Hammerstein's work?

Prior to *Showboat*, musicals were essentially collections of jokes and songs, and even after *Showboat* most of them were. Hammerstein virtually alone pioneered the idea of trying to tell a story through music, trying to meld the European operetta influence and the American freewheeling jazz musical-comedy influence—I shouldn't say influence, but, he melded those two streams of presentation into one. Which resulted in a kind of American operetta. From *Showboat* to *Music in the Air* and through the 1930s, his star rose and fell, and he resuscitated it with *Oklahoma!* when he teamed up with Richard Rodgers, who brought a different kind of sensibility. Jerome Kern, with whom he did most of the shows, was very much a European composer. Rodgers was much more a kind of American vernacular composer. And the result of that was *Oklahoma!* And *Oklahoma!*, though today it seems very naive as a story and rather naive in terms of the depth of the characters, nevertheless, because of its enormous success, influenced musicals ever since. Innovative musicals mean nothing if they aren't successful, because nobody pays attention to them. If, for example, *Threepenny Opera* had been a success in this country, musicals might have matured much more quickly. It was only when it was done off-Broadway in the early fifties that the Brechtian musical came into being. But the book musical really can almost solely be attributed to Hammerstein's efforts.

He was a playwright first?

Yes, he wrote a couple of plays, but I don't even know if any of them got on. I think he wrote one called *The Lighthouse* first, something like that. But he was into lyric-writing almost immediately. He had a mentor named Otto Harbach, who was a well-known lyric writer and got him into the music field.

What he brought to the musical presumably were the criteria that he applied to plays?

That's deceptive, because a lot of the musicals of the thirties were written by playwrights like George Kaufman and Moss Hart, and they weren't interested in writing musicals that told stories through character. They were interested in satires, light-hearted revues. Things like *As Thousands Cheer*. Hammerstein was using the same principles but in a so-called serious way. He picked serious stories, that is stories which are supposed to involve the viewer and make you feel emotional connections with the people on stage. In that sense exactly what a playwright attempts to do. Whereas Kaufman, Hart and the others, Lindsay and Crouse, they were not applying their playwriting gifts or sensibilities—they were applying a kind of—I don't want to say joke-writing because that reduces it too much—sketch-writing ability.

Hammerstein introduced the idea that a song could actually be a manifestation of character?

And could explore character. Songs as pioneered by Hammerstein are often the equivalents of soliloquies, in that they're direct address to the audience by a character either explaining or self-exploring himself. The watershed of that probably is the soliloquy from *Carousel*, which is the first time that technique had been used. But even in *Oklahoma!*, 'Lonely Room'—the song that Judd sings—could be considered a soliloquy if a playwright were doing it. I think the essential difference, of course, between a musical and a play is that the fourth wall is broken all the time even in the most dramatic or serious musicals. People are rarely just involved with each other on stage; there's always—particularly in songs—a direct connection with the audience.

Would you argue that a musical is as much a personal statement as a play, it's just a collaborative one?

Not most musicals. I think most musicals are not personal statements. Although in fact it's a *reductio ad absurdum*: people wouldn't write the musicals unless there was something in the story that interested them to begin with. If you write something it's got to be an expression of what you're about. So I wouldn't say that it's any different for musicals than for plays or anything else. A little less personal probably for musicals, because most musicals are written so much with an audience in mind, and most plays are written essentially with the play in mind, I think.

Is it a question that can be answered with the book musical whether the music or the book comes first?

No, I think the book always comes first in this kind of musical. It has to be the story and the characters that propel both the song aspect and the need for song. Why should they sing? It has to be a group of characters and a story that you're not just enhancing by adding songs but in which musical expression becomes intrinsic. I think any good musical starts with the book, the libretto, the idea, the story, the characters. I can't work on anything until I've discussed for weeks and sometimes months with my collaborator what the story is, why is music needed, why is music intrinsic as opposed to decorative, and what will music do to the story. When I was writing *Sunday in the Park with George*, I was really frightened that the music would tear the delicate fabric of what James Lapine was trying to get at in terms of the creation of a painting. You must start with libretto, all the strong musicals have strong stories. One of the reasons that *West Side Story* attained its popularity—apart from the success of the movie, because it was not all that popular when it was done on the stage on Broadway—is that the story is such a good story. Something happens all the time.

You came into West Side Story *when Arthur and Leonard Bernstein had—*

Jerome Robbins, Leonard Bernstein and Arthur Laurents had been working on an idea that had to do first with Catholics and Jews but that one didn't work out. Then, because of the headlines about street gangs, they got together many years later, and they started writing this version of *Romeo and Juliet*. I came in on it when Arthur had a three-page outline. And Lennie had actually written the tune to 'Cool'. And that was it.

What age were you?

Twenty-five. And it took us over a period of two years, although there was a six-month hiatus in there, when they each did a different show and I worked for television. It took about a year and a half to write.

Did you draw on Shakespeare at all?

Very little—by the time I joined it Arthur had transmogrified the plot into pretty much what you see now. There was a fake suicide—Anita committed a fake suicide. There was a more careful parallel to the whole interrupted message and the deaths in the tombs: that was simplified. Generally it was pretty well-formed by the time I got there in terms of what the plotting would be. Arthur had found parallels for the plotting throughout.

So were you given a pretty precise remit for the lyrics?

Well, no. Arthur showed me about two and a half closely typewritten pages outlining the plot and then we talked about it and how songs would function. I don't think we ever referred again to Shakespeare. Arthur really was mostly interested in the plotting, the melodrama of it and how to keep that much action. The triumph of *West Side Story*'s book is not only this kind of made-up language that he did to prevent the shelflife from deteriorating too quickly, but the conciseness of the plotting. *West Side Story*'s probably the shortest book ever written for a musical that isn't a sung-through musical, with the possible exception of *Follies*—the lovers meet and fall in love in eight lines and you completely believe it.

It's one of the few musicals—outside your own—that don't let you down in the sense it doesn't offer a highly sentimental conclusion.

It parallels Shakespeare, drawing the two houses together, but it is sentimental—not so much sentimental, it's what? For example, is *My Fair Lady* sentimental? It may not be what Shaw intended but it doesn't seem like pandering. The word 'sentimental' implies that you're pandering, that you're watering down something so the audience can swallow the pill or something like that. I suppose in that sense *West Side Story* isn't sentimental. We really were trying to tell the story, and probably in those days we believed that you could make peace between two warring houses. I don't know that I would feel that today. But we lived in a more sentimental time, or a more optimistic one.

When Arthur talks about it he says this was a musical that was made without any sense of calculation about the audience.

That's deceptive. You can't look at a number like 'America' and say that was done without the audience in mind. I mean, it was written that way, yes, but it was presented—and we all knew the way it was gonna be presented—with numbers with buttons. We spent a lot of time finding buttons for numbers—you know, a 'button' being a moment that allows the audience or encourages the audience to applaud. We knew it was a musical, and we knew it was a musical meant to please. In fact, one of the terrifying moments was opening night in New York City. For the first forty minutes the audience sat as if they were in church: they'd heard that this was a great work of art—capital 'G', capital 'W', capital 'A'. So they sat on their hands; they did not realise that we were out to entertain them. Not entertain them with, you know, rabbits out of hats and dancing girls—although there're a lot of dancing girls—but entertain them by absorbing them in a story. And only when 'America' was done and the sort of fourth wall was burst open by something they recognised—a bezazzy dancing number—that they felt they were entitled to have a good time and applaud if they chose or gasp if they chose, and they did. And from there on they had a very good time. But we were dismayed, and that's the proof to me that we all wanted to communicate. I mean, why do you write except to communicate? I've never written anything where I was consciously pandering, and I don't think many of my peers or contemporaries have either. We generally write what we want, but you're always aware that an audience is there. How can you design a musical number without being aware of bringing it to an ending because if you don't, the audience won't applaud? If you don't let them applaud in a musical—and this is the really important point—then they're not ready for the next moment, because the unspoken contract between an audience and a musical is that they're allowed to applaud. When I wrote *Passion* I deliberately killed all the applause, because I didn't want to break the mood. I wanted them to applaud a lot at the end, but we were asking them to accept a very peculiar story, which did not lend itself to show-stopping numbers. So I decided: no applause at all. And I still think it was the right decision. But generally that is what an audience expects, and if you don't let 'em do it, they won't listen.

So there's an unbreakable syntax in musicals?

I'll give you a very good example. When we did *Gypsy* in Philadelphia, it ends with this breakdown that the leading character has. Madame Rose has a nervous breakdown in song. I wanted it to end and designed it to end on a high violent harmonic that was a dissonant chord, because I thought you don't applaud a woman having a nervous breakdown: that's just wrong. There's then a two-minute scene after that, in which her daughter comes on stage, and they have a forgiveness scene in which the daughter becomes the mother and the mother becomes the daughter, which is the idea of the evening. And then they go off arm in arm and the curtain comes down, and I thought then the audience could applaud. And when Oscar Hammerstein came to see it—now this Oscar Hammerstein who was the one who transformed the musical from frivolity into seriousness—he said: 'You've got to give Ethel Merman a hand at the end of the number,' and I said: 'But all you've taught me all my life is...' And he said: 'No, no, it's not dishonest, Steve, if they don't applaud her they won't listen to the last two minutes. They're waiting to applaud Ethel Merman. If you don't let them off the hook, you might as well bring the curtain down there.' And he was dead right. So I put a fake ending on Rose's turn—meaning an ending that is okay but it's not the one I believed in—and the audience went berserk with applause, and the dead silence for the last two minutes was exactly what you hope for in the theatre. They listened to those last two pages with such ferocious intensity, and they got the point of the evening. And that would not happen in a play.

But you've spent really since then—the whole of your career—subverting these golden rules.

You have to. There's another thing too. The third show that Rodgers and Hammerstein wrote after *Oklahoma!* and *Carousel* was a show called *Allegro*, in which Oscar really tried to subvert the rules. It was an abstract show: it had no scenery, it had merely an S-shaped curtain, and it told the story of a man's entire life from the day he was born till he was about forty years old, at which point he'd reached a moral crisis and had solved it. And it was a flop. It subverted too many rules. It didn't tell a linear story. It told a chronological one, but it didn't have a plot. It isn't until quite recently that I realised how much my experience on *Allegro* counted, because I was Oscar's assistant on that. He wanted me to learn the practical side of the business—it was during the summer when I wasn't at school—and I became his gopher and his typist and all that. And I think I was very, very lucky that that was the show. Because I learned things about how not do a show, because I could see what was going wrong—or in hindsight I could anyway: you could probably say I wasn't smart enough to know it at the time. But there were all kinds of artistic conflicts as well as the practical conflicts that happen with directors and authors and things like that. And all those things combined. Oscar had a skewed vision of what he was writing, and he always wanted to rewrite it right up to the day he died.

With the exception of you taking the musical in a different direction, why did the book musical die?

Oh, it hasn't died it's merely gotten swollen. The so-called sung-through musicals... *Les Mis* is a book musical. If you're talking about the musical in which there's speech and song, speech and song, it didn't die so much as become subsumed by the success of the sung-through musicals, mainly stemming from Britain. And audiences now are very used to the sung-through musical. But whatever you think of the book, the Disney musicals have books. And *Ragtime* is a book. It's not dead: in fact, more likely, the sung-through musical is on the way to either being transformed or being dropped for a while.

It got disconnected from popular culture with the coming of rock 'n' roll.

The effect of rock 'n' roll on musicals is the equivalent of the effect of television on theatre or movies on theatre. It's made both musicals and theatre in general—I don't say a cottage industry, but you know, it's no longer the only game in town, it's not even the major game in town, theatre. It's a—I want to avoid the word 'elitist'—but it does appeal to and attract fewer people, at least in this country [USA] than it used to. I mean, what's deplorable about the American theatre on Broadway is: you look at the list and it's twenty-four musicals and two plays. And in London the last time I counted it was fourteen musicals and eight plays. That's not good. Now the off-Broadway theatre and the fringe theatre is very much alive, and people are writing plays, but not an awful lot of people can fit into a two-hundred-and-fifty-seat house—two hundred and fifty people can fit in—for six weeks, which is what you have in London in the fringe theatres. So how many people are gonna get to see that play? Unless it transfers to the West End, which few of them do. And the same thing is true here. So I fear it's not so much the death of the book musical as the gradual fade of theatre and musical theatre. I don't think that we'll ever fade entirely, because I think there's always a hunger for live storytelling. But it's never going to be kind of the central entertainment again, it just isn't.

Arthur Laurents
1 9 1 8—2 0 1 1

Playwright and director. Arthur Laurents wrote the book for West Side Story *and for* Gypsy *and numerous plays and screenplays. He appeared before the House Un-American Activities Committee and was blacklisted. I interviewed him in New York in his brownstone in Chelsea when he was eighty-two, still working as a director and as indiscreet and caustic as ever.*

What were the origins of the book musical?

Oh, I think it came from operetta originally. Then they had the musical comedy, which you could say had a book, but it really was a collection of bad jokes between songs. And then I think it began to take shape actually with Rodgers and Hart, rather than with Rodgers and Hammerstein. Shows like *Pal Joey* and *On Your Toes* do have a book.

What about Showboat, *wasn't that before?*

Oh, *Showboat* I forgot. *Showboat* is wonderful, though it's endless. I mean, as I said someplace else, everything is too long except life. I said that as a joke but I think it's true.

What distinguishes a book musical from a play with songs?

I remember when Steve Sondheim read the book of *Gypsy* he said: 'Well, this is a play.' I said: 'No, it wouldn't work as a play.' The reason it wouldn't, first of all: everything is heightened enormously. You don't jump into music, you seamlessly step into it. That has to be in the style of the writing and the characters have to be larger than life and larger than 'play' life.

What is it that gives the licence to a character to sing?

I used to think that you could only sing if you got to the point where the emotion was so high that it could only be sung. I don't think that's so any more. I think you can make any character sing so long as that character has some passion. If they don't bleed, they don't sing.

Do songs have to have a narrative within them?

I think they have to. They have to get some place, that's my taste. I mean, there's a song—I always use it as an example—in *Camelot*: 'If ever I would or should leave you'—I forget which—'It wouldn't be in summer.' The minute you hear that, you know: well, we're in for the four seasons. And that's what we get and it doesn't go any place. It would be a surprise if they didn't get through winter. Then it would be a good song.

So the book always comes first.

Must. Must. The book gets all the blame and none of the credit, but a good score cannot survive a bad book. And vice versa.

You're saying that all the elements are interdependent.

They are. The music is most important, because it is a musical. But it's like providing the fertile soil for a song. If you don't have a character and a situation to get the song out of, particularly for the actors, they're just stuck, saying: what are we going to do, face front and just, you know, show off a beautiful voice? It's boring. It's not theatre

Is there any significance in the fact that most of the people who invented the American musical are Jewish?

Or dead.

Or both. What is the Jewish contribution?

I remember a man came to me to talk about *West Side Story* with a very different point of view: that all four collaborators were gay. And I said: that has nothing to do with the show. What did have to do with the show was that we're all four Jewish. But that had to do with a feeling of a fight against injustice which informs that show. Why there are so many Jews? I don't know. It's a profession that was allowed. The only Jewish theatre I ever saw—I went down to Second Avenue— it was very funny. They did musicals down there which were a compilation of everything that was on Broadway. It was all in Yiddish, which I didn't understand. I remember it had a destroyer or warship, because it was right after the war. And somebody—Menashe Skolnik, great comic—parachuted down on deck, and they all sang this song, and they all danced, and half the girls in the chorus had glasses. And an actor, who was in my first play *Home of the Brave*, Joe Pevney, who became a director, he translated it. It had vitality and warmth. And they were passionate about whatever it was. And I think that's a Jewish characteristic.

They also had a thing that they called 'baking', which was putting together the elements of the show. That smacks of the way that musicals are created.

Oh, I read about that in the Jacob Adler's book. But it seemed to me they were putting together routines. Comic routines. And they would throw them together and throw in a number. You think that's the origin of the musical?

Well, I think the process is collaborative.

You think it comes more, or at least as much, from that as from the operetta?

I'd say more. We've returned to the operetta with the sort of poperetta, Andrew-Lloyd-Webber thing.

Oh, that's a good word.

But the book musical seems to me something original. Was Hammerstein the prime influence?

I don't know who else. I remember when I was a kid, one of the ways I got interested in theatre was there was a stock company near where I lived, and my cousins and I, we'd go every Saturday. And one day we saw *No No Nanette*. Well, that was technically a book musical but all I remember was the parasols twirling. You know today it's a helicopter...

Did Oklahoma! *feel to you like a breakthrough?*

I didn't like *Oklahoma!*

What didn't you like about it?

The first image that comes to mind is tapdancing cowboys. I thought: this is arrant nonsense. It started off beautifully with a glorious song. And then I thought it was very hokey. The best thing about it to me was what Agnes de Mille [the choreographer] did. Because she made you think: why doesn't Laurie want this guy who was perfect, why doesn't she want him to go to the picnic with him? Because she's deeply sexual and ashamed of it, and she's drawn to Judd.

That was in Agnes's ballet. And that was something I had never seen in a musical, and I liked it for that. But the rest of it—'I'm just a girl who can't say no'—no.

Hammerstein was a playwright first, wasn't he? You were a playwright first.

Oscar Hammerstein was a playwright, was he? I didn't know that.

Yes, he was a playwright first, but we don't remember his plays. But we do remember your plays. Being a playwright, you've brought different criteria to the musical: meaning and content.

Oh yes, but without thinking. It was just the dramatic instincts of the playwright. I think if more playwrights did musicals we would have more good musicals, but as you know, playwrights don't want to do musicals, and for two reasons. One is, a lot of them start to lecture or to analyse why a song. You feel it. I don't believe there are rules for that. You either know where it is or you don't. The other reason is that the playwright takes a beating, the librettist takes a beating, and if you want to do a musical as a writer you really have to have a sensible ego, which very few people in the theatre have, writers or not. Obviously I think I do.

Well, West Side Story *was an astonishing collaboration of four egos that I'm not sure I'd describe as sensible: Bernstein, Jerome Robbins—*

I said it was the writer needs a sensible ego.

Oh, the writer. Ah…

Only the writer. He's the one that gets shafted. The others, oh, they were enormous.

What was the genesis of West Side Story*?*

Sometime in the late forties Jerry Robbins asked Lennie Bernstein and me to write a musical that would be a contemporary version of *Romeo and Juliet*. And the boy was to be Jewish, the girl was to be Catholic. It was to take place in the spring, when it was Easter and Passover. What attracted me was the idea of working with Lennie. Because I had seen *On the Town*. Well, I thought his music was the most exciting theatre music I'd heard, for a musical. But after we futzed around for a while, the whole thing reminded me of an old play I'd never seen called *Abie's Irish Rose*. And I thought this was *Abie's Irish Rose* with music, and I wasn't interested. Then several years passed and of all places to get inspiration Lennie and I were at the pool of the Beverly Hills Hotel. It was a time when juvenile delinquency had taken hold in this country. Gangs. And one morning I was there doing some terrible movie, and he was doing some concert—not terrible. And the headlines were all about Chicano gangs against so-called 'American' gangs. Lennie loved Latin American music and so did I. So we said we could do it about that. I didn't know Los Angeles or the Chicano situation. I knew New York. I knew Puerto Ricans. I knew Harlem. I said: let's do it there. He would've done it any place. We called Jerry [Robbins]and that's how it started. Then there's the classic story of how Steve [Sondheim] got into it.

Originally were you going to write book and lyrics?

No. Originally Lennie was going to write the lyrics, then he decided it was too much. And then I think they approached Comden and Green—because they had all worked together—who fortunately were busy. I say fortunately not to denigrate them, but they're just wrong for it. And Steve had auditioned for me with the score of a musical they were going to do called *Saturday Night*, which played in London. And as he remembers—he's a great injustice collector—I said I thought the lyrics were wonderful and I wasn't mad about the music. Well, a lot of time passed and there was an opening-night party. God-awful play called *The Isle of Goats* by Ugo Betti, with Uta Hagen. She was on her back downstage with her knees astride, moaning and groaning she wanted a goatherd. It was art. At the party for this fiasco there was Steve, and, as he says, I literally smote my forehead and said: why didn't I think of you? And I introduced him to Lennie and there we are. They started writing the lyrics together, you know. And talk about egos. But Lennie made the most magnanimous gesture I've ever heard anyone making in the theatre. We opened in Washington. Steve wasn't mentioned in the reviews because he was nobody. And Lennie said: I'll take my name off the lyrics because it means something to you and not to me. It was terrific of him.

Did you have to research the gang stuff?

No, I made it up. We had a producer who walked out on it. She was always after me. She'd say: 'Why don't they say, "That's how the cookie crumbles"?' And I said: 'Because by the time this show gets on, nobody will be saying that.' Also, you have to remember in those days you couldn't say four-letter words. I mean, one scene ended with 'Hey Officer Krupke—krup you!' Well, that was transferred to the end of the song because it's much more effective in music. But I realised I would have to find a language that sounded like street talk and wasn't. And also to lift it out of literally the gutter, which is where this play takes place. So I made up this stuff. What's interesting to me is the word 'cool'. It wasn't used then. It's one of the few words that I think is kept in usage, but the meaning changes every decade. So it doesn't seem dated even now. The rest of them I threw out, and made up a lot of talk that sounded like something.

You knew Romeo and Juliet *of course.*

I wanted to examine the story, which I read carefully, and I do have a kind of obeisance to Shakespeare that nobody picks up on. The balcony scene is full of the word 'hand'. And in the meeting scene in *West Side Story* there's a lot of hand talk and usage, except I use it sexually. And then I had to see what would work for our story, and I forgot him. Except one place where the English, I must say to my delight, picked up on. No American critic, lecturer, whatever, has even noticed. There's one place in the story I think is better than Shakespeare. It's why the message doesn't get through. In *Romeo* it's the plague, here it's the theme of the piece: prejudice. They don't know that over here—but they don't know Shakespeare in this country.

You set your ambitions for West Side Story *very high.*

The best thing about the writing of it was we had no self-censors. We just wanted it to be the best that we could make it. I frankly thought we were lucky it would run three months. I didn't give it a chance. I didn't care. I don't think any of us did. I don't think anybody worried about its commercial value or not. We were looking for a phrase to describe it, and we came up with 'lyric theatre', which was weak. But it was a way of saying: no, it's not like everything else. Oddly enough, people think *West Side Story* was very innovative. I think for the wrong reason. I think all the techniques in *West Side Story* had been used before. What hadn't been used was the content. That was the beginning of saying you can treat anything in a musical.

It never goes soft on you. Was that deliberate?

There was one place we had an argument. Nobody wanted a song written about Krupke but me. And they said I was being commercial and vulgar. So I got very grand and brought up Shakespeare's clowns and the porter scenes and that's how I sold it. But it does serve that purpose, to relieve the tension. In the movie oddly enough they took that song and put it early on, it doesn't work. It's a cheap comic song. When you put it in its dramatic space it works.

And so you actually cited Shakespeare in the discussions?

Yes, and another time too. Jerry wanted Maria to take sleeping pills, so I said: but now it's the twentieth century, and she breathes and everybody would see it. With Shakespeare they believe it; they wouldn't believe it today. So that got rid of that.

Was the collaboration an active one? I mean, did the four of you work together and criticise each other's work?

Eventually, yes. It started—I did an outline, then I would write scenes and then they began to write the songs. And then Jerry stepped in, and we all went over it. It was rather fast. I don't know why I think good musicals are written fast. I

know *Gypsy* was written very fast. And everything was very amicable until we opened.

And what happened then?

Well, to everyone's surprise at the first preview in Washington the audience went wild. It was madness. And that's when Jerry wanted it to be a 'Jerome Robbins Production'. And there was terrible behaviour from then on in. Opening night the three of us didn't speak to him, which is sad in a way.

There's nothing like the American musical before and probably, in fact, there's nothing after.

Yes, there is.

Is there?

I think there is. I think it will develop more.

The kind of musical we've been talking about lasted for about thirty, thirty-five years, ending round about Gypsy *or just after. Why did it die?*

I think because people tried to duplicate it. I don't think you can duplicate any form. I think anything has to be informed by a personal passion. Steve Sondheim's musicals are very individual; they're all his and attempts to imitate them are bad. And I hate to say it but there aren't until this moment genuine promising—and I'll use this dreaded word—'artists'. Well, maybe one is Adam Guettel, whom I think is going to write a musical that everybody will be glad to see. He's a composer lyricist and he's my godson, and I'm mentoring the musical. [*chuckles*] His songs are gorgeous. And they're fresh. It's individual, it's idiosyncratic, it's Adam. [Guettel has subsequently written *The Light in the Piazza* with book by Craig Lucas.]

Did it have anything to do with the fact that—

—he's Richard Rodgers's grandson!

Until about the mid-sixties the popular songs, the songs that people whistled on the street or heard on the radio, were also the songs that were in musicals. Then with rock 'n' roll that all split apart?

Rock 'n' roll songs don't lend themselves to musicals. And except for some songs, such as primarily those written by The Beatles, I think they're all asinine. The lyrics are primitive and they're childish. And in a musical you can't get up and sing that childish stuff. It has to have something, some emotion, some real thing, and they're not in those songs, so the musicals are no good.

Because they don't emerge from character and narrative.

Right. I think any first-class work in the theatre must have character. I can't think of one that doesn't. The great ones have great characters. Even an ensemble of characters. And those rock musicals, you know, they don't have anybody. They have a guy with a guitar, and a girl with stringy hair, and that's it.

And spectacle.

Oh, spectacle, well, if you call that spectacle. It's not spectacle to me because it's used in a very vulgar way. I remember—maybe because I was a kid, but I've never forgotten—the curtain for *On Your Toes*. They didn't know how to end it. There's a song in it called 'Small Hotel'. It ended with the hero and the heroine singing the song behind a window in a little house. And the walls of the proscenium started to close in closer and closer, the house came in, then the last thing was they pulled the shade and the whole stage was blacked out. It was thrilling. I never forgot it. That's spectacle to me, and it also had a purpose. Because it says in our small hotel we'll be alone together. It wasn't just aimless.

So that's married to character and narrative.

And situation and everything.

And wit.

Right, oh wit.

You haven't talked about wit.

In musicals?

Yes.

It's very hard. It's hard because, practically speaking, musical performances don't usually have wit. Someone like Steve Sondheim writes very witty lyrics. Not jokey. Most people write jokey lyrics. If a character is really witty what does he or she sing? A patter song. Well, maybe they can get away with one. But it doesn't lift you. Music should lift you.

Do you think that musicals are almost inevitably about ordinary people rather than people who are privileged by wealth or particular intelligence or gifts?

I don't think there's any limit. I mean, the plays today try to be about ordinary people. I don't think ordinary people are very interesting. We should write about extraordinary people. I don't mean that they have to, you know, rule the world. But extraordinary characters, let me put it that way.

Like Tennessee Williams's characters, for instance. What do you remember about the first performance of Streetcar?

I remember I had read the play first. Irene Selznick, who produced it, gave it to me to read. And I was surprised that she was producing it, because Blanche on or off paper is not attractive, unless you really understand what the play is about. I mean, what she wants in the world. She's the outsider. I think that's what his plays are about anyway.

And they use language in a very vivid way—not purple prose but hard-nosed.

Tennessee heightened language, and to me it's so individual it's absolutely right for the milieu. He always located his plays in odd places anyway. And those characters, it seemed to me, that that's how they would talk. I never thought it was anything you could even say was naturalistic—it was just natural to them. I never felt he was trying to aggrandise his words, his language. It's something that I think he was born with. And it's just beautiful. And I think [Elia] Kazan was the best director, American director, I have ever seen. Because he got thrilling performances out of the actors. And his productions looked theatrical. But what he did in that play, he distorted it. He made Blanche the villain. Kazan had very peculiar feelings about women anyway. I know that Jessica Tandy [who played Blanche] in New Haven said to Kazan: 'I beg you, don't make me the villain.' But he did. It was one of those rare things that happens in the theatre: the production and the introduction of Marlon Brando. Tennessee really arrived with that play, despite the success of *Glass Menagerie*.

What was he like?

You know you hear of a celebrity or a star or somebody and you think: oh, I want to meet that person. You should never have met Tennessee. He was usually drunk. He made silly jokes. I didn't know him all that well. He wasn't the kind of person you wanted to spend time with. For me particularly because I revered his work, so I didn't want to be disappointed in the person.

What did you say when you first met him?

I could say nothing, I was just thrilled to meet him, and was kind of surprised that he played the clown. I think he acted a lot in private, you know. He created a persona for himself. I was once in Key West—which I absolutely hated—and went to his house. When you read about his house you think: 'Tennessee Williams's house!' It was a dump. It was a tiny little bungalow, and I thought: well, you're an artist, yes, but you have all this money, why aren't you living in a decent house? I don't know why he wasn't, he didn't care. The booze was there, and there was Duvall Street, which I call the Street of Dreams, without going into what those dreams were. When I first met him, he said to me in one breath: 'Oh, you're Arthur Laurents, you're not much taller than I am.' And I thought: my God, this is Tennessee Williams and all—what is he thinking of? It was interesting enough; it was by Irene Selznick's pool, because that's what he loved to do, swim.

He seems to me every bit as much of a political writer as Arthur Miller.

Oh, I think he's very political. And he was political as a man. Just because the issues are not as obvious, but everything has a social base, as I believe it must. He was very political.

As were you. You were blacklisted, weren't you? Tell me about the atmosphere when the House of Un-American Activities Committee started their hearings.

Well, it started in Hollywood. I was always involved in left-wing causes, and it was exciting. Because we were idiots. We thought we were going to wipe them out: they were all dastardly, and we held a thing called the 'Thought Control Conference'. And where did we hold it? At the Beverly Hills Hotel. Very Hollywood. At first it didn't mean much. Then it got very serious. And there are endless stories: I won't go into all of them. But what happened was that the producers, partly because they were Jews, were frightened. And because the Committee was very anti-Semitic and openly so. And they felt it would reflect on them. After first saying there would be no blacklist, they enforced a blacklist, and the town was decimated. I think that's when pictures started to go bad, because of the talented people who were kicked out. It was frightening. And people informed who didn't have to. Like Kazan and like Jerry Robbins. Jerry, poor fellow, informed because he wanted to work in movies. Well, they didn't want him, so he should've saved himself the trouble. Kazan wanted to work in movies and did. And, again, I may be in the minority, but I don't think Kazan was a very good movie director. I think he was a great stage director. But that's what he wanted.

Was this a real moral choice—whether to inform or not?

It was a moral choice for almost everyone. It ends up a moral choice, I suppose, but there are the small fry, the people who would not be able to work. Not as a director or an actor even, but in some job in the studios. An agent for example. And that's the only thing they knew. Do you inform to feed your family or don't you? I suppose in the end it's a moral choice because you can find ways of getting a job. But there's nobody I know who informed who I approved of.

It seems a painful irony to me that not many years before that in Europe there were people who were having to make the same moral choice, people who weren't Jews being forced to inform on or willingly informing on people who were Jews.

I think the choice was easier in Europe because I think the Western world is largely anti-Semitic. So it wasn't so difficult to inform on a Jew. I think it is very difficult or was very difficult—still is—to inform on friends. These people just didn't inform on co-workers; they informed on friends. That is immoral—I don't care what your politics are. And particularly people like Kazan and Jerry Robbins. The theatre had no blacklist. I think part of that is because the theatre was not corporate. There were individual producers, so people followed their own conscience. And when you're on your own, you have a better conscience than when you're in a corporate set-up.

Do you think the theatre is corporate now?

I don't know what the theatre is. We lack producers. People say where are the writers? I think the biggest need in the theatre is producers. I'm on something called the Broadway Alliance, which I more or less started in one sense with the object of getting new American plays on Broadway. Because there were none. And at one time I had high hopes, because one of the things it did do, it started to make a dysfunctional theatre community a community again. But then it gets down to the dollars. And there is such insensate greed. My point was that unless everybody gives up something, we'll all have nothing. And I think that we're still headed there. The place to do a play is off-Broadway, but that's getting very expensive.

When the hearings started taking place, how did the climate change?

Slowly. It was curious. The first person who had an effect was the first star who testified, Larry Parks. And he made a mistake. He had named all the names, but when they asked him to name them in public he begged the Committee not to ask him. Well, that was neither standing up nor falling down, it was crawling. So they didn't like him. And he had informed to save his job. And they gave him a picture: it bombed. Sterling Hayden informed: he was a hero before. Later in his own memoir he hated himself for that. Brando. I saw Brando in Paris. (I had been blacklisted and they took my passport away and then I got it back and I went to Paris and lived there. Terrific time.) And I went to meet Marlon to have lunch one day, with Ellen Adler, Stella's daughter. And Kazan had taken an ad in the international edition of the *New York Times* proselytising for informers. Really. So I told that to Marlon, and he said: oh, that's not true, he would never say that. He was really upset. And he went back to this country and made *On the Waterfront*, which is an apologia for informing, written by an informer, Budd Schulberg.

The Committee had an effect for another reason. Federal employees had to take an oath that they were not Communists. So it was affecting the country on all levels besides the theatrical one. Where it hit New York was later, when they began calling theatre people. Well, except for, you know, people I've mentioned like Kazan and Robbins, people stood firm. The theatre community stood firm. Television buckled. No jobs. I don't think there ever was a period in the theatre where it was very prosperous for actors. So they were counting on television for jobs, and they couldn't get them. For me, when I came back to this country and was asked to give my name for something for the first time, I thought: wait a minute, dare I do it? And when I realised I had checked myself, I was horrified. Because it has an effect whether you know it or not. I think everybody is damaged.

So it created a sort of self-censorship?

Oh yes, absolutely. People were no longer willing to do things, because they thought: well, not here or not maybe not on this issue, but they're going to get me here. And, well, look at it today, in this country: 'liberal' is a dirty word. I think you could follow the line from that period to today.

Were you aware of Brecht when he was living in LA?

Yes. I met him. There was a woman named Salka Viertel, who was reputedly Garbo's lover. She also wrote scripts for Garbo's movies. And she had a salon for the refugees. Thomas Mann, Hanns Eisler, Heinrich Mann, Bertolt Brecht. Oh, it was very toney, you know, in the left-wing sense. I don't know what Brecht was like. He had very elegant leather jackets. That struck me and I thought: how left are you? And then, of course, I thought about his behaviour with the Un-American Committee. Well, that saved his neck. But he was no hero.

Did you see Galileo?

I saw it when Charles Laughton did it out there. Yeah, terrific play.

What was Laughton like?

Well, it depends what you think of Laughton. I thought Laughton was a wildly amusing ham. I mean, he was over the top, and I thought he was mad. Really.

So did he obscure the play?

Oh, of course he obscured the play. It wasn't about Galileo; it was about Charles Laughton's return to the stage, in a tiny theatre on La Brea [Los Angeles]. Everybody came, and you know it was as though the Maharishi of some place had come, and they all bowed down as they did years later in the ashram. But still it was worth seeing and worth doing. That's theatre.

Arthur Miller

1 9 1 5—2 0 0 5

Playwright. Arthur Miller wrote All My Sons, Death of a Salesman, A View from the Bridge, The Crucible, The Price *and many other plays and short stories. When I interviewed him he was eighty-four and very energetic, physically and mentally unbowed. With* Death of a Salesman *running on Broadway and* The Price *about to open, both in new productions—he was undergoing a total rehabilitation after years of being patronised by the New York critics while being much performed and respected in Britain. This exchange was in the* New York Times*:*

> CRITIC ONE: *Arthur Miller is celebrated there.*
> CRITIC TWO: *He's so cynical about American culture and American politics. The English love that.*

Of course, these critics got it wrong on all scores—about the English, who were (and are) in thrall to American culture, and about Miller, in whom they mistook disappointment for cynicism. My interview with him was long—over two hours— and took place in his apartment on the Upper East Side in New York. After the interview we went for a walk in Brooklyn, which is where he used to live (in Brooklyn Heights) and work (in the US Navy yard). We walked down to the riverfront to be filmed in the shadow of the pillars of the Brooklyn Bridge looking out over the East River. 'These are our cathedrals,' said Arthur, looking up at the bridge. 'I thought those were,' I said, pointing across the river to the Business District and the twin towers of the World Trade Center. 'Oh sure. "The business of America is business." That's what Calvin Coolidge used to say. He was the first President I can remember.' *Then he stared at the buildings. 'None of them were here when I lived here. Not one.'*

You were fourteen when the '29 Crash happened. Was the Depression your 'sentimental education'?

I walked into it when I was a kid, and I think that fracture of optimism that we had lived in for so long was a cataclysm, not just for me but for the whole country. It destroyed the idea that we had a system, an economic system. It showed that God had not created what we were living in. That it was not something that had sprung up with the forests and the rivers. And this mutability of everything was a shock. The disillusion was simply unbelievable. What it did for me was to objectify life. I began to see that everything was capable of destruction and indeed was on the verge of destruction. So it's basically a tragic view of existence: we live at the edge of a thread—you just shake that structure and it all comes apart. I think the Americans in general live on the edge of a cliff. Fundamentally they're waiting for the other shoe to drop. I don't care who they are, even the most optimistic of them. It's part of the vitality of the country, maybe, that they're always working against this disaster that's about to happen.

Your starting point in the theatre was a period of great optimism, with the foundation of Federal Theatre Project. How did that come about?

The Federal Theatre Project was basically a relief operation. A woman named Hallie Flanagan got to Roosevelt and convinced him and Mrs Roosevelt that, instead of putting writers, artists and scene designers into road building or something, it would be better to let them make art. And it was a phenomenal thing. It lasted I guess about seven years, but it created immense art in this country. Painting, dance, theatre. We got paid twenty-two dollars a week. Twenty-two dollars and seventy-seven cents, that was my salary, and I was only on it for about five months.

What was your job?

I was on a so-called playwriting project, which was a new invention. I was among the first and the last to be on it; you were supposed to go home and write plays. I think I was the only one of about forty of them that really wrote anything! But they all had a good time, and they were writing stuff. A lot of radical plays. One of them I remember was about the building of the railroads, which was full of corruption; they had a great time on stage playing with the corruption idea. It was dreadful stuff. But the basic invention there was the Federal Theatre Living Newspaper, which has never been repeated anywhere that I know about. This was written, not by one man, but by committees of men and women, the way movies are made. They'd pick a subject—let's say, medicine, or housing—they'd get six writers, everybody busy writing stuff, and an editor. And he'd edit the whole thing and stage it.

Day by day?

Day by day. And it was very exciting. Electricity, the production of electricity. Farming. Tremendous social subjects. Electrification of the farms. Of rural areas.

You could be talking about Russia, from this distance.

Oh, it was right out of Russia. I'm sure that the Russian example was very influential in the creation of the project.

Did the project die because it smacked of Socialism?

I'll tell you exactly why the project died. There was a play called *The Revolt of the Beavers*. [*laughs*] It was a children's play. The children were beavers: they were building this dam, and they went on strike because they didn't get enough pay. And the boss beaver was very cruel to them. A friend of mine wrote it; it was a marvellous children's play. The kids in the theatre, they were in heaven. And then Congress heard about it, and they regarded it as a Communist thing, which in a way it was. So they closed down the whole thing, that was the excuse. But mind you, this was '39 and the war was coming—and the end of the Depression, as a result of the war. So, the pressure on the government to create jobs of this kind was slackening. And that ended it.

Did it have the effect of making you think that art could change society?

It was one of the things. When I was growing up—by '32, '33, somewhere like that—a number of people were writing very socially activist plays. Odets' play *Waiting for Lefty* was probably the best of them all and the most effective. In it he called upon the audience to go on strike. In fact, the actor would stand there and the audience was yelling: 'Strike! Strike!' About what, we never knew, but there was a spirit of militant rebellion. And this spread through the younger generation of people. I myself couldn't write them because—I don't know—it just didn't work for me; I wasn't able to latch on to that kind of a formula. And it *was* a formula that soon died because it got very repetitious. You began with somebody who was stupid, and he gradually learned that the system was bad, and then he grew militantly opposed to the system. It was a bit like the Catholic Church's rituals in the Middle Ages where somebody found God.

We were still doing plays like that in the seventies in Britain.

Oh...

You mentioned Clifford Odets. He was the creation of another utopian movement, The Group. What was The Group, and what was its importance for you?

The Group was certainly the most important influence that I know about. The reasons were several. One was that first of all, the acting was amazing. This was a whole different kind of acting. See, you've got to remember that most plays were acted by actor laddies who knew all the tricks and did them very well, and most of the plays were completely trivial. Suddenly, there was this group of people who were dealing with real life as one knew it. The power of it came out of the art. Of course, the art came out of a lot of political and philosophical thought. And it was terribly stimulating. You really wanted to become part of some kind of theatre. I was still in college and I envied all of them, that they could be part of this movement.

And they were an ensemble.

Oh, they were an ensemble, they were a real company. But the organisation was chaotic and they missed a lot of opportunities, because there was nobody with an organisational ability. They were a lot of crazy actors. And consequently they flew apart far earlier than they needed to.

You've described Broadway in those days as a Shakespearean ideal. Why was Broadway everything that it isn't now?

I think primarily there were maybe three or four producers, businessmen who normally did all kinds of trivial stuff. But they all had in their hearts the idea that they were there to promote art. And these guys would take a chance on a young writer, on a new play, in the commercial theatre. Because there was no other theatre, see, there was no off-Broadway. The theatre outside New York was simply waiting to see what New York had done and then they would reproduce New York in Pittsburgh or Detroit. The Broadway theatre was the centre of new theatre for the whole United States, and it was paid for by these entrepreneurs who were insane people who believed that it was their job to do this. One of them was this crazy man, Billy Rose, who produced big extravaganzas like *Dumbo* and, you know, blue elephants. He was married to Gypsy Rose Lee and was an ex-songwriter and a screwball. But he thought Odets was God. And whatever Odets wrote—he hardly read it, I'm not sure he could read—he put up whatever money was needed. Those guys, they don't exist any more.

Who put up the money for All My Sons?

That was... bah, it's hard to remember. See, the money would be raised and maybe twenty people would get together and put up $500 here and $300 there and $1,000, because the whole production cost of *All My Sons*, I'll bet, was no more than $25,000, $30,000. Well, *Salesman* was under $40,000. So you could get, let's say, ten people—sometimes there were more—who put up small amounts, so nobody had very much to say about what was going to happen except the producer and, usually, the director and the actors. The authority was gone; there was no authority to start with. It was a wonderful, creative chaos. And then the costs started to go up and that was the end of it. I mean, now, to do *Salesman* again here, reproduce a production already in being in Chicago, simply move it here, was a million dollars, $800,000. Same actors. Same sets. That production, at the time I'm talking of, would maybe be $35,000. Well, you can't raise a million dollars with a couple of folks. So, the name of the game is different.

Was it pure coincidence that both you with Willy Loman and O'Neill with Hickey in The Iceman Cometh *took on that profession?*

I don't know how that happened. But, of course, the salesman is king of America. I never thought of it that way, but later on I had to think of it in that way. We realised that we were both reaching for that central figure. And it turns out everybody's father was a salesman. I can't tell you the hundreds of letters that I have gotten over the years starting: 'My father was a salesman.' You know, we're a society based on the advertising of goods and the consumption of goods, that's all we're about.

Was there a salesman who you had in mind, who you'd met?

The origin of the play was an uncle of mine, although he'd never recognise himself in this play. He was a road man, who would go out on the road and sell stuff. Anything from church bells or whatever it was. It didn't matter what they were selling, it was just… the idea of selling was holy. I have to tell you that when I did the play in China, they had no salesmen, because Mao had just died and the Communist system was there. The only thing they had that was remotely like it was that they had guys who were buyers who were competing with each other because factories needed to buy raw materials for their factories. And the actor playing it said: I can't figure out a way to approximate Willy's tremendous feeling for other salesmen until I remember that, when the railroad started in China, it was a very dangerous thing to go on a train because there were bandits. So, a group of men arose who guarded the railroads by riding horses next to the train, and these guys had a certain camaraderie, one with the other; and the profession of guarding trains was very highly regarded! So he says: whenever I think of how I would feel if I were guarding against bandits, that's how I become Willy.

Salesman had a wonderfully inventive scenic idea, being able to be able to walk from the past to the present, with a set that had no solid walls.

When I wrote the play I couldn't imagine a set. So I wrote the play for three platforms: one was the stage platform, one was a slightly raised platform to be the bedroom of Willy's wife, and one would be a higher platform for the boys' bedroom. What Mielziner, the designer, did was: he took those three platforms, but he embedded them in this marvellous… what would you call it? It looked like it was going to be blown away. It had the outlines of a building of a house, but a strong wind would simply turn it into powder. It was a great design, and maybe the best single set that I know of to express both the reality and the impermanence of the salesman's brain.

What was the original title of the play?

Inside of his Head. When I first showed it to Kazan, I think that was the title. What I wanted was the inside of a skull, and there would be platforms in it, but somehow you would have a face there too. I didn't know how you would do that. But of course I gave that up because it got to be so cumbersome, it was stupid!

Salesman *opened in New Haven.*

No, it opened in Philadelphia in the middle of winter, and I should add that we were very nervous about it, more than we liked to remember, for one basic reason: We were afraid—well, I wasn't, but they were—that the audience wouldn't know whether he was in the present or whether he was thirty years ago. And, one man in particular, Josh Logan, who was a considerable director, had put in a thousand-dollar investment in the play until he read the script, and then he took back five hundred because he said: they're never going to know where you are. And indeed, in the making of the set, Mielziner created a leaf effect, so that, when Willy went back in time, this projection of leaves on the stage would tip them, the audience, that we were now no longer in the present, we were back there. Of course, I doubt very much if anybody knew what was being projected there, because the projection was very vague: it was just a lot of blotches, all over the place. In any case, the audience followed it perfectly easily.

What happened on the first night, the first performance?

Well, it was simply unbelievable. The play ended, and there was a dead silence. I remember being in the back of the house with Kazan, and nothing happened. The people didn't get up either. I thought we were sunk. Excepting, I'd heard sobbing in the audience, from men. Men were simply burying their faces in their handkerchiefs. All over the audience. It was like a great funeral. Really, it was like being at a funeral. And the reason they didn't applaud, I believe, is that you don't applaud at a funeral. And then, when it, the cyclone hit, it was overwhelming. I was weeping myself at the idea of the power of this damn thing. It came in like a great big truck! Then one or two got up and picked up their coats. Some of them sat down again. It was chaos. The normal routine of theatre-going had been disrupted. And then somebody clapped, and then the house fell apart and they kept applauding for God knows how long. I remember an old man being helped up the aisle, who turned out to be Bernard Gimbel, who ran one of the biggest department store chains in the United States. It turned out that he had been swept away by the play, and the next day issued an order that no one in his stores—I don't know, eight or ten stores all over the United States—was to be fired for being overage! [*laughs*]

Were you influenced by seeing Tennessee Williams's work?

Streetcar was a marvellous invention as far as I was concerned. For one basic reason. You see, the attitude towards plays as I had come to understand it was that the playwright had to vanish into the scenery: nobody wrote these plays. One shied away from style—language-style of any kind—in order to make the thing totally real. Then Tennessee came along, and he turned it all around. There was suddenly a *writer* here; this stuff was manifestly *written*. People didn't talk that way, and if they did, they didn't talk exactly that way. That was a liberating idea. You felt licensed to create your own language.

You felt licensed to write a kind of poetry—language that's rhythmic and intense and distilled?

It was a liberation for me. That's why I could write that whole first act in, I don't know what, two days. Because you could now spin it out with all the full force of your imagination, without hiding behind this curtain of anonymity.

So you could write a line like: 'the woods are burning boys'.

Yeah.

And not feel: I wonder if people would say that.

Nobody would say that. However, it sprang from his gut.

Was there something in the production of Streetcar *that also encouraged you?*

Of course, that was Kazan's genius. He could seize the lyricism of something, but organise it. And his use of lighting was something marvellous. Everything was brilliantly theatrical, instead of imitating some kind of reality. His influence on the theatre was tremendous at that time, but of course he had come out of the Group Theatre, because he wouldn't have existed without the Group Theatre. That kind of imagination. You see, the Group actor was hopefully trained as a dancer, as a singer, as a philosopher, God help us. They would sit around reading some abstruse piece of philosophy in order to explain to the brain to take in the whole complex of this world, and it all mysteriously became available in *Streetcar*.

Particularly in Brando's performance.

And Brando was sprung loose. I'd seen Brando before: he was always magnificent. I mean, I remember the first time I saw him, it was unbelievable. He had an animal force: you felt that a lion had been let out of his cage, and nobody had to teach him anything. I think Kazan would be the first to say that. But here Brando was given a form that was new, and it was terrific.

He emerged from the Actors Studio, didn't he? Which emerged from the Group, didn't it?

I happen to know this because I was working with Kazan at that time when he and a couple of other people thought that they could recreate the conditions of the Group Theatre. It was as simple as that. This was the late forties. The idea was that they would learn from their past mistakes and create a school which would employ Stanislavsky methods and attract the younger generation. The problem was who should head this up. Well, the one unemployable man around was Lee Strasberg. I'm not exaggerating. Kazan worked with the Actors Studio from time to time, but he was a busy director in Hollywood, so he wasn't there very much. And the thing gradually became a way for people to learn how to behave on the stage in a way that had nothing to do with text. The text was the enemy of acting, put it that way. I have had actors say to me: well, the main thing is the actor's emotion. And I would say: well, what do you do if you are going to act Chekhov and everybody knows what the text is, or Shakespeare or Ibsen, are you going to forget those lines? What Lee was doing was playing to the actor's weakness. Everybody wants to just *express*; the idea of being an actor who combines the text, his emotions, and the rest of it was too difficult, so they simply eliminated the text. I couldn't bear the whole idea from day one. It just seemed to me to be a fraud.

The Crucible came out of contemporary events. What did it feel like when the McCarthy plague hit?

I think the main feeling I had in, oh, about '52, was that we were in a kind of spell that was being cast over the country. I couldn't be very specific about it at the time. All I knew to start with was the idea of the citizen being completely untrustworthy. And everybody was hiding something, whatever it might be. It was a problem, everywhere. I'll give you an example. I was in a lawyer's office, and they called in another lawyer to sign something as a witness. I was in the midst of talking to my lawyer and mentioning that the Broadway theatre had become terribly corrupt, that all that mattered any more was money, that the generation of producers who were willing to take chances with young people was practically over, and that it was a show shop now, etc. And this other lawyer, who had been brought in just to sign something, looked up and said: well, that's a Communist position. And my lawyer, who was a Republican, I guess, was as astonished as I was. The point was that neither of us argued with this guy. We thought he was slightly touched. At the same time, he seemed to be in power. If you were going to take him on, you never knew where that was going to lead. There was a kind of terror, a rippling terror, that you didn't know from what angle accusations would come from, and to start to argue positions was quite a kind of a ballet, where you went around positions that might conceivably have been Communist positions at some point. Political positions. Or literary ones. My generation came out of a depression which had ended only about twenty years earlier—or less, really, ten years earlier. And, the idea of radical solutions to things was perfectly normal. I mean, everybody got involved with that. Truman himself had said: this whole Communist thing is simply a way for the Republicans to get back into the White House. But such was the force of this thing that even he had to back off and establish an investigative apparatus—to track down Communists in government.

Did it feel like being Jewish in Germany?

I think it was very close to that. I think it was very close to that. You had the feeling that from unknown corners of the universe could spring this monster who would consume you alive. The reason I say that is, for example, the teachers were particular victims or targets, because there were a lot of radical teachers for one thing, and they were vulnerable. The idea of teaching our children this Russian ideology was very inflammatory: I knew about three teachers who were fired summarily. There was no trial, nothing. Just accused of something and they've gone.

Did you feel particularly vulnerable, being Jewish?

That went along with it. The anti-Semitism involved was quite obvious. And a lot of Jews had been left people. To give you an example: in the early fifties, the *Holiday Magazine*, which was then quite a well-known magazine, was sending writers out to their alma mater to write about the changes that had taken place at Yale, Harvard, Princeton, all the great universities, since their graduation ten or fifteen or twenty years earlier. And the editor, Ted Patrick, whom I didn't know, called me and asked me if I'd go back to the University of Michigan and write about the changes since the thirties: so this was '39 to '52—that's the spread. So I went back, and my former English teacher was now the Dean of the university; and there was a man with a striped suit and a good tie, but formerly, when I knew him, he was a mess, as an English teacher, and a wonderful man. And he said: 'Well, you're going to find it quite different now, there's less standing around the lamp-post, talking. The corporations are here at the end of every graduation period, picking up the people with the best grades. Everything is being sliced like cheese, and it's quite sad, but why don't you talk to the man who is the Head of Orientation? There is a department in the university, not a department but a man, who takes the young as they come in. He just spends a week with them, with a group of them and teaches them where the gymnasium is and where the English department is. He leads them through the university.' And so I got talking with him and he said: 'It's quite different now than when you were here.' I said: 'What specifically?' He says: 'Well, the FBI hires, pays certain students to report on the teachers.' I said: 'Report what?' He said: 'Well, any sort of left-wing lectures. But, of course, at the same time they're paying the professors to report on the students.'

I'd been a reporter on a newspaper, and I went to the newspaper one day. There sat a middle-aged man writing down things from the papers. I talked to one of the reporters—the young guys—and he said: 'He's the State Police, this guy. And whenever he sees any statement by anybody that's at all liberal or left, he writes down the guy's name. They have a list.' Now, mind you, the Governor of the State of Michigan at that time was a man named 'Soapy' Williams—Mennen Williams Shaving Cream? That was his family—and Soapy had been in my class. He had been the head of the peace movement, and as I'm talking to this guy, I was looking at old newspapers from my generation, and there was a letter in this paper from Soapy Williams. Earlier, a guy signing himself 'Conservative' had said: 'Why is it that all the meetings of the peace movement are full of Communists?' And Soapy replied: 'Why don't you come to one of the meetings, and instead of all these Communists, we'll have a Conservative too.' Soapy was now, x years later, the Governor of the State, and it was his State Policeman who was sitting there and taking down the names of possible radicals. If Soapy had been around they would have added his name, you see? It was that kind of stuff. It was madness.

You were subpoenaed by the committee.

Not until later.

What did it feel like when you received the subpoena?

It felt like a dead weight had been dropped on my head, because I knew what they wanted to do with me, and I knew what I was going to do with them, and it was all a gigantic waste of time.

You didn't vacillate, thinking: do I have the courage?

No. The reason was that I was so disgusted by this time, that was 1956, that's four years after what I've just been describing. By that time, let me put it this way: the full force of the Red Scare was diminishing. I knew perfectly well by that time why they had subpoenaed me. It was because I was engaged to Marilyn Monroe. Had I not done that, they would never have thought of me. See, they had been through the writers long before. They'd never touched me, they'd never reached for me. Once I became famous as her possible husband, this was a great possibility for publicity. I'll finish this particular historical moment by saying that when I got to Washington preparing to appear before that committee, my lawyer received a message from the Chairman of the Committee saying that if it could be arranged that he could have a photograph taken with Marilyn, he would cancel the whole hearing. I mean, the cynicism of this thing was so total, it was asphyxiating.

You didn't have to make a painful moral choice?

No, there was no choice. How could one deal any other way than simply to say: I'm not going to talk about anybody else, except myself. I didn't appeal on any constitutional grounds. I just said: you ask me anything you want about me, I'll tell you.

But other people made bad choices.

I think part of my reaction was that I was an independent person. I didn't have a company; I didn't report to a producer; I wasn't writing movies. See, if you were in the movie business you were helpless because you had to work for a studio, and if they said you're not going to work, that's the end of your life. There goes your entire career. That didn't exist for me. I could always put a play on, where—I don't know: England or Germany or France or not at all, the hell with it. But nobody could fire me because nobody had hired me. So the result was that I could really talk for myself without fear of that kind of retribution, whereas these other poor people—you know, a cinematographer, a director, a writer in films—were totally at the mercy of these corporations which had caved in. Earlier on they had resisted the Committee, they had felt that it was immoral for them to be running a blacklist. Of course they collapsed after the Committee really put the screws on them, and now they were red-hunting along with the Committee. It was disgraceful.

If ever I had to make a moral choice, I'd like to think I'd have the courage of John Proctor in The Crucible. *Do you think his position is a romantic or a realistic one?*

I think it's realistic in one sense. A man like him would literally shrivel up and die if he found himself dragging other people into this nest of vipers. In a way, there's little choice for a guy like that, although the agony involved is tremendous. It's romantic in the sense that he has an idea of himself which is that of a leader of a sort, a moral example, perhaps, for others, so he's letting down a lot of people, if he should accede to the committee.

What he has in common with many of your other heroes is a desire to preserve his name: 'How may I live without my name?'

Right.

And Eddie Carbone says: 'I want my name!'

Yes.

And Willy Loman says: 'I am not a dime a dozen, I am Willy Loman.'

It's himself, it's his very identity, apart from other people or apart from the class that he is living in. Really, it's his one claim to moral identity, I suppose.

It seems a very American thing: the idea of the name, the individualism. I can't imagine a British writer writing that.

Oh, really? It seemed to me to be the most natural thing in the world at that time. I wouldn't have thought that that was in any way a particularly American thing to be saying.

To me, it's the individual saying: I have a right to own my own life, and at the same time we're all dependent on each other. How do you connect the two?

In order to connect you have to be somebody to start with! [*laughs*] If you're nobody, there's nothing to connect. See, what's left out of a lot of American ideology is the rest of us. I think the governing idea, which we got from the Puritans, is that man is an individual in a battle with everybody else. And that he's got to carve his identity out of the jungle or the forest. At the same time we Americans are more dependent on society probably than anybody else in the world. People say that the taxes are too high, that you shouldn't have to be paying taxes. These same people are riding on terrific roads—somebody's got to pay for these roads. They want great schools, but they don't want to pay any taxes for them. I think the Greeks had a word: Idiot. It is the Id. We call it the Id, that is the essential, sexual centre, but it was applied to people who had no idea that they lived in this society. And we really cultivate idiots at a tremendous rate, we've got a Congress now [1999] which I think is sociopathic. They really think that the government is the evil. But government in itself isn't evil.

But do you still believe that we can improve society?

I've seen it improved from time to time. If we got rid of these jokers, it would certainly be an improvement. We've got some guys there who haven't passed the first civics lesson. It's terrifying. I mean, for example, this Test Ban Treaty they found to be intolerable: that anybody should tell the United States not to do something.

Do you expect people when they see The Crucible *to reflect on the way that they live their lives?*

I would hope so. God knows whether they do or not. I get a certain amount of mail from people who feel they've been confronted with stuff that they would prefer not to have seen and they're glad finally they have seen it. What is really good theatre? It's really a battle with denial. This is what it comes down to. The stage shows you stuff that you didn't dare want to look at before.

Do you think The Crucible *had an influence?*

Initially it landed at the height of the McCarthy terror. It was greeted with real questioning: some didn't get the thing at all, some reviewers; others resented the play, they wanted to feel like nothing like this had ever happened in the world before. We were really in a special position, historically: menaced by Communism. And what I was saying in the play was: this had been going on since the beginning of time. They didn't want to think about that and consequently, the play was not a great success, initially. Oddly enough, McCarthy died a couple of years later. I can't remember the dates, but about four or five years later a group of young actors put it on in a ballroom in a hotel in New York—it wasn't even in a theatre—and that's when that play was really launched. It was launched by young actors, far too young to be playing these roles in some cases. And suddenly, McCarthy was dead and the whole issue had cooled off, so there was now time to look back on it. When it was really hot, society didn't feel it could confront this fire!

Was it difficult to write about events in the present tense?

I wished I could do something else like that. See, [*laughs*] I wasn't given the material to do it with, but I didn't regret for a minute that it happened, because it gave heart to a certain number of people who figured: yes, the thing is still alive, the civilisation. There is still hope of some kind of rational attack on this miasma we're living in.

You created a new dramatic language for the play. What were its component parts?

I tell you, I went up to Salem at that time because that's where they had the original records. Now, during the Salem witchcraft trials, ministers acted as stenographers and they had a primitive shorthand system. It wasn't really shorthand, it was just abbreviations, so you could read pretty much what people had said, and I was completely absorbed in this way of speaking. Of course, a lot of it you couldn't directly use because we wouldn't understand it, so I had to adapt it into a kind of muscular English which was reflective of that original. And it was great fun to be able to do that. I learned, by the way, in writing the play, I thought: oh, now I know how Shakespeare could write all those plays, you see, because when you run out of juice, you just flick open the book and you see: here's some more stuff! You know what I used to do years ago? I would take any of Shakespeare's plays and simply copy them. Pretending that I was him, you see. You know, it's a marvellous exercise. Just copy the speeches, and you gradually realise the concision, the packing together of experience. [*chuckles*] Which is hard to do just with your ear, but if you have to work it with a pen or a piece of paper, and you see that stuff coming together in that intense inner connection of sound and meaning, it's exhausting, just the thought of it.

August Wilson
1 9 4 5—2 0 0 5

Playwright. He wrote The Pittsburgh Cycle, *ten plays about the African-American experience in the twentieth century, each one set in a different decade. I had produced one of them*—Ma Rainey's Black Bottom—*at the National Theatre a few years earlier. I interviewed him in a hotel in New York.*

I got involved in theatre in 1968. It was the height of the Black Power movement, and the idea of theatre being able to communicate ideas is what attracted me to it originally. I started a community theatre in Pittsburgh with the idea of using theatre as a tool to politicise the community or, as we said in those days, to 'raise the consciousness of the community'. And perhaps, even more importantly, to alter the shared expectations of ourselves. I saw theatre as a way of doing that. I couldn't write plays then, but I made an abortive attempt. I had a couple of guys talking, and one guy says: 'What's happening?' and the other guy says: 'Nothing.' I sat there for twenty minutes trying to think of what else to write, and I said: I'm not a playwright.

You had a hard schooling in Pittsburgh?

I dropped out of high school.

You were at a high school with a thousand white kids and you were the only black kid, is that right?

Yes, they decided that they didn't think I should be going to school there, and after a while I agreed with them and I left.

You've said that you took refuge by crawling inside words.

When I first learned the word 'breakfast' and saw that it was two words to make one word, there was hope from then on. I tried to invent words by putting two words together and, yeah, sometimes the words were just so beautiful that I wanted to crawl up inside them. But when I left school I went to the library, and it never ceased to amaze me that they didn't charge me for the books, that they were free. And then I discovered that in formal schooling you have to achieve a certain level of proficiency in a subject in order to advance, but you go to the library and you say: give me a book on calculus, and they don't even ask if you can read, they just give you the book. I found a great sense of freedom in that.

When Black Power came along you identified with that. Why didn't you start writing prose?

Well, I was a poet at the time; you do poetry readings and you have an audience. And I was influenced by the fact that LeRoi Jones was writing plays at that time. The plays were designed to politicise the community, and theatre was a way of disseminating the ideas.

Who influenced you as a playwright?

The largest influence has been the Blues, as I see that as the best literature that Black Americans have. And rooted inside the Blues is an entire philosophical system at work. In order to pass along information, you have to make it memorable, you have to make the story memorable, so someone will go and tell someone else. And the songs were like that, and I became intrigued with that idea of uncovering the social manners of Black America through the Blues.

Were you trying to make a new form of theatre?

Well, the theatre that I participate in is essentially a European art form: it's based on the age-old drama that's been handed down from the Greeks. But what I bring to that, and what Black Americans bring to that, is an African-American sensibility. It's very similar to jazz. Jazz is created using European marching band instruments; the availability of the instruments came about because of the Civil War and the marching bands. Blacks took those instruments and, because of their sensibility, they created entirely different music out of the European instruments. I see theatres the same way. If you have the theatres in which to develop the playwrights then you don't take anything away from American theatre; what you add is an aesthetic so that eventually you'll arrive at something that is truly and uniquely an American theatre. Right now, the theatre that we have in America is still based on European-American cultural values, and yet America is made up of an amalgamation of various races and cultural groups that are other than European, and they have a contribution to make. If you throw all that in the mix and allow these aesthetic statements to be made, then I think you'll truly have something that is vibrant and of the twenty-first century.

So, when you started to write plays, did you have a model, in the way, let's say, when Arthur Miller started to write plays he looked to Ibsen?

I count myself fortunate because I didn't have a model. I say that because, when I was twenty and decided that I wanted to be a poet, it took me eight years to find my own voice as a poet, because I read anyone and everyone and did a fair amount of imitation of almost any poet you can name. So consequently, when I started writing plays, I didn't know the literature of the theatre or the history of American theatre, and I thought: I just want to feel my way through this and go at it on my own. I didn't want to spend eight years trying to find my voice as a playwright, so I just more or less forged ahead with my own sense of what the story should be, or what the play should be.

All your plays seem to me to be about trying to connect people with their past, trying to give people a sense of continuity.

Certainly a large part of my work deals with the idea that you have to go back. As one of the characters says: 'You have to go back and pick up the ball. If you make it to an end zone and you don't have the ball, it's not a touchdown.' This is what I've found: that with my generation, particularly of black Americans, there seemed to be a disconnection, a connection that was lost with our grandparents. I remember kids would come and they would say: my grand-mother died and we have some land down south. And I would assume that they were going to move. But they would sell the land—they had no sense of how they connected to their grandparents. I thought this was important: in order to understand who you are, you must know who you have been in order to determine who you are going to be. Even though it has been a difficult history in America, it's a history of triumph, because we've managed to survive and in some instances to prosper, and we're still culturally sound and robust.

But is part of your hope that you educate the white audience? It seems to me, not being American, that slavery is still very little understood.

It's very little understood and, of course, you can see evidence of slavery all around you. Whites generally seem to want to forget their involvement and their part of it. So they sort of gloss over and say things are better now and let's proceed on. But the history is one of triumph for us, and we can't forget that, because it is what has enabled us to survive and to make the contributions that we have made.

You came into theatre for polemical reasons but, although your work is strongly politicised, it's never polemical.

That's not what I'm about; I don't want to write a polemical play. I work as an artist, and I have something that I want to say as an artist. So for me the aesthetic statement is the most important thing of the work. Whatever themes or whatnot that touches, that's fine, but I still always imagine myself as Picasso, you know, standing in front of a blank canvas. You don't paint for a particular audience, you work as an artist to satisfy and make your aesthetic statement. When I sit down and write, I'm trying to write the best play that's ever been written. Or at least I used to try to do that until I ran across a quote from Frank Lloyd Wright which said that he didn't want to be the best architect that ever lived, he wanted to be the best architect who was ever born to live. I had to raise my sights and say: now, I'm trying to write the best play that's ever *going* to be written!

You don't try and second-guess an audience, or have a picture of your audience?

I don't have a particular audience in mind when I write, other than an audience of one, which is myself. If I did, it would probably be my contemporary playwrights. That's probably who I would write for—the same way I think Michael Jordan played basketball. Like, hey, look, I can do this, you know? Or, what do you think of that move?

When you talked of an African-American aesthetic, is that a singular way of telling stories?

Oh, absolutely. And I think this arises from the fact that we have come from an oral tradition, and we pass along information orally. At one time it was a crime to teach a black person how to read or write in the United States of America. Africa has the oral storytelling tradition—that's where we come from—and in certain African cultures the mark of a good personality is how long can you keep the story going and keep it interesting. You have to keep it memorable in order for someone to remember the story to pass it along. This is the way information was kept alive, as opposed to it being written down and recorded in a book. It's not a bad way of passing along information, yeah?

You grew up in the South. Were you familiar with Tennessee Williams's writing?

I don't ever recall seeing a Tennessee Williams play, although I saw the movies. I saw *Cat on a Hot Tin Roof*, and I saw *Streetcar Named Desire*, and I've heard it called 'poetic realism'—I'm not sure if that's the phrase. I just thought it was a very good play, and I identify with that. I think: boy, I wish I could write one like that, you know? *Streetcar*, in particular, yes.

Williams writes about dispossessed people, people on the edge of society; you write about a fault line at the heart of American society.

Ah, well, absolutely. I write about Black American culture. I have a tremendous amount of respect for the painter, Romare Bearden, who said when someone asked him about his work: I try to explore in terms of the life I know best, those things which are common to all culture. I thought; aha! That's what I'll do: I'll explore the commonalities of culture to the specifics of the black American tradition.

When you wanted to become a playwright, you said you wrote two lines of dialogue and then couldn't think what to say next. What released you into thinking you could write a conversation?

Sometime later, it was in '68… I think what was happening was that I didn't always value and respect the way that black Americans talked. I thought in order to create art out of it you had to change the way that they talked. And so I was writing plays with what you might call 'poetic dialogue'—for instance, I had an old man and an old woman on the park bench, and the man walks up and he says: 'Our lives, frozen in the deepest heat and spiritual turbulence.' She moves away, and he says: 'Terror hangs over the night like a hog.' That's not the way that I write now, you see. Partly what happened is I moved from Pittsburgh to St Paul in 1978. When I moved to St Paul, I missed the voices of the people, but I began to *hear* them for the first time. And I wrote the play *Jitney*, in which I just decided I'm going to let the characters talk and say whatever they wanted to say. And I sort of turned a corner and never looked back, because I found it very liberating and I couldn't wait then to write the next one.

You were concretising experience, learned experience?

Yeah, exactly. I love that word 'concretise'. I got involved with writing because it was concretised thought. You could actually make your thought concrete and show someone: hey, this is what I was thinking. You see, that just fascinates me, still does, you know?

And that's what draws you to the theatre rather than writing fiction?

It's real and it's immediate. I don't know how many novelists, I guess not many, ever walked on the bus and saw seven people reading their novel, but I can go into a theatre, and there's like seven hundred people watching my play all at one time, you see. And I find that very thrilling; it's a community experience. Reading is a solitary act that's done in a wide variety of places—you never know what the response of the reader is. In the theatre, it's an immediate experience and you find out right away, you know.

Is it also that you like the space between the words in the theatre—what people don't say to each other?

I hadn't thought about that, although certainly if you talk about silence in music or the space between notes, it's very important; otherwise you won't have music.

I just find the theatre so liberating. People say you can do more in the movies, and I go: well, I'm not sure. There's a lot of things that you can do in the theatre that are as inventive. You can do things in a theatre that you can do on film too. You can show, for instance, a field of blackbirds flying off in a movie, but I can also describe it on stage and make you see it perhaps more vividly, because you're bringing something to the experience, you're inventing this field of blackbirds, so you see it maybe better than film, because film maybe is too literal a thing.

What has to happen to help theatre flourish and to help to grow an African-American theatre?

Well, I think the tools have to be made available to the artists in order to work. By tools I mean that we need some of the sixty-six LORT theatres—the League of Resident Theatres—in America. Only one of those is black; I would like to see four, five, eight, nine. If you had nine, for instance, you'd get a five-play season. That's forty-five plays—that's forty-five playwrights—getting productions they're not getting now. Forty-five directors directing plays, forty-five designers, etc. Five years from now that's five times forty-five, and then, you know, you learn by doing. That is bound to strengthen the skills and the abilities of the artists who have all the ideas and all the talent, but they don't always find an opportunity to exploit that talent, because we simply don't have the theatres.

How do you change that?

I'm not sure. What has to happen is that we in the black theatre have to strengthen ourselves, we have to take an honest look at where our failures are, and we have to begin to build relationships with the funding institutions who fund these other sixty-five theatres. But if you look at any one of those theatres you will see that it didn't just happen overnight. A group of committed people came together and decided that they wanted to have a theatre, and they pushed and pulled and otherwise provoked that theatre into being. People didn't just give their money. This group went out, and they were persistent, and I salute that. This kind of thing has to happen more in the black community if we're going to have that kind of theatre. I think that the government can be supportive, but I don't want to rely on government, I think the artists have a responsibility themselves to go out and make their art, and make it happen, on their own.

Jason Robards

Actor. Jason Robards appeared in over sixty films and many plays on Broadway, including several by Eugene O'Neill, most notably The Iceman Cometh *and* Long Day's Journey into Night. *He was a sharp but tired seventy-eight when I interviewed him in a hotel in New York. He died later that year.*

———•—•———

A lot of people take a long time to get to like O'Neill's work. What about you, was it love at first sight?

Yes. I read O'Neill in the Navy in World War Two. I was in the Pacific: I got on a ship which had a small library, and I saw a book that said *Strange Interlude*. I thought: this is going to be a real hot book. But it was a play, and it was a play in which people would freeze and speak what they really thought. Then they'd stop. It fascinated me, so I guess it was love at first sight. I did see the original *Iceman*—with a dinner break and everything—when I was going to the American Academy of Dramatic Arts in New York. They had us go to a preview, and it too just fascinated me. I did *The Iceman* ten years later.

Was it the characterisation or the language that you found so attractive about Iceman?

When I heard that José [Quintero] was going to direct this play, I begged him to be in it. I said, I want to play Hickey. I saw the face of Hickey. I saw the face of James Barton, who had played it originally, even though the whole production was kind of messed up. José said: I must ask you to read this, read for me. So I read part of the end of the play for him. It just fell in. I don't know why it fell in;

I could see, feel, be that person. Then he said to me: 'Now do the funny part.' That was very easy for me because I was that guy. It was almost as if I drove on a road that I always knew and knew every corner. The script seemed to lead me exactly down the emotional road if I stuck with the script and oddly enough stuck with the stage directions. There are a lot in these plays, as you know. When the guy who was playing Willie and I were rehearsing, he said: 'Let's erase all these things, you know. We don't want to do this, we don't want to do this, this is baloney. Let's go it on our own.' So the next day we crossed them out. But we studied that script every day, and finally we started taking an eraser and erasing the crossings out, because everything in the stage directions set up the atmosphere. All the specifics were there. It's almost a play in itself, some of those stage directions. I found that in every play of his that I did.

Perhaps he wrote these very elaborate stage directions because he thought: I've seen the way my father's generation treat plays, and I don't want my writing to be treated like that.

Yes, but you know the thing that amazes me is what he must have read in his sort of itinerant life. His knowledge, where did he get this gift? I mean, how can you study that much and know that much and not live that long? He wrote a play about the plight of Italian Communism, all kinds of stuff—*Lazarus Laughed* and all that stuff, the references, everything.

You performed The Iceman *in a bar, didn't you?*

It was the Greenwich Village Nightclub. The part that the stage was on was the dance floor that they'd had in the club, and then there were some steps down to a bar. We left the bar there—you could get drinks there in the intermission.

You probably know Long Day's Journey *better than anybody on Earth, because you've been in two productions, you've also directed it, and you were in the Sidney Lumet movie.*

I played Jamie in the original for almost two years. Then I played the old man, James Tyrone, in two, three productions. I do know it pretty well, I guess.

You must feel you know O'Neill, the man, very well.

I realise now I know O'Neill so well that I feel that I'm part of him. I know his life. His life and mine are the same, because we both had actor fathers, and we both had mothers who were away. All the family things. My mother was in a sense not there, and the brother, the younger brother, came along. And the jealousies... All the things that are in the plays suddenly I'd see: it's my life. My father was an actor in a play in Chicago. My mother went out to visit, and I was born in Chicago. Then they took me back to New York. And then they were on the road for about four years until they settled down in New York again. All these things. And being at sea for so long—I was in the Navy—and being a drunk, you know. I drank like a crazy man and never faced what was bothering me by blotting it out, not having fun drinking. All these things... I guess I got it almost out of my system by acting in these plays.

Did you ever meet him?

No, I wish, oh God, I wish I had. My cousin was the Entertainment Editor of *Life* magazine, wrote a number of books, wrote a wonderful book on Ellen Terry, and he knew the theatre very well and the opera. He died recently. He was a critic, and actually I hold him in great respect for writing about the theatre around the country, all the regional theatres. He was the only one that ever knew they existed. He did a great interview with O'Neill. O'Neill liked him very much. That's the nearest I came.

What did he say about O'Neill?

He just thought he was the greatest guy he'd ever met, and they had a great time together. They spent, I don't know, an hour or two maybe, and he wrote this article on him.

So he wasn't miserable company, O'Neill.

No. E.G. Marshall, who I knew very well, was in the original *Iceman*. He loved him. He went out with him a couple of times, and they said: 'You can't go out with him because he's not supposed to be drinking.' The wife got mad with him for going out with him. But he was great fun, he played the piano, had a lot of fun.

When O'Neill was growing up and his father was touring in The Count of Monte Cristo, *do you think he thought: what I do in the theatre is going to be exactly the opposite of what my dad is doing in the theatre?*

I think he was very upset with the kind of theatre that was going on, but O'Neill at that time was too small to know much about it. Things were breaking, you know; his family was in such disarray; he was sent away to school. He must have just thought: 'I don't want this, I don't want this life.' I never wanted to be an actor, and when I saw my father disintegrate and self-destruct in the land-of-the-living-dead Hollywood, I thought: 'Well, I'd better get out of here, get to the Navy, do something.' I hated to see him self-destruct, which he did. I'm sure that O'Neill said: 'I don't want this kind of life,' if his great desire was to write. He always wrote poetry; he wrote for a paper when he was in his teens up in New London. I didn't write.

What does it feel like when you're an actor, when you've got to do one of those arias which can go on for pages and pages.

136

Well, what I do is learn those first. I did that in *The Iceman*, I did it in *Long Day's Journey*, I did it in *Moon for the Misbegotten*—that's a beautiful play, man, that's the one, I'll tell you. Anyway, I learned them, I learned them, just put the book up on the mantelpiece, blah blah blah blah. My wife says she hears me at night going blah blah blah, I'd wake her and say: is that right to you? I've got to get all the words, everything; and I'd keep that, and try it every night. And then you've got the monologue in your pocket. Then you do them, and it breaks time. You know, time is broken on the stage. Stage life is so different from real life. I was doing *Moon for the Misbegotten* with Colleen [Dewhurst] and she said before the show: 'You know I'm tired tonight.' We were doing eight a week—that's a long play, and she never gets off the stage. I said: 'I am too, I may just coast and get through it.' She says: 'That's fine.' Would you believe that within twenty minutes into the play it was like somebody put their hand on her back, and she just went: the whole thing lasted three minutes. We were soaring, somewhere else. That is the greatest thing that happens in these plays. If you know it well enough, it's always there and then it just takes off. Three minutes and it's over, a lifetime in three minutes. It's weird.

And you have these endless repetitions in some of the plays.

There are repetitions, but each time it's different. You know, it's a symphony: you have repetitions but each time it's repeated it's under different emotional circumstances and it means something more. We didn't cut *Iceman* or *Long Day's Journey* when O'Neill gave us those plays. There were no cuts in fact. He had an agent come down to look at us to see that we weren't cutting when we were rehearsing. And the reason *Long Day's Journey* ran over four hours: we had to keep every poem and everything. And actually we did six a week. We couldn't do eight because of union rules—the stage hands were getting golden time if we went too long.

O'Neill's father once said: 'What are you trying to do, make the audience go home and commit suicide?' But you don't feel that way. How do you explain that?

That you don't go home and commit suicide?

You feel elated.

Because he said: 'In the dream is the hope.' We don't kill Harry in *The Iceman*, we don't kill Harry Hope. He doesn't kill Hope is what it is, Harry Hope or our hope. Do you know that during *Moon for the Misbegotten* I had letters, hundreds and hundreds of letters, from people writing to me as if we had solved their psychiatric problems. They took them out of heartache and despair, these plays. I couldn't believe it; I said: 'What are these people writing to me for? I can't help anybody!' Brian Dennehy [the actor] even told me he came to see it three times.

Once when he was working in his father's butcher shop, he came in his butcher outfit to see it: he still had some of the blood on his butcher's apron. Three times he wanted to sit there, a lot of people did.

But what about the saddest play ever written, Long Day's Journey?

Oh God, that's sad.

But for all its melancholy and its despair, you don't feel suicidal when you watch it.

No, and you know, there is a tremendous amount of humour. In all his plays there's great humour, great laughs sometimes—especially, you know, the argument between the father and the older son about acting. He's sending him up. In the end they're all there—mother's going on, but still they love one another very, very deeply. You say: well, I have hope for that family, they're still there and they are still together even though she may be hallucinating. The first time in the play we see the father put his arms around Jamie and say: 'Don't cry,' you realise that they are close. And of course the one guy we know is the survivor is the young O'Neill, Edmund in the play; he survives, and he survives to tell us this.

So it's about persistence—love and persistence?

Love is great, it's in there big. It's in there big; it's a beautiful play. *The Iceman* is a real big symphony, and *Long Day's* is the most beautiful string quartet that could be.

O'Neill always talked about doing the 'big thing' in the way that some American novelists talk about the 'great American novel'. What do you think 'the big thing' was?

Oh, I know what it was. O'Neill spoke—or wrote—more than once of 'eleven plays', a cycle of the two hundred years of an Irish family in the United States. He never finished them. These plays—had they been finished, and he had not suffered from this nervous ailment, whatever he had—they would have been like Shakespeare's *Henrys*. They'd be a whole series of plays that all tie into one another. The one play that survives out of the cycle is *A Touch of the Poet*, followed by *More Stately Mansions*, which is not a completed play and there's no point in doing it. In this Irish family one of the ladies survives to become a mother of an Irish President of the United States, which I often think is Rose Kennedy. I said: my God, this guy, he didn't know who Kennedy was, he'd never heard of him, but he wrote this whole thing about the beginnings in *A Touch of the Poet*. That's the thing, I think, the 'big thing' that he meant. But maybe he meant *Long Day's Journey*, I don't know.

Kim Hunter
1 9 2 2—2 0 0 2

Actor. Kim Hunter had a distinguished career in the theatre and in film. She played Stella in the original Broadway production and the film of A Streetcar Named Desire.

What did you think when you read Streetcar?

It seemed like a good play, a nice part, you know. I was happy to audition for it.

Jessica Tandy had been cast by then, but not Brando?

No, no. His part was going to a famous film actor. One of the questions that they asked me before they gave the part to me was: how tall was I, because he was short and I was fortunately shorter. It was John Garfield, who of course had played in theatre years before, but was a big film star at that time. I don't quite know how he got out of this contract, but I think he decided that, coming back to the theatre after so many years, it should be *his* play. So he kind of dropped out, and that was when they hunted around, and Marlon Brando became Stanley.

What were rehearsals like? I don't imagine they were all absolutely plain sailing.

Actually it was a remarkable rehearsal period. Our first rehearsal we were on stage, the actors were in a semicircle facing the audience, there was a big table in front of us, and [Elia] Kazan, [Tennessee] Williams, [Irene] Selznick [the producer], our stage manager and all had their backs to the audience. I remember Kazan saying: 'Just read it; don't try to bring things to it yet; just if something

139

happens fine, good, but just read; I mean, talk and listen reading the play.' And we read it. Then we started rehearsing. And when I say rehearsing, it was kind of trying to discover who we were as characters, what the scenes were about, what our relationships were with the other characters in the play. We stayed in that semicircle for ten days rehearsing. If we desperately needed to get closer to someone we were having moments with, Kazan allowed us to get up and move over but then get back. After ten days our stage manager taped out the set on the stage, we got on our feet for the first time, and Kazan didn't really have to block it: we all knew where we were, except for the fight scene—yes, that had to be blocked and kind of changed a bit.

What was Tennessee's part in rehearsals?

He was at rehearsals every day. Once we got on our feet, and Kazan sat in the auditorium, Tennessee sat way far back but was there watching. Every now and then he'd have an idea, he'd write a note and bring it down and kind of tuck it in Kazan's upper pocket and then go back. Finally Kazan grabbed him by the scruff of the neck and said: 'Sit down, I want you next to me. Don't keep going back there.' There was only one area I think that we wanted him to write things for us, and that was the fight scene, where there was supposed to be a great deal of ad libbing. As a whole company we said: 'No, we want Tennessee Williams's words, not ours please.' And so he did. He wrote all the ad libs for us, and that was marvellous.

Was Kazan very fastidious about the text?

We had a company that honoured our playwright and therefore wanted it to be absolutely true to what Tennessee Williams wrote.

The company sounds like a close-knit one. Was Brando very much part of the company?

Definitely. As we got, you know, playing month after month, Marlon would make alterations in movements and that kind of thing, not words. But I think Jessica Tandy got a little disturbed by a lot of the things that he would do. Didn't bother me a whit. He was just absolutely a marvellous actor to work with. His sense of truth about what he was doing just came to you like a fireball. It brought the best out of you.

Was he generous towards you?

Oh yes, and very thoughtful. I went through a bad period in my life in the course of the run. I actually burst into tears on stage, and he came up to my dressing room shortly after and suggested that I might be interested in seeing a psychiatrist—but terribly concerned. He didn't want me to fall apart and was very thoughtful. Bless his heart, I think he may well have saved my life.

What about Kazan?

I think he's the best director I've ever worked with. He had this capacity and need and way of getting to know his performers very closely—and much of their personal lives—so that when he needed a particular area of your emotional background and being, he would know each button to push to get what he needed out of you. He was ruthless in that way, but also extremely generous and kind, because he would never do it in front of a company if he got that personal; he was always very private. One of the reasons he was such a very good director was that he knew how to get the best out of all his performers.

What was the response the first time an audience saw the play in New York?

When we got back from Philadelphia, our reviews kept getting better and better and better. We got to New York, and Kazan said: 'Now look, all of you, forget about those reviews. Yeah, we all think it's a bloody good play, but it's a little like oysters—not everybody likes oysters, so just do your damnedest, and we'll see how it turns out.' Well, we did get extraordinarily good reviews, but the response to the play was mixed from the audience point of view, because it was very unusual. For the times, it was an extraordinarily unusual play, and maybe a little more open, more honest and daring than most plays up to that time.

And sexy.

And sexy, yes. That it was.

What was it like being on stage with Brando?

It was marvellous being on stage with Brando. Every now and then crazy things would happen. One performance, at some point a repetition of lines came up, and when we both realised it, it was all we could do to keep from laughing and not carrying on with the scene. I noticed if Marlon didn't like what he was doing he would downstage himself, and there was one time that both of us very nearly fell into the pit because I had a tendency to do the same thing myself. One night, after the fight scene, when he called me downstairs from Eunice's apartment, and I came down the stairs into his arms and we went off into the bedroom and into the bed, the lights didn't go out. So we quickly got our feet off the floor, and I was saying: 'How far do we have to carry this reality on stage? Do we actually have to have sex?' I don't think either one of us would have minded it very much, but we really didn't want to get undressed. There was another time when he carried Jessica Tandy to the bedroom for the rape scene, and the curtain didn't come down when it was supposed to, so he just carried her right on into the closet. Jessica said: 'You gonna hang me up on the wall and rape me?'

Did it seem odd that he became a by-word for Method acting?

I don't know quite why Marlon should have been pegged as the leader of the Method, but he certainly did bring everything from within himself to whatever role he did. I think Karl Malden said once about Marlon that he can make wrong choices, and even bad choices sometimes, but the one thing he can never be is false. That incredible capacity for truth is of course the heart of the Method, and not everybody has it.

What did Method acting mean to you?

The Actors Studio was formed just a few days before we started rehearsing *Streetcar*. Once the play had opened Kazan came to me: 'Stella is your audition for the Actors Studio,' he said, 'Get up there and work.' At that time there were two groups: Kazan was the monitor of one, and the other was Bobby [Robert] Lewis. And Bobby Lewis's group was filled with actors with a little more experience; Kazan's group were all of us younger ones who just sort of hadn't been around that long. So I was in Kazan's group and Marlon was in Bobby Lewis's group, and so was Karl Malden. And both Lewis and Kazan virtually introduced us all to Stanislavsky's method. Eventually I learned that the Method is a technique to help you when you're in trouble, when you can't trust your own instincts about what is true and right for the role—for the performance for the play. You shouldn't just use it as the only way to go about the work.

Do you think it became a cult, that it started to damage actors who weren't very good?

Yes. I did *Dark at the Top of the Stairs* [by William Inge] down in San Juan, Puerto Rico. It was mostly a cast that was brought from the States down there to do it. This girl-child in it suddenly one performance started to leave the stage before the scene was over. And I grab her and bring her back, and we finally finish the scene. Afterwards I said: 'What the hell did you think you were doing?' She said: 'Well, I felt I wasn't feeling it properly.' She was a student of Lee Strasberg, who frequently made that point: you must feel it to do it, kind of thing; she was a young actress who had not enough experience to be able to put it in its proper category. Instead she just took it absolutely literally, which is insane.

According to Arthur Miller, Strasberg was something of an embarrassment for the Group. They had to find him a job, and they found him the Actors Studio.

Yes, thanks a lot. For me it destroyed the Studio. I finally left after five years.

Tennessee Williams is a man that I wish I'd met, but then people who knew him very well have said: you wouldn't wish you'd met him.

Oh yes, you would have. He was a dear, loving man with a crazy sense of humour. Then, of course, as the years went by, he drank too much, but still we'd run into each other all the time after *Streetcar* closed, and we'd hug, and be happy to see each other.

Was he an entertaining raconteur?

Well, yes and no. We had one interesting evening in New Haven, which was our first time of *Streetcar*'s being on stage with an audience. It was only a split week: I think we opened on Thursday. Friday night Thornton Wilder came to the play, because at that time he was teaching at Yale in New Haven. Irene Selznick had a gathering in her suite in a hotel afterwards, so the company was there and Thornton Wilder and, of course, Tennessee. It was a lovely party, but then at one point, of course, absolute silence to allow Thornton to give his review of the play, which he did—and a very talkative and intelligent chap he was. He had one complaint about the play: 'I think the character of Blanche is just much too complex for the theatre, to be on stage.' And Tennessee said: 'But Thornton, people are complex.' Then later in the evening Irene said: 'You know, it's marvellous to have these two marvellous playwrights in the same room at the same time. Can't we hear each of you tell us how you work?' Well, with Thornton it was no problem at all, being a professor. He explained that he gets his idea and then he does his research and then he does his outline of a play; the dialogue is the last thing that comes. And I saw Tennessee was getting down further and further into the couch he was sitting on because he knew his turn was coming up. Finally it did, and he said: 'Well,' he said, 'I get a couple of people together, and I get them talking and eventually I'll see the point I want to make and I'll make it. And if there's a joke, I'll make it too.'

Tony Kushner
1 9 5 6—

Playwright. Tony Kushner wrote Angels in America—*a play in two parts. The first part was called* Millennium Approaches, *the second* Perestroika. *If you run a theatre you hope for the sort of luck that Peter Hall had when* Waiting for Godot *dropped on his desk at the Arts, or Brendan Behan's* The Quare Fellow *on Joan Littlewood's. For me at the National Theatre it was* Angels in America, *which seemed Shakespearean in its ambition. It is still a fearful indictment of New York producers that his play wasn't produced there until after its National Theatre opening. I interviewed him in his bottle-green clapboard house on the banks of the Hudson River in New York State, a hundred yards from where Washington put a chain across the river to stop the British from getting to New York.*

You started going to the theatre quite young?

I think the very first play that I was aware of as a great play was *Death of a Salesman*. My mother was an actress. She did Linda Loman in the local amateur theatre production of *Death of a Salesman* in 1960 when I was four years old. It had an enormous impact on me.

When you were four?

When I was four. I think maybe not so much the play itself because I couldn't really follow it, and I was confused by certain things, but I thought it was very sad: I was very alarmed that she was crying. It was done in the round—which was a sort of a big innovation at that point—and so I could see the people opposite

144

crying at the end of the play, and I knew that my mother was making them cry. I think that that impressed me enormously. I'm sure that's why I went into the theatre: because my mother had done it and had done it rather well—she was actually a good actress. I remember the figure of Willy Loman too, very, very powerfully.

What was it about Willy Loman that impressed you?

I got the idea that he was a very sad person, that he was a defeated person, that he was someone who was extremely tired, that life had sort of beaten him down. I remember thinking that he looked a lot like my grandfather, who was a small businessman and had had a hard time as a businessman. I think that kind of stoop, carrying the briefcase and the sample cases... It was a figure from the working world, and there was something not great about the working world. I come from a family of artists, who at that point were having to go into business to make ends meet. I think I was beginning to understand that there was something unpleasant about the world of commerce. And so, in a sense, I think I got the political meaning of the play. I mean, the genius of the play is that there's absolutely no way to separate out the economic man from the psychological man from the political man—the story combines all three so spectacularly. I was struck with that all over again watching the revival on Broadway.

So was Death of a Salesman *responsible for your political education?*

I came from a family who were left-leaning, New Deal liberals. I wouldn't say that *Death of a Salesman* was responsible for my political education, but it was very much a part of the political and cultural worlds of my parents. It was transmitted to me from the earliest days of my interest in the theatre that American theatre had a political dimension to it, and that it had a progressive political dimension, and that it was in some sense opposed to the political economy, opposed to capitalism and critical of it. I mean, *Streetcar* and *Long Day's Journey* and *Salesman* are irreducibly political plays. I think that *Salesman* is the medium through which I learned to read American drama in a political fashion.

Did Salesman *encourage you to think that theatre was an instrument for changing society?*

What really had the biggest impact in terms of that was Brecht. But you have to look for models from your own soil and your own time and place. And so I had the example of Miller, his career and *Salesman*, absolutely. It took me a lot longer to understand how good some of the other Miller plays were. For a long time I sniffed at them as melodramas, but now that I've tried to write plays myself, I've come to realise how incredibly hard it is to do what he did so spectacularly well. For a long time I shared with Brecht a sort of anathema for catharsis, but I realise now that there is such a thing as catharsis in drama, that there is such a thing as tragedy, and that the tragedy is not necessarily anti-political or apolitical, or politically reactionary. And *Salesman* manages that and so does *Streetcar* and *Long Day's Journey*. That scene where Willy and Biff fight, where he says: 'You're nothing, you're nothing, you're nothing'—there's liberation in that 'nothing'. That's an incredible moment of theatre; it's real genius, and it's arrived at also in *Streetcar*.

You grew up in Louisiana, so in many ways it seemed that you would've been drawn to Tennessee Williams, if for no other reason than that he spoke the local language?

I didn't see any Williams when I was a young kid. He was too racy. When I finally read *Streetcar*, I was absolutely floored by it. I think it was the first time that I understood that it was possible to be an American and to write in an American idiom and still write poetry for the stage that really worked. Maybe because I'm from the South, it was easier for me to hear it not as some kind of filthy Gothic nonsense, which is what a lot of people criticised Williams for when he was first writing. There's an incredible richness and floridity to Southern speech. There's a slower pace to the society, and when they tend to express themselves people can talk more expansively—in Louisiana especially with the mix of Creole and English and Caribbean cultures. It's a very lively verbal mix. It's real poetry in the sense that it creates spaces in between words in which meaning exists.

What about his sensibility?

Obviously the fact that he was gay is a subject of all of his plays. Any gay kid reading *Glass Menagerie* knows what's going on with Tom, even though it's never discussed. In *Streetcar* it is discussed, and in *Cat on a Hot Tin Roof* it becomes the subject of the play—to the extent that he was capable of. There's a kind of lushness and a kind of theatricality, a kind of artificiality, a kind of a willingness to reach too far and to push at the boundaries of what's considered good taste to get somewhere—a certain kind of excitability and emotionality. These are clichés, but these are qualities that you can identify immediately in Williams. And the powerful presence in all of his writing of human sexuality, which, for instance, you can't say is the case in Miller. There's sex, especially in some of Miller's later plays, but in *Salesman* and in *All My Sons* it's really packed down and sort of fifties, square-jaw and clenched. And the treatment is somewhat Calvinist: it's a sort of good-and-evil and committing sins, and so on, whereas in Williams it's this absolutely inescapable, unavoidable life-force that's beating through everything.

And the sympathy for the dispossessed?

Yes, the sympathy for the dispossessed, the sympathy for the underdog in the sexual battle. That whole thing feels gay. Of course on one level, an absolute identification with female desire—or with desire incarnated in women and in women's sexuality—makes *Streetcar*, in terms of gender issues, absolutely decades ahead of its time. That play is a play about rape and about violence against women. Blanche is a woman who has stayed unmarried too long for her society's standards, for what's permissible according to her society's sexist standards: a woman who doesn't have money, a woman who's economically vulnerable and who becomes desperate because between her and prostitution is not very much. It's the same dynamic as in *Mother Courage*—all that stands between me and selling my body is the wagon.

Did Williams think of himself as a political writer?

This was a time of enormous national redefinition and questioning, and out of that questioning would come the civil rights movement and feminism and the gay civil rights movement and the anti-war movement. Williams is right in there asking all of those questions.

O'Neill dealt explicitly with all those subjects in the twenties, didn't he?

It took me a really long time to get him, because he's in some ways such an incredibly bad writer. That great thing that Mary McCarthy said when *Iceman Cometh* opened on Broadway: 'We mark tonight a solemn occasion, the return to Broadway of a very great writer, who, let's face it, doesn't write very well.' And it's true, he's incredibly clunky, it's corny, the way that the main themes will be beaten over and over and over again. As Ezra Pound says about Whitman: you broke the wood, and now the time has come for carving. O'Neill broke the wood; he wasn't a delicate shaper, and he never became one. He was the first American playwright. He arrived: no one was doing anything of any interest whatsoever, and he created serious American theatre. I think the kind of violent dichotomies and the brute dialectics of resurrection and damnation—all that Catholic stuff that he turns up—makes for a very clunky playwriting. Nonetheless, because he was a very great genius, it devastates you at the end of almost any evening, even though half the time you're sort of screwing your face up because it sounds so dumb line by line. The one play that may not be true of is *Long Day's Journey*. They used to say it's the longest apprenticeship in the history of world theatre—it took him his entire life, and then finally at the end he got it right. It's a play that has a level of linguistic fluency that none of the other plays has. He was as great a player with idiom as Dickens was in a way. He really used a staggering amount of American verbal expression in those plays.

He never bent to the will of Broadway, never compromised in any way. Was that an inspiration for you?

The first O'Neill I encountered as an icon was that letter about him writing *Long Day's Journey*, that he would sit at the typewriter and weep for hours and hours and hours. While he was typing the tears would flow down his face. I found that repulsive and thought it was deeply un-Brechtian—he'd, of course, have sneered at the idea that you should be weeping while you're writing. It took a long time for me to get what O'Neill was after and what he was about, and to understand both the political dimensions and also the theatricality of it. His plays are almost always about actors, and they're plays about theatre. He was heroic. That terrifying courage that he had to go away and to write: he was probably the loneliest playwright in American history. He probably didn't even give himself the comfort of rehearsal rooms and production. He wound up sort of hating actors and directors and the whole thing, and really just wanted to be alone and kill himself with work. That stark example gives you a certain kind of courage. There's a great letter where he writes about these vultures flying from their dark beyond and tormenting him endlessly, and he says now at the end of my life they've given me an exchange for all of this torment, some small germ of a soul. That was really what mattered to him.

Angels in America *was commissioned by the Eureka Theatre Company in San Francisco, yes?*

Yes. It's a small, really terrific, left-wing theatre. It was in a sort of rebuilt garage in the Mission District, which is an economically and racially very diverse area. The Eureka did all sorts of great progressive political theatre like the first Caryl Churchill on the West Coast and David Hare and Edward Bond and Howard Brenton and a lot of Brecht.

Did you know what it was going to be about before you started to write it?

I knew that I wanted to write about Roy Cohn, who had just died of AIDS in '86. I had a dream about an angel crashing through the ceiling over the bedroom of a man in a pair of pyjamas, and I knew that I wanted to call it *Angels in America*, I didn't know why. I was interested in Mormons for all sorts of reasons, so I knew I wanted them to be in the play, and I knew that I wanted it to be in America during the time that I was writing, or at least only a couple of years prior. It came out of a very dark and terrible time. It came during a period when the President of the United States had been President for seven years before he had uttered a word about AIDS. When I wrote the play nothing had been said about it. When Roy Cohn—who was a person I always hated—had died, even the Left indulged in a great deal of homophobic, AIDS-phobic gloating about the manner of his death. There was an ugly current all around the world that this was a visitation of evil on a group of people who had really deserved it, who had earned it by their misbehaviour. And there seemed to me to be a certain kind of consonance, and also a kind of an irony, that this powerful, conservative counter-revolution was taking place at exactly the moment when we were being hit by the greatest biological disaster of the twentieth century. When people were more than ever having to explore the extent to which we were really interconnected, the reigning ideology was one of complete selfishness and disconnection. It felt incredibly important to write specifically about the moment that we were living through, and to try and make some sense of it.

O'Neill said: 'I don't think you can write anything of value or understanding about the present. You can only write about life if it's far enough in the past. The present is too mixed up with superficial values; you can't know which thing is important and which is not.' What made you so confident about writing about the present?

I'm not confident about anything, but what he says is actually probably true. I felt a sort of terrible pressure at the time; I was very, very angry when I started writing. Virginia Woolf says you shouldn't write out of anger, or if you do it's going to weaken what you do, and I think she's probably right about that. I thought that Reagan's behaviour during the AIDS epidemic was especially monstrous and that he was in every other way monstrous. I thought Margaret Thatcher was and continues to be monstrous. I was annihilated by the epidemic, by friends dying, and a politically grounded oppression with a biological disaster of these proportions was overwhelming. I felt an incredible need to deal with that and to write also about being gay, which I hadn't done. You could say that O'Neill in writing *Long Day's Journey* is writing about something that happened thirty or forty years before the time that he wrote it, but it's got an immediacy. And Miller and Williams were writing absolutely about their moment. You could also say that Shakespeare uses an incredibly transparent kind of metaphor that only just barely disguises the fact he's really writing about Elizabethan and Jacobean England. Writing real historical drama seems to me to be very hard and risks losing a kind of direct communication.

In a sense, you were also drawing on the century drawing to a close and the collapse of Communism in Eastern Europe?

I was a Medieval Studies Major while I was an undergraduate at Columbia, so I started thinking about the millennium very early on, because I had read a great deal about what had happened at the last millennium and have always been very interested in the sort of ambiguous figuration of the 'end of time' in Christian apocalyptic literature—the way that the end of the world is either the Day of Wrath or the beginning of the Kingdom of God: it has both a positive and negative charge. By the mid-eighties I was thinking a lot about the fact that the millennium was approaching. Then the beginnings of *glasnost* and *perestroika* took me completely by surprise, as they had taken everybody—I was so exhilarated and disturbed and excited by everything that was going on. We'll never in our lifetime see anything quite like it. It seemed that a great necessity and a great good was being accomplished, and also it was terrifying.

You argue in the plays that America needs to change as profoundly as Russia.

In a certain sense one could say that America and Europe had already gone through their own *perestroika* in the sixties. But I think that we're in a time now when grand theories about the history and purpose and direction of human life as a whole have lost their lustre. People don't trust them any more. So we're fighting now to maintain some sense of progress and some sense of human dignity and worth in the face of an absolute dearth of real theory to explain where we're going to go. *Perestroika* continues to be a kind of a model for that: that one is not allowed to stop moving simply because one does not know where one is going, and yet one must be aware of the fact that not knowing where one is going makes forward motion genuinely perilous.

You mentioned the conservative 'counter-revolution'. What did you make of Margaret Thatcher's statement that there's no such thing as society?

I would like to think that all plays and all theatre have a refutation of that evil and moronic statement. All one has to do is sit in a theatre, to be an actor on a stage or to work in a theatre and see the way that human beings within a microsecond of the house lights going down coalesce into a society, into a discrete entity that didn't exist before. People have a great innate genius for communalising, for collectivising. There's no better illustration that I know of in the world than watching an audience describe its personality almost instantly, enter into a complicated relationship with the thing on stage and develop it along the course of the evening. And then dissolve afterwards but not completely, because what everybody takes from the theatre is not their own individual experience of the play but something that's been profoundly shaped by that collective beast. The audience and the actor and the play, it's an instant community. Theatre is an irreducibly communal event, and it's proof, I think, of what Marx says: that the smallest human unit is not one but two people, that one person is a fiction; there's never been—and there never will be anywhere in time—one person.

You think the theatre is uniquely well equipped to deal with society?

I've said this a lot, and it comes from Brecht. Theatre is inherently dialectical because the illusion/reality paradigm is unavoidable in the theatrical experience. What is on stage also isn't. It's always a transparent illusion; you always have to see double when you're watching anything on stage; you're always aware that the dead body is breathing; you're always aware that the angel is hanging from a wire. The trees always look fake, and there's a point past which the illusion can't be carried in the moment on stage. So people always have to see double, which is critical consciousness, and it teaches you to see dialectically. It teaches you to understand both the manifest appearance of things and also their actual content. Theatre can't help but be a politically useful art form. Also because it's a gathering of people, it's always that sort of platform for the discussion of events. There's this great thing that Schiller said to Goethe: in a Shakespeare play you don't feel trapped while the parade moves in front of you. The parade is there and you're moving around in it, and you have room to turn around. That's a great thing to strive for in the sense that a whole world is contained in a play.

Is that true of Beckett? Did he mean much to you?

Yes and no. I just feel that I'm so completely lacking the qualities that make Beckett Beckett.

What are the qualities?

A kind of terrifying interiority. He's a very strange playwright, because he started out by writing two completely perfect plays and then became a great experimenter. I'm completely tied to narrative, I'm a traditional narrative realist, and so I've gravitated much more towards Brecht than Beckett. I've always thought of myself as a sort of a popular writer, and clearly Beckett didn't. In a certain sense he's not a writer for audiences. Audiences become progressively less and less important. I mean, I don't know where you go after you write *Endgame*. I don't know where you go after you write *Waiting for Godot*.

What did you take from Brecht?

Brecht was the first writer that I'd read who synthesised what was really great and exciting about Marx with a specific aesthetic. I was very excited by that: it gave me a way of thinking of myself as a writer who remained politically engaged. Brecht had shown a way of doing that in both the plays and the poetry and in his life.

In what sense in his life?

He had been involved first in Communist and then in anti-Fascist struggles before and during the war. The sharpness with which he saw what was going on! *Mother Courage* is the play that analyses, on exactly the same lines that Trotsky does, what was going to happen in Germany—that this shaky petty bourgeoisie was going to do anything to avoid losing the little bit that it had, and that included voting for Hitler. I think *Mother Courage* is the great play of the twentieth century.

What about Galileo?

I think *Galileo* is very simplistic. It's a wonderful play; it's very exciting in this time of all of these fundamentalist nutbags running all over the place. It's great that you can see a play which says 'I hate the Church, I hate anything that's irrational.' I don't quite believe in Brecht's great faith in science, which even he began to question after the atom bomb fell. Even Brecht said *Galileo* is a piece of fun. He didn't consider it one of his great plays. It's got a great main character, but I find it not complicated and twisty enough.

What about the influence of British writers?

I started thinking about being a playwright in the mid-eighties when there was this obnoxious but nonetheless awe-inspiring influx of British playwriting. Most specifically [Howard] Brenton and [Edward] Bond and Caryl Churchill. Also Trevor Griffiths. It suddenly became completely unacceptable not to grapple with social realities. You know that you could defy the O'Neill interdict and just say: I don't care if it works or not. All of this British playwriting was irritating to us. We thought: stop producing Brits and do Americans. We were always saying that. But the most recent invasion of British theatre in America seems to be coming primarily from a kind of Anglophilia, a sense that if it had been a hit in England that it'll be a hit here. It's about money now. But when Joe Papp was bringing in a lot of it, you saw *Top Girls* or *Fen*, and you had no choice. You had to go out and try and write like that. I don't think there's any writer that's been more of an influence on me than Caryl Churchill, who I really think is one of the great playwrights of the century, and I know so many playwrights who feel that way. The gauntlet was thrown. And of course these were all British writers deeply influenced by Brecht.

What do you make of the fact that the longest-running musical and a successful Broadway play are both Socialist parables, Les Misérables *and* An Inspector Calls? [*This was 1999.*]

I've never actually seen *Les Misérables*. I think *Inspector Calls* was kind of amazing. It's an incredibly simple and clear parable about responsibility and about the desire to distance oneself from the evils that afford one the luxury of living the way one lives.

But do you think, is it an indication that people want something more than just a complacent entertainment?

Well, *The Lion King* is a right-wing fantasy about social domination and the supremacy of men everywhere. It's a completely beautifully packaged, neo-con parable for neo-con times and neo-con audiences and their creepy little children. The ideology Brecht says is there: the absence of an ideology *is* an ideology. It's just a conservative ideology, and everything that you see has it.

Do you think American musicals are essentially right-wing?

Most American musicals are sort of classic liberal-progressive parables. They all have their little political song, you know: you have to be taught to hate. They're all about communities and outsiders and strangers being welcomed. They deal with all the great American themes and actually deal with them very, very well, very movingly. They're about slavery, they're about race, they're about business. Rodgers and Hammerstein would never have put a show together that didn't have a kind of socially conscious dimension. Even in the way they're about love they make an interesting attempt in the way that they address love to connect individual feelings with community.

There's something un-British in them, which is that they're optimistic. You're distinctively American in that respect.

I've come to believe that optimism is a moral responsibility in artists. I'm a sentient being who reads the newspapers, and of course I feel great pessimism every day about what's going to happen to this planet, but I think it's incredibly important, especially for artists, to search for plausible occasions for hope. That's very different from the cheesy, Andrew-Lloyd-Webber-sort-of—processed, pasteurised hope, which you can tell is really mostly a shriek of despair. I think that you have to look for it. And I also find hope always in the fact that I really believe that at any point in history about forty per cent of the population of any country is sane and moral and looking for justice. If there is any hope anywhere, I think that's where hope comes from. And I think if you write about those people and their problems and their struggles and explore that and how they encounter the other sixty per cent, then you write plays that have a certain dimension of optimism. There's a cliché that Americans have this kind of blind-faith optimism and don't want to look at the dark side. I don't think that that's true. There's no writer more insanely optimistic than Dickens, and the great cornerstone of American literature, *Moby Dick*, is a work of terrible darkness and despair. There's a real sense that this country has always had of an impending holocaust or disaster where all of us will be wiped out. There's a great deal of darkness in America. I like to think that my optimism is more internationalist and comes more from a kind of Socialist progressive position—you know, pessimism of the spirit and optimism of the will.

Luise Rainer

1 9 1 0—

Actor. Luise Rainer became an actress at the age of sixteen in defiance of her parents'
wishes, acted in Max Reinhardt's company in Vienna, went to Hollywood, won two
Oscars in a row, and married Clifford Odets, the hugely successful left-wing
playwright (Waiting for Lefty, Awake and Sing, Golden Boy, The Country
Girl) *and screenwriter* (Sweet Smell of Success). *She withdrew from movies,*
having crossed Louis B. Mayer, and barely acted again—the odd play and a happy
life with a new (publisher) husband in New York and London. Yes, she told me,
she had regrets, but she gave no sign of bitterness: 'Never look back.' She was
extraordinarily lively—bird-like, bright, funny, a Pierrot face, with the large, deep
eyes of a marmoset. And still beautiful, wonderful cheekbones, and when she turned
away from the camera as she spoke, the light perfectly sculpted a shape unchanged
since her Hollywood days. She still had a strong Viennese accent rolling her r's as
she spoke of Brecht: 'Hoorrrible.' I interviewed her in her eighty-ninth year in an
airy flat in Eaton Square—in a house, as the blue plaque told me, where Vivien
Leigh once lived. Before I left she showed me a photograph of a man with frizzy grey
hair and a large moustache, white beach trousers rolled up to the knees and a smile
of pure contentment on his face. Close beside him, also in white, was the heart-
stoppingly beautiful twenty-six-year-old Luise Rainer. 'Albert Einstein,' she said,
'was a very nice man.'

I think you met Clifford Odets in 1936, is that right? What was he like when you first met
him?

To me, there was something incredibly beautiful about him, yes. There was a wonderful alertness and... I tell you all about it. I had come as you know from Europe, and I was very, very emphatic in my work. I very, very much wanted to, oh, I wanted to become the greatest actress ever, and of course I found it rather difficult in America. But I was not in America but in Hollywood. I had already, very soon, very dear friends and one of them was George Gershwin, another one was Harold Arlen, the songwriter, and another one was Yip Harburg [also a writer of many classic songs, including all the ones in *The Wizard of Oz*]. We had dinner together, and suddenly there came an extraordinary silence into the room. It was already late at night, everybody chatting, and everybody looked to the door, and it was really quite extraordinary because I didn't know who that man was that came in. But he came in, and he was greeted by various tables. Then he looked around, and he made his way to our table. He knew Gershwin of course, and Gershwin asked him to sit down. And he happened to sit next to me. He never spoke a word to me, and it was very strange because I felt something, I don't know, it was like an electricity. I took my chair and I moved it a little bit away, and then he looked at me and... I knew.

What did you know about him at the time?

Nothing.

He had done Waiting for Lefty.

He did *Waiting for Lefty* and he was declared the new O'Neill. He had obviously made an enormous impact, but it was absolutely unknown to me, and it wasn't any part of what attracted me. He was so different from all the people that I had known up to that time.

Waiting for Lefty *was an agitprop play?*

Yes.

Did it surprise you that this man had become well-known in America for writing a piece of political theatre?

No, because we all felt that way during those days. You must understand there was already this terrific turmoil in Europe. One was aware of that, and everybody in a way had a feeling about it. Most people took a stand about it: it was part of our time. I was never a political animal. I knew the beauty from the not-beauty and the good from the bad; I knew the poor from the rich; and I knew also the million things in between. And so that was not part of any of our lives. His and mine together. He had the intuition and the instinct of the artist, and he was immensely sensitive. He was very involved with everything, and he was very differentiated at the same time. He was very aloof and held everything away from him. He worked all night. He lived in a wave of music; he had always music about him.

He was very wrapped up in himself?

Totally, totally. I mean, he didn't even know in many ways what he was doing, you know. In my case, I was a slave. He had made me a slave, I was never that before. I was a wild girl, but I was not a slave, and he always said he wanted an equal. Well, he didn't want an equal at all. I mean, criticism was out of order completely.

But you had a huge respect for his talent?

I had a huge respect for him. And, yes, call it his talent: it was him. It was not something separate from the man, you know. His miseries and his sorrows were very manifold because he was very, very sensitive. He also suffered a great many things that many people would not even realise.

In his childhood.

He had a very perturbed one.

Can you describe Clifford?

He looked like a disciple, he had large grey eyes and a very strong face and very serious face, very intelligent face, and there was beauty about him. And he had a great charisma. It didn't matter what woman there was, if it was Marlene Dietrich or Clare Boothe Luce, they all went for him, and they went for him because he had something very, very outstanding and very strong. That was Clifford.

He had one suicide attempt when he was a teenager or in his early twenties?

He never told me about his suicide attempt. Later, when I left, he'd run with the car off to Mexico and run into a tree but nothing happened to him. He always said: 'I can't stomach it any more'—and he died of cancer of the stomach. I felt that he ate his miseries.

He had a surrogate family which was the Group.

He lived with the Group.

And the Group seemed to be almost like a cult.

Yes, it was like a cult. They felt that they were part of a cult. They were immensely secure in themselves as long as they were within this group which they had founded—Clifford and, of course, [Harold] Clurman and [Elia] Kazan.

I felt that they were very, very much too much enclosed in themselves, and they didn't see enough of the world. I had come already from far away, and I had seen a great deal already. I had also belonged to a great group, and so I could evaluate the importance this way and that way.

And they resented you?

They resented me very much, yes.

Particularly Harold Clurman?

Oh, Harold was very worried about me. You see, he would say: you can't take our Clifford away from us. I didn't intend to take his Clifford away, but Cliff was there and that was it. He didn't want me to come to his openings—even *Golden Boy*, which he had dedicated to me. So the opening night I walked around and I was walking the streets alone and I came past the Algonquin Hotel and a taxi stopped and a tall black woman came out and I just stared at her and said: 'Marian Anderson [great African-American classical singer].' And she looked at me and she said: 'Luise Rainer.' Then we got together upstairs and I had the most marvellous time because she was singing for me. That was the one time I remember that I didn't go to his opening. I never went any other time after that, and then of course I lived in California and he lived in New York.

You were very busy.

I made eight films in three years.

And he wrote almost as many plays in that time. I know very few playwrights who were so prolific over such a short time. After that he stopped and he went to Hollywood.

His life got very confused. Well, confused is the wrong word. He wasn't confused, he was irritated and he was unhappy, unhappy, unhappy.

The Actors Studio was an offshoot of the Group. What were your impressions of it?

Unfortunately it was very negative. I knew Lee Strasberg very, very well, but I personally could never have worked that way, wouldn't have wanted to work that way—it was absolutely psychoanalytical. I thought they were all a little bit nuts.

They were very literal-minded about what Stanislavsky was teaching. One of the consequences of the Actors Studio was to downgrade the importance of technique.

Yes, because there was that ego also that came in the training. There's much too much emphasis on 'What am I doing?' instead of doing it, do you know? There was a consciousness of: '*I* do this, *I* do that,' do you know?

But there are some actors who just transcend it—like Marlon Brando.

Marlon Brando, yes, he overcame it. Because he was very direct and very elemental. We all know about technique: we throw it away, it becomes an unconscious thing, and it is important to throw it away.

It's important to throw it away, but of course it's important to have it in the first place.

Yes, sure. It's like driving a car.

You knew Brecht, didn't you?

Brecht wrote to me when he was in Sweden or Norway—I am not quite sure. I didn't know all his plays. I only knew *The Threepenny Opera* very well. I knew about him, I knew his poetry which I liked very much. When he needed an affidavit for America it was easy for me to be of help, and I helped him—I in those days was known or whatever it is. I helped him—and all the lady folk that he brought along with him. And when he came to America, naturally because of that, he wanted to meet me.

And you asked him if he would write a version of your favourite play.

No, I didn't ask him at all. No, we went on a walk one day, and he said he would like to write a play for me. Then he asked me what would I like to do? And I talked to him about a certain play that I knew from Europe—a beautiful play that was, as a matter of fact, the first play that I ever saw and made me want to become an actress. And I told him about this play, and he was quite amazed and he looked at me. The play was called *Der Kreidekreis*. He was amazed because he told me that Klabund—a beautiful poet, who died very early—had given him this idea. And Brecht said: that is what I am going to write for you. And so he set out to write *The Caucasian Circle of Chalk* for me.

But he only wrote a page and a half?

Yes. I went into the war, and I was away. The thing is he had no money, so I got him together with a very dear old producer who had great belief in me and said: anything I want to do, I could do with him. So I called this man and I said: look, here is Bert Brecht, he is a great playwright—in case he didn't know—he probably didn't know. I put Brecht on this man's payroll, and then I went away. I went into the war [as an ambulance driver in Alexandria], and I stayed away for quite a long time. After about four or five months I came back, and the producer called me—or I called him, I don't remember—and he said: 'Do you know, I pay this man all the time. I paid him and paid him and never saw a piece of paper and never saw what he wrote.' He was very upset. So I then got in contact with Brecht and I said: 'Listen, this is not right. You've got money from this man all the time, and how is it possible that you don't answer this man when he wrote to you and asked you for seeing something of the play?' And Brecht said to me: 'I am going to send it to you.' And the next day came two double-spaced pages. I looked at it, and on top was the title: *Caucasian Circle of Chalk*. I thought half of it must have gotten lost or something. No, I read it, and of course I couldn't make anything out of it. And then Brecht telephoned the next day and said: 'What do you think of it?' And I said: 'What do I think of it? Nothing, I haven't seen it. I have seen only two pages of it. I haven't seen anything.' So there was a long silence. Well, shortly later I met him again. This time it was in New York and as a matter of fact I went to his place. There were many doors—I guess in my mind there were many doors—and out of every door fled a lady. And I was then alone with Brecht, and he said: 'Well now, what do you think?' And I said: 'Well, I don't.' He said: 'Now come on, say something about this, read it to me.' And I thought: well, my God, what is this man doing? He wants to write a play for me, what does he know, has he not seen any work I have done or what? And I just stared at him and I said: 'Mr Brecht, I don't know what you are doing, I don't know what you want.' And he looked at me and he named a great actress and he said: 'She would be on her knees to me.' And I said to Brecht: 'I wouldn't, and I think you better write your play without me. Just write. Bye, bye.' And I never saw him again.

Can you describe him?

Yes, I can describe him. If you see a spider, then I have described him. That's what he looked like to me. He was very thin, I think he had red hair. I am not quite sure if he had red hair, but red-haired people always worried me because when I was a youngster a red-haired boy was very mean to me once.

You didn't like Brecht.

Oh, he was very unlikeable, very, very unlikeable. Horrible. Of course I have terrific fights with Ken Tynan over Brecht, who thought Brecht was everything, but I felt that life was so different than Brecht saw it. I must say I love his poetry. He was a very, very good poet, but in his plays everything was black and white: the rich were black, the poor were white.

Except in Galileo.

But in *Galileo* he had a human being to work on, a human being that existed, and therefore there was no way for him to describe things differently. But otherwise everything was black and white, and I didn't appreciate it. And anyway I disliked him, I disliked him very much.

You came to live in London in the fifties?

I came here with my second husband in '56.

Did you see Look Back in Anger *then?*

I saw *Look Back in Anger*.

And what did you think?

It was very angry. It was very funny. I must tell you something: I saw it now again, and it's a completely different play. It's not that we have changed, but the character has changed very much. Then it was a young fellow who was destructive, and he knocked about, and I felt somebody should give him a slap left and right and be done with, do you know? I really couldn't understand what was this extraordinary success. But when I saw it now again, I felt it was a very poor human being, and there was an extraordinary thing about the man and the woman and the inability of the getting together. Which I felt did not come out in the first version which was shown here at the Royal Court.

Alan Bennett

1 9 3 4—

Playwright and actor. Author of Forty Years On, Habeas Corpus, Enjoy, Single Spies, The Madness of George III, The History Boys *and others. Alan Bennett has become part of the (quintessentially English) family, a familiar face, a national institution, adjectival: 'Very Alan Bennett,' people say. I interviewed him in the basement kitchen of my house. He wasn't at his happiest when talking about his own work. He's revealed a 'self' in his plays and his diaries, but when he was sitting in my kitchen uneasily facing the prospect of an interrogation, the 'self' couldn't be disguised as a fictional persona. But he rallied generously and answered my questions with a practised ease.*

What did you have in mind when you did Beyond the Fringe?

I think we didn't want it to be like all the other revues that used to go on then, which were a staple of the West End and consisted of sketches about showbiz, and sort of silly sketches like 'How would it be if such and such,' interspersed with songs. I really enjoyed them myself, but anyway we decided that this wasn't what we wanted to do. We didn't really formulate any aims other than that. Of course, in that sense it was very successful, because it put paid to that sort of revue, which never recovered from the blow. We wanted it to be funny; we wanted it to be relevant, I think. All the business about satire and so on, which people talked about, was analysing it afterwards, really. It wasn't something that we had any notion of doing when we were putting it together.

So you weren't a small group of politically motivated men.

Far from it. I think I was the most serious, but I wasn't politically serious. I mean, I was just dull, I think, really. We were quite silly. Apart from Peter's imitation of Harold Macmillan, his contribution wasn't political at all really, nor was Jonathan's. We wanted to talk about the world as it was, and that was something the revues didn't do. So in that sense it was different.

Were you influenced in any way by the Royal Court—in the sense that realism had infected the British theatre?

I'd actually not seen *Look Back in Anger*. I think I'd only been a couple of times to the Court before *Beyond the Fringe*. I think I'd seen *The Chairs*, the Ionesco play, but it didn't mean anything to me, the Court, at the time. It meant a lot to me in the seventies but not in its first flowering. There was talk subsequently about German cabaret and the influence of Brecht and of American comedians like Mort Sahl, but it was all… it was all *post hoc*.

At the same time as the Royal Court was making waves, so was Joan Littlewood in Stratford East. Were you aware of her work?

I saw *Oh! What a Lovely War*, and I think maybe the form of that affected *Forty Years On* a bit—the sense that theatre could be quite free-form. And certainly the use of well-known tunes. Another thing which tends to be forgotten now is that there used to be a World Theatre Season every year at the Aldwych run by Peter Daubeny, and plays from all over the place came to London. In 1967, the year before *Forty Years On*, I saw a play there called *The Glorious Resurrection of Our Lord*, a Polish play, in which there was a kind of choir screen across the stage with the characters on the stage and on a gallery formed, as it were, by the screen. That certainly affected the form of *Forty Years On*.

Forty Years On *seems quite influenced by Brecht.*

Well, I'd never seen any Brecht, and I don't think I'd read any. *Forty Years On* was a transition from writing revue, i.e. sketches, to writing what I think of as a proper play. Its form was absurdly complicated: it's a play within a play within a play. I'd never attempt it now, but I didn't realise then what writing a play involved.

A lot of writers say: 'Well, I needed something to look at because I didn't know what a play was.'

Mm.

Was Rattigan or Coward your idea of a proper play?

When I was a boy in Leeds I used to go every Saturday matinée and see whatever it was that was on offer. Nowadays that would mean very little, because I think it's mostly opera now and plays don't tour in the way they did. But in those days you would get West End plays with their original cast coming round after their West End production. I saw a very peculiar collection of plays there. Of course, in my mind they weren't distinguished one from the other; they were just things that turned up at the Grand every Saturday afternoon. They were all mixed together in my mind. I didn't see them as school of this or school of that. They were just plays. I saw some Shakespeare, plays like *Black Chiffon* with Flora Robson, *Daphne Laureola* with Edith Evans, a play about a Labour colonial Governor with Eric Portman, *His Excellency*. And then I began to see plays like *Waiting for Godot*.

What impression did that make?

I didn't find it at all mystifying, and I didn't find it so plotless. I may have found it a bit dull, but then I often found plays dull. I found it quite funny as well.

But did you have any sense that it was a play about post-war Europe?

I was too young probably to think in those terms then. I just thought it was a play about very peculiar people, but then so was *Black Chiffon* in my view. They weren't like people I knew.

In the fifties were you at all conscious of the Holocaust and the Bomb?

I remember in August 1945, when we were living in Guildford very briefly, coming back with the *Evening News* and reading about the first atomic bomb. And also in Guildford I saw the terrible newsreels not of Auschwitz, of Dachau, because I can remember it went up on the screen that children should be taken out of the cinema. And the trouble was in those days you had to queue for the cinema so long that nobody left—they didn't want to lose their seats. So I saw that. But in a way the consciousness both of the Bomb and of the Holocaust occurred in a way ten, fifteen years after they happened. CND and so on. I once or twice went on CND marches.

Did you think about Noël Coward when you were writing Forty Years On?

I read and thought about *Cavalcade*. I think it was Philip Hope-Wallace [drama critic of the *Guardian*] who said *Forty Years On* bore some relation to *Cavalcade*. I met Noël Coward and said this to him, which was not the right thing to say. [*laughs*] There was quite a definite silence after that.

Did Coward regard you as a raging intellectual?

No, no, he was very nice to me. He came to the previews of *Forty Years On* when John Gielgud was still very uncertain whether he should be doing the play. Noël Coward went in and really gave him a shot in the arm and said: you know you're very funny, and this is a good play, and it's sad and funny, and so on. This was only a few days before we opened. So I was very grateful to him for that. And then he took me out to supper at the Savoy, where we had sausages and mash, and he was just very nice. I mean, I was so nervous. I was much more shy in those days than I am now. I'm bad enough now, but then I was so inarticulate. But he really drew me out and was lovely to me. So I've always had a lot of time for him. I think some of his plays are wonderful. *Hay Fever* which I saw in 1964 revived at the National—just a most wonderful play.

And Rattigan?

I saw *The Browning Version* in an amateur production in Leeds and thought it was a wonderful play. I still do. Probably it's the best one, better than *The Winslow Boy*. Of course, nowadays there's, there's all the analysis of Rattigan as smuggling his homosexuality across. And to some extent that's true in *The Browning Version*, because of the dried-up schoolmaster or donnish figure, who's suddenly revealed as having these deep wells of feeling for the boy who gives him the book. It's a very homosexual notion, really. It's rather like A.E. Housman. That certainly made a big impression on me. It's also beautifully constructed.

Do you simply follow your nose with subject matter?

It seems to me what happens is that you've got something that niggles you, you've got something that you can't resolve. In *Forty Years On* I think it was knowing that I was very conservative with a small 'c' and radical in other ways—knowing that these two feelings and concerns existed and not being able to reconcile them. And the play is an attempt to reconcile them. It's also an attempt to write a funny play about a school. The plays about spies, I suppose, are an attempt to settle my ambiguous feelings about England. Of affection and identification, but at the same time feeling alienated from it. Every play I've written seems to me slightly to the side of the play I wanted to write. Maybe if you ever wrote a play that you actually intended to write then you won't write any more plays. I always think that about *The Importance of Being Earnest*. It's an absolutely perfect play, and I know it was Wilde's last play because of the circumstances, but I think it probably would have been his last play anyway. Most plays are nearly completed circles and the production completes the circle, makes it a whole. *The Importance of Being Earnest* is completed there on the page; there's nothing much you can do with it. It's a wonderful play and absolutely perfect, but for that reason I think it marks the end of his artistic endeavour.

Wilde claimed that he had turned what he said was the most objective art form that existed into an art form as subjective as the lyric poem. You do a similar thing to Wilde—you put your own sensibility and voice very clearly into the heart of your plays.

I don't really know how else to do it. I'm less and less bothered about concealment and smuggling things across than I used to be. I don't like going to see productions of plays that I've done, apart from the one that I'm currently doing, as it were. But I often find that I'm embarrassed by my plays to the extent that sometimes I lie on the floor of the theatre behind the seats, because they come too close to home. Actually it's embarrassing to me; it's kind of undigested. It's probably what I mean by saying that it's always to the side of the kind of play that I wanted to write.

The thing that all your plays have in common is a view about class as the sort of engine of English society. Have you always felt that you're imprisoned in it?

It's never bothered me, I don't long for a classless society. Since my strength is in dialogue, in the sense of hearing the cadences of people's speech and so on, which is ineluctably bound up with class, you can't separate the two. Of course, it would be disastrous if everything were flattened out. It used to bother me when I was younger; I'm still very awkward for some reason in the presence of the aristocracy—they reduce me to being seventeen again—but it's not out of any undue respect for them. [*laughs*] I don't know, but there's something goes wrong there. But class doesn't really bother me. I'm not a crusader anyway, but it's not something that I'd want to see the end of. I can't see how somebody of my generation writes as if one were outside it.

What did the 1945 election mean to you in the fifties? Did you have a sense that life was going to get better?

I was a terrible Tory when I was young. I was awful: conformist and censorious and full of religiosity. I was an awful youth, looking back. But I look back to the period 1945–51 as a kind of golden age. It's absurd to say that, because it was the most drab and austere period. There was no colour in the world really, and there was no choice in the shops. Life seemed to be very simple then, and people very innocent. Again and again I find that period crops up. The pictures I like are often pictures from the late forties. And then, of course, at the end of the decade there's this wonderful explosion of the Festival of Britain, when suddenly there was colour and design, and you thought that this was a vision of what the world was going to be like, when it wasn't quite, of course. But it occurs in *Getting On*, my second play, where there's a long speech about what life was like then and about the making of the Health Service. It's deeply nostalgic, but it is something that I do feel strongly about.

But you're very acerbic about the way in which that innocence and that optimism have been corrupted.

Well, yes, I suppose I am but [*laughs*] I don't know what to say to that.

'Yes'?

Yes.

I suppose what I'm saying is that, although you'd say you're not a political writer, you are— in the sense that to be an English playwright is to deal with political matters.

Yes. I'm not a political playwright in the way that David Hare is. I don't tackle, as it were, political problems, but I think some of the stuff that I write—particularly in *An Englishman Abroad* and plays like *A Question of Attribution*—is political. And *Getting On* is a very political play in the sense it's about a politician. I think I'm probably quite naive in my political assumptions and in what I want to say. I don't have much contact with politicians or with journalists, but I'm always shocked when I do by how seemingly unconcerned they are about the moral issues. What they're concerned about always is gossip in a very English way—they're concerned about the latest political scandal and so on, and when you put a, as it were, moral point of view they look at you as if you're slightly touched. That shocks me.

Is it another characteristic of Englishness that we shy away from ideology?

Well, it may be; that's a charitable way of looking at it. I think the English are just concerned with gossip… I know he's totally discredited, as it were, now, but I belong to a generation that thought that JFK was a great leader and a great force for good—however shoddy he's been made to seem since. I mean, the death of Kennedy was a blow in English terms not simply in terms of American politics. You just felt that some kind of idealism had been snuffed out.

Painters always say: after Picasso, what can you do? But Shakespeare is an even greater thing. As a playwright, do you feel that you're in any way in the shadow of Shakespeare or that it's just a sort of marvellous bonus?

When you're reading a book or whatever or seeing a play, and you come across a sentiment or a thought which you think is unique to you and personal to you, and then here it is put in the mouth of somebody else, you feel connected. You feel as if somebody's taken your hand. Now what I feel with Shakespeare is that whatever you do and however different the circumstances, he has been there first. Somewhere he will have expressed whatever unique thought you've had. So he's not like another writer, he's almost like a force of nature. I can't imagine a writer who would think of Shakespeare as a rival in the way that you do think of other writers as rivals.

So it's just a particular gift of the landscape.

Yes, yes. My knowledge of Shakespeare is confined to going to see the plays. I've never acted them. Well, I played Katarina in the *Taming of the Shrew* when I was a boy, but I'd not the faintest idea what the play was about. I learned my lines and my cues, and I didn't read the play at all. I fear there's a bit of that still in me. [*laughs*]

What is it about theatre that attracts you?

I suppose I go to the theatre thinking anything may happen. I mean, quite apart from the play, somebody might collapse on the stage. I know that seems frivolous, but I think that's an element in what an audience is there for—the possibility of disaster. And the possibility of triumph as well, but it's the uncertainty. Having performed, I know the sheer terror of it: it is quite a perilous proceeding. If you're in an audience and something goes wrong on the stage—you know, somebody dries, say, or whatever—the audience is like a cat suddenly seeing a bird: it's on to it. There's a huge tension in the auditorium. Quite frightening. I do think of an audience as slightly like a wild beast.

What is it that draws you to writing for the theatre?

I suppose it's writing dialogue—I mean, plots are far harder to write for me than dialogue. And if you're writing dialogue then obviously—unless you want to write like Henry Green, say, and write novels entirely in dialogue—you're drawn to the theatre or to television. It's as simple as that, really.

Is it also that whatever you do in the theatre it can't be abstracted? There's always going to be a human being.

There has to be a human being from my point of view, because they talk, and talk is what I'm interested in, and talk is what I deal in. It seems to me, when you talk about the future of the theatre and so on, it has a future so long as somebody's going into a room and sitting down with a blank sheet of paper and trying to write lines that somebody else is going to say.

Harold Pinter
1 9 3 0—2 0 0 8

Playwright, actor and director. Author of The Birthday Party, The Caretaker, The Homecoming, No Man's Land, Betrayal *and others. I interviewed him on the stage of the Almeida Theatre, where his play* Celebration *had recently opened. For a man who had a reputation for being somewhat curmudgeonly in talking about his work and himself, he was wholly forthcoming.*

———•—•———

When were you first aware of Beckett's work?

I was in Ireland, working as an actor, in about 1951, and I came across a copy of a magazine called *Irish Writing*. There was an extract from Beckett's novel, *Watt*, which knocked me sideways. So when I got back to London, I went to the Westminster Library, which was the biggest library in London: they'd never heard of Beckett. Nor had any other library, in fact. I then went back to Westminster Library and pursued the matter, and found there was a copy of a something called *Murphy* in the Bermondsey Public Reserve Library, and I insisted on getting it out of the Bermondsey Public Reserve Library, and in fact it had last been—read—borrowed, you know, in 1939. This was 1952, I think, by this time. So I decided on that basis I was justified in taking the book and keeping it. It was my one criminal act, as far as I know, and I still have it. So that's when I started to read Beckett: '50/'52.

And did you try and get in touch with the author?

No, good Lord no. No, I read all his novels. I read *Watt*, *Molloy*, *Malone Dies* and a lot of his short stories. I got hold of everything I could, which was pretty difficult, but I got a lot of it from Paris.

And then presumably you heard that he'd written Waiting for Godot?

Yeah, I heard about that. I was in rep at the time, acting again in England. In 1955 that was, but I finally got to see it, and was very… pretty stirred by it.

You saw it in Paris?

No, no, no.

What did you think when you saw it?

I thought it was the kind of theatre that I'd been waiting to see. It seemed to me there were no holds barred, there were no constraints, that the fellow could stand on his head and do what he liked—which he did—twice, [*laughs*] and I was very excited by it. By that time I'd read all his novels, I knew the kind of imagination that I was looking at, so *Waiting for Godot* didn't really surprise me. It certainly excited me, but it was nothing that I didn't in a sense expect, that kind of exploration.

But it surprised you that somebody could do that in a theatre?

Yes, I don't think it was really being done in that way at all. For example, there's a great deal that I admired and admire about John Osborne, but the kind of revolution that is often attributed to him, I've always really thought was actually Beckett's. You know, Beckett opened up the theatre in a way that Osborne I don't think did. That wasn't the point about Osborne; he just stirred everything up, I think, you know, touching on nerve ends of our society at the time. But Beckett—it seems to me the leap he took in theatrical terms was quite singular.

And for somebody who'd worked as an actor and had presumably been in a lot of plays with sets where the walls shook, the fact you could do a play without setting it in a domestic context must have seemed remarkable.

That's absolutely true, and, of course, the tree, which is naked and then has leaves… this kind of theatrical image was wonderful, and I'd never seen it before.

Did you find the language very alluring?

Well, yes. The point, however, I'd like to make is that—without in any way, and by a long, long chalk, comparing myself to Beckett, which I certainly wouldn't do—I was really always interested in language myself, and had been since I had been a boy. I mean, I had already written a novel by the way, and a lot of poems, but no plays in fact, at that time. But I had that kind of concern about language, and how to distil experience as economically as possible had been my passion since I was about fifteen. So there were roughly ten years in which I had been doing my own thing anyway. So it wasn't a question of: 'This bloke is really doing something that nobody else can do,' but: 'I somehow find myself on the same track.'

And presumably you'd thought the same of Shakespeare?

Well, Shakespeare did everything, anything he liked, that's the thing about Shakespeare. He had a range of operation which is surely without equal, because he could do that, he could do that, and he could do that, and he could do that. He could really stand the world upside down. As a matter of fact, I'm glad you mentioned Shakespeare, because I was very, very, very engaged with Shakespeare, and the Elizabethans, and the Jacobeans, from all my teens and all my youth and throughout my twenties. I still am, really. *[laughs]* Webster left an enormous impression on me, and I read Shakespeare long before I read Beckett. I was a great reader, you know. One of the things that I'd like to point out is that my own, for what it's worth, my own cultural history was mostly to do with novels, prose. It's true that I read Shakespeare, and I read Webster, and Tourneur, and Ford and so on, but I read a great deal of poetry, and I read a great deal of prose. Joyce had an enormous effect on me, and actually Kafka and Hemingway. You don't live in a vacuum, not if you're that passionately interested in literature. What was on my mind at the time really was a whole configuration of voices, which were coming into me.

What about the climate in which this configuration was taking place? You grew up between two absolutes. The absolute of the Holocaust and the absolute of the Bomb. What did that mean to you as a teenager?

[*pause*]

Well, both things meant a great deal to me. I…

[*pause*]

…the Holocaust was actually a very… I mean, as it gradually was revealed, what had really happened… I must say the Jewish community, of which I was a part, in London, knew much earlier than was recognised or acknowledged in other circles, what was going on in Germany and right through Europe. That had a very strong and visceral impact on me. I was about fifteen when the war ended, and the horror, knowing that many, many people, who were vaguely relations of mine, were dead, had been murdered…

[*pause*]

Because with every Jew who lives in England, there was also the precariousness of how close we all were to precisely that fate. And there were so many other incidents to do with that. What government did, and how they treated Jewish refugees and so on, this was all known to us. But as for the Bomb, it didn't take me more than twelve hours to recognise it as a tragedy for the human race, and I certainly still believe that's the case. Consequently in 1948, I was a conscientious objector against National Service. I was just a boy, you know, but there it is, and I refused to join the army because it seemed to me that here we were: the whole propaganda was to do with another war, you know, and you've just left the last one five minutes ago. Everyone was ready to go. We were being encouraged and all the boys were joining the army; and here we go again, and so on. And I thought, to hell with it, I'm simply having nothing to do with it. I was prepared to go to prison. In fact, I had two tribunals and two trials, and the magistrate fined me twice—or rather my father, who had to find money that he didn't actually have. But I took my toothbrush along to the trial. It was my first, if you like, overt political act. So, well, these terrible things had an effect on me that's never left me. I've never recovered from either, and what interests me now is the way it's very easy for so many people, particularly politicians, to pretend it more or less never happened.

Does Waiting for Godot *grow out of the experience of the war and its aftermath?*

I've never seen it in those terms. *Endgame* I see much more as the end result if you like of a catastrophe, of a world catastrophe. I certainly think the desolation and the survival of the human spirit in *Godot* remains very stirring and very moving: the fundamental thing of being disoriented, dispossessed, disembodied, not knowing where you actually are in a landscape which will, as it were, go on for ever without any boundaries: no walls, no comfort, no security. That extraordinary mixture in Beckett of absolute despair, but not quite absolute, because there's also the immeasurable tenderness of the man in his work, which is acting against that despair.

Everyone speaks of him with great warmth.

He was delightful—I knew him quite well—and he loved gossip. 'What's the latest?' he would say. And he also loved cricket.

[laughs] Yes, of course. You became politicised in a very fundamental way. What about the optimism of the '45 government? What did that mean to you and, correspondingly, the failure to live up to it?

It meant a great deal. In fact, I wrote a poem about it recently, called 'Requiem for 1945'. It was published without consulting me actually. The editor, with the best will in the world, wrote as an introduction to the poem, that 'this is a requiem for the war'. But that's not what I meant at all. It was a requiem for the hopes of 1945 and that extraordinary landslide. Anyway, I can't quote the poem—it's pretty good, I strongly recommend it—but I'm simply saying that it was crushed. I talk in the poem about these people who found the portholes of their room smashed by a sea that snarled at them. In other words, that this could not be maintained, because the powers, the general powers in the world—if you like, capitalism—said 'No.' And [*claps hands*] does that. All my friends at the time were very, very, excited and followed what the Labour government was doing in 1945 with total respect. We found suddenly we were possibly living in a decent society. All those ex-servicemen who voted for the Labour government and overthrew a structure which was redundant and therefore doing a great deal of harm. We had tremendous hopes, yes. I have to tell you I have very considerable contempt for the way New Labour regards and refers to the true Labour Party, and what it was doing. I think it is quite disgraceful.

A writer of the period who had a lifelong battle against capitalism was Brecht.

Yes, I'm a great admirer of Brecht. I like some of Brecht's plays better than others. I think he was a remarkable writer and a totally, really extraordinary, individual voice, and technically an innovator of the first order, really a pioneer. I know Brecht's poems extremely well. And I think he's a much underrated poet—so succinct, and so telling, and so beautiful. I think Brecht is a great artist. He's clearly slightly unpopular now because he belonged to the wrong side. He took the long view—the wrong view, and so on. Because now, that kind of political correctness, as you know, is a disease, and everyone who had the least—seems to me, both as men and as artists—the least [*sighs*] desire for something called 'social justice', and for looking rigorously at what is actually going on in the world, is discredited very easily. They're regarded as unrealistic, naive and romantic—and also, more than that, subversive. So I'm a great admirer of Brecht.

I saw a production of The Birthday Party *that was the most politicised piece of theatre I've ever seen. It was in Prague in 1969, shortly after the Russians had moved in. In the Činoherní Theatre. It was an unambiguous political allegory. But perhaps to you it's not layered with political subtext?*

Oh. Well, actually, I think it is [*laughs*] slightly layered with subtext. [*laughs*] This was not the view about *The Birthday Party* taken in England in 1958. They just said: 'This is a total load of rubbish, this is incoherent and meaningless.' It's only been much later in this country that another view was taken at all about the play. I did write a letter before rehearsals started to the director, Peter Wood. I think this is quite important from my point of view: the letter does exist, it's been published. He actually asked me, before rehearsals started, to write a short speech of some kind, explaining what the whole damn thing was about, you know. And I wrote the letter saying: 'There's no one in the play who's going to stand up and say, "Now, you've been wondering what was going on here. And now I'm going to give you the message." It has to speak for itself, and it does speak for itself.' And I said: 'Just put it on the table that Goldberg and McCann are the socio-politico-religious monsters with whom we are faced, and the pressures on any given individual.' I saw it very, very strongly and very, very clearly at the time. So I did realise that it was political. I knew it was political, but I wouldn't just stand on a soapbox and say so.

Did you think that by making it explicit you would diminish the power of the metaphor?

Yes. It would be an extramural statement. I feel that theatre is a living thing. Let the thing live and breathe and speak.

It seems to me so bizarre that it was treated with such disdain. Do you have any explanation?

[*laughs*] No, not really. I think you'd better ask the people who treated it with disdain. But, it nearly put me off writing for the theatre, of course, it was such a total... We all suffer from the critics in this. It's part of the job, isn't it? It's part of the whole enterprise, but I don't think anyone's received a worse body of reviews than I did in 1958. But in actual fact it was a very good education for me, because it was such a cold shower. I had two courses: one was to give the whole thing up, which I thought about, but then, did not. The BBC actually came to my rescue, BBC Radio. I wrote a play called *A Slight Ache*, and then I went on doing it. I must say in my experience—which does go back now over forty years of writing for the theatre, and my plays are done in many other countries—I find that the English reception, both critical and public, is much the most reluctant, much the most guarded, much the most suspicious, much the most irritated.

Is that because we're still dug into some form of social realism?

[*coughs*] I don't see it that way. I couldn't say whether that is the case. What I would propose is that the whole idea of—dare I use the word?—'art' theatre is really a tradition in England which is subjected always to another tradition, which is the tradition of mockery. Particularly if it involves any kind of real, imaginative exploration. Or any political input, you know. Whereas, in my experience in Italy, and in Spain, and in Greece, and in France, it's a totally different story.

Is it a fear of seriousness?

Yes, I think it is.

George Devine was someone who tried very hard to put seriousness on the map.

The project of the Royal Court?

173

And I would have thought that he'd come along to Harold Pinter after The Birthday Party *and say: 'This is absolutely wonderful, It's totally original. I'd like to do your work.'*

[*laughs*] I think the answer to that is he didn't love my work. And he didn't find me totally original. I liked him, but he didn't like me, [*laughs*] as it were. I liked the Royal Court and what it was doing, but I simply didn't fit in. And the only time I did fit in with the Royal Court was as an understudy. You know, I understudied in John Osborne's play *Epitaph for George Dillon*. I earned a little living at that point, about seven pounds a week as far as I recall, and so I *was* part of the Royal Court. I worked as an understudy in the N.F. Simpson plays, and that was my one relationship, really. Two plays of mine were done at the Royal Court, but they came from Hampstead, and George Devine didn't like them very much. He was quite entitled not to like them. Well, he was obviously a funny bloke. I had no real relationship with him myself, although I admired very much what he did and the way he stood up for the theatre. I remember very well he said, you know, 'Failure, you have to have...'—what was it?—'you have the right to fail.' I admire that very much, and I think that that tradition has been carried on. It's the one thing, the one light we have left in an increasingly dimming theatrical society here: the right to do something which didn't sell out, as it were. Not necessarily fail—two very, very different things, of course.

The right not to have to succeed every time?

Yes, yes, yes. I think that's extremely important. In fact, it's the lifebelt, it's the only lifebelt we have.

But you had a commercial producer at a crucial time, who was your champion.

Well, I did have a commercial producer, Michael Codron, who put on *The Birthday Party*, which was a catastrophe. He did, however, put on *The Caretaker*, three years later, which was not a catastrophe, so that was very gratifying. But I left the commercial thing and went to the Royal Shakespeare Company. Because the Royal Shakespeare Company was a very, very lively place in the sixties at the Aldwych. It was wonderful. And I do remember that Peter Hall, with whom I've had a very long association—we've had a few ups and downs here and there, but he's a remarkable man, I think—took *The Homecoming* to his committee, his artistic committee, at the RSC in the Aldwych in 1964, and they all said—very distinguished people—'Yes, very interesting, but no. No, I don't think this will do. I don't think it's right to do a play with six actors. We've got a big company, and I'm not too sure about all this.' And Peter apparently said: 'Well, I've taken all your views and I'm going to do it.' Which he did. And I've always, [*laughs*] you know, liked that very much.

With Look Back in Anger *at the Royal Court in 1956, there was a play that finally wore its heart on its sleeve. But the great American plays*—Death of a Salesman, The

Crucible, View from the Bridge, Streetcar, Glass Menagerie—*had been written almost ten years before that but somehow hadn't penetrated British theatre. You knew of these plays?*

I did, yes. I was very excited when I saw *View from the Bridge* in its first production here. I thought it was terrific, yes, absolutely terrific. *Streetcar* I saw very shortly afterwards. I'm very glad to say that I knew Tennessee Williams quite well, and I thought he was the most delightful man, and I know Arthur Miller very well, and I think he's a hell of a fellow. I mean, there he is in his eighties, as young as ever, and there's no stopping him at all, really.

Was it their use of language that excited you?

I think Tennessee Williams could take wing in a way that nobody else dares really even now, you know. I say 'even now': now, at any time. But in terms of language, again I must come back to my own experience and my own history and my own education, and that was, as I've said, American literature, prose literature, modern novels. They meant a great deal to me in my youth, long before I knew any of these playwrights. John Dos Passos and Ernest Hemingway made an enormous impression on me. I still think that Hemingway is, at his best, incomparable. The question of sinew, of language: it's right there in Hemingway, you know.

And what about O'Neill?

He can never be kept out of history for one very good reason. He wrote the greatest last line that's ever been written—apart from 'Go bid the soldiers shoot'— in *Long Day's Journey into Night*: when she says to her husband, and her two sons: 'That was in the winter of the senior year. Then in the spring something happened to me. Yes, I remember. I fell in love with James Tyrone and was so happy for a time.'

What is it about theatre that you find so alluring?

Well, you see, I started as an actor nearly fifty years ago, and my first experience was with an audience, and I developed a very... tense relationship with the audience. In other words I found myself born into a situation where, as a young actor, it was either them or me—if you see what I mean. And I still understand that kind of tension between what happens on the stage and what happens in the audience. It's very, very strong. I'm talking about when the audience laughs, and you don't want them to laugh. When they rattle their coins in their pockets and you don't want them to do so. When they yawn. When they cough. When they say, 'What the hell am I doing here?' You can't let them win. You've got to say: 'I'll tell you what you're doing here. You're going to shut up and listen to me as an actor,' you know. And you have to also assert that kind of authority—I'm not going to say foul means or fair—but by all means at your disposal. As a writer, and I think also as a director, you've got to understand what the hell that means. Now, it would be stupid to say that all audiences are hostile bodies of people. They're not. But there is a very, very odd chemistry, as you know, in audiences. So, I want to make it quite clear that there are many audiences that I've really loved. But there are other audiences I have quite detested. What I learnt as an actor was that the tension has to be addressed. Now, what I've just said is probably extremely old-fashioned, because now, in half the things we see in the theatre, the audience is a part of the action. And the actors are part of the audience, and so on. I find those boundaries rather... when they're loosened, I don't really like it very much. But I'm getting on, you know. I remember once, [*laughs*] when I went to see a production of *Nicholas Nickleby* at the RSC at the Aldwych, an actor I had actually directed was prancing around before the show, pretending to sell hot coconuts or something, whatever the hell he was doing. He came up to me and waved a hot coconut in my face, and I said: 'Bugger off.' He went away, and then just as the whole thing was about to start, he danced down the aisle and thrust a hot coconut in my lap... [*laughs*] and I cursed him all the way back to the stage. I've never been one for that mixture of audiences and actors, so, in that sense, I know that I'm very traditional and old-fashioned.

You mentioned before we started that you wanted to say something about the media.

Ah, the media, yes. Well, [*sighs*] I think one of the really crucial elements in our lives is the media, it's the press, as we all know, because you read what it says in the papers and that's what life is. That's what truth is, we're told. That's what we're educated to understand. But, without going into it in too much detail, I'd like to tell one little story, which brings in perhaps a number of elements here. Finally it's very simple. I wrote a thing on the bombing of Iraq, just before it happened. I wrote what I called 'Open Letter to the Prime Minister'. A piece, just very sober, but I do believe, very objective and quite clinical, and also ironic, shall we say—pointing out to the Prime Minister, that our ally, the United States of America, had an absolutely appalling record in terms of human rights and national proceedings and domination of the world, this, that and the other. So I thought he might be interested in knowing these facts, which possibly people hadn't told him, you know. So I sent it to the *Guardian*, and they said, 'Yes, we'll publish it.' So I opened the *Guardian* newspaper a couple of days later, and there it was, except 'Open Letter to the Prime Minister' had been changed to 'Writer Outraged'. Now if you examine that, it does two things. It says: 'Oh my God, here's a writer outraged, can I turn over to the next page.' It predisposes the reader; it makes it not an objective account. Even if you read the damn thing, you think: 'Oh, he's outraged, he's outraged.' And also, the interesting thing is that it's 'writer' outraged. Who are these writers? They're always outraged. We didn't say: 'Busman Outraged' or 'Bus Conductor Outraged' or 'Carpet Salesman Outraged'. But 'Writer'... It's the... I think it has... I'm not sure that I'm being totally articulate here, but I do believe that there's a thought about how a writer is actually perceived in this country. I assure you that if I'd sent my open letter to the Prime Minister of any other country in the world, they would have called it 'Open Letter to the Prime Minister'. I think that speaks for itself.

Tom Stoppard

1 9 3 7—

Playwright. Author of, among other plays, Rosencrantz and Guildenstern Are Dead, Jumpers, Travesties, The Real Thing, Arcadia, The Invention of Love *(which I directed at the National Theatre),* The Coast of Utopia *and* Rock 'n' Roll. *I interviewed him in a corner of the foyer of the National Theatre. Before we started, we looked around the cathedral-like front of house of the National Theatre and talked about whether buildings outlast the expansionist impulse to create them. Later we wandered into the bookshop, where there was a full shelf of his work. 'You've written more than Proust,' I said to him. 'More jokes too,' he said.*

Who were you influenced by when you wrote Rosencrantz and Guildenstern?

Beckett. An embarrassing thing happened to me actually very recently. One of my sons went to see *Waiting for Godot*, and afterwards in a rather sort of bewildered, slightly embarrassed sort of way, he asked me whether I had realised that there was some similarity of rhythm and cadence and back-and-forthness about the dialogue. The first thing he said afterwards: 'Did you know about this play when you were writing?' And because he came at this innocently I suddenly felt exposed as a major plagiarist. I'd always been very happy to concede the homage, of course.

But was it the rhythms of the dialogue or were you emancipated by seeing that plays don't have to be about society or set in rooms?

I never took from Beckett what I found in him later on. In other words, later on I found the philosopher. The first time round it was the poet, it was the person who made language do this. I also responded to the comedy, I mean, literally to the jokes. I just loved the small scale of the jokes, the tiny shifts of emphasis that made you smile. Seeing *Waiting for Godot* was an amazing experience for me, and it was to do with a redefinition of theatrical validity. It held up, kept you amused, absorbed, occasionally puzzled, and it seemed to do so without really having any cards to play. Even now the thing which I enjoy most about Beckett plays is that they recurrently come to a point where there seems to be no way forward from there—and then he finds a tiny way forward, and then you're off again.

It was a sense of playfulness that attracted you.

There's a sly acknowledgement of the watchers, you know, us out there.

Did you read his philosophy as nihilism when you saw it?

Well, I don't eagerly or easily apply the word nihilism to Beckett. Nihilism doesn't in fact mean believing in nothing in that loose sense. It's actually more like a conviction that none of the answers are good, that none of them are anything. And in a funny sort of way, Beckett's plays are not nihilistic plays, they find tiny, tiny solaces, even if they are just wisps of hope in all that bleakness and despair. The whole point is that it is actually uplifting, there's a sort of extraordinary courage and stoicism in these characters who are legless, headless, in dustbins, lost, deserted.

Did he license you to think you could write about anything? Or to write with the sort of fearlessness that Shakespeare did where scenery wasn't a problem. He thinks: I'm going to write this play about a tempest—there's a storm, a shipwreck, and then you cut to the island. Hasn't the twentieth-century theatre been struggling to get back to that sort of freedom?

To get out of the room?

To chuck out the scenery.

In the early sixties, when I was a journalist, I interviewed a designer called Sean Kenny. People of my generation remember and revere him. I think I must have perhaps mentioned shyly that I'd written a play or tried to write a play. He said: 'Oh, go and write a play where somebody jumps out of a window onto a horse and gallops across the field chased by all the people in the town.' And I felt completely liberated and turned on by the way he spoke—that there were no barriers, everything was possible. I feel that we are the beneficiaries of some evolution in the way theatre is conceived by directors and designers as well as by writers. It's a troika. My generation are the beneficiaries of a huge but quite unique advance in what theatre can present to the eye and to the ear. And, of course, people like me now blithely write stage directions which call upon extraordinary feats of imagination from designers and directors.

Do you think Shakespeare introduced the idea of putting his own life into plays as you suggested in Shakespeare in Love? *Or is that notion introduced by Wilde as you propose in* The Invention of Love?

I think that Wilde found himself as a playwright when he discovered that he was his own main character. His first play was called *Vera; or, The Nihilists* and was a melodrama about the assassination of the Tsar of Russia set in 1790s. He invented different Tsars and he messed about with the historical period, but he never actually wrote out of doctrine. He wrote out of a kind of Hegelian interaction between a posture and its opposite, and found a way forward when they clashed. It's an appalling play, but between the revolutionaries and the aristocrats there's the minor character of the sceptic. He's a young man, and he's like a little harbinger of the Wilde to come. He never cracked it until he realised he should be writing about this minor character to the exclusion almost of everybody else. So you end up with plays which are highly personal in more than one way, I mean, they are personal in the sense that he's in them, but they are also personal in the sense that they're coded works of art about the social world he moved in.

Was that irony born out of a) being Irish and b) being gay?

You don't have to look that hard in *The Importance of Being Earnest*, for example, to find what appears to be a coded homosexual play underneath. But I personally don't go with that thesis. I think something else is going on which is much more frivolous—mischief and jokes were going on. He would name a character after somebody in his social circle; he would pay off little scores. In that way, Wilde was combining two aspects of his character—one was the artist, who was there to do a serious job no matter how comical it might be, but the other was a public figure, who was drawing on his social life but also drawing it in to the plays and commenting almost as an aside. But this is an aspect of somebody who is very, very rich in gifts; he doesn't have to be po-faced about what he is doing. The whole thing about people like Wilde is that there's plenty more where that came from. They don't have to make the most of each one. When you act a Wilde character or when you act Wilde himself, I always feel it's a mistake to deliver the *bon mots* as if they are little treasures. I think actually that the point is there is plenty more where they came from: they are just thrown out.

What's his influence been?

He's had a tremendous influence in the world of social politics. He's been adopted, if you like. He's been invested with a self-consciousness, a purpose, an awareness which he possibly took more lightly than we would like to believe now. But I think Wilde is one of those rare cases who were the beginning and end of something. There was nothing like a Wilde play before there was a Wilde play, and there has been nothing really quite like a Wilde play since then.

Your Wilde says in The Invention of Love: *'I made my life into my art and it was an unqualified success.'*

The Wilde personality fictionalised, given a name, and set going in a Wilde play opened the door to a path which we're all still following. It showed that if you had something to say, you could actually say it almost in person; you didn't have to sort of filter it through some other kind of person or a bunch of people. You could actually give yourself a name on a hat, hire somebody to walk on stage and say it, just say it directly. You go from the Shavian protagonist, like John Tanner in *Man and Superman*, who's the spokesman for the author, all the way to Jimmy Porter. It's a component of what defines the modern theatre, you know. Perhaps Wilde, whom we think of as earning this high place because of style and wit, actually earns it for a rather deeper reason: that he saw that the theatre could be simply the dinner table at which he spoke after dinner.

You mentioned Jimmy Porter. What did Look Back in Anger *mean to you?*

I think *Look Back in Anger* is talked of as a watershed by the people who went regularly to the theatre for the previous ten years or twenty years. It was one of the first plays I saw. It was only much later that I understood the context. After the war there was a great vogue for verse theatre, I think as a reaction to the austerity of the times. There was a sort of richness available and, as that really became less relevant, something else was needed and *Look Back in Anger* was what happened. It was, of course, exciting, but speaking for myself I wasn't aware that it was the first time that people of this generation or class had spoken. I just thought it was a wonderfully well-written, exciting play and, yes, you felt: here is a man who is speaking for us, who also reads the posh papers on Sunday and lives like students. I admire the play very much but I don't attach to it enormous significance other than as a social phenomenon. We were speaking earlier about seeing Beckett for the first time. That was a completely different experience, because you felt that different things were now possible. *Look Back in Anger* was about different people, but the rhetoric was the rhetoric of English drama.

Did you think Joan Littlewood's work showed that different things were possible?

I was at the first night of *Oh! What a Lovely War*, which I am guessing now would have been 1962, and next to me was a veteran of that war, a very old man with no teeth. I didn't know him, but in the interval he turned to me weeping and said: 'I was there. That's what it was like.' And I was very moved by the play too as well as uplifted by it because it's very funny as well. I was also aware that it broke forms and somehow managed to do something almost impossible: to convey the sense of what it must have been like but to do it as a kind of music hall. I think that it did lead to quite a lot of important work. The supposed connection between [Joan Littlewood's] Theatre Workshop and Brecht I find puzzling. Joan's theatre wasn't alienating. It was actually what Aristotle is: pity and terror. It was: 'Get in there, feel it, empathise.' That's how it got to me. As a matter of fact, I think by definition theatre has to draw you in, you have to suddenly lose yourself, and you have to be prepared to laugh, cry and forget who you are. The notion that it's a didactic form and that you must be constantly reminded that you are in an, as it were, extremely elaborate and entertaining classroom is in conflict with what theatre is. It's connected to the child watching the conjurer, to the child actually listening to words in a pantomime.

David Hare

1 9 4 7—

Playwright and director. Author of Slag, Plenty, Fanshen, Teeth 'n' Smiles, The Secret Rapture, Racing Demon, The Absence of War, Skylight, Amy's View, The Vertical Hour, Gethsemane *and others. I have known David Hare since the late sixties and have directed six of his plays. He's a practised master of the role of interviewee: fluent sentences with beginnings, middles and ends, Christian names always attached to surnames, and passion attached to ideas. I interviewed him in his workplace in Hampstead, which was once the studio of the painter, Mark Gertler.*

When did you first hear about Brecht?

Properly, at university. I'd gone to study with a Marxist, Raymond Williams, and he thought that Brecht was the inheritor of the great tradition of twentieth-century drama—in fact, he wrote a book which went from Ibsen to Brecht, so Brecht was the important figure. But Brecht doesn't actually deal with the two great events that mark the twentieth century.

Which are?

Which are the failure of Communism and the killing of six million people in the camps.

What about the Bomb?

Well, he'd already conceived *Galileo* before the dropping of the Bomb, so he dealt with it by changing the end of the play. I only began to get interested in him in middle age. Like a lot of political playwrights I dealt with Brecht by not dealing with him, because the world into which I was born was so different from the world into which he was born. He's basically a prophet of doom when he's writing in Germany in the twenties and thirties. He's got that zap and zing of someone who knows that something terrible is going to happen. When something terrible does happen he writes what I think are his masterpieces which I take to be *Galileo* and *Mother Courage*. They're two plays about people behaving badly—plays about bad faith—and maybe you only get interested in bad faith when you get into middle age. They are plays about times when there's no right way of behaving, when it's impossible to behave well. He's very clear, both in *Galileo* and in *Mother Courage* that these people adopt strategies to try and survive in difficult times. It's his great subject: how do you get by when there is no right course?

For a man who would claim objectivity, he dealt very subjectively with these issues.

There's plainly an autobiographical element in the sense that he, if you like, justifies cowardice, and plainly he did do some fairly cowardly things in his own life. I think they're the greatest works that have been written in the theatre on the subject of compromise, bad faith, getting by, not being able to do what you would wish and, if you like, the irrelevance of idealism. He writes about situations in which it doesn't much matter what happens to your ideals, because history itself is blowing through the room and turning everything to matchsticks.

If one accepts your thesis, he's been terribly misrepresented because he's invariably spoken of as a polemicist and a didactic writer.

Yes, 'didactic' is a word that critics use about anyone who puts politics in their work. They don't want the theatre to be grown-up. I mean, Gorky is called a didactic playwright by critics, but Gorky was crucified by the Russian Revolution. He knew more about the failings, intricacies, workings, pluses and minuses of that revolution and tried to write honestly about it. For his pains he's called didactic. But that's just a smear word that's thrown at all political playwrights.

Brecht's clearly influenced you.

His influence on me is simply that he's the great exemplar of politics being an adult subject, but secondly, he's an exemplar of seeing historical incidents as being incredibly complicated and not reducible to simple ideas. Galileo is someone who, with the very best intentions, ends up doing the wrong thing. Galileo and Mother Courage are two of the cleverest people to appear on the twentieth-century stage: they both know what's happening to them, and it's their self-awareness, it's their sophistication about their own dilemmas, that's new. Even in the 'new drama', so-called, of Ibsen and Chekhov there's a degree of self-ignorance; there are places where the audiences laugh because they know the characters better than they know themselves. You never laugh at a Brechtian character for not knowing themselves; they know themselves inside out.

But I'd argue that his influence on our theatre has been much greater as a director and as a thinker about theatre than as a writer.

Well, the decision to sweep the stage clean of junk, which was a completely liberating thing in the British theatre, happened in the early sixties as a result of a series of very talented directors—mainly John Dexter, Bill Gaskill, Peter Hall—and designers—John Bury, Jocelyn Herbert—going to see those Berliner Ensemble productions and being profoundly influenced by them. He cleared the clutter off the British stage, and we started again with the lights in view and on bare boards. That in itself became a style, and it became eventually a decadent style, but, in the productions by the best of the Brechtian British directors, the questions about what was the social status of the characters and what was the nature of the class transaction going on between the characters produced some very great work—much greater work than was being done by those people who were only asking the old questions about psychology.

So was Brecht in some way the godfather of the seventies?

If you're talking about my own crop of political playwrights then I don't think that you can say that Caryl Churchill, Howard Brenton, Trevor Griffiths have in common the sense of being part of a Brechtian legacy. On the contrary, I feel that I was born into a world completely changed. The failure of Communism wasn't my generation's fault; it wasn't something that we felt personally. We were born into a world much more affected by the nuclear bomb, by American foreign policy, and by the failure of leftist governments in the West. You don't find those things dealt with in Brecht's work. But there's a machismo about Brecht, which I find unattractive. This determination not to be caught out in any kind of humanist stance, not to wear your heart on your sleeve, not to show passion, not to show feeling, rarely to show love, rarely to write about the heart. I think by the time writers of my age were writing in the seventies, we found that rather old-fashioned and contrived, that pretence that you're nobody's fool and 'you're not going to catch me being sincere'. I think a dose of sincerity was rather a wonderful thing in the seventies.

Why has the political play died out, with rare exceptions, in this country?

Because I think young people's attitude to life is different. In other words, it's a reflection of the different approach to life that young people now have. I don't think that they believe that formal politics of the kind that my generation believed in can deliver the improvements in people's lives. You know, political writing is always socially progressive: it always thinks that there are things that you can do about problems and that by taking the following course you can improve life in the following ways. The audience yearns for such plays to be written again, and is overjoyed when they find them, but those plays come out of a need. If the young people don't feel that need, then they won't write plays in that form. The other thing that has gone is a zeal to portray the whole society. This younger generation of writers for some reason doesn't have this descriptive zeal. I regret it because I think one of the things the theatre does best is be the social secretary—the Balzacian sense that you're meant to record what's going on in the society at the time. Perhaps young playwrights feel that television and film does that, but I don't feel it does.

Do you think it's got anything to do with the fact that we were born into a generation with a '45 election that felt not only that the world could be changed but that the world would change?

Yes, I think the possibility of practical things to be done which will alleviate human pain and suffering and the channel for that desire to change things being through formal, organised or street politics, that's gone, and it only will come back if the need is there in the young to change the society that they live in and the belief is there in the possibility of changing it.

Somebody whose work would be inexplicable in any other period of history but the aftermath of the Second World War is Beckett. When did you first become aware of him?

I think *Godot* was done as the school play as it's been done, you know, in thousands of schools, because it was the dominant avant-garde work of its time in a way that I don't think any play has been since.

What did you think when you first saw it?

I was taken aback by it because of all the usual reasons: I couldn't understand how a play could not make sense and yet make sense. Its methods were so radical. We're so familiar with it now that it's impossible to see how radical it was to have people talking what is effectively gibberish on the stage and yet for it not to seem cute or gimmicky but for it to seem emotionally felt.

You felt very strongly about it and yet you weren't influenced?

Beckett was so original and so overwhelming that you can't take his achievement away, but finally what he's saying isn't what I believe.

Which is?

I think that to try to write under the eye of eternity, as he does, finally flattens everything out, and to take up a writerly posture which is above action rather than in the action is finally not a method that I preferred as a playwright. In Beckett's case, I'm sorry but it finally becomes quite boring. *Waiting for Godot* is unplayably boring now, I think. I'd run a mile rather than ever see it again. There's that famous story of Philip Larkin finally writing the poem he wants to write about death; and when he writes it, he then can't write any more poems: that's the last poem he can write. Now if you take death as your subject and the meaninglessness of life—which is Beckett's essential subject—and you say we're born astride the grave... if you believe that, then it both has a very flattening effect on your writing but also hasn't much to say beyond that. So in other words he writes a few great plays—*Krapp's Last Tape* is his best work, and *Endgame*—and then everything is essentially commentary, because there is one idea in his work which is so overwhelming and dominant that he never finds another way of writing after it.

But isn't he like a painter? Like Francis Bacon?

I think Bacon found more variety within his subject than Beckett did and I think that Beckett's work doesn't develop. My mother has Alzheimer's; when I go to see her she speaks Beckett monologues, she speaks late Beckett. That interests me, but I don't know what to do with that information. It doesn't help me, and Beckett doesn't want me to have any particular response to seeing the accuracy with which he can do Alzheimer's dialogue. So in his later work, as a member of the audience I'm lost for a response, and he doesn't lead me anywhere. I'm mystified by having been lucky enough to meet Beckett on occasions and him being a character who could talk about anything, and who was so interested in everything, who was so deeply interested in people and would talk, as I have heard him talk, on Ireland or meteorology or—

Cricket?

—the theatre or cricket. A fascinating man, I mean, a great man to talk to, with this incredible zest for the detail of life—and yet where is it in his plays? Here's a man who fought in the French Resistance—my God, I would love to see Beckett's play on the French Resistance—and yet by eliminating ninety-eight per cent of subject matter he's actually guilty of what political playwrights are accused of: being more keen to put across his message than to describe. A writer who doesn't have the basic urge to describe—which he does have in his early novels, but which he doesn't have in his late plays—is a writer that I don't quite know what to do with.

What's his influence been on the theatre in this country?

I think his influence was obviously bad at first, in the sense that a lot of writers came along who thought that it wasn't necessary to have a plot. He appeared to reduce plays to something terribly basic. But in fact, because he was a genius and undoubtedly he is a paradoxical genius—meaning great revolutionary, but not finally very rewarding playwright—he was able to construct the cleverest non-plot of all time: i.e. they wait, he doesn't come but plenty actually happens. Lots happens in *Waiting for Godot*, lots happens in *Endgame*, and it's structured like a musical piece, but inferior playwrights looked at his work and thought that it was formless. Far from it, it was incredibly formal, but he encouraged a lot of very lazy, very sloppy, structureless playwriting that was virtually stream of consciousness. But I think Pinter is a rare example of where the pupil takes something from the master and makes it into something more powerful. In other words, when Pinter roots some of the discoveries of Beckett in a real social context, when he puts them in a boarding house in a seaside town or he puts them in the East End with more familiarly characterised people, then I think the view becomes even more powerful.

What about Peter Hall's thesis that of the Brechtians and Beckettians it's the Beckettians that will survive?

The Beckettians will survive, and the Brechtians won't? Oh really? Are they going down the pan of history? I think the split in twentieth-century drama starts with Chekhov and Gorky: in other words, Chekhov is accepted as the master, but actually he was in an argument with Gorky. Chekhov pretends to a level of disengagement as writer. He hoped that you would see the characters, but you wouldn't see him, whereas you can see Gorky in his own work. You might say that one approach is classical: you are detached, you are God. Well, Chekhov and Beckett both play God. The writers to whom I am temperamentally drawn don't pretend to play God: they're in there with their characters as messed up, as passionate, as mucky as they are.

Isn't there a strain that is in someway untainted by either Brecht or Beckett?

As a playwright I don't think about influences. I'm not conscious of influences. I don't think of myself as having any legacy either from Brecht or Beckett. To take it right back: Ibsen and Chekhov invent a new kind of social play, don't they? They invent a play in which the characterisation is much more complex, and which is affected by the social ideas of the time—particularly feminism and an interest in social problems. And a representation of the middle class as not just people floating outside time but people who actually take actions which have consequences which are felt very hard by poorer people. That social view arrives with Chekhov and Ibsen and Gorky, and it happens that in this country it arrives in the form of a particularly garrulous Irishman called George Bernard Shaw. And because his bent is for comedy and for a certain kind of stylised dialogue, this new social drama is hidden both by its Irish accent and by the sheer length of its sentences and the difficulty of its playing, but it arrives all the same. And there arrives something called the 'state of the nation' play, and, because the twentieth century is particularly interesting because of the rise and fall of the British Empire and because of the enemies that we had to fight both in the First World War and in the Second World War, the 'state of the nation' play in my view is much the richest strain in twentieth-century drama. It starts with *Heartbreak House*, which is very influenced by Chekhov and Gorky, and it runs right through D.H. Lawrence to *Look Back in Anger* to *Saved* to Caryl Churchill and Howard Brenton. I think it's the richest single strain in modern theatre.

Do you think it's justified to regard Look Back in Anger *as the watershed, the start of a revolution?*

Oh yes. I think *Look Back in Anger* is the most significant debut of the twentieth century. It's the biggest splash a playwright ever makes with his first play, and it makes other things possible. I don't say that those other things wouldn't have happened, and yet John Osborne is the gatekeeper: he opens the gate and everyone else comes pouring through afterwards. That means not just in terms of the subject matter that he is dealing with but the tone of voice in which he is dealing with it. People had predicted in the forties that there was going to be a revival of poetic theatre, and there was a revival of poetic theatre. It's just that the poetry happened to be the poetry of John's beautiful monologues, and it was cast in a dialect that nobody was expecting but, my God, it's poetry.

What was John Osborne doing that hadn't been done before by Rattigan and Coward?

Expressing strong feeling without embarrassment. Showing people in the grip of passion, not to be mocked. You know, when anybody in Noël Coward becomes passionate they are insulted by the playwright for expressing it. Coward behaves as if it's non-U to admit you feel things. I can't stand all that awful posing, both in his diaries and in his plays when he keeps saying sex is overrated. Oh yeah? Who's he trying to fool? Or was Coward genuinely sexless, and threatened by people who weren't? That's why it's exhilarating when Jimmy Porter arrives. Raging round the stage is a man who greatly feels, and though we are invited to find him at times ridiculous for greatly feeling, we are meant to identify with his feeling. And there's no doubt that the audience at the time did. Where Osborne was different, and I think radically different, was that the subject of the work is sex. In *Look Back in Anger* you have a woman—Helena—who's standing there saying to Jimmy Porter: 'I hate you,' and then she suddenly turns round and wants to go to bed with him. And similarly Jimmy Porter's relationship with Alison is only explicable in terms of the sex they have. So that suddenly in a Lawrentian way you have a British play which is about sex. I don't think people recognised that at the time, but I think any good revival of the play makes that clear. It foreshadows everything that's to happen in terms of the explicitness about sex and the emphasis on sex that you get in the following years.

And in that sense it was anomalous in the Royal Court?

The more you think about George Devine, the more admirable he is. He was interested in mime; he was interested in French theatre; he was interested in getting novelists to write for his theatre; and a script arrives through the post from a young man, and he says: 'This is much better than anything else we can put on at this theatre.' And suddenly the theatre that he's dreamed of, which would be rather sort of avant-garde, he has to throw out the window because he's so committed to putting on this young man. He brilliantly straddled the theatre director's dilemma: keeping true to your principles while at the same time doing the best work that is offered to you.

Don't you find it odd that this was happening in Britain years after Tennessee Williams's best plays, Arthur Miller's best plays, Eugene O'Neill's best plays, Clifford Odets' best plays had been played in the US? How do you explain that?

It's a mystery, isn't it? Arthur Miller plainly was delighted by the arrival of John Osborne because he was effectively saying: at last the infection has spread to England, and at last in England you're going to have socially engaged, passionate writers of the kind that we've had in America for years. Why it took so long to cross the Atlantic I don't understand. But you might equally ask why did it take so long for the American theatre to be influenced by the British. American playwrights used to come to England in the seventies and eighties, see these works and say: you know I must go back to America and create this kind of political work. But it isn't until Tony Kushner with *Angels in America* and Wallace Shawn with *The Designated Mourner* and *The Fever* that you get American playwrights who are deeply influenced by the British theatre.

Let's get to Shakespeare.

[*laughs*] Aren't you meant to do a bit of a segue?

What's original about Shakespeare?

What I admire about Shakespeare is that he puts everything on the stage. He's the great originator of the idea that the stage actually shows everything. In Greek drama people talk about everything—and they bring reports of it—but what Shakespeare does is throw the whole thing onto the stage. Now Chekhov has been the dominant influence of twentieth-century theatre: he invented or reinvented this idea that you could portray a whole society by putting people in a room, and the claim is made that you can feel, just by the way they talk, that the Russian Revolution is coming. What's so great about Shakespeare is: he says nonsense to that. I will put the Russian Revolution on the stage. If there's a battle, the battle's on the stage; if the tempest comes, the tempest doesn't beat at the window, the tempest is on the stage, the ship is on the stage; murders are on the stage—unless for a particular reason in one play he chooses to have the murder offstage for a very specific reason—but by and large he shows you things, and he doesn't worry about the problem of how they are going to be shown. You can't imagine Chekhov writing: 'Exit pursued by a bear.' That's a uniquely Shakespearean stage direction. He says: 'I'll have the bear; it'll be on the stage; and it's up to the director or the actors to work out how they do it.' That desire to put the whole of society on the stage—every class from king, bourgeoisie, courtiers, right down the middle class, working class—and show interaction not only between the classes but among the classes, among the people in each class as well. That's sensational. He shows history on the stage.

So you think that for a British playwright having Shakespeare as a legacy is a unique gift?

I also think that his role in British life is very extraordinary. He didn't go to university, he went to grammar school, and yet his work is profoundly serious. It represents what I think of as the middle way of Britishness, which is expressed through the theatre because it's didactic. The number of actors I know who can complete *The Times* crossword... Not because they've wasted so much time in their lives, but because they've educated themselves through performing the plays of British playwrights, which are in themselves an education. In society today to one side lies academia with all its potential for aridity and pretentiousness, and to the other side what's called the media with all it's potential for stupidity. Down the middle of the road drives the British theatre, where people, through a mixture of high-mindedness and auto-didacticism, present something which is both sensible and idealistic. And that's Shakespeare, the man who teaches himself through the theatre, who participates in the theatre. He's an actor in the theatre, he's effectively the director at times, and he's also learning all the time by reading all the time and adapting. 'Self-taught' is almost the most beautiful term of praise I can think of for a writer.

Jocelyn Herbert
1 9 1 7—2 0 0 3

---

*Designer. Jocelyn Herbert learned from Motley—the sisters Margaret ('Percy')
and Sophie Harris with Elizabeth Montgomery. Trained as a painter, she worked
initially as a costume designer. She started designing sets in 1956 at the Royal
Court, becoming George Devine's collaborator and later living with him. Her
epitaph of him sums up what he gave to the Royal Court: 'For a brief period our
work, and our lives, had a centre.' She developed a style of humane
minimalism—designs without clutter that concentrated attention on the actors
and the text. At the time of our interview I had known her for over thirty years.
She had barely changed in that time, always with the beauty of a Gothic saint.
We talked in her studio, surrounded by her designs and masks and photographs
and memorabilia, the silt of nearly sixty years' work in the theatre. 'If I was
rich,' she mused, 'I would have a huge room with a billiards table. I've always
longed to have that…'*

When did you first hear about Brecht?

I was in France, and I heard that his company were playing in Paris, so I got a bus
up to Paris and went to see *The Caucasian Chalk Circle*. The funny thing was that
I had to go without any shoes because I'd walked all round somewhere and got
terrible blisters.

And what did you think?

I'd never seen anything as wonderful.

What was it that was so wonderful about it?

The sheer beauty of it, but also the play itself was so full of different meanings and saying so many different things. Everybody says he's too political, but I never found so because I rather agreed with his politics.

So it was the combination of the politics and the aesthetics?

And the humour, of course. And that wonderful scene when there's a bare stage and just a few reeds across—and there's the girl and her friend, with the river dividing these two people; it's wonderful that. And then also the way they did their speeches: they suddenly came out and talked to the audience. I thought that was quite wonderful.

Did you know anything about Brecht's theories?

I didn't really know much about him then at all, but then I did start, you know, being interested. I responded so much to his ideas and his attitude to classics: that you have to look at them like a new play. They all had a contemporary feel without being gimmicky in any way.

You went to Berlin.

Yes.

Did you meet Brecht?

I never did; he died before I…

But you met the company?

I met the company and his daughter and all the actors and the young directors. He died just before the company came to London in '55, was it?

'56.

I'll never forget going to the Palace Theatre. It was absolutely crammed: and to see this play—*Mother Courage*—in German. I think the first act lasted two hours or something, but you could hear a pin drop. Nobody stirred, everybody was completely riveted. That was quite something, you know.

What do you think it was about the event that so stirred people?

It was wonderfully acted. It's a wonderful play, of course, and it was beautifully staged. But I suppose it was the surprise of the quality of the whole thing compared to what we were used to here. One wasn't thinking like that during the performance: you were just absorbing it. It was only afterwards I realised how in sympathy I had been with everything he seemed to want to do or did, in fact.

Did you go away from seeing Brecht's productions thinking 'I must change my approach to theatre'?

I really went into the theatre to try and get rid of a lot of scenery. At that time it was all decorative scenery and painted cloths, and I wanted to bring some of the abstraction that had happened to painting and music and poetry and things like that into the theatre. I mean, you can't abstract people, but you can approach a design in a more abstract way, giving indications of things rather than making it naturalistic. I think it was the sort of revolt against naturalism really that impressed me. What was wonderful with Brecht was, you know, that everything was utterly real but utterly poetic as well.

How do you start designing a play?

I always start with a bare canvas, but it's three dimensional. It's a very collaborative art, the theatre, and designers only form a little part of it. I always tell students this story: if you're on tour and the actors are there but the scenery doesn't arrive, you can have a show, but if the scenery arrives and the actors don't come, you haven't got anything. I think that's a very salutary thought for young designers. They don't like it very much. When you have spareness the actors and the text emerge with much more strength than if they're surrounded by a lot of stuff which doesn't really have any meaning. It may look very beautiful, but it's not helpful.

What's Brecht's legacy?

I think he was by far the biggest influence on design this century and perhaps on production. There was Craig, but he hadn't got the technical skill. If Craig was alive today all his amazing things would work, but because they didn't at the time, he didn't make the impact he might have done. I think a lot of designers have been influenced by Brecht. The trouble is that so few people like seeing his plays. They get annoyed because they're a bit Socialist or Communist or something and they don't see the poetry in them. I think they think it's dogmatic, no, not dogmatic...

Didactic?

Didactic, yes; and actually that isn't good in the theatre usually, but I thought he managed it. His plays were caring about people, which is really the basis of it all, isn't it?

What did you think when you first saw Waiting for Godot?

I loved it. Actually I took Laurie Lee and he didn't like it at all. We had a terrible argument all through dinner, I don't know why.

What did you like about it?

The sort of mixture of clown, the loneliness and hopelessness of life and everything. I respond to that: you know, people are so alone and abandoned, and yet they find ways of getting through the day.

Beckett seems to me a paradox: everybody describes him as very warm and absolutely delightful company, and yet there's this very bleak, pessimistic work.

I don't think people always are in the flesh what they write. They can be terribly different from what they write—and they can be very disappointing. I remember growing up and meeting someone who I admired very much and not liking them at all. With Beckett it was the reverse: he was the most courteous, charming, wonderful man. But I think the problem is that although he was so incredibly erudite—he'd read everything and he was so articulate— his work is incredibly simple. He used to get terribly irritated when people asked him, you know the sort of thing: 'Is Godot meant to be God?' And he'd say: 'Well, no, if I wanted it to be God I would have called it God.' He hated intellectual discussions about his work. But we all spent a wonderful evening— George [Devine] and I. It was Christmas in Paris, and we were wandering from bar to bar as they closed: we ended up at the Falstaff. Beckett was talking to George about trying to write a play without a person. This was the birth of *Not I* in fact—you know, with just the mouth. They were sort of discussing whether this was possible or not.

But it's not a play without a person.

Well, you only see the mouth. It's just the words; he regarded the words as the... well, they are the vital thing of every play, aren't they really? I mean, without words we wouldn't have any theatre at all.

But on the other hand, he seems to me to approach the theatre like a painter.

He did love painting; he loved to go and look at paintings. And he loved walking. He had a little house in the country—a very sparse little house—just with trees and grass, rather like it might have been a set. I've never met anyone quite like him. I mean, he... he, I suppose, was one of the most lovely men. He taught me to play billiards!

Did he ever talk to you about the war, what it was like being in the Resistance?

No, not really, hardly at all. I think he had to, you know, live very sparsely—gather wood for fuel, work on the farm—and it was a very tough life I think. But he didn't say very much about it.

For a writer thought of as very private, he had an eventful life.

I think so. Of course, he had this long friendship with Joyce. He wasn't actually his secretary, but he helped him a lot, especially as he got blind.

Did he talk about Joyce?

He did a bit, yes, because he had this problem with Joyce's daughter, who was very much in love with him. He was very nice to her, and he liked women, but he didn't sort of realise she was falling in love with him. It's difficult, I don't know how to talk about him. I just think I was just so lucky to have known him. It's difficult to describe someone like that, isn't it? You can't, really.

Did he talk to you about his stage pictures?

The thing is that he actually envisaged every movement on the stage and where people would stand or be, and where a light would be; that's why if you design, it's terribly important to listen to what he says in his directions—the very few that he gives. If you just say: 'Oh, well, I won't have an all-dark room; I'll have something else,' then you're denying the play something essential. It's not that it won't play: it'll play, but it won't be as beautiful and as complete as it would be if you do try to do what he envisages. Of course, often you don't have authors who have a vision when they write. They don't really know, or they don't mind terribly, perhaps.

His plays are like musical scores in the sense they have to be played as they're scored.

Yes, I think so. You know, people laugh and say: 'Well, that has three commas [*laughs*] and not four, two and not…' Billie Whitelaw used to get demented when he rang her up and said: 'There's only two commas now, you know.' It does seem crazy, but musically for him it was rhythm. I mean, in *Happy Days* he knew exactly where the bags should be and the things Winnie took out of it and what they should look like. I saw a production once where they had a full bottle of medicine—the whole point is that she throws it away because it's empty.

Brecht and Beckett both had very, very strong ideas about how their plays should look and be presented.

Well, they were both exceptional, weren't they? Don't you think? I mean, they are two great people. I think Brecht and Beckett are the two great people of the theatre of our time, of the century probably. They certainly mean more to me than anyone else. They both gave so much of themselves and their own beliefs to the theatre, which is wonderful.

What do you think the Beckett's legacy is?

Perfectionism, really. Beautiful writing, demanding a very careful and beautiful production. It's very extraordinary: I don't know if you went to the Barbican when they had that *Godot* there, directed by the German man [Walter Asmus] who worked with him. It was rather wonderful to see that huge theatre crammed to the roof with young people absolutely loving it. It shows that things win through if they're good enough.

Do you think that Beckett influenced people to write in a way that they hadn't written before?

Probably, but I think it doesn't quite work when people try to write like him; they've got to find a way of using what he said or the way he wrote. Every word to him, you know, was examined. He used to know the plays by heart when he came to rehearsal: once he got up and did the whole of *Krapp* right through because the person who'd rehearsed it was so awful. They said: 'Oh, did you like it?' He said: 'Well, it's not quite what I meant,' and the actor said, 'Well, why don't you do it?' And to my amazement he said: 'Well, would you like me to show you?' And he got up on stage and he played the whole thing. [*laughs*]

How good an actor was he?

Beckett? Oh, wonderful.

You were in at the foundation of the English Stage Company at the Royal Court. What was the aim of the company?

The aim was to try and encourage young people—or not necessarily young—to write plays for today and not just drawing-room comedies. It was to combat the horror of the West End at the time, the sort of emptiness of it all. Of course, when we began, there weren't many new plays. It was only when *Look Back in Anger* came along—as George [Devine] said when he read it, how lucky we were to have such a play. Mind you, it had very bad notices to start with until Ken Tynan gave it a good notice, and then it took off. We started with a company, and we always believed we should have a company, but of course we found that if we wanted to do a new play—I think it was every six weeks—we couldn't exploit a success because the company were rehearsing the next play. So in the end we gave up the idea, and of course all the young directors said: 'Oh, shocking thing!', you know, and George said: 'Well, we have to survive.' And through John's *Look Back in Anger* we made money, so we were able to put on things by John Arden and [N.F.] Simpson and all these people. We just lost thousands every time, and

Neville Blond [chairman] would say: 'You know, George, why are we doing these plays?', and George would say: 'Well, I think he's a good writer and I've asked him to do another one.' [*laughs*] And Neville just accepted that, you know.

You had a visual aesthetic that you wanted to bring to the theatre, the bare stage, but actually the first success was in a box set.

Well, it was. When we started, we wanted to clear the stage and get rid of all the borders and show the lights and have this pale surround and try to just put things inside that, but they were all sort of domestic plays. You can't just do any old play on a bare stage. There are some need walls or windows or doors, but you can do it in a way that isn't completely naturalistic, you know. John [Osborne], of course, always wanted more scenery. In *Luther* I was gradually taking scenery away, you know, and there's one bit he hung on to which wasn't necessary at all. But he was wonderful in the sense that all his research was so interesting and because of the pictures he had; he was very responsive to the look of things, funnily enough.

What happened when Look Back in Anger *was a success?*

Well, it was very exciting, of course. Many more people came to the theatre, and it also brought in a lot of other writers gradually. And, of course, it took on a flavour of that awful saying 'angry young men' and all that, which was fine in a way. I think it was the beginning of the revolution. I mean, we all felt we were really on a crusade: we had to struggle to have the money to put on a play, but nobody minded; everybody worked all night. I remember I earned seven pounds a week painting the scenery. And the stagehands were all taxi drivers or things in the daytime. It was partly due to George, of course. He just had this wonderful way of encouraging talent wherever it was, and because he knew about running a theatre, and he knew about lighting, and he knew about carpentry; he just involved everybody in some way. It was an amazing time. Everybody really believed that the text was the basis of the work and that everything you did should be geared to making that live. And so everything was sort of geared to the play and to the actors and not to the look of the thing. I think the thing is that, although all the directors and designers and people who worked there are all different in ways, they all still have that kind of belief and their work did really show it. Funnily enough, they all fought like cats and dogs, of course, but if people started attacking the Court they ganged up on them. I remember Lindsay [Anderson] and Bill [Gaskill] and John [Osborne] were all saying: 'Oh, we should have a company again,' so George said: 'Well, come round and we'll talk about it.' I was up on my balcony in the studio working away, and there they were downstairs—and they couldn't agree on a single actor, the three of them. When Bill took over the Court, he did have a company again, but of course he had to do exactly what we did because he couldn't make it pay.

What was the crusade for?

It was to create a new audience if possible, and also to have plays about all the terrible things that matter. It didn't have to be political. That's where Beckett was such a wonderful thing because he was poetical, if you like. We wanted to make theatre interesting and hopefully make more people go to the theatre, not just the rich and bourgeois. But of course when we were absolutely broke once, Tony [Richardson] wanted to do—is it *Look After Lulu!*? [by Noël Coward]— with Vivien Leigh, and I must say we were all absolutely furious. But we were broke, and everyone said it would make some money. And of course it didn't; it was a flop. But people used to say: 'Oh, it's wonderful what you're doing at the Court,' and George would say: 'Oh good, I'm glad, what have you seen?' 'Oh well, we saw *Look After Lulu!*' It was a terrible struggle, and he always felt that he'd failed: he hadn't got a new audience. I mean, more young people did come, but not what he'd hoped. It was very sad, really.

William Gaskill

1 9 3 0—

Director. Bill Gaskill worked with George Devine and Tony Richardson at the Royal Court and was its Artistic Director from 1965 to 1972. He was also appointed one of the founding directors of the National Theatre by Laurence Olivier. In 1974 he started Joint Stock Theatre Company with Max Stafford-Clark. A precise and fastidious director, he stared at me with characteristic disdain when I asked my first, lumbering question: 'When you were growing up, did you feel that you were caught between two absolutes, the Bomb and the Holocaust?' After an implicitly critical silence lasting several years, he answered: 'No.'

Were you politicised when you started working in the theatre?

I was an aesthete; there was no question about it. What I wanted to do was make culture.

What was your cultural background?

Oh, my father was a French teacher, so my grounding was essentially European; after I left university, I went to Paris, because I was very excited by the French theatre. That's where it all seemed to be happening. So the whole cult of existentialism, but more particularly the whole stylishness of the French theatre, had an enormous influence. It was only really with the arrival of Brecht, which was about five years later, that I altered my whole viewpoint.

So how did you first hear about Brecht?

There used to be a kind of left magazine called *New Theatre* during the war and afterwards, and they very much promoted the whole idea of Brecht. And so one knew a great deal about it, and even when I was at university I had plans to do a production of *The Threepenny Opera*. I got a 78 of the original production, with Ernst Busch singing 'Mack the Knife', which I used to play endlessly, so my whole image of it was all really fixed. And then I read *The Caucasian Chalk Circle* and *The Good Woman of Setzuan* in the [Eric] Bentley translations, which were the first things that you could actually read in English. And they didn't have a big influence. I remember saying at the time that if we saw the way they were done— because we'd already heard that they were done in a very particular way—then we might understand why he was considered so remarkable.

So was it the aesthetics that drew you to Brecht?

When I first saw the plays on stage, I think it was then that one realised that the theatre could be about something serious. And one knew that absolutely instantaneously when the curtain went up on *Mother Courage*, and you saw her pulling the wagon round the stage, and they sang the song. You knew that it was quite different and that they'd thought about the moment, and the way they sang the song, and the way it was presented. It was immediately clear that the theatre was being used for some kind of purpose, unlike anything that we'd ever seen before, whether that was aesthetic or political didn't seem to be really definable. In fac, it was both: I mean, the two are obviously very closely interlocked, and I still think that.

When did you first see the Berliner Ensemble?

I didn't see the Ensemble till they came to London in 1956. Of course, 1956 was also the year in which the Royal Court opened, so the two events more or less coincided. And the two things became very significant simultaneously.

Which productions did you see then?

Mother Courage, *The Caucasian Chalk Circle* and *Trumpets and Drums*.

You directed Mother Courage *at the National Theatre several years later, and you did the production from Brecht's 'model book', the photographic record, moment by moment, of his Berliner Ensemble production. Why did you do that?*

I suppose because I really didn't think it could be bettered. I didn't have any kind of desire to rethink it. I think now that was a mistake, not because the model book was wrong, but because I didn't take the actors with me. I mean, there's no point in doing that unless somehow the actors belong to an ensemble and have an approach to the work: then it makes sense. But it seemed ridiculous to impose it on a group of actors who had no real feeling. Looking back on it, I don't think any of the productions I did of Brecht really had the sort of vitality that they should have had.

But was that because you were so in awe of the original productions?

I suppose so, yes.

What did you learn from Brecht?

I learned most of all, I suppose, the use of space, the sense of the empty stage: that everything on the stage should be essential, and there should be nothing unnecessary—which didn't mean that it shouldn't be rich or colourful or vital— and the use of space should be not just for aesthetic reasons but to make political moral points, if you like. That was a complete eye-opener to me. And I think it has been with me ever since—rather to a fault, they say! You know: 'The work is twenty-six boards and no passion.' But I feel the excitement when the stage is empty and you put an actor onto it, and a piece of furniture or a prop: you already are in a dramatic situation of tremendous importance and relevance. That was a complete eye-opener to me; I'd never understood that before. And ever since then I've not seen theatre any other way. I've always thought: start with the empty stage and work from there.

That's close to Peter Brook's epigram. But you don't share Peter's aesthetic, do you?

No, because I suppose I have quite deep down a sense that theatre might have a moral purpose rather than, if you like, a didactic purpose. I don't think Brook would reject that. One reason, for instance, why I did *Courage* like the model book was that there are certain groupings on the stage which mean one thing and one thing only; if you alter them it means something different. If you put a chair in the middle of the stage it means one thing; if you move it to the side it means another.

When I saw the Berliner Ensemble productions ten years later, having boned up on all the theory, what struck me was the simplicity and truthfulness of the acting.

Yes, yes.

And intensely moving. Did you find that?

Well, yes, but in a very odd way. I mean, the bit where [Helene] Weigel [as Mother Courage] crosses the stage with that fake smile and looks at the boy [the body of her dead son] and then turns round and the corners of the mouth drop completely was absolutely artificial. In no sense was she identifying with the mother's feelings; she was presenting a series of fixed masks to represent that emotion. And even so, it was very powerful and in an odd way very moving, but her method of achieving that was not at all what Edith Evans would have done, for instance.

It was cold-hearted.

Well, I think it was ruthless.

Would you say that Brecht's method as a director was ruthlessly dictatorial?

Oh yes, I'm sure, yes. Of course, in his first company he had people already very experienced, but I think the younger actors became absolutely controlled by him.

When did you meet Helene Weigel?

When we were starting the National Theatre. Olivier and his wife, with Ken Tynan, John Dexter and I, went over to Berlin, really to look at the ensemble as a model of an exciting European theatre which we all admired. We wanted very much to see how it was run, and Weigel entertained us and, of course, made a lot of propaganda out of Larry being there.

Did you watch the company rehearse?

No, we only saw them perform.

And the theatre: what did you think of that theatre?

Oh, it was, of course… it's a marvellous theatre, a marvellous, heavily baroque theatre. A lot of the greatest experimental theatres have been made in wonderful old buildings like the Royal Court and the Old Vic.

And so there is some creative tension between the architecture and—

Yes.

—the aesthetic.

Yes, absolutely.

What do you think Brecht's influence in this country has been?

He obviously influenced a great deal of staging and design. I guess the Peter Brook *Lear*, the RSC *Wars of the Roses*, all that is completely Brecht-influenced. Certainly Jocelyn Herbert's work at the Royal Court. In the actual look of theatre and its staging, unquestionably. Politically, we did a play with a group called Joint Stock—*Fanshen* by David Hare—which was about the Chinese Revolution: I guess that was the most Brechtian thing that I ever did. But I think Brecht was a poet. I don't know German, but he was probably a great poet. And one of the most remarkable things about the plays are the songs and the poetry in them. Hardly any writer nowadays is a poet. David Hare is not a poet—the last thing he is is a poet. You can reproduce everything else, but you can't reproduce the lyric element, and that, I think, is crucial to our understanding of Brecht.

His minimalism—or the minimalism that you translated into your minimalism and Jocelyn Herbert's minimalism—has become a sort of common syntax of theatre.

Well, not very common: it's already wildly old-fashioned, isn't it?

Some of it, I suppose. The other contribution that you referred to was that he took the theatre seriously.

We'd always been looking for someone to lead us into serious theatre, and he certainly did that. Later on there were all sorts of other influences. I think the American influence is very important—and how that got all mixed up with the English radical tradition. But I don't think that actually was very Brechtian. And there was Joan Littlewood, but I'm sure Joan would never claim really to have been influenced by Brecht, though perhaps she was. She'd evolved her own way of looking at theatre from the radical days of the thirties, of which Brecht may have been part, but it grew out of something much more indigenous. The interesting thing about Brecht is that the underlying feeling of the plays is very sombre. There's something really romantically tragic underneath the Brecht plays, and the feeling that gets you is not: 'We must go out and change the world.' But I think we hoped it would be, and we tried to make it that.

So, in that sense, Beckett and Brecht are really quite close together in sensibility.

Yes, I think that's true. Of course, Brecht was an intellectual and would have fought any such concept. But I think there is something... There's no natural division, really.

When were you first aware of Beckett's work?

I was in weekly rep with Harold Pinter, and he used to speak about this writer who was influencing him. It sounded like a load of absolute rubbish to me.

Was this 1956, after Godot *had been on at the Arts?*

No, before. I think Harold knew of his work before then. I think he'd read the novels.

And what did you think when you first saw Godot?

I thought it was wonderful. It didn't have a huge impact on me. I didn't think 'Oh, this is going to change my life' or anything, because one didn't know where

else it would go; it seemed like a dead end, really. And then George Devine did
Endgame at the Court, and, yes, it was remarkable and all that, but one never
thought that it would become central in the way that we thought Brecht was
central.

What was 'remarkable' and 'wonderful'?

I suppose the language really—the sense of the language not being poetic in any
traditional sense but in the choice of words, and their juxtaposition making a
kind of different sense.

*You didn't think here is somebody who has decided to use the theatre in a way that is quite
new—like a painter?*

No, I didn't think that. It took me a long time to realise that at all. I thought it
was marginal in the way that, say, when we first saw Merce Cunningham, that
was also a revelation: but how it was applicable, one never quite knew. And I still
don't quite know.

What did George Devine see in Beckett?

George loved the French, loved the fact that Beckett wrote in French. And there
was something about Beckett's incredible authority as a writer which George
just responded to. But I don't think it became part of all our work. In fact, it's
only much more recently that I've felt its absolute centrality to the last fifty years
of the twentieth century—where you suddenly think: oh yes, the writer is
Beckett.

*Do you buy this thesis of Peter Hall's that there are the Brechtians and the Beckettians, and
it's the Beckettians who will have had the greater influence on the theatre?*

Obviously Beckett's had an influence on Pinter, and Pinter has survived very
well. I think in general it's true that Beckett is in and Brecht is out. The length
of Brecht plays—the massive scale of them, the epic quality if you like—is not
something any longer that we can quite digest. Something about it now creaks,
whereas we demand things which are more concentrated and more compressed,
which last an hour and a quarter and which you can sit through without an
interval. Our whole attitude to what makes a work of art in that sense has altered.

But is part of the allure of Beckett the total distillation, the minimalism?

I think it's the metaphor for hopelessness, for despair, which we respond to. And
we don't respond to writers who have a positive belief in the future. I think it's
as simple as that. Particularly after the fall of Communism. We've lost our
idealism. Perhaps it wasn't very strong, if it could go so easily.

Did Beckett encourage writers to think: I don't have to have four walls, I don't have to have plot. Two blokes stand on stage and talk about nothing, the moon comes up, the moon goes down?

No, I think writers just got lazy. Writers started writing plays for television, and when they weren't accepted by television, they would do them for the stage—and pretend they were epic plays, because they took place in lots of different venues.

What was your attitude to Joan Littlewood's work?

We were rather envious of some of their dedication: she had a group of actors who worked for almost nothing and lived in the theatre and were completely part of the same work and did improvisations together. They were a kind of theatre that we in a way wished we could be, but at the same time knew that we couldn't. I remember once being in the bar at Stratford East [where Littlewood's Theatre Workshop was based], and Gerry Raffles, who was the Theatre Workshop manager, said of me: 'Oh, look, the enemy is here.' And Joan Littlewood said the most marvellous thing: 'Gerry, there are so few people who love the theatre that we can't quarrel amongst ourselves, can we?' Which was a bit rich coming from her, I know, but it was very emotional and direct.

But she wrote viciously about George Devine.

I know, but she's like that, isn't she? She was capable of great warmth.

But did she think that she was neglected?

Obviously she was treated abominably by the Arts Council—she didn't have a subsidy. I thought the saddest thing was that, when she became commercially successful—because *Oh! What a Lovely War* was tremendously successful—having to maintain it lost the very tight, very concentrated group that she'd had at Stratford East.

Did you ever feel corrupted by success at the Royal Court?

No, we were never successful enough to be corrupted. We didn't have enough integrity to be corrupted, you know.

How did the English Stage Company start?

I wasn't in on the very beginning; I didn't really join till after about a year. But I was a close friend of Tony Richardson and met George Devine, of course. It originally started as an attempt to create a serious ensemble theatre, such as you might have in Europe. They would do those plays that had never been done, the sort of plays that are now done at the Almeida—the Wedekinds and the Lorcas, all those what I call 'Eric Bentley' plays. And perhaps encourage new writing as well. But there was no new writing: it was very much a stab in the dark. We said: we want new plays, but whether they would come or not, we didn't know. But they arrived, and then the fact that they arrived altered the whole nature of what it would be, you know. Also the idea of it being an ensemble with a directorial style went out of the window because the plays were so different and so varied. We were going to do a West Indian play [*Skyvers* by Barry Reckord, 1963], and therefore we had to find black actors. We hadn't ever had a play with a group of black actors before. So immediately you had to make new decisions depending on the plays that were written. Any play that we liked, we did. So, immediately after the success of Osborne, there was a flood of writers for whom the Royal Court was the only theatre that would do their plays. That was very exciting, you know. Every year you would say: 'What's John on?' 'He's writing a new play.' 'What's it like? What's it about?' The excitement was tremendous. It lasted for about four or five years, and then gradually, of course, the other people started doing new plays. The National and the RSC were formed, and other theatres started doing modern plays. So the Royal Court lost its absolute focus, but for a time it was the only theatre where an exciting writer could have his plays done.

What did you think when you first saw Look Back in Anger?

I thought it was shattering, really, but I read it before I saw it. I was excited by the language more than anything else. I thought the language was so amazing—the richness and the violence of the rhetoric, which now may seem nowhere near as strong, but then seemed wonderfully different in kind. Here was somebody who was speaking quite personally with passion. Terence Rattigan doesn't speak with passion about anything, really. Of course it was socially critical in a way but in a very anarchistic way. But the actual passion of it was what excited us.

But there had been tremendously passionate writers in the English language—O'Neill, Odets, Williams, Miller—who'd all been seen in London.

Yes, but Osborne was an English writer. Arthur Miller came to the Royal Court and said the English theatre was hermetically sealed; and it was true. We thought the style and the elegance would come from France and the passion would come from America. So it was important that there was an English writer.

How did you find out about Edward Bond?

Very early on, George Devine started a writers' group, which was to meet every week and discuss and share ideas. George handed it over to me. The group of writers were very, very keen. They included [John] Arden and [Arnold] Wesker and Ann Jellicoe, Keith Johnstone and Wole Soyinka, and one or two others. We decided that we wouldn't work on the plays that were being written; we would work on theatrical exploration. So we did a lot of improvisation. One week we would work on what we thought was Brechtian theory. And one week we would work on masks, and so on. The writers were exploring different ways of making theatre. If it fed into their work, well and good; if not, it didn't matter. All those writers who'd written plays which had not yet been done but which we thought were interesting were invited to join the group. And one of those was Edward Bond, a very silent, taciturn, young man whose origins were a mystery as he spoke very little about himself, but he was obviously very, very serious, and took part in all the improvisations with total dedication. And then eventually his first play was done on a Sunday night [in the smaller Theatre Upstairs].

Which was?

The Pope's Wedding [1962]. That was in George's time. The important thing about the Court was the continuity. When I took over in 1965, I went on working with those writers who had been discovered by George Devine. That seemed to be part of the process. Certain writers were only really developed by the Court over a period of time—the last one to be done regularly was Christopher Hampton. After that, writers started hawking their plays round to whoever would take them. But to begin with, a writer would come to the Court, and his first three, four, five plays would be done at the Court.

What was the genesis of Saved?

It was commissioned. But I said: if I don't like it, I'll do *The Pope's Wedding* in the main bill. But *Saved* arrived, and I immediately liked it. I said: 'Oh yes, this is the play I want to do.' But why or how he came to write it, apart from the fact that it was a commission, I don't know.

And is there a sense in which you would say this is the fruits of a man who's looked at Brecht or looked at Beckett? Some of his plays—like Narrow Road to the Deep North—*almost seem like a pastiche of Brecht. Did you talk with Edward about influences?*

He always had a very clear idea about how it would look on the stage and how it should be staged. He accepted completely that there should be no scenery, or minimal scenery. That was written into the stage directions. I've never seen it done any other way, really. I suppose he must have got some of that from Brecht. But not from Beckett, I think.

What happened with Early Morning?

Well, *Saved* [staged in 1965] was the subject of a court case because it was banned by the censor—or major scenes were banned by the censor—and so we did it under what we thought was a legal protection, which was as a theatre club. But it was considered not: we were taken to court and were found guilty.

You weren't sent to prison.

We weren't sent to prison but fined £50 costs. I think that was all.

The offence in Saved was the scene of the stoning of the baby?

And one other scene between the boy and the mother.

What was it specifically that was felt to be offensive?

Well, in the scene with the boy and the mother it was that it had sexual implications which were unacceptable, and with the stoning of the baby it was its violence and partly its language—not so much its language, mainly the violence of it. The whole scene was banned. But when we came to do *Early Morning* [1968], which was a strange sort of fantasy piece about Queen Victoria having a lesbian relationship with Florence Nightingale amongst many other things—the last act was set in heaven—the play was banned outright. That was very unusual: to have a play banned completely. Normally you would have indications of certain passages or certain scenes. But the Chamberlain said: the whole play's banned. We thought it was mainly because it was about royalty. The Lord Chamberlain, whose main job was looking after the royal household (and so he was, of course, quite close to the Royal Family), would not have wanted to offend them. And the thought of Queen Victoria having a lesbian affair was obviously revolting to everybody. They were very intolerant. But we decided we would go ahead and do some single private performances of it.

It aroused extraordinarily powerful emotions in Parliament and within the theatrical profession, didn't it?

Yes, but the theatre for a brief period of time was very central to people's lives. It was headline news. I don't think anything that happens in the theatre has that centrality now, I don't think so at all. When John Osborne wrote [his open letter] 'Damn You England', it was major news; and the banning of a play at the Royal Court and the police being in the theatre was known by everybody.

The major news now is when The Lion King *gets a three-million-pound advance. I had just started working in the theatre then but was very conscious of this group of people at the Royal Court who were extraordinarily combative and strong in their views. How had that come about?*

I think because we'd been attacked by the censor, and by the critics, so we felt all the time everyone was against us and the only way was to close ranks. We were genuinely embattled, but after a time we became paranoid. Funnily enough, I think that when the censor disappeared [1968], something went out of our lives. We didn't have anything to fight any more, you know.

So did you then move the battleground to, as it were, aesthetic grounds? The scorn the Royal Court had for the Royal Shakespeare Company's work, for instance, was really quite legendary. Things mattered then in a way that they don't matter now. Nowadays it's hard to imagine that people's lives are at stake in the way it seemed that it was for you then.

Well, now you've said it, haven't you?

When you were running the Royal Court, what were your feelings about the theatre in general?

When you're running a theatre you don't think very much about anything except running a theatre—you don't need me to tell you that. You want it to go in a certain way, but you can't control it. You are finally at the mercy of what plays are written, and to some extent the kind of directors you have and the response they have to the plays. I was still haunted by the idea of having a company and an ensemble, which is almost impossible to maintain if you want to concentrate on new writing. Every director at some point wants to evolve some kind of style, but finally it's not what it's about. What it's about is what the writer is trying to say.

And does that become increasingly difficult?

Yes, yes, it does, it does.

Arnold Wesker

1 9 3 2—

Playwright. Arnold Wesker's plays include The Kitchen, *his trilogy*—Chicken Soup with Barley, Roots *and* I'm Talking About Jerusalem—Chips with Everything, Shylock, Love Letters on Blue Paper *and many more. He was very politically engaged in the sixties with CND and with a campaign for making the arts accessible to working-class audiences, which led to the foundation of Centre 42. He organised festivals and raised funds to convert a disused railway shed into a theatre venue: it became the Roundhouse. He has long regarded himself as a combative outsider in British theatre, railing against the power of directors—including me. Although I produced* Chips with Everything *at the National Theatre I had, in his view, been blind to the qualities of his later work. In his autobiography he indicted me: 'The "powers-that-be" give you the power to be, not us, no one judges your work before it has been seen by a public as you judge ours before the public has seen it.' But when he came to my house to be interviewed he was charming and emollient: he brought me a bunch of flowers.*

What was your apprenticeship?

I wanted to be a film director and I worked in this kitchen in Paris and saved up enough money for six months' study at the London School of Film Technique where I met Lindsay Anderson and he read *Chicken Soup with Barley* and said: 'You really are a playwright, aren't you?' He put it to the Court, and the Court turned it down and gave it to the Belgrade Theatre in Coventry, who did it for a week there and then brought it to the Court.

211

You were in very good company because Harold Pinter was turned down by the Royal Court. Why do you think they didn't go for it?

I owe the Royal Court everything in the end, but they turned down all the plays. They commissioned *Roots* and then wanted me to rewrite it thinking that Ronnie ought to appear and I said I think you've missed the point, and I thought that was the end of my playwriting career. Peggy Ashcroft read it and loved it and said Joan [Plowright] had to do it. *The Kitchen* they thought couldn't work because it had thirty-one people on stage all doing work. I've often wondered whether there was just a tone of voice in the plays that was alien to them. I thought it may be a Jewish tone of voice, but I don't know, one would have to really dissect it very closely to identify what it was, but they weren't comfortable with me, and I can remember John Dexter saying: you know, you've no idea how they talk about you—and me. I think also because we weren't university boys. It didn't worry me—it seemed to me that writing plays was kind of better than anything, but I think they did view me with, not suspicion, but as a certain upstart that didn't quite belong.

What inspired you to write Chicken Soup with Barley?

My family. It's the story of my mother, my father, my sister and me. As *Roots* is the story of Dusty, my wife, and her family and *Talking About Jerusalem* is the story of my sister and brother-in-law, who lived that life out in the country. I don't have great powers of invention. I used to say I don't have much imagination, but that isn't strictly speaking true—I do have a sort of imagination but I'm not very good at inventing.

And what were your playwriting models?

I didn't have any—the cinema was my model, which is why I wanted to be a film director. I used to go to the movies, we couldn't afford the theatre, and the only theatre I saw was the plays that the amateur company to which I belonged put on and those in which I performed. That was really the extent of my theatregoing experience.

Did you do the West End plays—Coward and Rattigan, for instance?

Yes, we did because I played in Rattigan. I played Taplow in *The Browning Version*.

Were you good?

I wasn't bad actually. [*laughs*]

How did you first hear of Look Back in Anger?

While I was a student at the London School of Film Technique it came to the theatre in Streatham and I suppose we went to see it because we'd all heard about it. Watching it I thought: yeah, this is where things are happening.

Because?

It had an energy. It had an energy that I found familiar—I mean, if only those Sunday bells... I'd written a story in which I'd observed the maddening sound of Sunday morning bells while I was working in the Bell Hotel in Norwich. I don't know what you think *Look Back in Anger* is about, but it seemed to me a love story and a very passionate love story and a play that seemed to care about the sort of old-fashioned values like loyalty and compassion and friendship. And I think all these things touched me, and, of course, what touched me was what touched everybody. There was just a freshness about it. It wasn't an original play in terms of structure, any more than my trilogy was original. They were old-fashioned three-act plays. But I suppose we were young and there was a freshness about the way we were looking at the world. The ending of the play worried me. It seemed a little twee and sentimental about rabbits, squirrels, and I felt something stronger was needed to end the play. There was a feebleness about it.

Did you miss a political sensibility in the play?

I had a political background—I mean, my parents were members of the Communist party and I had aunts and uncles who were members of the Communist party and my aunt Sarah, who's one of the characters in the trilogy, was one of the first women trade-union organisers. She was a very fiery, dynamic woman. I was very concerned about my parents and the way they quarrelled, and I had a sense of the family breaking up over the years and what struck me was that here was a family breaking up against a background of a political ideology breaking up.

Your plays have a Socialist agenda in the sense that they argue that the working class are badly treated and given second-rate treatment.

That's a perception that has no foundation if you actually look at the plays. I've personally been very ambivalent about the British working class and, without going into details, you can see that there is this ambivalence in all the plays. I imagined that I was a Socialist. I wasn't a joiner. I was never a member of a political party. I think between the age of fifteen and sixteen for about six months I was a member of the Young Communist League, but I'm not very good as a committee man or in a team and I really couldn't submit to party discipline. But I always thought I was a Socialist until that word just began to be meaningless.

You were you a member of CND?

A member of CND and subsequently the Committee of a Hundred, which was the follow-on from CND, and had this rather embarrassing month in prison— I say embarrassing because when you think of all the people who have spent lifetimes in prison, it was kind of silly. But, you see, even with CND, with the Committee of a Hundred, after that month in prison I said we must now all resign because we shouldn't create heroes and anyway the next sentences will be twice as severe. But no one agreed with me and the result was that people did go to prison the second time for much longer periods and one woman hung herself in Holloway jail. I was never someone that could be relied upon to go with the majority.

You were described as an 'angry young man'.

It's a dreadful phrase, isn't it? I mean, you've read John's autobiography and he explains how the line came up. This journalist attached to the Court invented that line. I keep getting asked this question wherever I travel around the world. 'Are you still an angry young man, Mr Wesker?' and I have to say I never was an angry young man, none of us were angry, we were all very happy. We were successful, earning money, people were taking notice of us.

It must have been flattering to be thought of as part of sort of a vanguard?

What was flattering was having one's plays done. I was very conscious of the danger ahead and right from the beginning I was saying: you know, this is not a revolution, it's just a cycle, we're part of a cycle, it happens this way. I don't know why it happens, I don't know if anyone has ever written a book explaining why there was a period of Italian cinema, a period of the English novel, the thirties poets, but that's the way it seems to happen. I was always very worried that I would be very quickly dismissed because I was very conscious of what had happened to the thirties poets and I thought: I don't want to be sent down that road. And so I struggled all the time against the notion that we were just a group of angry young men who would come and go.

What was the climate at the Court like?

It was exciting—the excitement of *Roots* being done at the Belgrade Coventry, moments I shall never forget: the first night at Coventry, with the cast doing exactly what John [Dexter] had rehearsed them to do—don't be pushed by the audience to go faster than this slow pace—and then came the first laugh and he turned to me and there were tears in his eyes. It was happening, and then the next morning after the reviews, George Devine negotiating with Brian Bailey to bring it to the Royal Court Theatre—I mean, these were heady days. Then *The Kitchen* being done for a Sunday-night production. I wasn't there on the first Sunday night because my father had died but the second Sunday night just sitting in the audience—they had seen *Roots* and you got a sense that people were here knowing that something exciting was going to happen, and this was true for almost every one of the players at the time. There were hiccups—I can remember Dusty [his wife] was in George Devine's little room giving the breast to our firstborn, and this disturbed George and he said to someone outside: 'For God's sake get that woman out of my office suckling this child'—which seemed very odd considering who George was. I mean, George was a gentleman. He was paternal. I can remember my mother, who was very fussy about people, adored him and we took him to the Yiddish theatre, which he'd never seen. It was quite a revelation for him—dreadful theatre, awful, awful theatre, but it was sort of exotic and he was interested. The great thing about George was that he was prepared to let other people's enthusiasm take over and this would apply to writers as well as directors.

When he said he wouldn't do Chips with Everything *what reasons did he give for not doing it?*

I can't remember. He didn't like it, didn't think it could work. I don't even know. Maybe there exists a letter—they've all gone off to Texas now [where Wesker's papers are now held].

Why was the Royal Court so combative with its rivals?

I don't remember feeling that or sharing a view that the Court was above all—I don't see how you could do with Joan Littlewood and her incredible achievements. You know, it's often forgotten. The Court's credited with this so-called revolution which really wasn't a revolution, but before the Court there was Joan Littlewood.

Did you know Joan?

Not seriously. I think she was very worried about me—the way she liked to work was with a very unfinished script. Whereas there are always changes in rehearsals in my plays, I couldn't be as unfinished as she would have liked. The first one I saw was *A Taste of Honey* [by Shelagh Delaney]. I loved it. It seemed to me that here was a play that was about five outsiders, really, and it wasn't treated sensationally. It was lovely and innocent and very moving. *Lion in Love,* her next play, was flawed and not as successful as *Taste of Honey*, but much more ambitious and I thought the critics were very cruel. She was trying to do something more, which is what one expects of writers, to not stand still. I was sorry that she was clobbered for *Lion in Love* and didn't really do anything much after that.

You say that there wasn't a revolution and if there was, it had occurred before with Joan Littlewood's Theatre Workshop. Surely you can say that the working-class voice or the non-received-pronunciation voice actually got into the theatre for more or less the first time?

Well, there was Sean O'Casey and there were the Victorians. I suppose I tend to think of cinema. You know, American and British cinema were full of working-class types. I wasn't conscious when I was writing that I was putting working-class people on the stage. I was simply recreating my experience or that part of my experience which seemed to me might have resonance. Far more unusual—as far as my play is concerned—is that I actually took Communists seriously and although they're severely criticised in *Chicken Soup* there is a history of idealism there which had to be respected. There is another aspect—and it's very difficult to say this—but there's a sense in which although there is a Jewish working class and there was certainly Jewish poverty, the Jews were never really working-class in the sense of the British working class were working-class, because they cared passionately about the arts and literature and politics and you found that only in small bastions of the British working class like the Welsh miners or Nottingham miners or Scottish miners. So I just didn't think that I was writing working-class plays.

Maybe nobody ever does think 'I'm smashing the mould' but it is true that British theatre was in a sort of cocoon as compared to the American theatre. So even if you didn't think you were breaking new ground, a new voice came into the theatre.

One's very pleased to have a new voice but you're right, one isn't conscious, I certainly wasn't conscious of smashing moulds. I don't know if you read the article in the *New York Times* that said that what we were really smashing was the homosexual group of playwrights of Rattigan and Coward, which seemed to me very silly.

You weren't stamping on the reputations of Coward and Rattigan?

The accusation that our generation was trying to stamp on a homosexual elite is sort of crazy. I was very naive. I don't think I was aware that Coward was gay or Rattigan was gay. Anyway, I'd subsequently developed a nice relationship with Coward, who I went to see in Switzerland because I wanted him to help with Centre 42 and it was a glorious encounter. We had dinner—it was the first time I'd ever been anywhere where someone unpacked my case for me—and I think I had fondue for the first time in my life. And then he took me away to his room—I think his boyfriend had travelled down with me—and he threw a whole number of questions 'Are you gay?', 'Are you married?', 'Are you happily married?', 'Do you have children?', bang bang bang, and I gave the right replies, and then finally he said: 'Dear boy, I would not dream of helping you with those dreary Centre 42 festivals. You were born with talent, you're wasting your time—like me. I was born with talent, I was born with bags of talent,' which was him being the *enfant terrible*. Then some weeks later he wrote an article in which he suggested that I was being insulting to those people in the provinces who had come to see plays. I mean, he was full of contradictions, he was a worried man, but a lovely charming man and he finally came to the show that I had wanted him to give his support to, and then, of course, he was in *The Kitchen*, that fundraising event [at the Royal Court for one night]. Rattigan became a friend of Centre 42, he gave us his name along with many others. There's this biography that's just been written about him in which the author says that Rattigan wrote a nice letter to me about *Chicken Soup with Barley* and that I was rude back. I have no memory of this—it's just not my style to be rude in that way. And the fact that he became a friend of Centre 42 suggests that there was nothing untoward in our relationship. I think I admired Rattigan more than Coward. Even now I have difficulty—his songs are incredibly witty, wonderful songs, but the plays... I sort of wince at the lightness and sometimes the silliness of them.

Peter Gill

1 9 3 9—

Director and playwright. Peter Gill's plays include Small Change, Mean Tears *and* Cardiff East. *He became an Assistant Director at the Royal Court Theatre in 1964 and then an Associate Director in 1970. He was the founder director of Riverside Studios in 1976, became Associate Director of the National Theatre in 1980 and was the founding Director of the National Theatre Studio in 1984. His productions of the D.H. Lawrence Trilogy—*A Collier's Friday Night, The Daughter-in-Law *and* The Widowing of Mrs Holroyd—*at the Royal Court in 1968 formed one of the landmarks of post-war theatre. I interviewed Peter Gill in his flat on the top floor of a house in Hammersmith on the edge of the Thames.*

What's remarkable about Lawrence's plays?

I think the fact that he uniquely represented what they call the 'working class'—or used to—as the heroes of their own lives; but they weren't a Fabian or liberal cause for him. He's writing about the Hamlets of their own lives.

Was Lawrence the first English writer to write truthfully about the working class?

He was probably the first English *playwright* to write truthfully about the working class. Nobody had written like that: making no apology for why you were writing about them. He wrote about these apparently poor people as something he wanted to write about, not something he had to write about. So it's not from a class position: it's from a position of equality—though funnily enough in *The Daughter-in-Law* he's writing about a class slightly lower than the one he writes about in *A Collier's Friday Night*, which is why it's more heavily in dialect than some of the others.

All the plays are written in Nottinghamshire dialect?

One of my views on why *The Daughter-in-Law* took particularly long to be performed is that, when I first read it, it was like reading Lallans Scots. I think people were always put off because it was a hard read.

What do you find surprising about Lawrence's plays?

That it's a poet writing a realistic play. It's as if Ted Hughes wrote a realistic play—except Lawrence was a better poet than Ted Hughes. It was as if Yeats wrote a realistic play. It's a complete collision of astonishment.

Why would a novelist—or a poet—decide to write for the theatre?

Because of the power that Shakespeare had on our country, everybody of any talent wrote a play—except Jane Austen and the Brontës: unfortunately the women didn't. I'm not certain that George Eliot didn't write one, but Wordsworth wrote a play, Shelley wrote a play, Conrad wrote a play. It was only Bloomsbury that put the stop to that. They sort of despised the theatre, if it wasn't the Ballets Russes. But Lawrence loved the theatre.

But there was nothing in the theatre that was like what he wanted to write?

I think he wanted to write for no reason but that he wanted to write a play and that he was free. I can't think of any other reason.

Shaw was writing plays about working-class people and even had working-class characters in his work. In what way were Lawrence's characters different from Shaw's?

For Shaw they were there to prove a point. In *Major Barbara* in the second act they're rather beautifully realised in the Dickensian manner. They were minor characters, amusing, slightly caricatured.

What happens in Lawrence's plays?

The perfection of *A Collier's Friday Night* is that he simply tells, in narrative form, the story of this particular evening—a Friday night, which is pay night in a collier's home. It's constantly in movement, constantly active, although the actions are minute. Of course, it did relate to his novels because *A Collier's Friday Night* is almost word for word a chapter from *Sons and Lovers*.

What physical actions occur in his play?

They're all domestic, they're all things that people couldn't have seen and that have very rarely been seen on a British stage—certainly not in the West End. I mean, there have been no kitchen sinks on the West End stage. I've only ever seen one, which was when Arnold Wesker's *Roots* transferred briefly to the Duke of York's Theatre from the Royal Court. I defy anybody to tell me that they've ever seen a kitchen sink in any theatre in Shaftesbury Avenue. They [Lawrence's plays] were domestic scenes of bread-baking, laying of tables, the ironing of shirts, the washing of miners' bodies, the washing of dead miners' bodies, the putting of children to bed, the doing of homework, the making of tea. Our generation thought we'd invented this sort of theatre through a kind of imitation of American and French realism, and then we found out to our astonishment we'd had this playwright all along.

Lawrence was a revolutionary in the sense that, like Ibsen, he put women at the centre of plays. What are the characteristics of his female characters? What are their qualities?

Lawrence's women? Well, they are powers in their homes, but there's a paradox because they seem to be more powerful while being politically unemancipated. When I did the plays, at one time I found that the actresses weren't living up to the strength of the characters. So I did an exercise in which the men sat in the auditorium and the women had to stand on the stage. And the men had to tell the women how the women had no power, in the process of which the actresses got rather angry and took on that curious Lawrentian quality of being powerfully enraged by their impotence and yet having an influence, particularly on their sons. I suppose it's a class situation—they had to be powerful or life couldn't have gone on. People often say that the miners' strike—Mrs Thatcher's strike—was the first time women were active, but that's nonsense. In 1926 how could the men in South Wales, where I come from, have stayed out of work without their wives' backing? Those women were always powerful. Lawrence documented it without being conscious that that's what he was doing; that's what makes him so brilliant. The women are not ciphers; they're not there to prove a point.

Does Lawrence sentimentalise the women at all?

No. He's a Romantic writer.

What do you mean by that?

He comes from a tradition that comes through from Shakespeare through all the writers that went before him. But he's not in any way a kind of Tennysonian. He's an English Puritan Romantic, that's the only way I can put it. A bit like George Eliot's feeling for women.

Is it justified to call them heroines?

Oh yes, they're heroines, they're definitely heroines. Whatever anyone says about him, women were clearly very important to him, so that's what he wrote about. And he writes about a variety of women—there are some wonderfully drawn women comic characters in his plays. They're not all tortured and wronged. They're terrifically good parts for actresses to play. You get a sense in Chekhov that he really loved women, but slightly thought they were silly. And Ibsen had this extraordinary relationship to women but what's he writing about? He's obviously writing about his relationship with women and he almost *is* them, isn't he?

Why were the plays neglected for years?

Well, it's a terribly unfashionable thing to say, but it's a sort of English self-hatred, right? It's simply class-based—you're not supposed to say this in Tony Blair's world. Some of them were tentatively done, but it would have been like asking a West End manager to put on an African folk play. It was beyond the pale that you could have a woman like Minnie Gascoigne or Mrs Holroyd or the mother in *A Collier's Friday Night* or the girls in *The Merry-Go-Round* as leading characters. Who would have played them?

But O'Casey's plays were performed in England pretty soon after they'd been written and then were consistently revived. What's the difference between O'Casey's treatment of the working class and Lawrence's treatment of the working class?

I think that O'Casey, like most of the Irish writers, has a slightly satirical line—Lawrence is not a ironist in that sense. His characters, as I said, are the Hamlets of their own lives. Of course, had he been Irish, he'd have been safe. Lady Gregory and Yeats would have put the plays on: they would have been about the Irish at a time when the Irish had to be listened to. But the English working class didn't have to be listened to except as creatures to be patronised. I recently was asked to do a play of J.B. Priestley, and I had to send it back because it said: '*Enter a maid of all works, note very well that she is not to be patronised.*' Now, I admire Priestley for saying it, but I don't want to be part of anything like that. In *An Inspector Calls*, Priestley doesn't write about the main character, she's not in the play. Who could have played her? There has to be a middle-class family, whereas the actual tragedy has happened to a girl who is never seen.

Put aside the issue that the English are always going to be interested in Ireland because of guilt, are you saying that what Lawrence lacked was a producer?

I don't know what happened. They did do a sort of tour of *The Daughter-in-Law*, altered by Walter Greenwood, which Sybil Thorndike was in. It had another title—a line from the play which I can't remember—which immediately diminished the play. And there was a reading or some kind of Sunday night performance of *The Widowing of Mrs Holroyd*. Nobody knew about *A Collier's Friday Night* until I discovered it by accident.

You did the three plays—A Collier's Friday Night, The Daughter-in-Law *and* The Widowing of Mrs Holroyd—*in repertoire. What was the reaction to them?*

It was a sort of astonishment. People couldn't bear it, they cried so much... The last scene in *Mrs Holroyd* is probably one of the great scenes in English. It may not be one of the great plays, but it's one of the great scenes: the wife is going to leave her husband, and he gets killed in an accident, and she and his mother are left to wash the body. We did it as they would have done it.

People were astonished by the physical reality.

I observed everything that Lawrence said we were to do, so I took enormously long pauses while people washed. There was a two-minute pause at one point when the younger brother in *The Daughter-in-Law* was in a rocking chair eating a piece of Yorkshire pudding, which he'd put jam on...

These were the stage directions?

I think that Lawrence imagined that they would take place offstage, and in my productions I let you see through to the kitchen. We took the wall away and they ate meals and cooked on the stage: that's always shocking. The thing about the theatre is that when somebody's stabbed you don't get shocked, but when somebody makes a cup of tea and drinks it, there's something very shockingly real about it.

The Lawrence plays were obviously very much in a great tradition at the Royal Court—from Granville Barker to George Devine. What was the significance of the foundation of the English Stage Company in 1956?

It was the beginning of what they call the sixties, which lasts from Suez to Mrs Thatcher's election. At the moment, people are reappraising and praising Rattigan and Coward without remembering that, at the time when I first came into the theatre, they wrote things like *South Sea Bubble*. I was in *Nude With Violin*—right?—and I saw Coward rehearse *Waiting in the Wings*. And Terence Rattigan wrote a terrible play called *Bequest to the Nation*. They were all done in the West End, and they had an element of going to tea with the Queen Mother about them—you felt the writers had been to Clarence House—and we weren't particularly interested in that. [*laughs*]

So what did George Devine and his writers bring to the theatre?

The war. You can never get away from the Second World War. George Devine had been in Burma, where he had had an experience that was very profound. He wanted a serious theatre—I don't mean a smug theatre or an unhumorous theatre. They didn't want an art theatre, they certainly didn't want a boulevard theatre: they wanted a serious theatre. They started with a more literary view— it was going to be a permanent company on a permanent set that was to represent the world, and on it would be literary works. It was called the English Stage Company because there had been something called the English Opera Company, which Benjamin Britten started. But this play by John Osborne came through the post and declared itself.

What is it about the stage of the Royal Court Theatre that encourages these radical plays?

Well, it's a stern stage, which is narrow and tall and quite deep and it sets you problems of sight lines, but figures look very beautiful on it. It's a Victorian theatre based on an eighteenth-century theatre, and therefore there's a wonderful dialectic, rather like the Berliner Ensemble's theatre in Berlin.

Do you think that Joan Littlewood's revolution was as important as what went on at the Royal Court?

Where Joan Littlewood differed from the Court was that her theatre was about one artist really: her. Whereas the Royal Court Theatre, under George Devine, was about a group of people. But what Joan had done, which the Court didn't do, was that she came out of the tradition of touring to places where people didn't have theatre. The Court was more metropolitan and, if you like, elitist. When I was a young man, the Court had much more affection for Theatre Workshop than Theatre Workshop had for the Court.

Did you regard the Court as upper-middle-class?

Yes. But then Joan was a bit of a figure in that respect, because she hung around with all the smarties in the Labour Party. If you were young at that period there were only two theatres that you wanted to belong to. George's theatre was more welcoming than Joan's, where to be working-class had to be an ostentatious statement. Somebody like me—who actually, for what it's worth, comes from a council estate and didn't look as though I had won the First War single-handed— I auditioned for Stratford East, but I wasn't her type of thing.

Do you think the theatre will endure?

Yes. Some form of live performance cannot but endure. What form it will take I don't know, but there's no way it can die. For one thing, paradoxically the theatre is, in its way, the least artificial art. It can't completely control the audience (which is rather why I'm against mic-ing actors). You can't cut away, as you can in a film. There will be always be an intuitive response between the audience and the play, and that's a sort of unique human experience. And the theatre is a moral art in a way. When you read *Sons and Lovers*, Lawrence is able to manipulate you, to make you feel what he wants you feel about the father. When I did *A Collier's Friday Night*, I had a wonderful actor playing the father, and the playwright couldn't make you dislike him: you just saw his tragedy as being equal to the mother's and the son's.

Christopher Hampton

1 9 4 6—

Playwright. Christopher Hampton was born in the Azores and lived for a while in Egypt, in Alexandria, where he set much of his autobiographical play White Chameleon, *which I directed at the National Theatre. His other plays include* The Philanthropist, Savages, Les Liaisons Dangereuses *and* Tales from Hollywood. *He was, for a while in the late sixties, the Literary Manager at the Royal Court. I interviewed him where he writes—a book-cluttered room in a flat at the top of a large late-Victorian mansion in Notting Hill.*

You were much too young to have been around for Look Back in Anger. How did you get into the Royal Court?

I got into the Royal Court really only because of Peggy Ramsay, my agent, who, when she received my first play and summoned me to London, said to me: 'How would you like to have your play done at the Royal Court, dear?' Well, I knew about the Royal Court, of course, so I said: 'Yes, I'd love to.' But what I didn't tell her, or indeed anyone at the Royal Court when I eventually met them, was that I had never seen a play there.

Did you know what the Royal Court represented?

Yes, I knew absolutely, and I particularly admired John Osborne and indeed anyone who'd cast an eye over my first play would see that I was not only an admirer but an imitator of John Osborne insofar as someone of such a different temperament as I am to his could possibly be. I imitated what seemed to me the energy of those plays, which we'd all read at school.

What was it about his work you so admired?

I loved its intemperance, really, and its energy and its unreasonableness. Its raw emotion. A lot has been made about how English John was, and how he virtually became a kind of embodiment of the Union Jack in later years, but what was un-English about him was this real energy of feeling.

And so when you did get taken up, did you feel that there was pressure on you to be a 'Royal Court writer'?

When I first came to work at the Royal Court, it was run by a triumvirate of directors: William Gaskill, Lindsay Anderson and Anthony Page. The three of them were such different personalities that in that period of time—it was the end of the sixties and the beginning of the seventies—the Royal Court was really rather eclectic in its tastes, although there were certain things that were outlawed, certain kinds of actors who had done very well on television—the place was rampant with prejudice of one kind or another. But there was in general a sort of embracing of more than one kind of play. And in particular a sort of system in which different writers started up relationships with different directors: Anthony Page with John Osborne, Lindsay Anderson with David Storey, Bill Gaskill with Edward Bond.

There were people who were acceptable and there were people who were absolutely beyond the pale. What fuelled that Calvinistic fervour?

I think what happened was that those people who were running the Court had had a difficult time in all sorts of ways. They'd come into a moribund institution—the theatre—and there'd been this huge struggle not only to do the kind of work that they were interested in, but also to do it without the interference of censors and nannies of one sort or another. The fact of the Lord Chamberlain shouldn't really be underestimated: people were threatened with prison, and there were police at the back of the auditorium, and all of that sort of thing. I can remember with my play *Total Eclipse* [1967], the police coming in to previews and so on. It was much more of a struggle for that particular generation than it was for us, because they'd fought all those battles, and then we strolled in and benefited from the work that they'd done. But it meant that they were very rigorous and sort of combative; there was a lot of conflict and shouting about what sort of work people should be doing. When, in later years, I went to work for the Royal Shakespeare Company, one of the things I found very mysterious about it was that everyone was so nice to one another. I didn't associate this with theatre at all. Theatre to me was people quarrelling in back corridors and absolutely condemning in terms of the most thoroughgoing contempt anybody who didn't agree with them. Those of us like myself and David Hare and Howard Brenton, who came in very young, I suppose one of the things we felt was that we had to somehow quarrel back in some kind of way.

Would you have been excommunicated if you'd expressed admiration for an RSC production?

We used to go to the RSC shows in small bands, and generally we left at the interval; it was much frowned upon if you expressed a wish to see the second half. [*chuckles*] And people would talk very loudly during the production. People would say: 'I can't follow the plot, can you?' when some piece of elaborate staging had obscured some point. As I now think back on it, one of the things that the Royal Court stood for was lucidity and plainness and a kind of austerity, which somehow I feel came to them through Beckett and George Devine and Jocelyn Herbert. It was felt that anything fancy, like people dressed in black and silver or standing on tables in jockstraps or whatever might be of the fashion of the day, was nothing to do with real theatre.

It was very anti-camp, wasn't it?

It was very serious, if that's the same thing. People were very, very rigorous in the way they thought of the staging of plays. I'm sure that also went back to Beckett's work as a director, which was so meticulous that famously actors were driven mad by the absolute necessity to pause here and not pause there, and breathe here and not breathe there. All of that was something new in the theatre, and something that people hung on to as a kind of talisman.

Were you influenced by Beckett in any way?

I had seen a school production of *Waiting for Godot*, which was not the best circumstances under which to see it for the first time. It did seem a rather long play, which I still think it is, actually. It slightly overstays its welcome in the theatre. It's one of those plays that reads wonderfully.

You mean that it's like a one-act play that's been extended?

No, because part of the point of it is the waiting. It seemed wonderfully original because it wasn't like anything else that had gone before, and it apparently had no social concerns at all. The mistake of Beckett imitators was to think you put two people on a park bench and that was all there was to it. But that seeming absence of social context didn't mean that it wasn't profoundly engaged with all the most important questions you could think of. What struck me most was that the work was as pessimistic as you could imagine, but on the other hand it was sort of bracing, simply because the language was deployed so brilliantly and the turns of phrase were so unusual. Of course, you should've been tipped the wink by the fact that he was a writer who wrote in two languages, which hardly anyone has ever been able to do. That should've alerted you to the fact that it was the language itself which somehow engaged his energy, and that the quality of the plays and the novels had to do with somebody who just used language in a more precise and imaginative way than practically any contemporary writer.

Isn't that true of all Irish writers, who are in a sense writing in two languages?

It's certainly true that for some reason Irish writers have a particular skill and relish for dialogue. There's any number of examples: in fact, if you're English, a dispiriting number of examples. Because I have a sort of remote Irish ancestry, I always try to pretend when I'm writing that I'm Irish. It has to do with that, that relish for language, I guess. They devote a great deal of energy to making what they say sound good and making their imagery more interesting than most of us are able to.

What was your first brush with Brecht?

I wrote a sort of dissertation on Brecht when I was at school. I studied French and German, and you had to choose a subject. The first long piece of critical writing that I ever undertook was on Brecht, and I came out of it feeling quite different about him from the way I felt when I went in. Because his virtues are sort of unexpected and are slightly opposite to the virtues that he proclaimed himself.

Which are?

He presented himself as the apostle of clear thinking in the theatre and of posing the problems of the particular subject he was dealing with so vividly that the spectator calmly sitting in the back row smoking a cigar would be able to work out for him or herself exactly what the issues were, in order to make their own decisions about them. That's what he said he was doing, and I imagine that's what he thought he was doing. On the other hand, if you study the plays with any sort of care at all you'll see that he loads the arguments so inescapably that there is only one conclusion to draw from the facts that he puts in front of you. So there's some sort of fraudulent relationship between his theory and his work. Where his work really is remarkable—at least this is what I thought—is in his poetic quality, his use of language. His mastery of all kinds of different dialects, of theatrical dialects of one sort or another, and his enthusiastic 'borrowing' from all the writers that he admired, makes for a very interesting mishmash in his work. If you're a tremendous admirer of Chinese poetry and of Kipling, what's going to come out is likely to be quite original and interesting.

As a director he seems to have written the grammar of late twentieth-century staging.

This is a terrible thing to say, but in a sense the persecution that he suffered, and being hounded from pillar to post and so on, allowed him a period of time, roughly leading up to and during the war, when he was able to sit and—although he wasn't a brooder—work out a whole new way of thinking about staging plays. So he did this extraordinary thing once he was presented with his kingdom in East Berlin after the war: he was able to walk in with a ready-made set of absolutely original ideas. And was provided with an enormous amount of resources to be able to present all that. In other words, he was in a tremendously powerful position. And although that position involved a certain amount of foot-shuffling and shabbiness and double-talk, he nevertheless used it in a very beneficial way.

He seems to have suffered a great deal of depression when he was in Los Angeles.

Well, you do if you go through those periods of time where you can't, you're not allowed to work. But he was a tremendously productive man and he wrote incessantly through all that period. Of course, his optimism was dashed as far as the cinema was concerned, because he was very anxious to apply a whole range of new ideas to the cinema. When he sat down to work with Fritz Lang, for example, he was deeply disappointed by the sort of criteria that reigned in Hollywood. And he was a little bit unsophisticated about the place where they go 'to sell lies in the marketplace'. I think he and Beckett are very useful poles in this discussion, because, whereas Brecht believed more than anything else in the social usefulness of theatre, the idea of the theatre being socially useful would have been one that would have sent Beckett screaming to the oculist.

Everybody talks about Beckett as very amiable, terribly good company, and Brecht as a completely unclubbable, solitary, difficult man.

You've probably hit on the exact definition of the difference between optimist and pessimist. It's very, very liberating being a pessimist: you are then able to be as pleasant to other people as you feel they deserve. If, on the other hand, you're an optimist, the constant bad behaviour of everybody that you wish to push in a certain direction is bound to make you ill-tempered.

When Brecht was in Los Angeles did he make all the other expatriates' lives a misery?

He was a terrible bully, Brecht, but I think that the accusations have slightly got out of hand lately: people are now saying that most of his girlfriends wrote his plays, which I can't believe can possibly be true. But he certainly was a person who had no hesitation in using people to achieve his aims. And some of those people reacted very violently. W.H. Auden said that Brecht was one of the only purely evil men he had ever met. And he did have that effect on some people. I think if you didn't surrender to his will, he was not the easiest man in the world to be around.

RICHARD EYRE

You grew up at the end of the British Empire. Did that influence you as a writer?

I suppose that growing up at the fag end of the Empire in various places which had been red or pinkish in the map is bound to affect you in one way or another. One of the paradoxical ways it affects you is that, in order to exist as an English child in a foreign environment, it tends to make you more English than the English. It also means, however, that the English experience didn't impinge. You didn't have all those cultural reference points like rationing and the post-war Labour government and all of that; you tended to breeze in and out of the country like a tourist for a couple of months every three years. So that when, after the Suez crisis, when my family were in Egypt, we had to leave and I came back to school in England, I found England on the one hand extremely exotic and peculiar in that there were a certain number of codes that I didn't really understand—partly to do with that sort of reticence or politeness or whatever it is, that English thing—and on the other hand there were certain ways in which I found myself absolutely at home, and certain things that I'd instinctively taken from my family. So there was an odd feeling of being simultaneously a homecomer and an outsider.

Is that a characteristic of your writing, that you're able to write within an English tradition and yet stand outside it?

I don't know about that. What I do know is that I felt, as we moved into the seventies, that a certain kind of play was what was required, and that wasn't necessarily the kind of play that I was able to write. It wasn't that I disapproved of plays which were about social issues and political issues and improving people's lives and all the rest of it, it was just that I had a kind of temperamental inability towards proposing solutions, and it seemed to me that the seventies was an era in which, if you didn't propose solutions and discuss big issues, you might as well shut up and go and do something else. So I found myself towards the end of that decade stopping writing for the theatre for a while, because the theatre does move in these great seven-league-boot spasms—it's in the grip of fashion, in short, and somehow one of the things you need to be able to do is to recognise when you're likely to be in fashion and when you're not. And so the kind of work that was being done in the seventies propelled me in another direction, which was the cinema.

Did you feel a sympathy with the writers who were reviled by the Royal Court generation? That's to say, what are your feelings about Coward and Rattigan?

When I first came to the Royal Court, the Kenneth Tynan line on Terence Rattigan was that nobody should be seen dead going to his plays. One of the things I'm ashamed of is that I rather accepted that. And the one time I met Rattigan, I felt a complicated mix of things. Now, of course, I think his skills were astonishing. And it can only have been the prejudice that was in the air that made me feel that he wasn't as good a writer as I now think he is. I mean, he, of all people, was the person who encapsulated Englishness and its woes and its qualities in a sort of pure way. Coward, I'm slightly more ambivalent about I enjoy his work very much, but I don't much like that kind of jingoistic, sentimental side of Coward. But he was a consummate entertainer.

Which is now seen as a cardinal virtue. Has the theatre now has lost a sense of believing in itself?

Believing in itself? No, I'm sure that the young believe just as strongly in what they're doing as we did. What people need is a kind of context or environment in which to flourish. It's like the British film industry, which in the seventies and eighties just died on its feet. But it didn't mean that there weren't talented people; it simply meant that there weren't the means of production, that there simply weren't the means available to make films, however much you wanted to. If you wanted to make a film you'd better go and be a Frenchman, because you weren't going to be able to do it here. I think that theatre is extremely vulnerable to these kinds of pressures, and while individuals of talent and originality will always make their mark in one way or another, it's very, very helpful to be part of a group of people who are heading in one direction or another.

What do you think the theatre does uniquely well?

A theatre audience is quite different from a cinema audience. When a theatre audience knows what is being said to it—and the context in which that is being said—and feels that what is being said is both interesting and valuable and worth saying, then a certain atmosphere arrives that you don't get anywhere else. I've been very interested over the last few years to read a number of attacks in quality newspapers by novelists of one sort or another explaining how the theatre is not worth anything, and how going to the theatre is a contemptible exercise, and it's all overrated nonsense, and there are no good writers in the theatre. You'd imagine that these people are quite sophisticated and intelligent and would not, if they thought for two minutes, say anything as stupid as that. You can't say: 'Well, I don't like sculpture, sculpture is absolutely boring; of course, painting is wonderful, but, you know, sculpture is a lot of noisy banging on stone, and of course no one with any sense wants to go anywhere near a sculpture.' It's an art form! The theatre is an art form; it's worked for thousands of years in a particular way that no other art form works; and therefore it's completely, shamefully foolish-making to say: 'I don't believe in the theatre, and I don't think there's any point in going to the theatre.'

Peter Shaffer

1 9 2 6—

Playwright. Peter Shaffer's plays include Five Finger Exercise, The Royal Hunt of the Sun, Equus and Amadeus. He has long talked of writing a play about Tchaikovsky and his brother. Sadly I (and others) have been unable to persuade the play out of him. Shaffer's twin brother, Anthony, was the author of Sleuth. Peter got a scholarship to Cambridge, after which he worked as a miner—a Bevin boy (named after Ernest Bevin, then Minister of Labour)—during the war. I interviewed him in a hotel in New York, where he lives most of the year.

I was called up as a Bevin boy. I saved my pennies, and when I had the time, I would go up to London and see theatre. I was very lucky to have grown up in the age of great acting, really great acting—the word 'great' is used now all the time, I'm afraid, to define very little, but in those days... Think of that cataract of great names: Olivier, Richardson, Gielgud, the young Scofield, Alec Guinness, Edith Evans, Peggy Ashcroft—and all of them acting all over London on the stage, live, in a variety of great plays. I caught the bug from that wonderful experience. I remember the great seasons that Olivier and Richardson played at the New Theatre [1944–49]. I remember seeing Gielgud's Hamlet, a magnificent performance. I've never ever seen or heard, and I emphasise heard, better than that performance. I remember the first time I ever felt the power of great theatre was when I was twelve, and I had gone to see John Gielgud play Richard II [1937/8], of course at that age one was in love with the whole idea of panoply and robes and crowns and tragic figures falling from great emotional heights, and it was all thrilling. But what I think principally excited me was the sound, and of course, in the case of John Gielgud, I never departed from my absolute, astonished adoration at the way John spoke lines endlessly with a transparency as well as musicality. Everyone talks of Gielgud's music, as if it was a narcissistic singing: it was much more than that. He provided a clear pane of glass through which you, the hearer, could see the meaning, as it were, could hear the meaning.

These days, this period is usually characterised, or caricatured, as a dead era until everything woke up in 1956. Is that a perversion of history?

It's a perversion of *my* history. I was very, very excited by classical theatre, certainly by Shakespeare. In fact, I spent quite a lot of time in the coal mines hauling great tubs of coal around and, in the endless nasty boredom of that, playing all the parts of all those plays in my head. I sort of knew them almost by heart—it's a vainglorious thing to say, but I did. It's also a perversion because in the forties and fifies there *were* remarkable plays, but there were much more remarkable actors than ever there has been since, I would say. I think perhaps that I was very caught up with the desire to write for such people.

Did you want to write like Rattigan?

No, I don't think I had any playwright models at all, other than the great comedies, say of the eighteenth century. Sheridan was a model in a way; not Congreve, I found his plots incomprehensible. I think Wilde certainly, certainly *The Importance of Being Earnest*. It seemed to me such an astounding thing to read that play or hear that play. The verbal music of Wilde, the wit of those epigrams— they are not even epigrams really—the comedic wit of the individual voice excited me very much.

And was it the fact that the tone of voice is so very strong in Wilde?

'Come, dear—we have already missed five, if not six, trains. To miss any more might expose us to comment on the platform.' The music of that, as well as the delight of its complete nonsense, enchanted me, and I was besotted by what writers in the past had been able to do on the stage, spoken in public by investing characters with lines of great pliability, immediacy and unforgettability.

What about Shaw?

I loved some of the plays. I loved the challenge of plays like *Major Barbara*. I love the ambition of Shaw; I love the ambition of the complete *Man and Superman* with the 'Don Juan in Hell' scene; I loved the early comedies like *Arms and the Man*; and some of *Heartbreak House* I liked very much.

But did it make you feel that it was possible to combine emotion and big ideas in the theatre?

It took me some time, because my first play or plays were naturalistic plays. *Five Finger Exercise* [1958] was virtually—I suppose, totally—a realistic play of the times, and I'm sure it was fashioned very much on the plays I knew of that time, which were called, sometimes derisorily, the 'well-made play'. It's a perfectly absurd expression to use as an insult, since if a play is well-made that has to be one of its greatest virtues. If it's called sneeringly a 'well-made play', then it means it's not been well-made enough.

You mean you're too conscious of—

—of the carpentry and construction, yes. I was always terribly impressed with the middle period of plays of Ibsen—how he mixed reality, realism and symbolism together with extraordinary subtle and efficient carpentry, so you didn't notice. He wasn't saying: look how well this is constructed, but you were excited by the fact it had been constructed so that every one of the four acts led to a mini climax, and finally to a major climax. I read those plays over and over again, because it seemed to me deeply exciting to me to try and do that oneself.

Five Finger Exercise *was presented by Binkie Beaumont [who ran H.M. Tennent, the leading West End theatre producer of the day]?*

Yes, indeed.

Now, how did that come about?

One day the phone rang: Could I come in and see Mr Perry? Mr Perry was Binkie's partner—wonderful figure, Anglo-Irish figure, beautifully, impeccably dressed. He looked at me and said: 'You've got to have a maid.' I don't know what I said, 'I can't afford one,' or something like that. He said: 'In your play, dear, I mean,' and I said: 'Does this mean you're going to read it, produce it… are you interested in producing it?' And he said 'Yes, very much. Would John Gielgud be acceptable to you as a director?' And of course Gielgud was my idol in many ways, not necessarily as a director. So it came about, and he cast Michael Bryant as the German boy, and Brian Bedford as the son, and it was an extraordinary experience. I remember my first day, I suppose my first day in the English theatre. I went to the rehearsal, very much the new boy, incredibly nervous, and John directed a move, put in a move, a physical move, on every single line of the first, say, fifteen minutes. 'You can stand up there, you can sit down there, it would be amusing if you took the dishes out there,' and so on, but on every single line. And then, just as we were closing the rehearsal, he said: 'Oh well, let's just run it; it'll be fun.' Everything was either 'fun' or 'amusing'. So, they indeed ran the first ten minutes, and it was horrendous in the sense that they all looked like a lot of mice on amphetamines, racing and running about. And John suddenly rose, one of those quasi-passionate exclamations of his, and said, 'This is a nightmare, stop it, what are you all doing?' and Brian Bedford fearlessly came down and said: 'We are doing, John, or trying to do, the moves you have given us.' And John looked genuinely puzzled and said: 'What on earth for? Everyone knows I can't direct.' That was my first day in the theatre.

What about Binkie Beaumont, was he in the background?

I always found him extraordinary. Not just courteous but extremely helpful and encouraging and intelligent, very intelligent. The first performance of *Five Finger Exercise* had not gone particularly well—it was at the Arts Theatre in Cambridge—and they were a bit sort of giggly, the audience. I was sitting rather depressed at the end thinking I'd got it all wrong, this is not going to succeed, and suddenly Binkie was standing behind me. He said: 'That blue vase is hideous, it must go. What do you say?', and I said: 'Well, yes, I suppose so. I think there is rather more to worry about: they didn't like it, they didn't like the play.' And he explained: 'There were a lot of rather silly nurses. They were having a good time, but it wasn't quite the kind of good time you wanted them to have. Deal with the things one can deal with: you cannot remove a nurse's laugh; you can remove that vase.'

So it would be unfair to describe the combination of Binkie Beaumont and the Lord Chamberlain as a repressive force?

I think the Lord Chamberlain *was* a repressive force. In fact, *Five Finger Exercise* was the last play done at what was the Watergate Theatre Company, avoiding the censor by calling it a club. Binkie himself was an old-fashioned romantic, and some of the productions were too varnished and too manicured, maybe too timid. But I gave him the manuscript of *The Royal Hunt of the Sun*, my play about the conquest of Peru. I'd written a line that became notorious as a stage direction: '*They now climb the Andes.*' I was staying the weekend with Binkie—John Perry was there, the partner—and I had heard nothing: they had referred to the manuscript not at all. I went to get myself a drink, came back and heard through the door as I was approaching it John Perry describing to Binkie that scene in *The Royal Hunt of the Sun*. John was saying: 'Well, dear, they climb up the Andes, do they? And what do they do then? They climb down them, dear. Fancy!' And I thought: 'I don't think this is quite the management for this play.'

It looks as though between Five Finger Exercise *and* The Royal Hunt of the Sun *you had an injection both of Shakespeare and Brecht. What actually happened?*

The first draft of *The Royal Hunt of the Sun* had been written, in note form, before *Five Finger Exercise* was produced. In the meantime, I had done a double-bill of plays, also naturalistic, called *The Private Ear* and *The Public Eye*, with Maggie Smith, which were still in that mould. I had sketched out a draft of *The Royal*

Hunt, which had a much greater freedom, and indeed it was, I suppose, Shakespearean in the way that it had many interlocking short scenes of an epic nature with armies on the move and massacres and great treasures being brought from all over Peru and piled up and put on stage and so forth. It was gestural as well as verbal—I suppose to some extent influenced by Brecht's use of gesture, certainly in a play like *The Caucasian Chalk Circle*, which is I think my favourite of his plays, partly because it is so spectacularly theatrical. I suddenly plucked up my courage to flesh out *The Royal Hunt* as a full play. The National Theatre had just then been founded, and I thought: perhaps I should send it to the National and indeed to John Dexter, who'd finally direct it with great brilliance and panache. A very scary man in a way, like a small prizefighter, he called me on the telephone and said: 'I'm coming round to your house; I want to read your play to you.' And he came and sat and read. He had been an actor himself, I think, at Derby Playhouse.

With John Osborne.

Yes, exactly. He read Act One one Saturday, and the second act the second Saturday. He was directing Olivier's *Othello* at the time. He read it very fairly. He could have read it sending up or edging me towards disapproving the bits he'd disapproved of or wanted excised, but he didn't. He read the bits he didn't like with equal conviction. He would stop at the end of every scene and ask my comments, and I would say: 'That's a bit redundant'—whatever it was—and my comments almost all corresponded with his notes. But as we approached that notorious line '*They climb the Andes*,' I thought I must interrupt and explain what I meant by this. So, greatly daring, I said: 'John, could I interrupt here, at this moment?', just as he was turning the page; he saw this line, and he thought I meant I was going to remove it, and he said: 'If you take that line out, I'm not directing.' It was terrific moment for me, because I thought: we're on the same, identical wavelength. What I wanted to see was a kind of theatre that exercises the imaginative muscle of the audience.

John's inspiration had been Brecht. He'd gone to the Berliner Ensemble and thought: it is possible for armies to cross the stage—you only have to see Mother Courage *or* The Caucasian Chalk Circle *or* Galileo *to think you can put whole worlds on the stage.*

I knew the kind of play I wanted to see had nothing whatever to do with the living room in *Five Finger Exercise* or the office in *The Public Eye*, nothing at all. It had to do with the world that only live theatre can fulfil, which is the world of things unseen. I was thrilled with the idea of joining a band of people to make the visible invisible or the invisible visible.

And did you feel Beckett was part of that world? When you saw Godot *what did you think?*

I had a very extraordinary experience with it. The first time I saw it I came out very confused, and nothing seemed to happen—indeed nothing does happen. I was baffled, and yet I was vaguely stirred. Images of those tramps and that solitary tree kept returning. A month later or so it had transferred to the Piccadilly Theatre: I thought I'd like to see it again, and I had the most marvellous time. When I came out I thought: why did you find that so difficult the first time; it's a very, very clear play. I could see that it is an immensely animated play within this husk of nothing ever happens, no one comes, no one goes. It's an intensely moving and lyrical reflection on human history. I am a tremendous admirer of his work. I am not entirely so with Brecht for one reason: although I love the theatricalism, what I couldn't quite take is this didacticism. Brecht said at one point in an essay I read: 'I am not interested in the next scene; I am interested in this scene,' and I thought: that's rather a pretentious remark, actually. I *am* interested in this scene, because I am going to write the next scene. I believe in narrative very strongly: I think it's the spine of all drama. People come for this, to hear a tale. The other day I went to see Théâtre de Complicité in *Mnemonic*: its director, I think it's Simon McBurney, had written a preface in the programme saying that the age of the single tale was now at an end, and that, because of our lives being so fragmented, narrative is now not any more a single tale but a fragmentary, cross-referential mosaic. And I thought: bollocks! A single tale is the staple of the theatre for me. So when I saw *Mnemonic*, although I am a tremendous admirer of Théâtre de Complicité—I loved *The Street of Crocodiles*—I thought this needed a playwright; it needed a playwright in the sense W. R. I. G. H. T—it needed a cartwright, a wheelwright; it needed to be cobbled properly.

You worked with Joan Littlewood. What was that like?

Joan came up with the idea that she wanted to do a children's pantomime. She said: there is not enough theatre for kids. She had a meeting at Gerry Raffles' house in Blackheath one Sunday; I went along because I knew a lot of the members of the company, just to listen, really. And they were talking about, oh, I don't know, the standard plots of English pantomime—you know, *Jack and the Beanstalk* and *Dick Whittington* and *Cinderella*—and I got more and more interested, as they went on talking. And Joan, who I was fascinated by because she was immensely voluble and immensely all-including, said: what do you think? There was a slight tendency to send you up and say: 'Oh well, you come from the world of the West End,' and so on. And I said: 'I think that kids actually are bored by *Cinderella*. I think they really like the ugly sisters much more.' I would love to actually have a go at trying to do a kind of popular *Cinderella*, reversing some of the values and seeing what happens.

What was Joan like?

She was a very ambiguous figure. I liked her very much. I felt strange sometimes in her presence because she sometimes seemed to condescend even to her own company. She would call them 'my lovely nuts', 'my dear little nuts' and all that, and I thought: 'Yes, but they are actors and they are very talented people sometimes.' She was a benevolent dictator, but I'm not mad about dictators, benevolent or otherwise.

What was your reaction to the Royal Court and 1956—now talked about as this great watershed. What did you think at the time?

I was a friend of Kenneth Haigh—he played the first Jimmy Porter. He showed me the script while he was actually rehearsing *Look Back in Anger*, and I thought it was marvellous writing. I've never forgotten the deep pleasure, for example, of referring to the mother-in-law: 'I think she's a witch, and she's making a figure of me. Every week I'd bet you the wax arrives from Harrods.' I loved the verbal music, the rhetoric of it. And I loved the subversiveness and the whole attacking thing of Jimmy. At the same time, I had a feeling as I was reading it, that it was too one-sided. I got a little tired of the silence of Alison. I thought: that's evading it, surely she has a life and is a person? But I underrated John, because there's that marvellous scene when her father appears, and I thought: this is really wonderful playwriting. I did not find it revolutionary formally at all: it's a very well-made, three-act play. I didn't require it to be revolutionary and still don't. I don't require anything to be revolutionary: I require it to be itself. I think in some ways, not in all ways, it *was* revolutionary in the sense that it blazed a trail with the sort of things it was saying about society, and what one was permtted to say: because a lot of the effect of censorship was not about just referring to homosexuality and all that—I mean, it's been narrowed down to that—but the effect of the censorship was that you didn't make critical comments on society or the structure of society or the oppression of society at all.

Was it the tone of voice? It wasn't working-class, but it certainly wasn't the prevailing upper-middle-class voice?

No, it wasn't any of those classes of voice actually, it was John's individual voice that excited me: it always is with an author in the end. I don't think one can write embodying a working-class voice, or a this or that voice. It's the actual use of sentence structure—adverbs and adjectives, the whole business of writing—that makes either the far-off muted sound or the clarion call and John's was a clarion call. It was thrilling to hear—just as hearing Stoppard at his wonderful best thrills me. I like it more than any other public experience except possibly going to great concerts.

Frith Banbury

1 9 1 2—2 0 0 8

Director. During his very long career Frith Banbury worked almost exclusively in the commercial theatre, where he directed many successful productions for H.M. Tennent, including the premieres of N.C. Hunter's Waters of the Moon *and Terence Rattigan's* The Deep Blue Sea. *He also championed Robert Bolt, John Whiting and Rodney Ackland, whose play* The Pink Room *(aka* Absolute Hell) *was years ahead of its time. He was forever young and, in his way, iconoclastic. He said once to Simon Callow: 'I'm a homosexual, half-Jewish conchie. Just because my father was an admiral doesn't make me one of them.' I interviewed him in his flat looking over Regent's Park, the walls crowded with Hockneys that he'd bought before they became fashionable.*

You were born in 1912 so you were a child during the twenties. Did you go to the theatre then?

I was given a toy theatre at the age of six and was hooked from that moment on: I knew exactly what I was going to do with my life whatever anybody else said. It was pure enchantment; it didn't matter whether it was *Joy Bells* at the Hippodrome or *A Midsummer Night's Dream* or Flecker's *Hassan*. I always thought that the last thing was the best thing, so *Lady, Be Good* was better than *A Midsummer Night's Dream* until *Hamlet* came along. I didn't take any account of what other people thought; this wonderland was for me, you see.

239

When you say 'wonderland', do you mean that people had fantastic costumes and gave larger than life performances and the sets were very vivid?

Yes, absolutely, that's what I mean, it was very much more beautiful and exciting than real life. Actually it may be to do with the fact that although I had a privileged background, I can't say I had a very happy childhood. I had a father who was a naval officer and ended up as an admiral, so he was away from my earliest years, and the people who supported me in these ideas were my mother and my grandmother—two Australian Jewish ladies. By the time my father came back from the war, the deed was done, and I was on the wrong path, thank God.

And later on, in the thirties?

Later on I became a bit more conscious of what was perhaps missing from the theatre that I saw.

What was the prevailing style of acting?

The prevailing style was extremely naturalistic. If you take Gerald du Maurier as the example, he was an absolutely wonderful technician; but the stars of that period, particularly in modern plays, had a very narrow range but within that range the technical ability was something which was quite wonderful.

My impression of Gerald du Maurier is that he was a man who was very good at lighting a cigarette in a cigarette holder, but you describe him as 'naturalistic'. In what way 'naturalistic'? In what way did he mimic life as it was lived?

In that he was the epitome of the well-dressed, well-bred gentleman, I suppose you could say, and this was what the audiences of the time wanted to see.

He was considered to have brought a new style of relaxed naturalism to the stage?

That's true, that is true.

Which implies that by his standards everybody else was more exaggerated and more caricatured?

I used to go and see an actor called Matheson Lang with the deep throaty voice when he did *The Wandering Jew*. Well, du Maurier was a reaction against all that overly theatrical sort of style.

What about the productions?

It was very primitive, really. When I think of the sort of sets and the lighting, and when I think what lighting is now—it's as different as chalk from cheese. Later on in the thirties, people like Rex Whistler, and Basil Dean's designer, George W.

Harrison, produced things that were more imaginative. Of course, there was always Edward Gordon Craig in the background—but he never would come and work because he didn't like what was going on in the English theatre.

Craig was swimming against the stream?

Yes, but of course you don't swim against the stream if you never do anything. The fact is that he produced beautiful books about what ought to be, but if you don't get up and practise it, then what the hell use are you really?

You were too young to have seen The Vortex?

Well, of course, I was a boy. But my mother went to *The Vortex.* I said: 'What was it like, Mummy?' 'Well, not for you, dear, as yet.' And I said: 'Ooh, I want to see that.' Immediately. But it was not thought suitable—even by my mother, who was, you know, fairly liberal in her attitudes.

Is it fair to say that The Vortex *in its time had as much influence as* Look Back in Anger *did in the fifties?*

I suppose it is, though you see the interesting thing about *The Vortex* is that, although it deals with drugs and sex, the old woman with the younger lover, the drugs which get thrown out of the window and all that, it's not all that far away in construction and in attitude from plays like *The Second Mrs Tanqueray* or something of that sort—only it went a step further in what was permitted on the stage. It was, I think, quite dicey as to whether it would pass the censor. There was quite a bit of coming and going and 'cut this' and 'cut that'. But yes, I think *The Vortex* in particular, perhaps, but all the Coward plays were a challenge—but only up to a point.

And was Wilde revived?

The first time I saw *Lady Windermere's Fan* was at the Everyman [in Hampstead]. They were dressed in modern clothes, and it seemed rather strange, but I think this was already the early thirties. The one that was done was *The Importance,* of course.

Was there still a taint about Wilde?

Oh yes, yes.

You were in a play about him, but this doesn't reflect a sort of liberalism about homosexuality, does it?

Not at all, you see it was done at the Gate Theatre, a small, fringe house; it could never pass the censor. The fact was, you see, that homosexuality was against the law, so there was always that risk in dealing with it. You knew that the censor wouldn't pass a play on that subject. You could only put it on in a club theatre. So you didn't think about it—you didn't want to write plays that could only be done in a tiny theatre. The general attitude was: what's the point of doing a play about homosexuality when we know we can't get it on?

So the Lord Chamberlain was a very influential figure in British theatre in the forties and fifties?

I would say that the Lord Chamberlain had an effect on all plays that were written, because if you were wanting to earn your living as a playwright, it was no bloody good writing plays about homosexuality or even lesbianism.

Could you say 'bloody'?

I don't know about the word 'bloody'. Herbert Farjeon, who wrote revues, wrote a sketch in which the word 'constipation' occurred. It came back from the censor: cut the word 'constipation'. There followed a very funny correspondence between Herbert Farjeon and the Lord Chamberlain, and eventually Farjeon produced an eighteenth-century word, 'costive', saying we propose to say 'costive', is this all right? And the Lord Chamberlain eventually said: yes, you can say 'costive'. Presumably the idea was that nobody in the audience would understand what the word 'costive' meant. There was also a very funny bit in that correspondence where it said: 'We know that Mrs Hermione Baddeley, when she said the word "constipation", would say it in a very proper way, but who knows what a lesser actress, when asked to do it in the provinces, might make of the word?' Of course, the funny thing is that Miss Baddeley—a bit of a genius in my view—could put a more than naughty twist on anything if she put her mind to it. People were given the most ridiculous things. A note used to come back: 'You can say "God" once in the scene but not twice; you have three "Jesuses" in this scene, you can have two of them and not the third.' Quite ridiculous.

One writer who significantly swam against the stream was Rodney Ackland.

I became conscious of Rodney first in the thirties when I saw a play, *Strange Orchestra*, in its try-out at the Embassy Theatre, Swiss Cottage. This play had an enormous effect on me. I saw it twice. Rodney saw things truthfully, whereas most plays of that era were inclined to wrap up truths. On the whole, one could say that assumptions about life were shared by the people who put on plays, the people who watched them, the people who acted in them and the people who directed them or whatever, and those assumptions were that it was theatre of comfort, reassurance. You didn't show anything too unpleasant. I think Rodney's plays, because of their truth and their lack of sentimentality, made the audiences feel a bit uncomfortable: 'They are very funny people, why do they behave like that? Oh no, that woman, why is she dressed so strangely? I don't know if I like it very much.'

You directed the premiere of his play The Pink Room *in the fifties, didn't you? We know that play as* Absolute Hell. *It's set on the eve of the Labour victory at the end of the war, and it's about a number of, as it were, defectors—not only from middle-class life. All classes are in the play, which was extremely unusual, and it has a sort of eloquence and a kind of freedom of speech that only American writing had at the time.*

This is because Rodney had a great bee in his bonnet about escapism, people who escape from life. After all, the play *The Dark River* is all about that too, you see, although it was written before the war and only done during the war. *The Pink Room* originally had an alternative title—*The Escapists*. It was all about people who were escaping into the good life, as it were, at the end of the war: then suddenly into it comes the horrors of Buchenwald, etc. The girl doesn't want to face it when she's told that her great friend has died in a concentration camp. It's set in a club in between VE Day, the end of the European war, and VJ Day, the end of the Japanese war and the Bomb. There were two clubs at that time that you could say it was founded on—there was the French club, which was founded for the Free French, and the White Room, which was for people who really had bloody good wars, thoroughly enjoyed themselves, and got stinking drunk.

Coming from a generation who are interested in such plays, I think this is very much a 'state of the nation' play.

I think it was 'state of the nation'—this is why it unsettled people: because they didn't like to face facts. It was a proof of how good the play was, in my view, that it also got under people's skin. Many people were upset and shocked by it, and we had notices saying that this is a disgusting immoral play. And the other facet of it was that there were three homosexuals, two lesbians and five drunks all on the stage at the same time.

This play didn't find a champion in the way that four years later Look Back in Anger *found its champion in Kenneth Tynan. Do you think that was just accident?*

I think the time wasn't quite right. There was the class thing in *Look Back in Anger*, which there isn't specifically in *The Pink Room*, but I think that the success of *Look Back in Anger*—this is my theory—was because we all voted Labour in 1945. It was all going to be lovely—and we were immediately confronted with Stafford Cripps and rationing and hardships, and so on. We expected the Millennium to come and of course it didn't. There's a certain resemblance to what's happening now: people expected lots of loveliness to appear from this present Blair government, and they're rather waiting with their tongues hanging out still, and hoping. What happened in 1945 was that certain things did happen, such as the National Health Service and all the rest of it, but by 1951 the Tories came in again, and I think it could be said that the old sort of middle-class values were still there pretty much in the theatre and that the young ones, the generation of Osborne and co, got more and more frustrated. *Look Back in Anger* didn't make an enormous impact at first. I remember saying: this is a promising first play, etc. It wasn't until Kenneth Tynan went and said: this is the play of the moment and everybody must see it and made that wonderful statement—'I doubt if I could love anybody who did not wish to see *Look Back in Anger*,' that it became the thing. It did make a great impact, of course, but not as great an impact as it seems now, looking back.

But the Royal Court got the flywheel turning?

Yes, I think you could say that. But what people now seem to think was it all happened in one day. I mean, for me, *Look Back in Anger* was, oh, an interesting play: I must go and see it, went to see it, oh yes, it needs a lot of cutting, it does go on so, that father is just an Aunt Sally... To that extent the play is rigged: that is not the last word to be said about an old Indian Army colonel. That's an Aunt Sally put up to throw the coconuts at. What I have to say in criticism of Osborne is that he often did that, because he did exactly the same with the niece in the play about the solicitor—

—Inadmissible Evidence.

Inadmissible Evidence. Mr Osborne wished to say something about the inadequacies of the young, so he brings on a girl who's only got one line to say, if that, and she has to be talked at and told how the youth of today are simply beyond the pale. Well, that's not what I call good playwriting. That's why I think—this may be heresy—but the best thing Osborne ever wrote was the first volume of his autobiography. But there are marvellous things in all the plays.

George Devine was the godfather of the revolution that gave birth to Look Back in Anger. *Was he was a contemporary of yours?*

Yes, I knew him from very early on. Let's face it, he was a great man, in the sense that he did create this Royal Court. One has to say there was a revolution—no use pretending there wasn't—and George was the one who made it. But of course, you have to have tunnel vision to create a revolution, don't you? And what is interesting and amusing now is to think that George had many years in the theatre before this happened: he was in John Gielgud's company doing a lot of plays in the thirties and was responsible for directing the first production of *Rebecca* with Owen Nares and Celia Johnson—now if that isn't old style bourgeois theatre, I don't know what is. George was responsible for that. But he went to the war, and the years passed, and he had a reaction against what became known as 'West End' to the extent of being rather severe with Peggy Ashcroft for having done a play like *The Deep Blue Sea*. Which to me is a bit silly.

He introduced directors with widely different sensibilites, who were united in their rejection of everything which didn't coincide with their aesthetic views.

That's right, it mustn't be pretty, you see. I go along with that, but not to the same extent as they did. I would say that their productions were a damn sight better than their pronouncements, if you see what I mean. It was the fuss and the bother that was a bit boring: the productions were often very good.

The Royal Court and Beckett were really synonymous. Do you think that Beckett's arrival on the scene had an influence on the British theatre?

Yes I do, in the sense that it gave writers the feeling that they could experiment. I can't say that *Waiting for Godot* is my favourite play, depends who's doing it. It seems to me that *Waiting for Godot* depends absolutely on two actors: if you get two wonderful actors, then it's as good as music hall. Of course, that's not quite what one should be saying, is it? This is, of course, heresy to put it this way, but I think Beckett writes wonderful material for an actor.

To what extent did Ken Tynan influence theatre?

I think that he did turn the tide very much against Rattigan, but then, you see, Rattigan asked for it. Tynan was such a brilliant polemicist. He wrote about Rattigan's plays, and Rattigan answered him. Of course, Tynan always got the better of him in a revolting way, I thought, because it was horrid what he wrote, quite horrid really, but it did fulfil the frustrations of quite a lot of people of that era. One has to remember that Tynan was a bastard whose father had done the right thing by his mother—he went to Oxford and all the rest of it—but there was a very definite bitterness at the back there, and I think Rattigan played into his hands. Tynan obviously wanted to direct and wanted to act. He tried both with no success at either, but the one thing he could do was write wonderful prose and brilliant invective. And sometimes, of course, he was very, very good when he admired somebody. I mean, he praised Larry Olivier, didn't he? He wrote wonderful things in praise of Olivier.

And he then went to the National Theatre.

I don't think he was a very pleasant character. When it came to doing the thing, it always seemed to go a bit wrong, didn't it? I mean, it didn't go very well at the National when he was the whatever-he-was there—we never quite knew, really...

He was the dramaturg.

He would have been in the German theatre: what is the English word for 'dramaturg'?

Literary Manager?

Literary Manager, that's right. He seemed to quarrel with people or perhaps he was too cunning. I did know him a bit, but I've only learned how little he thought of me when his letters were published. But he did have an influence; oh yes, there's no question about it. But I still think that the thing that made the difference was the censorship and then the removal of the censorship.

But the censorship wasn't removed until 1968.

Right, exactly, but during this period it was all bubbling up. There were two plays, weren't there, that failed to pass the censorship: Tennessee Williams's *Cat on a Hot Tin Roof* and Arthur Miller's *View from the Bridge*. Well, Binkie Beaumont was brilliant: he took the Comedy Theatre, made it for the moment into a club so that it didn't have to pass the censorship and we could see those two plays. If he hadn't done that, we shouldn't have been able to see those plays in a public theatre, it was quite ridiculous. And you weren't allowed to say anything about royalty. This is why *Victoria Regina* [by Laurence Housman] failed to pass the censorship after it had been done at the Gate Theatre [a club theatre] here. Of course it went to New York and was a great hit there, but it couldn't be done here in public.

You could say that there was implicit censorship of the voice of the working class, and this was one of the things that you could say came in with the Royal Court revolution: that you started to hear working-class accents on stage, and you started to hear them spoken by working-class actors with a working-class background.

This is quite true. I quite agree about that. Actors who came from a lower class in the old days found it necessary to talk proper. People like Gertie Lawrence or Jessie Matthews, both from working-class backgrounds, realised that in order to get on they had to learn to talk posh—to learn to talk what we would call 'received pronunciation'.

When you started as a director were you aware of Granville Barker?

Oh yes. As a playwright. Is he the director who, as it were, threw out the French windows? I wouldn't say there was any director that did that. I would say simply that it came about slowly. The idea of productions that were poetic and expressionistic—that didn't have naturalistic scenery—really goes back much, much longer than the fifties or sixties. It's a mistake to think that these productions didn't exist in the twenties and thirties.

So although Gordon Craig never actually put his work into practice, his ideas—and Barker's—did come to be exemplified in a number of productions.

But Granville Barker never did a production that he acknowledged to be his once he left the theatre… during the First World War, wasn't it? He came and helped other people. It was John Gielgud who persuaded him to come and help. He'd come for one or two days and give notes, but he didn't say: this is directed by Granville Barker, nor did he have any say in the physical production, the sets and the costumes and lighting and stuff.

Would you say that the theatre is always renewing itself?

Oh yes.

And that there is nothing new under the sun?

Yes, I would, because I shouldn't be surprised if one day we see the old French windows appear again. In fact, one of the things that amused me about *Amy's View*, that play of David Hare's, when Judi Dench came on and patted the cushions: I thought, good heavens, we're back with old Marie Tempest—she always used to pat the cushions, and she played actresses. There was an air of that play that suddenly took me right back. I don't suppose David will be too pleased to hear me say that, but it did.

Alan Ayckbourn

1 9 3 9—

Writer and director. Alan Ayckbourn's plays include Relatively Speaking, How the Other Half Loves, Absurd Person Singular, The Norman Conquests, Absent Friends, Bedroom Farce, A Chorus of Disapproval, Woman in Mind, A Small Family Business, Man of the Moment, The Revengers' Comedies, House and Garden *and many others—seventy-three in all. He was Artistic Director at the Stephen Joseph Theatre in Scarborough from 1972 until 2008; during that time he provided at least one play a year for them. All his plays have been premiered in Yorkshire and forty of them have subsequently transferred to the West End or the National Theatre. I interviewed him in London, in his flat in Docklands.*

As a writer do you see yourself as a sort of social anthropologist?

I've been through so many different phases as a writer. I've had a very long writing career, you know. My first play was professionally produced in 1959, so it's forty years of writing. Most dramatists tend to drift away to television, or to do movies—even though they come back. Most of my contemporaries have. But I've never really gone anywhere, except theatre. I started off as 'Mr Light Ent'— you know, *Relatively Speaking, How the Other Half Loves*, very light plays. Then somebody told me I was a bit like Chekhov, so I started steaming that way, and that's a very dangerous pond you sail across, when you're told you're the English Chekhov. It almost inevitably causes you to sink slightly, because you begin to take yourself very, very seriously. I came out of that: I'd exhausted the domestic

cupboards by then. I began to look outwardly. Then I wrote a sort of series of—
I suppose you'd call them social plays: *Man of the Moment* ('social' to a certain
extent) and *Chorus of Disapproval*, *Small Family Business*. I think my little domestic
plays were about people who weren't really in control of their lives. There was
a sense of complete and utter hopelessness. Later on, when the long Thatcher
reign began, I began to develop a—what shall I say?—social awareness. It was a
very unfashionable thing, but I was aware that our spiritual dimensions seemed
to be disregarded, shrinking and lost. You know, the Church had lost its
dominance over us. There's nothing like a good world war for everybody to get
down together and pray, but, once that was over, the Church really got shoved
aside. But there was nothing really in its place except a series of moral codes that
seemed to be written on the back of envelopes, by various people, to suit
themselves. They'd say—and I began to try and reflect this in the plays: 'Well,
surely we've got to agree on certain things.' And: 'Well, no, it's okay to kill certain
people, it's okay to steal certain things, it's okay to treat certain people this way,'
which is what the code was threatening to do. It seemed to me we were in a very,
very dangerous world, where moral vacuums could cause things that happened
in Germany in the thirties and led to the war. The whole reason all that
happened, of course, was the way that the country got into such a terrible
economic and, in a certain sense, moral state. And in came someone who
appeared to be making it right, but they're never the ones you should elect!
[*laughs*]

*Did you start to see the theatre as in some way a refutation of Thatcher's 'There's no such
thing as society'?*

Yes I did. I never thought I'd be in that boat, because rather unashamedly I always
said—although I hope my plays did more than that—I was mainly there to
entertain. Also to inform and hope to make points, but they were mostly
domestic points about how men treat women, and women treat men, and so on.
Suddenly I did feel the need to say more than this. You do need something to
push against. But it's quite hard to be socially vigorous for very long. There was
a wonderful moment at the Establishment Club, who made absolute mockery of
the Tory government—the government did what the British always do, they
turned up at the Club. In the end, how can you fight the guys who are applauding
you on stage, saying: 'It's absolutely wonderful, can you do me again?' I think
that's what happens in this country. You get absorbed. You get asked to the palace,
and you get given a CBE. That shuts you up, doesn't it? [*laughs*]

*A few years ago, I saw a survey which showed you were the second most popular playwright
in the world, behind Shakespeare, but ahead of Brecht.*

[*laughs*]

What is it that you do that communicates universally?

I write about generalities. I mean, in a sense that I always explain myself as the births-deaths-and-marriages-column dramatist. I don't tend to write about issues very much, and I write about what people do to other people. What mothers and sons do to each other, and so on. And of course they're rather common. They happen in any society, and so, yes, in a sense, the plays are still recognisable to the Japanese, you know, who take to them. And I've seen productions of mine—on video—from Japan, which are quite fascinating, because somehow the whole grammar's changed, the performance style is totally different. Practically everything is unrecognisable and quite alien, and yet there are my characters still experiencing the same problems. Probably, the short answer is: I've written always for a specific theatre in a specific community. People say: 'Oh, you try your plays out here, don't you?' No, I do not 'try my plays out' in Scarborough: I write for Scarborough. I write for a community. I write for as wide a spectrum of that community as I can possibly manage. I've always said to myself, if I walk down the street to the theatre and someone stops me and says 'I'm coming to see your play, will I enjoy it?' and I look at them and say 'No'—then I've got something very, very wrong. Whether they're the local doctor or the local plumber, they should both find something in that play, and if they don't then I'm doing it wrong. And that has kept me as wide as I can get.

That's why the theatre is important to you, because there's that contact?

I've got quite evangelical in the last few years about theatre. It's arisen mainly because I've been asked so many times now, both by people in the press and by people I know: 'Do you think theatre will survive into the next millennium?' It's a question we all ask ourselves; we've been asking ourselves since the silent movies arrived: 'Oh, that's the end of theatre, isn't it?' Yet it's survived. And I think it will positively survive, simply because of that spiritual vacuum I was talking about. Without making it sound too grand, I think the theatre is a community—a Scarborough community, Nottingham, Leicester, wherever. It's the equivalent of our church. It's where we go now. We should go to look at ourselves, and to look at our neighbours, and to share things other than seedy details on the Internet. If you do a good play, whether it's a Shakespeare play or one of mine, and the play works, there's a sense that an audience shares it. That's why I'm very encouraged by theatre-in-the-round, because—when people say: 'I keep looking at the audience'—I think: 'You're supposed to.' It's a group activity, theatre. You're aware of your neighbour. If you go to a cinema, and you're pinned in your seat by huge images coming at you at a hundred and fifty miles an hour, and sounds that are now so loud that your ears bleed, and someone says when you come out: 'Was the cinema full?', you say: 'I've no idea, don't know if anyone was sitting there or not.' But if you go into a theatre—and certainly an open-stage theatre—you're aware of a live participation with others, and that's what makes it important. Over the years I've done sort of silly games occasionally—like plays with variable middles and variable endings—and they look pretty gimmicky, but what they are, in fact, is an attempt to say to the audience: this is happening tonight; this is happening now.

I've written a new play which they're doing at the National next year [this was in 2001]—*House and Garden*—which has an outrageous concept. It takes place in two theatres simultaneously—in this case the Olivier and the Lyttelton: the actors run between the two. There's absolutely no sense in doing this at all, except that when we did it in Scarborough—and I hope it will happen at the National— people got terribly excited by the idea. And they got very excited by the curtain call, when the actors ran from both buildings, in order to take two sets of bows; and then we carried the whole action out into the foyer. All you can do is strike matches; you can't ever light bonfires, but you can strike a match for a minute and make the theatre flare. I think if we can all do that occasionally, all us writers and directors, then it still lives.

Do you feel very much that you're working in an English tradition?

One of the things about being English—and I'm only aware of it because my plays have been translated into so many languages—is we have the most wonderful language for drama. I went to see *Norman Conquests* in German, and I said: 'What's the difference?' The translator said: 'We just find ourselves frustratedly using the same word where you've always chosen a different one.' The first line in *Relatively Speaking* is a man saying: 'I can't say I'm very taken with this marmalade.' Which describes his class. And the way he speaks shows a certain antagonism between him and his wife, a sort of distance. When the Americans tried to Americanise it, they came up with the equivalent, which is: 'This marmalade's a freak out.' Which said nothing. It's the same language, sort of. But I think it's the selection of words that's English. Then beyond that, there's the way we behave to each other. We are a very oblique nation. I like that. I mean that feeling that you can go home, and it's only when you're on the bus you realise you've been insulted. [*laughs*] Or snubbed. And one explores the displacement activity that goes on. I don't think any character in my play has ever said 'I love you' directly to anyone. They've always been building a cupboard, or something, at the time, you know, and they've said it. Usually misheard the first time. There's a feeling of indirection in a lot of our drama. My own *Relatively Speaking* is based on mistaken identities, which wouldn't exist in some cultures. Somebody comes in and says: 'Hello.' And you think: 'I don't know who you are.' But you don't say, as an American might: 'Who are you?' You just carry on, hoping you'll recognise them, and getting deeper and deeper into something. That's very English.

And class?

Class is very important. Its shifts. It's not middle/working/upper now. They're different classes. There's an urban and a rural class, and there's money. It's more the American model now. And there's that sort of—well, that class that I never mix with who go to clubs and whip round the West End a lot. They have their own class. If you put three—I always say—if you put three Englishmen into a room, they'd start a class system in about ten minutes. One of them would declare themselves slightly superior to the other two, and then the second one would sort themselves out. That's in our nature.

We English seem to be very good at acting, at theatre. Is that because it's second nature to us to act a role, a class role?

Once you create a class structure, you create frictions. You also create, from the comedy point of view, embarrassments—people don't know which knife to hold. I'm sure the people who put all those knives out did it in order to sort out the people who didn't know which knives to hold. 'Oh dear, dear, dear. He's eating his asparagus with a spoon.' You know: 'He's out. He's not part of us.' And there is obviously extraordinary resentment or, in my case, some sort of mild amusement. I was born with vaguely artistic parents. I was then projected into the middle class as a result of my mother's second marriage, and found myself a bank manager's son in Sussex. You can't get any more middle-class than that. But I remained rather detached from and rather amused by the games we play with each other. The fact that the bank manager's wife had all the staff up for sherry, asked them if they liked sherry, and they stood awkwardly round in a circle, wishing each other Happy Christmas… It was really the forming of a play there.

And is regionalism part of the knit of Englishness?

There's the north/south divide, which people keep saying doesn't exist. It damn well does. I'm aware of it because I spend more time in the north now. There's quite a strong feeling about the divide, certainly in independent Yorkshire. I suspect, though I don't know the other regions, there is elsewhere, too. There's certainly a very peculiar feeling whenever you go into East Anglia: you always feel like you're going into another country. Considering the island is quite so small, if you travel down from Yorkshire, through the Midlands, through the moneyed Cotswolds or whatever, into Sussex, they couldn't be more different. And yet we're the same nation. The identities are still there. Although I'm a natural southerner, I'm very fond of the north. It's taken me a hell of a long time to get to know what they're talking about—not understand their language, but understand the body language behind it. They're quite gentle, supportive people, but quite brusque occasionally. And they love to tell me: 'Well, it's not so bad'— you know, the play—and that's actually the big, big praise.

John Bury

1 9 2 5—2 0 0 0

Designer. He designed productions for Joan Littlewood for many years including Oh! What a Lovely War, *and for Peter Hall designed* The Wars of the Roses, The Homecoming *and* Amadeus *among many other productions. Along with Jocelyn Herbert he gave a visual syntax to much of British theatre for a generation. I interviewed him in his house in Burleigh, in Gloucestershire.*

You met Joan Littlewood and you saw the work of Theatre Workshop just at the end of the war. Well, how did it happen?

I'd met the company and seen their work when my family were in digs in Middlesbrough —Father had been taken up there during the war: he was a chemist, but had got involved in the Bomb, I think. I came home on leave from the Navy, and my mother had heard that this theatre company was playing. I saw their show, and I met them. And next year, when I was on leave again, I went to a summer school which they were taking part in. I turned up in full naval uniform, and Ewan MacColl [co-founder of Theatre Workshop with Joan Littlewood] took great delight in making me lie on the floor and roll over, do breathing exercises while giving me no moment to change out of my uniform. Billie Whitelaw was there at the age of about fourteen. She was laid on the floor with me. It was an eye-opener. At the end of the summer school, they said: 'When you're demobbed, what are you going to do?' That was really the end of me because I got absorbed, and that was that. Joan was there, and I became very fond of her. Although I wasn't any good as an actor—they tried me out for a couple of days, but decided there was no hope there—I was a terribly useful

253

chappie because I knew how to mend fuses and organise things, and it transpired that I could cook far more economically and better than anybody else.

But you became company lighting designer?

Unfortunately Ben Ellis, who had been the lighting designer, had a very bad time over Hamburg during the war and became highly schizophrenic. Just as he was setting off on our first tour, he had to be taken off lighting. So there I was, willy-nilly going off on tour with this huge great board, thousands of wires, not having lit a show in the professional theatre before. And I took also to the communal living, because, having been in the Navy for a long time, I could make things work. And, like me, very few of the company were actors in any sense of that word; very few of them had been trained.

Were they performers?

Joan made them perform. She turned people into performers. She took people and built them up into the fantasy. She had the knack of getting people moving. You daren't be late, to begin with. Joan was a great disciplinarian, particularly in the early years. She was very good, we were told; on the ball. She would take a situation, and she would run it and improvise us around it and try different people in different parts: everybody had to have a go. And you were looked out and pushed away and then, gradually, you'd realise she was getting somewhere. Sometimes when she was dealing with people like me, she had to show me what to do, how to stand and hold my breath, and the rest of it. She was always very bouncy, always totally alive and never inner, never private in any sense. She never went to talk to somebody else in the corner or anything. Everything was done out there on the floor, together. But she didn't keep me at acting long.

First of all you were an electrician, then a lighting designer, and then you became a stage designer?

Yes.

How did that transformation occur?

I began to take the problem of our switchboard and our equipment quite seriously. Most of it was pretty worn and derelict, picked up from various theatres around Yorkshire and Lancashire, and I made it work until I was really quite proud of it. And then I looked at the problems of rigging and unrigging and how long it took: so we made up cable runs and things, which were all quite new. I became hooked, as it were, on the lighting.

But how did you move from being a technician to an artist?

I pretty soon saw, when I was doing lighting, that lighting and the set were really the same problem, and I couldn't really light a show which I hadn't designed myself. So I got interested in surfaces, techniques, how to do it. And what made a set alive on stage. I could never manage to light somebody else's box set or painted set at all.

Is that when you started to develop a sort of sculptural use of space? And texture, which has always seems to have marked out your designs. You discovered this for yourself. You hadn't been to Germany and seen [Brecht's designer] Caspar Neher's work?

Later on I saw Caspar Neher's work, and later on I worked with the Berliner Ensemble for a bit—not worked, but observed—and it reinforced everything. I learned a few more tricks, taught them a few, you know: it was quite fun. But I worked it out myself. Everyone was getting terribly keen about Brecht and rushing off to Germany and then coming back and having white light and grey walls and things.

You had got there already?

Yes, I'd got to it already, yes.

Was Joan urging you to go in that direction?

Joan was a great critic, mainly by liking things that I did. 'That's fine, let's have a bit more of that, Camel,' she said—I was called 'Camel' in those days. I was encouraged and pushed in that direction.

You started to work on Shakespeare with Joan?

Joan was keen on language, of course, very keen on language. She was as big as Peter [Hall] is on getting the text right. She produced out of Harry II. Corbett, the younger Steptoe, the best Richard II that I think anybody's seen in this generation. George Cooper's Bolingbroke was good. She worked very hard with them. But we didn't have much of a set, if we did have a set at all. She just worked on the actors on what was going on, what they were meaning.

So you'd achieved the kind of minimalism that really didn't become widespread for twenty or thirty years in Shakespeare?

Yes, yes, yes, yes.

Joan was asked to do Henry IV, *both parts, at Stratford, when Peter Hall took over at Stratford [in 1958] and you went to design it.*

Yes.

And then you stayed and became a member of Peter's company?

I had nowhere to go. We were straight out of digs in East London and went up to Stratford [-upon-Avon] to help Joan, but she took off for Nigeria. Peter said to me: 'You'd better stay.' And I said: 'I think I'd better.' So that was that.

So it was accident rather than a sort of considered strategy on Peter's part to enlist you?

Ken Tynan, at the National Theatre, was putting out feelers about what I was going to do, and Peter Hall apparently had been putting out feelers. But on the whole Joan was the prize. I mean, they all wanted Joan; they weren't particularly after me.

So you go to design Wars of the Roses [1963]. *Did you know what you were doing?*

I knew quite a bit more than they thought I did. John Barton was a menace. He had no business sense at all: every time he tried to change something that I did, I nearly went through the roof because he always changed the wrong thing. So I had to be very firm with quite a lot of it. But Peter was very good, globally. They knew when I was doing a good job on the scene and when I wasn't.

There was a scene in Henry V, *the departure for France, where there was just a bollard at the front of the stage and a huge hawser that came down from the flies. You imagined this ship there, and there was absolutely nothing else on the stage. I'd hardly ever been to the theatre, and it was a revelation to me that you could suggest a whole world with minimal resources. Had that come to you out of years of working with Theatre Workshop?*

I didn't want to give them too much, you know.

I remember that rope as having real texture. And all that steel on the stage floor.

It was actually copperplate treated with sulphide to make it look steely. I had it on all the walls too. Everything was made of steel, that was the language of the production. Armour and steel. We had a long rehearsal period; we had the stage to ourselves, so we didn't have a repertoire to cope with. And going to Stratford was a great joy, because there was a very good army of technicians and friends— and their lighting designers. I've always been scared of the commercial, professional theatre because I like doing everything myself, and they don't always like you doing everything yourself. But at Stratford everybody was terribly helpful. The lighting team worked very well with me. And I became very attached to the whole scene at Stratford. It was like being back at Stratford East, you know, where they were all handpicked people.

You went back from Stratford-upon-Avon to Stratford East to Joan to do Oh! What a Lovely War?

Oh! What a Lovely War was great fun. Joan had been listening one night to a radio programme—Charles Chilton's—with the First World War songs. We both remembered them, and we felt there was something there that could be used. So Joan got a pianist and they were all banged out: the company was in pretty good shape for improvisation in those days. Joan and me went through the whole lot, and we built in the way that only Joan can: one minute it's absolute chaos and you don't know what you're doing; then suddenly you've got a show which you totally believe in. It's amazing the way it does work with Joan. All the big ones have just come, materialised, out of a lot of material, then suddenly she puts a finger on the right button, and you're there. Suddenly we had a show, a few scenes had to be changed occasionally, but it remained consistent. Of course that's why she loved it so much, and when other people started messing around with it she got absolutely furious—that silly film they made of it, you know.

Was it your idea to add the photographs on the screen?

I was wary of doing the photographs. We were going to have more photographs, but you can't act against photographs. It just didn't work when you put up endless pictures of the Western Front and had people doing things in front of it. Either you look at the photographs or you look at the show. I cut the photographs right down to the musical moments. So that we had a photo-sequence when they were singing, and then no more.

And what about the news panel?

We felt a need for factual contact, you know the 'FIVE THOUSAND DIED YESTERDAY' stuff. But again you couldn't use it all the time. You had to wait to the right moment: then you had the song, and then you had your newsflash. And then you went back to the show. It was going to be used far too much originally, but Joan and I between us cut right down to about four or five key moments.

Now, like a number of her shows, the success in a sense consumed Theatre Workshop, because The Hostage *transferred, so did* A Taste of Honey *I think,* Oh! What a Lovely War, Fings Ain't What They Used T'be, *all these shows were transferring and so the company was broken apart by its own success.*

Indeed, yes.

Was that part of the reason that Joan gave up?

Yes, Joan was very fed up. Every time she got a company together, it got split, and those bastards in the West End, as she referred to them, were stealing all her little chickens. And after a bit she gave up. I hung on as long as possible, in fact I two-timed for a bit at the end to keep Stratford East running.

Was she very bitter at the lack of support from the Arts Council?

Well, verbally, yes. 'Right bastards' she'd call them all. I think she provoked the opposition in that she would never give way to any artistic mentor. She would never have the Arts Council come down and discuss the problems with them. She was absolutely determined to be alone; she didn't want to be lectured or talked to or have it explained to her why she couldn't have any more money. But by the time she left she'd—well, she'd had it, I think, and she realised that she wasn't getting any further. When I first joined the company, I couldn't understand why we weren't the National Theatre of Great Britain.

You designed Happy Days *at the National?*

Yes, yes.

Did you have any strong feelings about Beckett?

I wouldn't sort of put Beckett down on my list of playwrights. He's got there without me.

Would you put Behan on your list of playwrights?

Oh yes, undoubtedly. Well, Behan/Littlewood. They manufactured text on the rehearsal floor. You couldn't do it without Brendan being there. Joan used to hold a pistol to his head, trying to make him write two more pages of dialogue. He was a wonderful chappie. He talked and he talked, and he wasn't frightened of anybody. Just drank too much, but he probably couldn't have written if he hadn't drunk as much as that.

What is it about the theatre that's always attracted you so much?

It gets me in touch with people, I think, because I'm a rather lonely sort of man.

Victor Spinetti

1 9 3 3—

Actor. Victor Spinetti appeared in many of Joan Littlewood's Theatre Workshop productions including The Hostage, Fings Ain't Wot They Used T'Be and Oh! What a Lovely War in the West End. I interviewed him in Brighton, within walking distance of the West Pier, which, in its heyday, housed the sort of Pierrot show on which Oh! What a Lovely War was based. While we were talking, as in a séance, I saw a woman over Victor's shoulder emerging on a balcony beyond the window at the end of the room in which were sitting. It was Joan Littlewood, haunting us. She was staying with Victor, as she often did, but refused to be interviewed. 'Nothing against you, love,' he said, 'but she says that talking about the past would be like a dog returning to its vomit.'

You first met Joan Littlewood when you auditioned for her?

I walked on stage and I expected a voice in the dark to say: yes, do something. But for the first time ever a director came down to the front and said: 'Hello, my name is Joan Littlewood, have we met?' I said: 'No, we've not met.' And she said: 'Well, what would you give me for this set?' I looked round, and it was half a beer barrel and a sort of a window frame and nothing much. And I said: 'Oh, I don't know, a fiver.' She said: 'This is a Sean Kenny set. If you owned this theatre and someone said they were going to pull it down and give you a million pounds'—I'm talking '59—'what would you do?' I said: 'Oh, I'd take the money and go on a cruise.' She said: 'You've got the part.'

You joined the Theatre Workshop Company to do The Hostage.

To do *The Hostage* in New York. I said to Brendan [Behan]: 'What can a Welsh-Italian play in your play, Brendan?' And he said: 'A fucking IRA officer, of course.' During rehearsal, Joan said to me: 'You're the IRA officer, right, so you have to bully us. So I want you just to be a bully. I want you to come into rehearsals and say: "Right, it's one o'clock lunch!" Bully us, make sure we break for tea, make sure we finish rehearsals on time.' Well, during a performance there was a laugh and without thinking, because of the way we'd been working, I swung round to the audience and said: 'Silence, this is a serious play.' Well, of course there was bigger laugh. Brendan, the next day, rang up and said: 'Keep that fucking line in because it's one of funniest fucking lines I never wrote.' And that's her way of working.

What was her attitude towards the script?

Brendan would come and tell stories. Rehearsals would stop, and he'd sit there, and he'd tell us yarn after yarn after yarn, and then go to the pub. He'd come back, and those stories would be in the play. And Brendan would say: 'Oh, that's good, I wish I'd thought of that in the first place.' And Joan said: 'Well, you did.'

What latitude were you allowed?

Well, you didn't have to do it if you didn't want to. You could withdraw. You could say: 'I'm not going to play this, bugger this,' and go and sit and watch. I used to go down, and I'd sit in the back of the stalls and watch Joan working in an area of pink light. 'I want my actors to look... actors are delicate...'—what's the word she used?—'they're birds' eggs, highly decorative but fragile. Gerry, for Christ's sake, take the bloody stage light out. Let's have pink light, let's make a warm light, I want you to feel good and look good in this light.' And we'd all sit in this light murmuring away and talking. And lots and lots and lots of laughter. With *Oh! What a Lovely War*, we sat in the green room, and she played the songs of the First World War, the tape of the Bud Flanagan programme. At the end of it she said: 'Well, what do you think?' And I said: 'Oh God, I hate those songs, I hate them so much my stomach's in a knot. When I was a kid, I used to watch those parades and see the poppies on the headmaster's car and the bonnet of his Riley—a big bunch of poppies—and I'd think: oh, I hate it.' And I said: 'I hate those songs, they give me the shivers.' Now most directors would say: 'Well, you can't be in this if you hate those songs.' She said: 'Oh, that's marvellous, darling. You can be the MC, then you won't have to sing them.' She worked on attitude.

She didn't impose?

Never. Never schematic. Peter Brook would spend six months telling you why there's a proscenium arch. Joan Littlewood asked me to demolish a proscenium arch, and I didn't even know that she'd done that. She said to me in *Oh! What a Lovely War*, at the very first performance, cigarette glowing in the wings, and I'm standing there on stage, soaking up the atmosphere—I like to be around where it's happening and waiting for the house to open: hush in the theatre—and suddenly she comes across and she says: 'We don't have an opening to the play really, darling; there's no opening.' I said: 'There's "Row, Row, Row".' She said: 'No, that's a song. I tell you what, go and talk to the audience.' I said: 'What about?' She said: 'Don't ask me. Just go and talk to the audience, take a risk. All right?' We were solid, we'd worked in a solid way: no walking on wreckage. And as she passed by to go to her usual seat in the gallery, she said: 'Oh, by the way, I can see your bald spot from the gallery.'

It sounds slapdash and yet when I saw the productions they appeared to be very fastidious. And you talk about being on very firm ground. How did that happen?

The actual work was amazing. It was solid, hard graft. When we did all the scenes in *A Lovely War*—the assassination scene, or the walking in the park scene—we would do that for hours. Walking through a park: we had to *see* it. When we rode through the orchard at the end of the show, we *were* in an orchard. We really had to do these exercises until we actually didn't have to say: we are now pretending to be in an orchard. We *were* on horseback.

How did the text get put together?

I have an original script somewhere: in fact, somebody borrowed it a few months ago to look at, and it's really not that much. All the songs are set, of course. Everything that Haig said was actually from his diaries, quoted absolutely correct. When we came to doing the scenes, for example, she said one day: 'Anyone been in the army?' And I said: 'Yeah, I did my National Service in the South Wales Borderers.' She said: 'What was that like?' 'Oh well,' I said, 'I remember we went to the padre's half-hour, and the padre was a little Welsh preacher: "Now, boys, seeing we're in the army, three things: don't drink, don't use bad language and keep away from the women." And we'd just been marched down from the bayonet practice, where this loony sergeant had stood with a bucket of hot pig's blood. He'd put the cup in the blood and, as you stuck the bayonet in the sandbag, he'd throw this in your face, to teach you that when you stick something in, something comes out.' So I told Joan this and she said: 'Oh well, we'll have a padre's half-hour, and we'll have a drill sergeant.' And she brought a drill sergeant down to drill us—we had umbrellas and walking sticks, we didn't have any rifles or anything like that—and he taught us the drill. When he left I can see her now coming through the stalls and saying: 'Oh, darling, I can't bear those licensed killers; what did he say?' I said: 'I never knew what they said to me in the army.' She said: 'Well, don't tell me, show me.' So I said: 'All right.' So we got some actors together, and I did just noises. And when I looked out she was falling about rolling about laughing. She said: 'You bastard, what are you doing working for me? That's a thousand-pound-a-week act at the London Palladium. Never rehearse it.' And of course I never rehearsed it. Some nights it would last two minutes, some nights three, if it went well, four. If it went too long, Joan would open the dressing room door and say: 'You're getting your laughs.' Boom boom.

When did she decide to turn it into a Pierrot show?

It was always going to be a Pierrot show. Because she had this idea from a kid. The interesting thing about that is no Pierrot costumes were made. No one made costumes. The costume designer wanted to do it: she wanted to make all this sort of stuff. But Joan said: 'No, don't make costumes till you see the actors and let them work first.' And there was no khaki except the second half in the one gas scene. I wore a hat for the drill sergeant, but that's all. And Haig wore the correct full uniform, yes. The way it came about—oh, you've opened up such a can of beans—she said: 'Right, let's do the trenches scene. Let's do war films.' So we played, oh, the bombs, the guns, the shells. We got all that out of our system doing scenes from *Journey's End* and all that. She said: 'All right, now split the company in half. Half of you go and sit in the back of the stalls. The other half stay on stage. Turn all the lights out in the theatre. Not only the lights but the exit signs too.' So the whole place was absolutely dark except for some grey light filtering through from the flies. 'Now I want someone to make a noise in the back of the stalls and I want someone on the stage to try and recognise who that person is.' She said: 'Right, that's it. When the shells are coming over and the machine guns start, you know where they'll be.' I knew at that moment we were there—we were in the trenches. And of course when the trenches scene came to be rehearsed, people talked quietly amongst themselves in the middle of all this mayhem. That's how she created that atmosphere which was there with us. That's what I mean about feeling solid in the scene.

Do you think she was thoughtful about her rehearsal process?

She watched a lot and listened a lot and used what was coming from us, but she had a framework in which to put that. Rehearsals went on for ever, and you didn't mind it. We weren't sitting round. Nobody did a crossword. We were all absolutely involved in this kind of mind-plugging-in, as she called her cybernetics, plugging in to this central mind, everything that we know.

Did you ever talk about the meaning of the piece as a whole?

No, no, we didn't.

Did you always rehearse on stage?

We always tried to do it on stage. And always tried to do it in very nice lighting.

What about the music?

In *Lovely War*, we never harmonised. Most productions afterwards made the mistake of putting in harmonies, we just sang it as the soldiers sang it, and of course Alfie Rowlston, the Musical Director, used to go mad because he wanted a little harmony now and then.

She wanted theatre that had the feeling of music hall.

Theatre of Joy. We had to say to people: 'Look, this is lovely, come and join us.' She said: 'We're here. Our business is to entertain: whatever message you have to put across unless you entertain, don't bother.' She was anti-Brecht, and people were very surprised by that. She thought he was a boring old bugger.

What happened the opening night, the press night in Stratford?

We didn't do flowers and cards and all that. We never knew when the press were coming, it was part of the rehearsal period. We were still, as far as we were concerned, in rehearsal.

Were there any old soldiers there?

Yes, and there were people who got up and threw their programmes at us. That tickertape at the back said: 'HUNDRED THOUSAND MEN KILLED FOR A GAIN OF TEN YARDS.' She had a letter from the War Office saying: 'Miss Littlewood, we must point out that it was a hundred thousand *officers* and men.' And she wrote back and said: 'I'm doing your officers the honour of calling them "men".' She received lots of hate mail.

Weren't there people who felt very strongly that you told the truth?

Princess Margaret. 'What's been said here tonight should have been said a long time ago, don't you agree, Lord Cobbold [Lord Chamberlain]?'

Did he?

Well, yes, we got her permission to go to the West End because of that.

What about people who'd fought in the war?

We had letters and support from people who had been through that war and literally engulfed us after the show. It was very moving. I've only had two shows I've been proud to be in—*The Hostage* and *Oh! What a Lovely War*.

263

What did Joan look like when she was rehearsing?

Always had a cap, always had a fag. Always walked about not quite catching your eye. Not looking up, walking about in this circle of light, and in the middle of that circle of light we'd be sitting and maybe somebody would be telling the story. She'd say: 'Just a minute, darling. If you actually knew the result of what had just happened to you, would you have changed your behaviour or anything like that?' Bit like in the psychiatrist's chair sort of thing, but it was easy, and there was a lot of laughter. Or she'd take her hat off and stamp it on the ground. 'You bastards!' Either with joy or anger, but her anger was always an act. She'd say: 'Our job is to entertain, we're seducers. The purpose of getting on the stage is to get off, preferably to be in time for the pubs to still be open. Don't hang about. You've got greasepaint on your heels. Get off.' And she would write her notes up for the cast. And then the next day as you come to the stage door, all along that wall there'd be notes. Halfway up the stairs there'd be notes, so everybody would read them: the cleaners that came in in the morning, the stage-door keeper, the fireman, knew exactly what she thought of us.

What three adjectives you would use to describe her?

Tempestuous. Loving. Laughing. Her laughter was wonderful.

What was her attitude to other theatres? What about the National Theatre?

She loathed the building. She said: 'I'll never go inside that building as long as I live.'

What about the Arts Council?

She never got a penny from them in the entire time that she was revered in the world. When she resigned from the theatre, or retired from the theatre, countries offered her whatever she wanted—not cities, countries. Germany offered her, Australia offered her, Canada offered her, they all offered her. But she felt: oh no, without Gerry [Raffles], who was really her guiding light, she couldn't do it. She said: 'I can't do it without him.' The support was all. I mean total. She never carried any money. She was like royalty. Gerry would do it for her. She was always into the work. She brought a life and an energy, whatever she was doing. The Fun Palace was her great dream, of course, on that stretch of land that's still empty. She should have done the Dome. She wanted to create a place of learning, to create a place of entertainment, to create a place rather like those gardens, Vauxhall Gardens. She thinks that everyone has genius, a sense of spirit, and that spirit should be brought out by education. She should run education. She should run RADA. She should run the National. She should run the Royal Shakespeare Company. She should run them all. Because of this life force that she has. This tremendous excitement about learning. Even now, she would be reading in a book in English and in French, both at the same time.

What do you think her influence on the theatre has been?

She says it doesn't exist.

I think she's completely wrong.

Well, I still try and work, if I can, in that way—to try and not walk on wreckage, which is what most actors do. I see them standing in the wings, and my heart breaks getting on stage like sort of a conveyor belt and then it's the end of Act One and you get off and then you get back on and it's the end of Act Two and you get off. Wreckage.

John McGrath

1 9 3 5—2 0 0 2

Playwright and director. Unusually for a left-wing playwright, John McGrath graduated from a theatre of doubt and ambiguity to the certainties of polemic and direct address. He started writing for television, initiating Z Cars, *later writing film and theatre—*Events While Guarding the Bofors Gun *and* Random Happenings in the Hebrides, *both of which I directed in the late sixties in Edinburgh. He started his own company in the early seventies and called it 7:84—its title based on a 1971 statistic: 7% of the population of the country own 84% of the wealth. The defining work of the company was the company's first show:* The Cheviot, the Stag and the Black, Black Oil, *about the Highlands clearances and the oil boom. With its mixture of sketches and songs, borrowed from the ceilidh, it played in towns and villages throughout the Highlands. A friend since the mid-sixties, I interviewed him in his home in London. For a man who had recovered from leukaemia a few years earlier, he was astonishingly vigorous on that day. Sadly the illness claimed him two years later.*

When did you first hear of Brecht's work?

I missed the 1956 visit because I was in France. When I came back everybody said: oh, there's this wonderful theatre which you've just missed.

What were people saying was so wonderful about it?

They weren't terribly sure—they were theatrical people so they weren't very articulate—but they were saying that they were really terribly impressed by the production. And that's what I think is interesting about Brecht, really: he's a great director, he's a great salesman, and he's a great self-publicist. And with these three attributes he managed to absolutely snow the whole theatrical establishment of England, because they then went round trying to imitate Brecht, which my lot—my sort of intellectuals, if you want to call them that—thought was hysterically funny. We went to see Peggy Ashcroft doing *The Good Woman of Setzuan*, directed by George Devine, and it was ridiculous, it was absurd, it was one of the funniest cabaret turns in history to hear Peggy Ashcroft pretending to be this peasant woman with these cut-glass vowels. It was rather like a Michael Powell movie, set in Scotland with a kind of Heather Sears-type actress all the way from Middlesex come to play a jolly Scottish lass. The absurdity was compounded when we started finding out what Brecht was actually writing about. Because what he was really writing about was a combination of political vulgar materialism and a sort of scientism—this kind of absurd belief that science was going to cure everything and, if he believed something to be scientifically correct, that that meant that it was a law, a rule, of life and of society—which actually relates directly to Stalin and Stalinism. It's that kind of mindset of the singular truthfulness of a verifiable assertion.

He travelled to Denmark and Los Angeles with the complete works of Hegel and of Lenin.

Did he ever read them?

They were marked up—every single volume. I saw them in his apartment in Berlin. So the Royal Court aesthetes—as opposed to you—in your view separated the politics and the aesthetics?

Yes. They were snowed by his power as a director and by the theatricality of what he achieved as a director, and to a certain extent by the theatricality of his writing. I don't think they had any clue what he was really saying.

When you did see his plays, were you simultaneously repelled by the politics and entranced by the aesthetics? Or did you see them as inseparable?

That's a very complex question, because I saw Brecht's politics as being highly dangerous, in that they didn't allow for humanity to creep in. It was all about scientific fact, and really this was the basis for the social engineering that killed ten million kulaks. It was a terrible way to think. I don't accuse Brecht of being entirely in favour of Stalin. Certainly in East Berlin, when that uprising came in June '53, he made his great remark: 'It would appear that the German people have elected the wrong government, and it's time that the government elected a new German people.' That was very good. But the aesthetics were the aesthetics of a kind of historical epic, which was very exciting on the one hand—good narrative qualities, very striking theatrical images—but with curiously little relationship to either his politics or his philosophy, in as far as I could tell. They seemed to just exist because he had huge theatrical instinct.

I'd say that the great thing we learn from Brecht is to go back to Shakespeare.

Well, that's what Brecht did in some of the finer productions. I mean, *Coriolan* was a wonderful production. *Arturo Ui* had some very striking theatrical ideas in it and was basically an attempt to go back to Shakespeare, and it was very, very good. But *Galileo* I find a curiously naive and simple-minded piece of philosophy—that's why I asked if he'd actually read Hegel. It has some wonderful theatrical effects, but, really, as a piece of writing it's lamentable.

I think he thought the same.

Did he? Well, at least he was a self-critic as well as a self-publicist.

If you look at our theatre—and I mean, particularly the theatre of the seventies, or today— what would you say Brecht's legacy has been?

I think Brecht's legacy to British theatre—Brecht amongst others—is in the theatricality that he achieved. I think it's in reintroducing music as integral to the way of telling a story, which was mediated through Joan Littlewood: Joan's use of music made what she was saying, what she was doing, much more approachable to a popular audience. Brecht was never really totally concerned about a popular audience. I think his attempt to reintroduce history into the theatre in the form of epic construction was a huge challenge to us. We lived under the shadow of Shakespeare, and anybody who writes in English since Shakespeare has been having to avoid being Shakespearean, because that's the trap that the Romantic poets fell into with a great thud. You have to avoid it, but Brecht showed that it was possible to write epic theatre without being mock-Shakespearean, which was terrific. I think his use of design in theatre, as mediated through many people—Jocelyn Herbert in particular—brought a fresh sense of the stage as a space with a relationship to the audience. That opened all kinds of possibilities to us for writing: it made a whole lot of things possible. On the whole I have to say—reluctantly—that Brecht did introduce a few ideas into theatre and a way of expressing ideas and a way of making them available to a larger public that really had not been seen in the British theatre. The way of handling ideas of Shaw and Galsworthy in the theatre was through conversation, through dialogue about the ideas. Brecht somehow was able—like a really good screenplay writer—to introduce concepts into theatre not through talking about them, but by showing them happening, showing their effects. This is what Brecht brought to us, and what I suppose I'm grateful for.

Were you also in France when Godot *opened in London, or did you see it in France?*

I saw *Waiting for Godot* in the Arts Theatre in the original production and absolutely loved it. Actually what I think I'd heard before *Godot*—though it may have been after—was a radio play called *All That Fall* [broadcast in January 1957]. I was at the time a great fan of James Joyce and loved that language—that relationship with the English language Joyce has. And Beckett inherited a lot of that from Joyce. He doesn't have the range and diversity, he doesn't have the wit of Joyce, but in the theatre he brought an awareness of just the power of words banging together, which was terrific. And again his ideas in the theatre I found sort of closer to home in many ways than I did those of Brecht. But Beckett's language, and his sense of the kind of grim realities of life, were quite liberating in a way.

How did that correspond to your own experience?

In my experience, Beckett is writing, as most Irish writers did, about the hard life of the Irish peasant, which is also my background: my family were all Irish peasants of one sort or another. But Beckett wrote about it in such a way as to universalise that bleakness, that sense of desolation, which somehow applied suddenly to all the millions of refugees wandering across Europe. When doing my National Service in Germany, I saw refugee camps, displaced persons... just terrible, the desolation and the ruin of lives and the ruin of cities, and the way that the world was, ten years after the end of the war, indeed fifteen years after the end of the war. East Berlin was rubble: there were still just bricks piled up on the pavement, and Hitler was still underneath his bunker. This terrible feeling that the world had gone wrong and was having to slowly and very painfully pull itself through a grim period. What Beckett was writing about... I don't know whether he was conscious of wanting to express that—I wouldn't accuse him of that—but I think his imagery was able to encompass that. And that made it mean a great deal to many, many people. Also the mental and psychological desolation of the fear of the Bomb, of these great superpowers, who could obliterate the world. Somehow, I don't know why, but it doesn't seem to loom so large in people's consciousnesses now, but it actually still exists. When it was new, from '45 onwards, we all felt that we were just keeping going on and that it could end, but at the end of it something would still tick on, that human hearts would still tick on. And I think that's what Beckett's imagery kind of contained.

Was it also a sort of theatrical emancipation?

I think Beckett's influence on the theatre has been largely deleterious, in that people have read him as being symbolic. I hate symbolic plays—particularly plays where there are people called 'The Woman' and 'The Husband' and 'The Giant'. But he liberated the language of theatre. The language of Beckett is so wonderful—the way the words bounce together, the kind of crispness and the crackle of the language.

Didn't he liberate the theatrical language, the language of physical imagery on the stage?

He did for himself, and it worked to a large extent. But I'm very cautious about his imitators. You either have people or events or argument or polemic or whatever, but symbols in the theatre—no, they don't work.

As Chekhov said.

Did he?

He said it in a critique of Ibsen. What did the Royal Court mean to you?

The Royal Court meant to me what it meant to a lot of people who were trying to write plays. A place where plays could be taken seriously and where you would have some feedback, and a place where plays were done—new plays about all kinds of things. It didn't have a particular ideological position, and it didn't have a particularly theatrical position, though of course George Devine brought a lot of the Michael Saint-Denis Parisian school of directing into the Royal Court.

Which was?

Which was liberation from the English tradition. What I got from George [Devine] was a wonderful sense of how much the actor could do without too much assistance. I used to go to classes that George Devine gave on trips and falls, and how to walk across the stage, and in the use of masks. What it was all about was the use of the naked actor, basically, without all the paraphernalia of theatre—narrowing theatre down to the one wonderful rich source, which was the actor.

So it was thoroughly humanist?

George was a complete humanist and that went through most of the plays, but he was so humanist that he wasn't exclusively humanist.

But is it possible to be anything else if you work in the theatre?

Yes, I think it is.

How? If it's this medium that puts human beings at the centre, and human beings communicating with other human beings, and everything depends upon the dimension of the human, how can it be anything else but humanist?

Well, for example, some of Brecht's plays are not humanist: they're anti-humanist. They're about the necessity of certain political acts which rise above the immediate human situation. And I think some of Beckett's imagery is anti-human: I mean, it's saying human beings are shit. But there is something that goes on, something that continues. A life force. George was a profoundly human, human being, and that's what made the Court so great because he was a very inclusive person: he understood a whole range of theatrical techniques and was able to embrace a whole new flood of new ideas into the theatre.

Look Back in Anger is held to be the watershed. What did you think at the time?

It's a typical sort of journalist's and academic's mistake, to identify the importance of the Royal Court with *Look Back in Anger*. It was an interesting play in that a whole generation of rather reactionary English people recognised themselves in a rather reactionary English play. But what was so important about the Royal Court wasn't *Look Back in Anger*. It put the Royal Court on the map, and it gave them headlines in the papers, and it made a furore and a *scandale*. What was important for playwrights was that the Court would take plays seriously, and that they had an all-inclusive policy of looking at any play that had talent and that had theatricality. And it was the production of a generation of writers: John Arden and Arnold Wesker and Keith Johnstone and ultimately Edward Bond, and before that Wally [N.F.] Simpson and Ann Jellicoe—the list goes on. And they introduced Brecht, in a rather lamentable way, but they tried. I found *Look Back in Anger* interesting, but not so great as a play. And the production was all right, but it wasn't so wonderful. What George Devine and his colleagues at the Royal Court achieved was to actually get some subsidy, to actually find ways of doing plays which didn't have to travel to the West End and satisfy that stultifying audience.

Joan Littlewood never got a subsidy but transformed British theatre. When did you first know about her work?

I was aware of *Uranium 235*, Ewan MacColl's play, which Joan had done for some time as part of her general awareness of plays about the Bomb, but I never actually saw Joan's work until Sean Kenny, who was a wonderful designer—who went on to design *Oliver!* for Lionel Bart—was going to design a play that I was doing in Oxford, based on Joyce's *Ulysses*, called *Bloom's Day*. Sean said: 'I want to paint the back wall of the Oxford Playhouse,' and I said: 'Well, you can't, what would that look like?' And he said: 'Well, I've just designed a show in Theatre Workshop. There's a dress rehearsal: you'd better come and have a look.' So I went down to the dress rehearsal with Sean, and it turned out that the show that Sean wanted me to go and see was in fact the dress rehearsal of *The Hostage*. And sure enough the back wall was painted black. But that wasn't what grabbed me about *The Hostage*; it was the whole style of the piece, the use of music, the brio, the sense of life about it, the wonderful use of language, the terrific performing skills of the actors. I've never really got over that particular evening. Brendan [Behan] was in the stalls, and the actors made a terrible mistake and said: 'Where is the author? He'll have to come and rewrite this.' And Brendan shouted from the stalls: 'I'm here, are you fucking blind?' That was very important to me because it transformed the whole theatre into one space—in which the audience took part in what was a celebration of life, but more specifically of popular styles of entertainment. And that was really where I found something that chimed with what I'd been missing, a connection between the stage—the language, the style of entertainment, what it was saying, what it was about, who was in it, what kind of people they were—and the audience: what they liked, and what they wanted for entertainment, and what their values were. And that was all there in that exchange with Brendan.

By that time Joan Littlewood had been doing that sort of theatre for twenty years. Do you know anything about her work in the thirties?

Ewan MacColl, when he was about fifteen, went with a mate to the Salford Amateur Dramatic Society, because they thought theatre might be interesting, and they decided in true apparatchik fashion that this was really boring and that they were going to take it over. So they took over the Salford Amateur Dramatics and renamed them the Red Megaphones—took them out on the streets to do street theatre in the markets. It was pure propaganda, because Ewan and the group then were in the Communist Party. Joan, I think, was working for the BBC in Manchester, saw what was going on and got quite enamoured of Ewan and drawn into that kind of theatre. And then, of course, she brought her own wonderful talent for drawing people in—entertaining people, challenging the actors to entertain people better, to make it more interesting—and her own intolerance of laziness and sloppiness and boredom in the theatre.

What was she like to be with?

She was quite challenging. By the time that I got to know her, she was on her way to becoming a grand lady of the theatre. But I imagine she was always kind of tough. There was an element of posing about the toughness, because she was really very soppy. But she had learned to... it was a sort of thirties/forties, left-wing posture of being gruff, and, I suppose, making up for not being working-class by being rude and gruff and tough. But she was wonderful: I mean, her smile was just worth a million dollars. She just brought so much humanity into her work—of her own humanity. She brought in this extraordinary sense of popular theatre—and that's the kind of work that I've tried to continue.

She was a great hater. Was that because she felt that everybody had cold-shouldered her?

I got the impression she was always very intolerant of people she considered fools. It seems to be a characteristic of everybody I've worked with. And she had a sharp edge to her tongue because she felt things were very urgent, that there were certain very urgent things to be done, and if people were impeding her or trying to stop her or mucking her about, or mucking about the show, she would be very sharp. But I don't think it was a spoilt-brat sort of sharpness.

Your own work—the 7:84 Company—was an attempt to create something like Joan Littlewood's work.

Yes. Yes and no.

What were the aims of 7:84?

I'd gone to the Everyman Theatre in Liverpool and seen an arty play at the Everyman. It was twenty per cent full, and I just thought this is wrong, wrong, wrong, wrong. There was a huge audience in Merseyside—which is where I'm from—for good theatre, but this isn't being it. And I wanted—having directed *Z Cars* on television, where we reached sixteen/seventeen million people—to make a theatre that would attract thousands, tens of thousands of people. Not by being vulgar and not by using all the commercial tricks, but it would be serious theatre, which would present itself in such a way that it was accessible to the people I grew up with. Most theatre was not accessible. So I started working with Alan Dossor at the Everyman. I began to get very committed to working in the Everyman to build up a local Merseyside audience. And that's what we did— and not just on the stage, but they ran a very successful bistro down below the theatre, which brought a lot of different kind of people in. It was cheap and cheerful and good. There was something about the Everyman that attracted the local audience—largely a working-class audience and a student audience, because it was also very close to the university. And, having seen that, I did a series of shows there which were designed, fairly crudely, to grow that audience. Having seen that work, I then began to want to not just play to working-class audiences on Merseyside and make just a local impression, but to make a kind of theatre that would travel to where working-class people, non-theatregoing people, liked to go for their entertainment. We took our work to them—we toured for a year and a half—and the reputation of the company [7:84] built up.

In what sense did your aims differ from someone who was trying to persuade an audience who previously hadn't gone to the theatre to see Phantom of the Opera, *for instance?*

It's a question of connection between the audience and what's happening in the theatre. A lot of writers who've had successful plays put on in the West End have sneered at what we've done and said: oh yes, but we play to more working-class people in a week than 7:84 plays to in a month. And it's perfectly true that they do play to them, but the experience of getting loaded onto a chara and driving into the West End of London and then sitting in a rather strange cathedral-like building… somehow their reception of what's on the stage is totally different; it's not a personalised reception. It's a kind of awe, really. What we were trying to do was break down all those mythologies: I mean, the mythology that you are actually experiencing something by going to *Phantom of the Opera* that might mean something to your life.

When you talk about a 'popular' theatre, what do you mean? Because the terms need defining a bit.

Yes, I've spent about twenty-five years trying to define them.

What do you mean by 'popular' theatre?

What I mean by popular theatre as opposed to what the commercial theatre means by popular theatre relates more to Gramsci's definition of the popular than to... I've forgotten his name: what's that guy who wrote *The Phantom of the Opera*?

Andrew Lloyd Webber.

Thank you. [*laughs*]

So how would you define popular theatre?

How I would define popular theatre as opposed to how Andrew Lloyd Webber would define popular theatre is: a theatre that speaks for and to a popular—i.e. a large, on the whole non-theatregoing—audience. In other words, an audience who are working-class or student or middle-class, but not living near a 'centre of excellence'. I think that a popular theatre has to use a language that relates to the entertainment language that people have come to enjoy and to appreciate. I love to use music. This is a very recognisable entertainment form for many, many people. I use pop music, or, in Scotland, folk music. I think it's very important to use comedy. People like to laugh: even in the most serious subjects, you can treat them with enough variety and comedy to hold an audience's attention. I think it's very important to use styles of performing that recognise that we are in a place and that don't try to convince the audience that they are actually somewhere else. I like the idea that the actors are actors and the audience know they're actors, can see that they're acting. And I like to cut from music to comedy to straight acting, sometimes to direct contact with the audience, to movement, to solo performance, to somebody coming on and being a comedian but carrying the story forward, somebody coming on and singing a song.

You could be describing the American musical.

What's wrong with American musicals? I think they're wonderful.

The key difference seems to be that you're taking your plays to the audience.

We're taking the play to the audience, but, unlike the American musical, our plays are about the audience and relate to the audience. My definition of popular theatre means that what we take to an audience in Clydebank means something much more direct to an audience in Clydebank than it would to an audience in Seattle. Though I must say, talking about Seattle, that what's been happening with the World Trade Organisation protests in Seattle and elsewhere is also a form of popular theatre.

You invoked the English tradition earlier. What do you mean by that?

It's very hard to define the English tradition. But it is something to do with the way that poetry was written in this century, which is a combination of modernism—i.e. the attempt to get away from Victorian values and to break new ground—with a kind of terrific diffidence about being ambitious, about saying big things. We really like to be quite contained and diffident and reserved about the size of our battles. My generation was so intensely sensitive about being pretentious that we actually never pretended to very much at all. I think that the English tradition is totally conditioned by a desire not to appear to be claiming too much, that what we achieve is achievable: you know, on the scale of Wagner to Tennyson, we're down at the Tennyson end.

But there was a big idea in the 1945 government. But then your generation inherited the defeat or the failure of that. Was the mockery to do with the sense that big ideas don't work—like Communism and Nazism?

I think the Labour government of '45 achieved a huge amount, and I don't think it's been defeated yet. It's affected everybody's lives, and it was one of the great sort of uncharacteristic moments in British life, that people did indulge in big ideas like a Welfare State, like making sure people didn't have to die in misery and didn't have to suffer because they couldn't pay the medical bill. That was huge and very uncharacteristic. It took a world war to bring it about. I don't think it's been entirely defeated, but ever since then we've been trying to trim back on that great idea. Of course, Thatcher brought in her own pretensions to a kind of remorseless market economy—and the monetarist idea that people's lives could be controlled by the manipulation of the money market—which were accompanied by vicious oppression of miners and strikers, the trade unions, and cracking people's heads, putting people in prison. That kind of pretension that she had towards intellectual superiority over the world was not part of the English tradition. Now we're getting back to the fifties. We're getting back to that sense of embarrassment at anything that might smack of a grand narrative.

Cameron Mackintosh

1 9 4 6—

Producer. Cameron Mackintosh has produced the premiere productions of The
Phantom of the Opera, Cats, Les Misérables, Miss Saigon, Mary Poppins
and revivals of Oliver! *amongst others. By using a team of resident assistant directors
and choreographers he has kept performances up to standard and created a brand
image—the 'Cameron Mackintosh musical'—which offers a worldwide guarantee
of quality. His spiritual ancestor is Florenz Ziegfeld, whose 'Follies' were
synonymous with his name, and whose shows were replicated for tour while still
playing on Broadway. With Ziegfeld, as with Cameron Mackintosh, there were
only two stars—the show and the producer. Constantly enthusiastic—even
evangelical—about musical theatre, he was interviewed in the auditorium of the
Palace Theatre, where* Les Misérables *had been playing for fifteen years.*

We're sitting in front of the set of one of your largest successes, Les Misérables. *Why do you
think it's been so popular?*

It didn't get very good reviews as a book when Hugo published it in France. In
fact, I've got a feeling that he published it in Belgium first, and then published
in France after a sixteen-year exile in the Channel Islands, but it immediately hit
a popular nerve. When we opened the show in America in Washington, I
discovered that the novel had gone to Robert E. Lee's troops and was so widely
read that his troops were nicknamed 'Lee's Miserables'. Hugo hit a nerve about
the spirit of humanity which has remained for ever, and I think the story has
been done in every language and appealed to everyone. The brilliant thing

276

Boublil and Schönberg [the composers] did was to find a way of retaining the essence of it and Trevor Nunn and John Caird [directors] and John Napier [designer] realised it in a completely different way. It's that rare thing where something is in its own way equal to the original source material, but it's complementary rather than watered down.

In many ways it's the last thing one would have predicted would be an everlasting success: it's a serious, rather earnest, piece. What is it that audiences come out feeling?

They come out feeling moved and exhilarated. One of the great things that Hugo did is that the characters are timeless—we'll know a Thénardier, we'll know a Javert, we've all seen an Eponine. It's very primal, and therefore it becomes an emotional rollercoaster. It's about the survival of the human spirit, which is the most basic instinct that any of us have.

Is part of its allure that these are general types rather than specific ones?

I think so, and, because they are general, the chances of a member of the audience recognising something of themselves in it is much higher.

Maybe that's a sort of definition of popular art, that the more specific it becomes, in a sense, the less popular. Do you think that's true?

The reason why Rodgers and Hammerstein's musicals have always appealed in Europe, and still are appealing today, is that they are always all about simple people—Maria, Anna, Curly in *Oklahoma!*, Billy in *Carousel*—and they teach people who should know better a lesson in life. That's something that never changes.

Cats is about simple, ordinary cats. What's the appeal? Is it just that it's a show that can appeal to children and parents simultaneously?

I'm sure Andrew Lloyd Webber would be the first to agree that it wouldn't work without the deceptive brilliance of T.S. Eliot's libretto. It's its simplicity which is its strength.

Is it Eliot that stops the simple from tipping into the facile?

Partly, but also it's a very clever score by Andrew. Before we knew what it was, he had understood that Eliot within his poetry had written the metre of popular songs. Often Eliot used to write them to well-known songs in the thirties. And although Andrew's music is completely different, he gave the sound of these poems a sense of the street. I remember Valerie Eliot [T.S. Eliot's widow] saying after she heard the first concert version we did at Andrew's home: 'Oh, at last, Tom would have loved this because Andrew understood it was the street he was writing about.'

These three shows, Cats, Les Misérables *and* Phantom of the Opera, *are successful beyond any show before. How successful are they?* Phantom, *for instance.*

Phantom has taken more money than any other musical in history. I believe it's taken in the stratosphere of nearly two billion dollars, you know, *Les Mis* and *Cats* are well over a billion dollars, and *Miss Saigon* was nearly a billion dollars. It's still unbelievable to me.

Phantom *isn't like American musicals. What are the antecedents of* Phantom?

It's very much a European operetta. Andrew said to me, as we were working on the show: 'You know this is going to be two steps backwards to go one step forwards.' And he was absolutely right. It lies in the heart of Viennese operetta: it's a great, Gothic, romantic musical, and it doesn't, like *Rocky Horror*, try and send up the genre. It embraces it and goes for it full-bloodedly, and people get lost in it.

Do you accept some sort of hierarchy of art by which people talk about operetta as sort of second-rate art and, as it were, Verdi and Mozart as first-rate art?

I always thought the best defence of that was a wonderful critic in the *Sunday Times* called Harold Hobson, who wrote about a Ray Cooney farce saying: 'This is on an equal par with *Hamlet*.' Because, you know, whatever the art is, as long it is absolutely of the best and true to what it is trying to do, then it is a marvellous piece of work. To me, there is absolutely no difference.

So can you put your finger on exactly what Andrew is trying to do in Phantom?

It's a mythic subject, which I think Andrew is always good at. I mean, *Cats* has a mythic quality, *Evita* has a mythic quality, *Jesus Christ Superstar* has a mythic quality, and *Phantom* is a great mythic part.

What's the substance of the myths?

Phantom of the Opera is *Beauty and the Beast*. *Evita* is a *Cinderella* story that's gone wrong. We all know how *Jesus Christ Superstar* is going to end when we go into the theatre, but, just as the film *Titanic* proved, knowing the end is actually part of the reason it's a success as long as you do it well and you retell the story in an original way.

So one of the distinctions between this generation of shows and the classic American musical could be that they don't have a mythic sense?

Yes, now I come to think of it. In hindsight there is a thread through many of these shows that I think has happened by coincidence. I believe most authors are catalysts: they often don't know why they are writing something at a particular time.

These musicals depend a great deal on spectacle. Is there an incompatibility between spectacle and subtlety?

I don't think the musical theatre on the whole thrives on subtlety. There has to be something larger than life. That's why Ethel Merman put her first foot forward. In theatre, on the whole, going into song is great for when you're dealing with certainty.

So doubt and ambiguity are difficult in musicals?

As the main thread, yes. You can have doubt, you can have concern, but in the end it needs to soar. And that's why the great popular songs are usually completely certain.

Patrick Marber

1 9 6 4—

Playwright, actor and director. Patrick Marber is the author of Dealer's Choice, Closer, Howard Katz *and adaptations of Strindberg's* Miss Julie *and Molière's* Don Juan. *I commissioned his first two plays when I was at the National Theatre. He says that I made him into a playwright. It's not true: he would have become a playwright regardless. Like everyone who runs a theatre, I was opportunistic and lucky enough to be in the road when he came by. I interviewed him at his flat in the City.*

Why are your generation often diffident or contemptuous of the theatre?

I think you have to define 'my generation'. Are you talking about the general public, or people working in movies or television or both?

Both.

I think theatre's too expensive, for a start: that is a major problem that must be addressed. And I think people perceive the theatre as stodgy and bourgeois, which it often is, and not relevant to their lives. We live in an age that celebrates celebrity, and people want to go to the movies and see movie stars.

But why will people sit through stodgy and deeply bourgeois movies but won't sit through theatre?

I don't know how the movies have managed this, but they are not perceived as stodgy and bourgeois. They are perceived as a good night out, whereas the theatre isn't. I think perhaps it stems from school trips, when we were all taken to the theatre because it was good for us and educational, whereas the movies were always seen as entertainment.

Why were you attracted to theatre?

I was taken at quite an early age, and I quite enjoyed it. I acted in school plays, and I just got an early taste for it through the route of being a performer. I got a big thrill out of the live experience of it, and I've never lost that feeling and commitment to a live experience, as opposed to a celluloid or video or transmitted experience.

So what is it particularly about the live experience?

The strange thing is I say 'live', but often one goes to the theatre and it doesn't feel live at all: it feels like it's stuck in a groove. But there's the feeling that this moment that you are observing will never occur again: there will never be this group of people sitting there in one space, this group of actors sitting there. It's not a case that something might go wrong, but something might—and so to some extent there's always the sense that it's a high-wire act. That's sounds terribly grandiose. It's not a high-wire act, of course: it has all been rehearsed, and it's pretty safe. But it's the experience of being with a group of people watching another group of people doing something.

But is that why a lot of people don't like it? Because they don't want to be part of a group of people?

No, I don't think so, I think people just perceive the theatre as intrinsically boring. And intrinsically irrelevant.

But you think the theatre isn't boring and isn't irrelevant?

Oh, I think sometimes it's deathly. I mean, we all know that the experience of watching a play that is boring you is… I mean, it's hell, it's terrible. If you're bored in the movies, you can scratch your arse and eat your popcorn and chat to your friend and slob about. In general when you go to the movies there's space and that counts for something. Whereas in the theatre in general you kind of feel cramped. Theatres aren't well enough designed. And if it's bad, it feels like the worse thing that's happened to you.

And when it is good?

And when it is good, there's a kind of euphoria in the audience, who are mutually experiencing something wonderful. And the applause at the end… that split second *before* the applause is a magical moment. I still find it magical to sit in the

281

audience, and the lights go down… the sense of the ritual of it. And I like the feeling that people have been doing this for thousands of years.

When you decided you wanted to write for the theatre, what were you aspiring to?

I think at the beginning, I just wanted to be part of it: so it was a groupie instinct. I just wanted to write a play and for someone to put it on. I just wanted to be able to walk into the stage door of a theatre. It wasn't really anything beyond that. I passionately wanted to write this play that I had an idea for; I wanted to express this idea in my head that wasn't appropriate for television. But I was a fan, really.

Was there a play or was there a writer who gave you that sense that you could do whatever you wanted?

No specific play or no specific writer, but a whole group of people. Harold Pinter, obviously, to any English writer post-war is absolutely formative. And Mamet. And all the obvious people.

What is it about Pinter's writing?

The precision of it, and the delight in language and its curiosity. It's theatrical writing—it couldn't exist in any other form. I've always been excited by language. I was a stand-up comedian, and obviously you learn very quickly the value of words: that certain words in the right order will produce an effect on a live audience. Pinter's language seemed full of these kind of bullets of language. I thought it was wonderful.

But when you started in the theatre, did you have an idea of form?

No, I just had a story I thought I could tell, and the story told me what form it would take. My second play is a lot more ambitious than my first, and I hope my third play will go a bit further. I was very influenced by Beckett in terms of wanting to explore forms, and I haven't really done that to my satisfaction. But I think of myself as a fledgling writer.

So what about Beckett do you find so alluring?

From the age of about thirteen/fourteen I read Beckett—the prose—and then I started reading his plays later. I just thought he had absolute integrity as a writer. He had his vision and took it as far as he possibly could and kind of wrote plays that were almost in a condition of silence by the end. I prefer the earlier, funny ones, but, you know, I think *Endgame* is kind of perfect as a piece of writing.

What is it about Beckett that is so singularly theatrical?

Well, he's damned funny when done right. And I suppose it just kind of creeps up on you: this strange thing happens inside of you when you're watching a good Beckett production. You absolutely feel your sense of being alive. It makes you feel your own humanity, which I think the best theatre always does. We live most of our lives in a kind of grey haze, so when you have a great artistic experience, it's not like you want to go and smell the flowers, but you kind of *do* want to go and smell the flowers! You just kind of think: yeah, I'm a human being, I'm alive, and there are these other people, and it's meaningful. At best.

Do you think we should be looking for new buildings for theatre?

No, I don't think so. I think the buildings are okay. Some of them could do with better air-conditioning, quieter air-conditioning. I like a play in a proscenium arch: I've got nothing against that. I think some plays are written for proscenium arches, some plays work beautifully in the round. It's not the buildings: we just need to do better work and get people interested.

What is it about a proscenium arch that attracts you?

I like the direct relationship with the audience: I like a play head on and I like an audience all looking in the same direction. That said, I staged my first play [*Dealer's Choice* at the NT, 1995] in traverse, so half the audience were looking at the other half. That seemed to suit that play. But for my second play [*Closer*, also at the NT, 1997] I knew I wanted the audience all facing the same direction, because I wanted them to experience the play in a kind of solitude. I think anything can be done on a proscenium, if you're inventive enough and you have a great designer.

What do you say to people who say the theatre is bound up in text and needs to liberated from the text?

Well, as a writer I'm obviously dubious about that. Many of my favourite things that I have seen in the theatre have been what is called 'physical theatre', but I don't know what physical theatre is. In the same way that I don't really know what 'text-based' theatre is. I think of the theatre as being live performance where words are spoken.

What do you want of an actor in a performance?

I want him—him or her—to serve the play, no more no less.

What does that mean?

I just want them to say the lines as agreed with the director and to always be pushing the action of the play forward rather than pushing the action of their character forward. I want them to take care of the play, not the character, which is a very tough thing to ask of actors. I want them to tell a story. I don't want them to worry so much about the back story of their character or that their mum hit them when they were five, which is something they invented in week two of rehearsal. I'm only interested in what serves the forward action of the piece of material.

But you presumably want the actor to absolutely live in the moment that the audience is sharing with the actor?

Yes, but not in a self-indulgent way. One person's definition of living in the moment is very different to another's. An actor who comes offstage and says: 'Yes, I took that one minute because I really felt that she would in that moment not be able to speak for a minute'—that seems to me an act of self-indulgence, unless it's agreed in rehearsal and with the other actors that it's a five-second pause, necessary because she is temporarily stumped. So I'm very cautious of who I cast and how I cast.

So what you're expecting of an actor is that they be conscious of themselves but not self-conscious?

Yes, I want teamwork, and teamwork sometimes means subjugating your ego to the greater good of the whole. And that is as much the case for the writer, the director, the actor: everyone has to eat a little shit sometimes to produce something decent.

What about design?

I want the design to serve the actors and to serve the play. I don't particularly want to make a statement with a design: I just want it to be simple, clear, and I don't want there to be anything on the set that isn't relevant to the action of the play. So I've tended to go for a rather stripped down, minimalist approach in the work that I have directed, either by me or by other people. Because I don't think you need that much.

Everything else is supplied by the imagination of the audience?

In an ideal world. I only need to see a chair to know what the room might look like. If you show me a battered wooden chair, I've got a fairly good idea of what the rest of the room might be like.

Is that the heart of the power of theatre—that you can put a chair on a stage and it can suggest a whole world?

In combination with a human being sitting on that chair saying some interesting words, yes. The theatre demands of its audience that it supplies the rest, and it joins the dots. It seems to me an imaginative act. It's a collusion between the production and the audience: everyone buys into this metaphor. You can do amazing things with that chair: it can become a boat, which can sink.

Do you think part of the reason people don't want to go to theatre is they're not prepared to enter into that collusion?

No, I don't think so, because I think that would be to suggest that human beings don't want to use their imaginations, and I think people have a deep need to use their imaginations. People want to be creative—just as when you read a novel, you create this whole world in your head, similarly when you go to the theatre, you create other worlds, you create back stories naturally, you create the room that we don't see on the stage that the characters refer to or go into. When I go to the theatre my mind is racing with possibilities: 'Well, when she goes out there, what does that room look like?' etc., etc. And the offstage characters who are referred to... I'm trying to think of a good example—well, yes: someone once said of *Glengarry Glen Ross* that Mrs Link is a very important character who is never seen. I know what Mrs Link looks like, this woman at home who's telling her husband: don't buy this property, don't get conned. I know exactly what she looks like, but I've never met her, and nor has David Mamet.

So what's the future of theatre?

I'm a naturally pessimistic person, but I'm actually rather optimistic about it, because I think people need to experience things collectively—be it rock concerts or comedy clubs, or the theatre or opera or ballet. I think people will crave more and more the live experience. The more we spend our lives sitting in front of computer screens, the more we're going to want to find reasons to get out of the house and be with other people. If we can just bring prices down, I think the theatre's product—God, I hate to call it a product!—is as good as the movies, as good as television, as good as any other art form.

Steven Berkoff

1 9 3 7—

Actor, playwright and director. Steven Berkoff has written, directed and performed his own verse plays, East, Greek, West, Decadence, Sink the Belgrano! *and others. He has also directed and performed Wilde's* Salomé *and adaptations of Kafka's* Metamorphosis *and* The Trial. *He has pursued his singular view of theatre doggedly for many years, defending and propagating his work with an evangelical zeal that has given him a not entirely justified reputation for being a theatrical Rottweiler. When I interviewed him, I felt it was a shame that he couldn't appear in three dimensions. As if to argue his case for the body as his instrument, he used his hands with sculptural expressiveness. The interview took place in a small studio, usually used for shooting commercials. After we'd finished, the studio technicians talked about theatre. 'It's dead, isn't it?' said one genially. Steven wasn't there to hear: he'd have refuted him with a lethal monologue.*

You saw The Living Theatre when they first came to London?

I first saw The Living Theatre in 1964. They were doing a play called *The Brig*, which was about life in a marine prison. Here was a company and a director, Julian Beck, who were typically obeying every rule of physical theatre. The subject was society, the community: the people were common men, the working class. Its theme was oppression, and it used movement, music, sound. You were engaged as the subject spoke to you: it addressed you as the ordinary man, and the sense of excitement in the theatre and what they did was extraordinarily intense and powerful. It showed what life was like in the brig, the military prison:

the daily routine, what people did when they got up, how they dressed, how they washed, how they scrubbed the floors, how they were punished. It was like an opera; it was like a drama. The British theatre expresses the dilemmas, the dynamics, the neuroses of the anguished middle class. Therefore they do a lot of Chekhov. Chekhov is very well written, but it deals almost exclusively with a kind of mourning, and an anguish. It deals with groups that are small; it deals with people who are enclosed; it deals with society that is tight, not mixed. So when I saw *The Brig*, it was phenomenal.

Did you see Grotowski's work?

I briefly saw Grotowski's work. There was an occasion, I think in the late sixties, when Grotowski was coming to London. We'd been hearing about Grotowski, and it was like a second coming. It was the late sixties, and everyone was waiting for Jesus, the Messiah. There were groups from America—La MaMa, The Living Theatre—and from Europe—this one and that one—and Grotowski, of course. People were in love with Antonin Artaud. Peter Brook was doing the Theatre of Cruelty. Everywhere there seemed to be some kind of almost millennium fervour: they were getting rid of the old theatre. So when people like Grotowski would come across, Peter Brook naturally seemed to be the Head Scout. And even when Living Theatre came, he was always outside the Roundhouse [where they performed]. He was the head prefect of all these turbulent, wild creatures. Because I think he envied them: he wanted to embrace that turbulence. Although he was a very, very clever and wonderful director, his direction came from a kind of eclecticism, while these people actually got it from the street, from their environment, from fighting with their own authorities. That was The Living Theatre.

So Grotowski came and of course said: 'If you want to see it, first of all we are looking for the right space.' Couldn't find a space in the whole of London. I thought: 'My God, this is very special. I mean, there's ten thousand halls in London, and he's only got a little play with six actors, but we couldn't find the space.' So they hunted high and low from Highgate to Hampstead, from Islington to East Ham, and there he was looking for this space, this special space. Eventually through some chance, going through the East End, hearing about that huge, wonderful church—the architect was Hawksmoor, and there were ley lines—and it seemed to appeal to Grotowski... Jack the Ripper, and all that stuff. So we [the audience] met at the ICA—Institute of Contemporary Arts. We got on a bus—only thirty-six people will be allowed to see it, no more, only thirty-six: a magic and rather cabalistic number. So we all went down to the East End, went down the hall into the basement, got our seats: one row of seats only. And then the head prefect said: 'Would you just be quiet for a moment: they'll come out; they are just warming up.' Well, I thought: they'd been warming up all day, but they are still warming up! And eventually they came on and did the performance, and it was exciting, but it wasn't that brilliant. I had the idea that they used no props, it was just body, but in fact, they used bits of rubbish and bits of props and jugs and pots, and not knowing the language was difficult for me. But I appreciated their devotion.

I was very taken by The Bread and Puppet Theatre. Did you see them?

I actually only glimpsed them on television documentaries, but I am familiar with a group called La MaMa, and they may be in a way very similar: very large, very gestural theatre. La MaMa came over here, and they did a series of plays, one of which was called *Futz* [by Rochelle Owens]. *Futz* was about a man who fell in love with a pig. Again, it obeyed all the rules of this physical, dynamic theatre. It was a group of simple people, common men, farmhands—and one man who fell in love with his pig and made love to his pig. And the message of the play was that love transcends everything: it's better than cruelty. The people around who heard this man make love to his pig were horrified, and they were going to burn him. And so the point of the play was what *they* were doing was a thousand times more horrifying… The actors were dressed in these dungarees, and they had long hair, and they came out with these things. And we as English, in our tepid theatre, we still had the remnants of Coward and Rattigan and little nudges of working-class spit in the form of John Osborne. Suddenly we saw this very kind of orgasmic powerful theatre, and we looked at these actors with muscle and hair, and that was kind of very influential when I saw that.

How did you start off in the theatre?

I had a desperate desire to go into the theatre, and I didn't have the background or the information on what really to do. Somebody said 'evening classes': it was a class for adults who have passed up the opportunity of going to university or formal training. Here was a little window of opportunity.

So I went to the City Literary Institute, and it was absolutely wonderful, because for the first time I could get rid of my shirt and tie and wear a rollneck sweater and a duffel coat. I thought: 'Now I am part of the club.' And then they said: 'Why don't you try and go to drama school?' So I went to a very formal drama school in London—quite a good school—and started training in a very formal way. I found it was too focused really on interpreting plays and on the ideas of the playwright and not the ideas of the performer. I was interested in trying to express myself more physically and more imaginatively. I decided that I wanted to expand what I knew. A woman called Claude Chagrin and her husband Julian were starting mime classes. So I went along, and it was a form of magic to me. With the mime you were an author, you were an inventor, a creator, and because of this, I went to the font, if you like, and studied with Jacques Lecoq. Mime became very much the kind of artillery I would use, as well as my other weapon, which would be a kind of psychological acting. But I always had in the back of my mind that movement was a key. I felt that the body became a piano, an instrument, and I would play this piano.

Was Jacques Lecoq useful to you?

He didn't necessarily want you to be a mimic, the white-faced mimic, forever climbing up endless stairs and going through endless walls. He wanted you to impersonate an environment, to be able to express yourself. He turned movement into a science. He was a great inventor and a great discoverer; one of the greatest things I learned from that was a form of mime whereby the actor became the environment. The actor's body was the set. I thought this was like a metaphysical form of theatre. It fascinated me, and I thought one day I want to be able to do this. I decided to stage Kafka's *The Trial*, where the actors were the set and the environment and furniture of Joseph K's house. K was being persecuted; his room was being searched; and the idea to me was your furniture, your room, is you, in a sense. So Joseph K became the drawers which the guards would search; he became the walls, the doors.

That was the birth of what you'd describe as 'poor theatre'?

I think 'poor theatre' is a kind of theatre which belongs to the people—although it is poor, it is very rich. It is very rich in a kind of self-awareness and discovery. Some of the greatest inventions can come out of the 'poor theatre': mime, street theatre, mechanics, robotic movement—all the things we find fascinating, even right up to Michael Jackson's Moonwalk, came out of the 'poor theatre'.

Would you describe Brecht's theatre as poor theatre?

Yes, oh yes.

In what sense? In that it required huge mechanics, and huge amounts of subsidy in order to present Brecht's work?

That may have come later after he was successful, but his earlier plays could be done in a factory. He used to advise his actors to go to factories, go to schools, go to any environment where you could get in: you could put on *The Good Woman of Setzuan* with very, very little money. As he became successful his ideas became more ambitious, and they gave him so much money to have great sets, great inventive designers. That's fine if you can afford it, but the origins of Brecht came from fairgrounds.

Do you think that money is the enemy of theatre? Does there come a point at which too many resources diminish the power of the meaning?

I tend to think that a lot of money diminishes the potential of theatre because you take away the risk. When I work—when I occasionally manage to get a job working for a formal theatre—the designer comes up, says: 'Well, we've got five weeks, and I've got this set.' I say: 'Well, I haven't really worked it out yet; I want to see what can happen.' And they say: 'We've got the carpenters waiting: if we don't build it and we don't spend the money, we won't be able to get the set built and what costumes do you want?' For most conventional theatre the costumes and the set come before the director has actually started rehearsing with the actors, so already he is throwing all this money, building the set, getting the costumes. He starts directing the play, and he thinks: 'Oh, it's so interesting with no set, it's marvellous. Oh, we've got this huge set with the stairs and this door you're going through: we'd better use it, I suppose.' I think the money diminishes the potential of theatre, which doesn't really need money. If you use the environment, if you are familiar with groupings, the ensemble, the body, then the body becomes the set. That becomes symbolic. It's far more interesting to the audience to have two bodies become doors, or a group of bodies become the room. The audience are more excited, because they have seen something that they have to interpret. The symbol is like playing a game, it's like a trick, whereas if you give them the reality of the set, they look at the set, and it's very nice, and very often they clap the set, but then after a few minutes they're still looking, and they get a bit tired, and the set is still there. So in ultra-bourgeois theatre—another simple generic term—in order to deal with this set they put in a revolve, so they can have another set the other side! Then they demand more and more money, denying all the time the possibility of the actors doing it. The actors become weaker, they become 'actrified', they can no longer move: they have no training because you don't need training, and the actor loses his athleticism.

So theatre is a poetic medium?

Theatre, first and foremost, has to be a poetic medium. I've seen some wonderful actors, and I've seen great performances from Scofield and Olivier and Richardson in naturalistic plays, but theatre should do something that cannot be reproduced on film, that cannot even be televised. It has to be symbolic, so that the audience are fascinated with the trick, with the idea, with the symbol, because the human imagination feeds on symbolism. When I try and stage theatre, I try to find the symbol for what the scene means. So I originally did *Coriolanus*, to briefly talk about my own production, and huge gates are mentioned in the play, huge gates: Coriolanus 'threads the gates'. And in every production I've seen they have a huge flaming gates! But I thought: 'What are the gates but wars, pressure, prevention, stopping?' So I just had all the actors behind me—ten actors—push against the gate: all these hands, arms, bodies. And then they opened the gates, and I merely stepped in and said: 'The gates are open'—to get a bit of a silly laugh. People appreciated the idea that you were stimulating their imagination and using symbols.

Willem Dafoe

1 9 5 5—

Actor. Willem Dafoe was a member of the Performance Group—an experimental theatre company which started in the late sixties. It was an 'environmental theatre'—each production took place in a found space and each was based on combinations of various texts, some new, some deconstructions of classics. When the Performance Group split up, several members of the company formed the Wooster Group under the direction of Dafoe's then partner, Elizabeth LeCompte. For more than thirty years, the Wooster Group has maintained an ensemble and made theatre out of modern and classic texts, found materials, films and videos, dance and movement, and fragments of sound and music: it's theatre as collage. Dafoe acts in movies to underwrite his theatre work, and he appeared to me to live an enviable life of a man unencumbered by ambition, liberated from the market and pursuing his passion. I interviewed him in Wooster Street in New York's Soho. After the interview, when we were chatting, I asked him what he thought were the special properties of theatre. 'Well,' he said, 'where else can you get spat on by an actor?'

I was attracted to the Wooster Group when I saw these people—the way they made work: it was a very romantic life to me. At that time, they weren't really dealing with playwrights; they were doing original work, and this work was coming from everything from tapes to their relatives. It was autobiographical work. The work that Liz [Elizabeth LeCompte] and Spalding [Gray] initially did was all autobiographical, and even though I didn't feel the urge to confess, I was struck by this ability to make your life into art and also just by the way they

291

lived. It was romantic for me at the time, so I just wanted to be with those people, because they were like… super-people. They were productive, and they were addressing their concerns in a real, immediate way.

In a way that you felt that conventional theatre wasn't addressing?

Right. Personal needs were addressed through personality [*laughs*] and through career. That's also tempered by what opportunities were presented to me as a young actor coming to New York—really wanting to pursue a commercial theatre career, but looking around and not only not being excited by what I was seeing, but also having it not be immediately available to me. Whereas, at the Wooster Group, I literally walked in there and said: 'I wanna work with you guys.' And they said: 'Okay, well, you go and sweep in the corner.' There was a kind of old-fashioned apprenticeship about coming into the group.

Part of the allure is being in a group—everybody participates, everybody contributes?

Everybody can participate, but the truth is there's a very strong central figure, and also, like any group, a natural hierarchy starts to form. There's a very strong centre there, and there are also very strong spheres of influence and responsibility. One thing that is special about the Wooster Group is that everybody's in the room at the same time. Nothing is departmentalised: you don't delegate this to someone else. We all get in the room. All the technicians. All the actors. The designer, the director, even to some degree, the administrators, are all in that room when we start making the piece.

How many people is that?

It depends from piece to piece, but it ends up, often, being heavy on technicians and sometimes can be twenty people.

Is that a very difficult size to manage?

No, because most people hang back. They're there to serve the thrust of what's going on that day. When we rehearse, we take a piece of text, or we take a dance, or we take a videotape, or something, and we try to put it on its feet, somehow. We try to find a way to present it, or to make something out of it; and that's the way we proceed.

The prime urge is to make statements, or to make art that is highly personal?

Ultimately we're trying to create a language that makes sense to us. [*laughs*] We're trying to express ourselves in a language that we think is, you know, playful and reflects our experience. The work started off from very autobiographical roots. Now, the form has changed a lot. Now, we're invested in a language. We've created a series of props and architecture and ways of dealing with technology. That's our language now. The impulse, I think, is to find those self-revelatory moments, find out what our relationship is, have fun and present something that we're interested in to these people in a room.

When you take, for instance, Chekhov's Three Sisters, *do you assume that the play's known by the audience?*

I've never selected the text, so the initial selection feels a little arbitrary. But when the director, or one of the performers, steers us towards a text, I just accept it, and then I try to find my relationship to it. I'm sure they have some sort of agenda. They're attracted to it for some reason. Sometimes there can be a fabulously practical reason. For example, when we started playing around with Arthur Miller's *The Crucible*, we had a lot of women in the company at the time, and not so many men. So that was a consideration—like a crass, really mundane consideration. In some ways we're like any other theatre company. [*laughs*]

You take a Chekhov text in order to reveal not so much truths about Chekhov's text, as truths about yourselves?

I think when we take a Chekhov text, we're trained to hear it. We tend to create a third thing between us: this group, our language, our history, the world we live in—and Chekhov. We aren't interpreting, we aren't illustrating, we're somewhere between, you know. The pitfalls of doing the classics are—you know about these pitfalls [*laughs*]—you either have a museum piece that you're scared to fool or play around with, or you find a different way to think than the accepted way. You have a museum piece that's basically impenetrable and doesn't live, or you try to blow apart the text so much that you get something that doesn't serve the impulse behind what the text came from. So hopefully we're creating something in the middle: something that's Chekhov, and something that's us.

What you're creating is a theatrical text that's made up of a number of sources?

Right. I think that's fair.

When the group talks, you're talking about how to bring the thing alive?

We never talk. We do very little talking. The only talking we tend to do is to structure activity, and when I say 'structure activity', it's to work with the text, so we know what part we're working on, or how we're going to work on it. But we never ever sit around and talk ideas, or what we intend to do, or what we think something means.

Can you describe a rehearsal?

293

RICHARD EYRE

You go into the room: everybody's there. They're waking up, they have their coffee and whatever, social pleasantries. Everybody kind of feels where everybody's at in the room. There's some sort of agenda: there's a piece of text that we want to deal with, and we're often kick-started by a piece of costume or the architecture of the space. Every time we rehearse, in my experience, it feels like we're creating something to show. Liz is like the audience: the director's like the audience. She sets up the scene. We contribute sometimes in creating that set-up, and then we play around with the text. When I say we play around in the text, we try and get it on its feet. We start out maybe doing something that is quite conventional, or we lay something over it that is like a difficulty or something that is related to it. The reason why we choose such and such a costume or a piece of the set isn't arbitrary: it comes from our history. Each piece sort of informs the next.

Is the aim to subvert the existing conventions of theatre, of the conventional play?

At the same time, we love the conventions. We're theatre. We are a theatre. We love the curtain going up. We love the curtain going down. We don't have a curtain. [*laughs*] Often we have to find out what that is and find what we love about it and do it in our own terms. Not because we're perverse and we have anything against having a curtain, we don't. It's just not that kind of space.

You have your own space. What is it about that space that's so good?

What's good about that space is it's ours. [*laughs*] It's a flexible space; it's basically a very large room. We perform to a hundred and fifty people, and we like the intimacy. We tour a lot—our bread and butter is international touring, so we're often getting new takes on the show by having to fit into another space. But to tell you the truth, the pieces are usually so designed that we prefer them in their original design—but not always.

Do you think there's a certain critical mass, a number of people in the audience, beyond which the show doesn't work?

Yes. Yes. On some level you could say: 'Well, they just experience it differently.' But, for example, we do use video monitors—sometimes they're information, sometimes they're visual noise. They function in a lot of different ways in the piece. The truth is if you can't see 'em, you can't see 'em. It's the same question I ask when I'm at a really huge theatre, and the actor's head is this big. I'm enjoying something, I'm enjoying the movements on stage, I am hearing the text, but ideally I'd like to be in the first row.

On the face of it, it would seem that the use of video technology would be incompatible with spontaneity, and yet the two seem to work to counterpoint each other. How did that come about?

294

They're basically tools. They're like a costume. They're like a hat. They're like a prop. They're things we work with. They're an extension of us. It isn't separation; it's really about integration and using what's available to you. For example, we use microphones quite extensively. It allows us to mix the sound in a way that we like: we feel less limited—there's more possibilities. I'd say that about all the technology. We can play around with the language of film: with live and recorded video we can have close-ups. We can play around with the ideas of perception, both for the audience and the performer. Those are all things that everybody tries to do in the conventional theatre, but they just have different conventions. We accept these conventions because we've worked with them: they've become part of our work. People that are familiar with our work don't say: 'Oh my God, there's TVs on the set!' Or: 'Oh my God, that person's holding a microphone!' You forget those things after a while; they become part of an extension of you.

Doesn't the video emphasise the liveness, the humanness of the humans? Is it a conscious aid to exaggerating the spontaneity?

When you ask about what's conscious, I throw up my hands, because, as an actor, I like being able to give myself over to somebody else's agenda. Liz, the director, doesn't articulate these things, but I think she knows a hell of a lot more what's going on than I know, that's all I'm saying. So about 'conscious', having an intention, my intentions are: deal with what's coming at me, or what I want to put out. Beyond that, I don't question. She's the one that says: 'Pick up that mic. Do the speech with it.' And I don't say: 'What does this mean? A mic?' Some people would say: 'What a drag. That sounds like you're a little slave boy.' But actually it's great because it frees me up to really invest what I'm doing with a certain kind of abandon and a certain kind of ferocity.

You seems to be entirely liberated from the Method?

I did have that training, and I was sort of repulsed by it, and it probably was because I wasn't very good at the psychology. People say, 'Have you ever trained in the Method?' Or: 'Are you a Method actor?' Well, when I think of the Method, I think Lee Strasberg, who popularised it here and to my understanding took one aspect of Stanislavsky and fashioned a whole technique out of it. It has a lot to do with emotional recall and substitution. The classic is: when you have a tearful moment, think of something from your life and substitute it. I think that's bullshit, because, as an actor, my job is to deal with what *is*. My deal is to find what's really going on—the is-ness and the such-ness of the story we're telling, of what our lives are about, and if I'm crying about my dog, it's about me and it's about my dog. It takes an intellectual choice to do that substitution and find it appropriate for when the king is going to lose his kingdom. It's not the same, so why do that substitution? For me, it doesn't work. I have an aversion to actors being rewarded for beating themselves up, and bearing their souls, because I think it makes a lousy contract with the audience. The audience has to sit there, and they get beat up by your 'bravery' in showing them your emotion. That's not what it's about for me. I'm much more interested in something that feels a little purer—the way dance is pure. I've always been attracted to the pure, childlike pretending of acting, as opposed to the technique.

Who's your audience?

When we do interviews, the director, Liz, used to say: 'We're a community theatre.' And I'd listen to that… [*laughs*] but she's right, we serve the community. It happens to be the community's filled with artists and painters and dancers and musicians, and that's our core audience. There was some discussion about maybe moving one of our shows to Broadway recently, and it just didn't feel like the right audience. And it has partly to do with economics—your average couple has a hard time scraping together two hundred and fifty bucks for an evening. So you get the older people that have had a hard day at work: they're very pressured people; they like the idea of getting some culture, but they get there, they're so bagged out, they fall asleep in their chairs. It's not a living theatre right now.

The problem with theatre is that the smaller it is, the greater the problem, because people say it's elitist.

I have a problem with this charge of elitism generally in the arts, because I think so much trickles down. It's not for everybody, but I think it affects everybody, and humanises the landscape. For example, we perform to very few people, but the people that we perform to are also making work. And they go out, and they present their work to people. It's like we're part of a community that radiates out. If our work is vital, we're touching lots of people. So, when I hear 'elitism', I get a little worried, because… look, I'm a regular guy; I grew up middle-class— very bad education—and I feel very down there with the people. But at the same time there have to be other people doing the laboratory work, doing the stuff that's not acceptable and maybe even that feels like it's basically useless now. What we do is maybe useless, but it's vital to us; and for people that respond to it, it's important to affect change. Otherwise a culture becomes totally stagnant and dies.

Maybe its uselessness is its great virtue.

I think so. I think so. [*laughs*]

Deborah Warner

1 9 5 9—

Director. Deborah Warner's productions include Titus Andronicus, Electra, The Good Person of Setzuan, Hedda Gabler, Richard II, Medea, Julius Caesar, Footfalls *and* Happy Days—*most of them collaborations with Fiona Shaw. She's keen on 'found spaces' and staging texts that appear to defy staging— such as Eliot's* The Waste Land, *which she initially staged in the near-derelict Wilton's Music Hall. My interview with Deborah was a characteristic exchange— certainties mitigated by an engaging bashfulness.*

What's an ideal space for you for theatre to take place in?

I think one that people haven't discovered before. And the difficulty comes for me when I use it the second time or the third time, because it becomes known by the audience. I think I used to annoy you by saying: if the National Theatre suddenly had an asbestos scare and was closed down, it would be the most desirable place in town, because it would be the one that you couldn't get to put on a show.

You want to consecrate each space anew?

I want the audience's expectations to be turned on their head the moment they walk through the door. That can be done in a space that they know very well by leading them into that space in an unusual manner. I suppose for me now choosing a space is as important as choosing a play or choosing a designer. And once that choice is made, the audience does not feel complacently that they know the order of the evening, what's going to happen once they've entered that space.

What do you make of the fact that most of the greatest advances, if you like, or inventions in theatre have happened precisely because there's a tension between conventional space and what's happening within the space?

I haven't had the privilege of seeing Brecht's theatre in Berlin but it goes to the heart of the issue, doesn't it? That we must be in a very strong, possibly political, relationship to space. I mean, space is political—it's either presented because the government chooses to say: right, this is where the culture will happen; or it's stolen by us and we run to the place where we're not meant to be; or we find an audience where we're not meant to find an audience; or we take a group of people on a pilgrimage where they never were supposed to go. And fundamentally this is what it's about. It's probably in the showmanship of that where many of the great theatre directors have made their name. We're not allowed to call it 'showmanship' perhaps, but I think part of Peter Brook's genius was showmanship. He was able to lead people from the city of Avignon all the way up a mountainside—and the last part of that journey on foot—to go and see *The Mahabharata*. Or choose Glasgow not London as the place the whole of England had to migrate to see it. And that became almost part of the event, didn't it?

What you're really talking about is the importance of the liveness of the event.

Yes. The uniqueness. It's unique every night, and it can never be repeated. That is what the theatre is.

You have to keep changing the frame?

You have to keep asking what theatre is, and you have to keep reinventing all the time. It can… [*chuckles*] it can be quite exhausting. Brought up researching the classics and how to present them to an audience anew, it took me a long time to realise that actually the very act of theatre has to be equally energetically looked at.

Do you think that plays are inevitably dependent on written text?

I did for a long time. Then by chance I was presented with an opportunity that taught me that there can be an act of theatre with no text at all. Obviously dance is an act of theatre with no text at all, but, you know, it becomes jolly interesting when there is text. I think everything, when it crosses the boundary, begins to burn very brightly. I was asked to do a piece for LIFT [London International Festival of Theatre]. I had to find a building in London that excited me and find something to put in it. And I discovered the abandoned St Pancras Hotel—the old Midland Grand Hotel above the station—and asked to do something there. The first thing that I did was to look for a text that somehow chimed with it. It's a wonderful, nineteenth-century building, and I looked for a nineteenth-century poem. Then I had notions that 'The Lady of Shalott' would sit happily in there. But of course it wouldn't sit at all happily in there, for there was nowhere for it to be and certainly nowhere for the audience to sit. I had notions of using this wonderful grand staircase and finding a way of putting the audience there, and the more I visited, the more I thought: this is nonsense. And the more I visited, the more I realised that the building itself, which is full of ghosts and a very, very strong sense of being caught between lives, had an incredibly potent text of its own that was speaking very loudly. I was very privileged to be alone there. I would go on a Sunday to desperately wrestle with what it was I could put in there. And then I thought: well, if only I could offer the audience the experience I'm having now, then what a nice time they'd have, [*chuckles*] really. And it developed into an idea of offering the audience a walk. They would come singly at ten-minute intervals, and they would follow a yellow road painted on the floor throughout the building. They'd walk through about one and a half miles of empty corridors. And their route was sometimes enhanced with objects placed in rooms, sometimes a fleeting image of a maid running away up a stairway or a canary singing. Or the canary stopped singing. It was so lonely: a bird hanging in space. And a room full of grass and a piano that played by itself. What I discovered was that everything was slightly turned on its head, which is that a space that is there to house an event *was* the event. That text which is normally witnessed by an audience somehow here was written by the audience. So it was described by some as being the audience's own poem. They wrote their own text as they made the journey. There was no question in my mind by the end of it that here was a piece of theatre.

You'd become the author of the event?

Yes, but what event was this? I'm in charge of guided walks now. Is this tourism? But then I began to think that tourism is quite an interesting form of theatre. When one is alone in a tourist site, one is extraordinarily privileged, and one is terribly conscious of oneself in a theatrical situation. If you're the first into St Peter's, Rome, in the morning, it's quite something. You may think: oh, it's like being in my own film, but in fact, it's not a film, it's very real. So it's very close to an act of theatre.

I infer from this a frustration with written text.

At that moment, yes. But I'm not frustrated by any of those things now. I'm just aware that one must keep on the move, and for one's own creative self one must all the time be working in different places. I had done a lot of work on written text. I hadn't done any work on newly written texts, and I've only recently worked with a writer for the first time—which was in fact on film.

Aren't there living writers who write things that speak to you?

If I've had a frustration with the writers writing for theatre, it may be that I've been frustrated by their vision of what the theatre could be: not by their words necessarily, but by feeling that there was nothing that I could particularly offer there that wouldn't be better offered by others. I've often said that had I been presented something that I did not even recognise as a play in text form I'd be very excited, and I guess that's where the Eliot poem came from. You pick it up and think: I can't stage that. I think my inspiration is often and inevitably something that doesn't have an obvious theatre form. I need the challenge of finding a new form, and it's dead handy if the thing is not already proscribed. I think a lot of our contemporary theatre writers have a version of the theatre in their heads which must perhaps be driven out and provoked differently. That's maybe my laziness that I haven't done that.

What about actors? In what sense can actors reinvent the theatre for themselves?

Well, they could probably reinvent theatre themselves if they didn't have a director there, couldn't they? [*laughs*]

Given that the most potent thing on a stage is always an actor, what do you put around the actor?

Things that are going to help the actor and not hinder. And no costume till very late in the day. Things to inspire the actor is the starting point. If they inspire correctly they might well serve to be an end point too. I think that's our job when our theatre is actor-led. One could say that is all that theatre is—although I have done a piece of theatre now with nobody in it.

What do you mean: our theatre being actor-led?

Text-based theatre is certainly actor-led. What I mean by that is that there is really nothing else that matters. The actor's ownership of the material has to be total for a good piece of theatre to be made. And when the director's ownership of the material is greater than the actor's, it becomes an act of academia probably. Or simply an act of bad theatre. One has to empower the actors totally.

Who are you making theatre for? Just to play devil's advocate: I could say you're a skilful, gifted person making theatre for a tiny group of people, whose tickets are being underwritten by the state to an enormous degree. Don't you have a responsibility to make theatre for a large number of people?

I'm beginning to think that I certainly do, but then I think that producers have the huge responsibility of making sure that it can run long enough for a large group of people. I feel pretty strongly that opera doesn't run for long enough, and there's no real reason why it shouldn't run longer. It's only the culture of those singers' diaries that stops it running longer. There's a lot of audience out there.

I went to see DV8's dance show [at the Royal Festival Hall]: it's quite astonishing that in that audience there was not a soul over thirty-five. And then you go next door to the National, and I fear it would be true to say that the vast majority of that audience is over forty-five or perhaps more. When the National this year projected films onto the Lyttelton flytower, it was incredibly interesting being out there on the terraces, because this group of people watching those films were not people that you saw in the National. So there's a lot of work to be done, I think, in making sure that the audience that is committed to live events does not start to run away from the more traditional form of theatre. They have, but they're there to get back: there's no question. I'm more concerned by this than ever, because I can recognise the audience. You see them and you think: oh dear, here we are.

What does Shakespeare do that no other writer does?

[*pause*]

Touches on every possible human emotion, every possible human feeling, every possible human story. And a complete love of the theatre, for those reasons. He left no stage directions, I think that was possibly his greatest gift [*chuckles*] to generations of theatre directors.

Simon McBurney

1 9 5 7—

Director, actor and playwright. Simon McBurney is a founder and the Artistic Director of Complicite (formerly Théâtre de Complicité). His productions include The Street of Crocodiles, The Three Lives of Lucie Cabrol, Mnemonic, The Elephant Vanishes and A Disappearing Number, which he also co-wrote. After the interview we were talking about the rise of movement-based theatre and the (possible) threat to the spoken word. He said: 'All this fascination with the spoken word is actually an interest in the nakedness of the human body. What could indicate a greater fascination with the human body than to concentrate only on the mouth in Beckett's Not I? People who say there's a division between the text and the body are actually talking out their arse.'

———•·•———

The actor, director, theorist, magus, madman and drug addict Antonin Artaud said that most theatre takes place in yesterday's buildings, the audience are detached, they're socially divided, there's a line between them and the actors, and we need bare, undecorated spaces.

My immediate response to that statement is that he is saying that, if theatre is a tree, something has happened to the root. That immediately makes me think that at the other end are the branches and the twigs. If I think about nineteenth-century theatre, I think about melodrama, about ballet, and the idea that somehow theatre at that age had reached the fingers of the body—it was sclerotic, just the decoration without the centre. It is a little bit like religious architecture— as the root, the faith, was lost, so the architecture itself became more and more decorated, until all you're left with is the Gothic revival, which is almost like a sort of advertisement for faith, but of course the faith itself has been lost.

You're trying to rediscover that faith?

Theatre at the end of the twentieth century, in order to exist, has to be necessary. Once theatre loses its connection with life, of course it immediately starts to die.

How do we reconnect?

Well, [*pause*] I suppose rather than thinking about how we reconnect it to life, I would rather think about why human beings need theatre. I would start with a human being's conception of time and the fact that we live in an age whereby a lot of the forms of artistic expression have to do with a perception of time, which is either to do with the present or the past. In the medium of film everything is to do with what will happen next. Film is a medium about the future, just as the photograph is about a moment disappearing into the past. The theatre is the only form which is to do with things happening in the present moment. My father was an archaeologist, and he always used to talk about the birth of language occurring around a communal event, specifically around the event of eating. Apart from wild dogs, human beings are the only creatures that we know who share their food with other than their immediate families. We seem to have this need to communicate around a shared event. And this shared event exists most intensely in our sharing of present time.

Artaud said that narrative and text were a prison, but you presumably feel entirely the opposite?

A play is not theatre of its own. A play is a sequence of words, which is like the blue touchpaper: you need somebody with fire to light it.

So the play has to be ignited by the actor. What is it that you want from actors?

There's only one question, which is whether what they are doing is alive or not. That's the only question. The curious thing about the theatre is that that life can come from so many different origins and in different ways. This has given rise to an enormous number of different theories of acting each of which claims to be the holy grail. The moment you work in theatre you realise that everybody comes to the life of it in a different way. I've had the experience of working— been fortunate enough to have the experience of working for a long time—with actors from very many different countries, and I've noticed, working often with Italian actors, that they do not come from the meaning of the words, as we would understand it in a naturalistic tradition, but from the rhythm and from the music. They hear it as music.

That's exactly what John Gielgud says about playing Shakespeare: that as an actor you don't necessarily need to understand what you're saying; it's the rhythm that is most important.

You might feel as an actor that you have to go through Hamlet's angst in order to communicate it, but equally an actor might be thinking about Coca-Cola. There was a night last week where we came off, and I thought it was a terrible performance. But of all the performances we have done, more people came up to us afterwards to say how moving it was: but the entire cast felt that we were completely empty. The meaning of the theatre exists in this space which is created between the audience and the actors. That makes it utterly unique. And something very, very mysterious.

This is an art form which ineradicably has a human being at its centre. But what do you put around the actor? What is design? What is mise en scène?

Everything flows from what the actor needs. And what the text means. And there are those things which you can design and construct and calculate, and then there are those things which you have no idea about. For example, I will sometimes in a rehearsal process place objects which I have a hunch will resonate somewhere, but I don't know how exactly. And I encourage the actors to pick them up to use. Actors will suddenly see something in a rehearsal room, and then it becomes *necessary*, because they need it for that particular scene—and then it adapts itself very quickly. Which if you were to perhaps suddenly rewind—*wooooow*—back twenty-five thousand years, you might see somebody beside a fire picking up a stick, and it becoming an axe and then something else. You can see someone telling the story. Very quickly the human imagination sees what it wants to see. We see it in children, of course. And an actor who has forgotten what it is like to play as a child should no longer be an actor. Because this element of the imagination is absolutely critical. Everything that occurs on the stage is linked to this idea of play and the word 'play'.

In what sense does Brecht indulge or encourage 'play'?

[*pause*]

Brecht is a very paradoxical figure. Very ambivalent, very, dare I say it, twentieth-century. With all the lies and the games of a twentieth-century artist. We don't know exactly where Brecht is telling the truth and where he isn't. And indeed the truth changed for him over the whole of his life. He started working in cabaret, and he ended up with the Berliner Ensemble. The difficulty with Brecht, in a sense, has occurred after the end of his life, because people take what he says as law. And the moment you apply law, something dies, and then you get the Brecht police. They say: well, this is how it should be played, and this is what the alienation technique is about. Brecht was changing his ideas as he went along. It so happened that he also had a monstrous ego, so he liked to think that what he'd thought up was the truth. We all like to think that somehow we've come across a new idea, and then of course a second person comes along and says:

well, I'll take that idea, and I'll apply it to this—oh, that works rather well! And then the third person comes, and they... and so it goes on. I think that Brecht was incredibly playful. We see that in the degree to which he shifted his emphasis all the time. He desperately wanted to make it in Hollywood: he never managed to. He wanted to write for Broadway: he never managed to. He found his way through all these different political situations. Politics for him was also a kind of survival. You see that most clearly of all when the House Un-American Activities Committee said to him: 'Mr Brecht, have you at any time in your life been a Communist?' And he said: 'No, no.' 'Or a member of the Communist Party?' 'No, no.' And then they read this poem which espouses Communism and said: 'Mr Brecht, do you recognise this poem?' It was one of his poems in translation. And he said: 'No, no, not the way you read it.'

When you do a piece of theatre, who are you doing it for?

One of the great difficulties of making theatre at the end of the second half of the twentieth century has been the problem that the theatre has become more and more elitist. It has become for a smaller and smaller number of people and more and more expensive. The number of people for whom you create it is very small in relation to an audience figure for the worst television programme, the most poorly listened-to radio programme. And so of course you say: well, what's the point? If we're only doing it for five hundred people in a run of ten weeks, that's perhaps going to be a maximum of twenty-five thousand people, or something in that order. It's absolutely true that we work for a very small number of wealthy people. That is absolutely true. But... [*pause*] if that is the case, why is it that amateur dramatics is such a widespread and continuingly popular activity all over this country and in America too? Why is it that people feel the need to come together in a school event when they go to see their own children performing? Why is it that at a certain point people feel the need to leave their houses and to gather together? Middle-class theatre is only a tiny drop in the ocean, but I would suggest that it is part of what I would call a pocket of resistance. A pocket of resistance grows outwards, and all its elements go outwards like dye in a big pot of water. What is interesting in my generation is the number of people who were at, for example, a concert of The Sex Pistols. The number of people is now several million who were actually at that concert... Which of course is not true. But the fact is that that event has spread out all over the globe. I did a piece which was an installation piece down in the Tube in the Aldwych. Now the number of people who saw it was about five hundred, but apparently the number who now *say* they've seen it is now somewhere in the region of three or four thousand. I believe that theatre now is a form of resistance. That might sound grandiose but in fact is actually relatively humble.

Robert Lepage

1 9 5 7—

Director, actor and playwright. Robert Lepage's productions include The Dragon's Trilogy, Vinci, Polygraph *and* Tectonic Plates, The Seven Streams of the River Ota, Elsinore, Geometry of Miracles, The Far Side of the Moon *and* Lipsynch. *In his work he threads together verbal and visual images, which succeed one another, grow and harmonise: the threads become themes, the themes become narrative. I interviewed him in Quebec, where he was born. We talked in what could be described as his theatrical laboratory—a converted fire station—the base of his company, Ex Machina, where he devises his shows with his collaborators.*

What is it about the theatre that draws you to it?

Frank Lloyd Wright said that theatre is the great mother art, because it's the ritual meeting place of all other forms of expressions, a place where music, literature, dance and architecture can express ideas. It's a total form of expression, and because of that you can't imprison it and say: well, this is what the theatre is. If you are an open-minded artist, you can wear theatres like you wear suits—you can use it for many different things.

Do you think that film is the language of the twentieth century?

Well, it's deeply rooted in the tradition of theatre—its narrative structures are always inspired by the narrative structures of theatre. The birth of cinema was an important event, but it's a very naive, a very thin form of expression. In many centuries' time, it will be as mature as theatre—or as music or as poetry—when it will have found its rules and broken them.

What do you mean, film is 'thin'?

I think that there is an infinite possibility of things you can do on film but the problem is that film is stuck with a lot of rules that it hasn't learned how to get rid of yet. We're always stuck with film realism. Film is about a camera showing you things that you can't see yourself or you can't come close to yourself. In order to be accessible, it chooses only one or two storylines. That's why I'm saying that film is still thin, and that with time, when it will have learned not to be stuck with realism and be more poetical, it will be a very rich and 'thick' form of art. In film the audience identify with actors; they don't identify with characters as much as they do in the theatre. In the theatre there's a series of conventions and rules that you impose on the actors and the audience, and there's an interactive phenomenon going on, where an audience in the theatre is ready to go on a poetical voyage with you. Film doesn't allow that as much.

To you, the idea of 'play' is very important?

In French when we talk about acting we say *'le jeu'*, which means 'the game'. There's very little of that going on nowadays in theatre, and I think that the most interesting—and the most exciting—theatre is when actors, directors and writers understand or reinvent that sense of 'playing'. It's not just having fun: it's a question of establishing rules, like the rules of a game, but it's also playing in the sport sense of playing. When we talk about performances, it's a word that we use also in the sport world. A play should be a place where you go and see people playing, and trying to surpass the limits of mankind. In the Olympics we're in awe of the poetry of the sports—the divers, for instance, who give the illusion for a moment that they're actually flying, that they're defying the different rules that usually burden mankind. I think that's what theatre should offer to the audience—humans who are trying their best to surpass themselves and, for a short moment, almost be God-like.

They should be transformed?

The stage seems to be the place of transformation. All of the best plays are about transformation—whether it is Bottom being translated into a donkey, or Medea, after having done her deed, being transformed into another Medea. I think that's probably the basic reason why the audience goes to the theatre—to witness transformation and to identify with that transformation, or try to invite it into their own lives.

And does the theatre itself have to keep transforming itself?

It's a very fugitive art form, and I'm very enamoured with that. It happens in a brief moment: you can never really properly record it. I think that its content has to be as ephemeral, too, and has to transform itself all the time. I'd compare it to a fugue by Bach—you try to grasp it, and it's already gone.

How are your shows created?

It's a strange process, because we write them collectively most of the time, but what we call writing is a very different process than an author who is alone in his room writing with a pen on a piece of paper. We are a group of people who devise things together, who improvise, research, do explorations: it could take all sorts of forms and shapes—it always depends on the subject matter. And even the subject matter isn't as defined: for example, when we did *The Seven Streams of the River Ota*, we never said we're doing something about the atomic bomb: we just did something about the word 'Hiroshima', and what that word triggered in the different participants' intuition or conscience. So you have to be very courageous and expect that it's going to go in a direction you cannot plan. The participants are very courageous, because they know that what we're doing today will probably be all in the trash bin tomorrow. So the process of writing is a very, very lengthy one. We work in steps, and we actually write with the audience in a certain way, because we present things that are still being developed. Eventually, by performing it, we end up writing it and often we come out with the play on the very last day that we've performed the very last performance.

The directing and the designing is done simultaneously with the writing of the dialogue?

Exactly. The space is always a very important element at the start, so the designing is meshed through the development. With time, the designer is asked to bring in some elements. He tries to see where we're going, and eventually designs something that at the end looks completely designed and sketched out, but it's actually something that grew out of the whole process.

What do you expect of actors?

The actor's role a long time ago was actually much more free-form and liberating and creative than it is today. I think that actors have to find a way to inject who they are, and what they know, and what they want to say, into the work. You have to believe in the actor's intelligence and in his intuition. All directors say that they buy into that but I don't think they really use it. I don't think they trust the actor's intelligence.

Do you see yourself principally as a storyteller?

I'm principally a storyteller, but I'm also an entertainer. I think that the ideal storyteller is a good entertainer.

Did you get your interest in the storytelling from your father?

My mother was a great joke-teller—not necessarily a good storyteller, but a joke-teller. She was a very funny woman. And my father was a great storyteller: not that he would have all these stories or these experiences to communicate, because on that he was quite a reserved person. But he was a cab driver, and he was one of the rare cab drivers in Quebec City who was bilingual, so he did a lot of tourist work. He'd visit Old Quebec, and, of course, he had all of these extraordinary stories to tell about old Quebec. Then he'd have to drive the tourists like twenty miles to the next place, and in between it'd be completely empty and lacking in any kind of interest, so he'd have to make up stuff. And, of course, he had this way of inventing stories for them not to be bored, until they got to the next site. He really knew how to keep an audience active, and he was very funny.

You always take fragmented stories and images and put them together. Are you most interested in trying to connect disparate things together?

You have to help the work find itself and try not to have this big ego attitude of: this is my work, this is me as an artist. I often compare what I do to these Inuit sculptures up north in Canada, where they approach work in a very humble way. They find a rock in a field, and they look at it, and then they see that on the surface there's something that looks like an elk. So they help the elk come out of the rock—just kind of bang it a little bit here—and then they do a little mark there. Then they just wait, and they're sure that there's a huge puzzle there somewhere, but they don't know how to put the pieces together. And one day it rains, and they look and, because the rock is wet, there's all this amazing background behind the elk. I think that working in the theatre allows me to do that kind of thing. There's this mass and mass and mass of information, of stories, and they're all kind of disconnected, and you just have to be patient and wait to see: well, wait a minute, this hand here actually fits with this glove here.

Do you think that audiences will change by better art being presented to them?

First of all, we have to acknowledge the intelligence of the audience. We're confronted with audiences whose narrative vocabulary has evolved in the past twenty to thirty years. The audience that we're performing to today have been challenged by the film vocabulary of storytelling, rock videos, commercials on television, the Internet. They can read stories backwards now and jump cut and flash forward.

What can you say to somebody who says that theatre will be dead in twenty-five years?

I think that I have to agree and disagree with that person. If the definition of theatre is what we see on stage nowadays in general: yes, that will continue to weaken and eventually die. But if we have a larger vision of what theatre is and really try to understand its profound essence, I think that theatre will always be there. In the next four or five years we'll be amazed how theatre and film will have to live together, because film cannot continue in the form it is, in the way it's presented. People want direct life, three-dimensional interaction, and that's something that belongs to the theatre. I think that the theatre will still continue to be the mother art, and it will with time have been enriched by so many aesthetic, technical, ideological revolutions that it will be even richer and even more alive. And even more ephemeral.

Appendix

John Johnston

1 9 2 2—2 0 0 6

Censor. Lieutenant-Colonel Sir John Johnston MC served in the Grenadier Guards during the war and after. In 1964 he became Assistant Comptroller and later Comptroller at the Lord Chamberlain's Office. Sometimes known as 'Stopwatch Johnnie', he was celebrated for his military attention to detail and for bringing an appreciation of the theatrical to royal ceremonies. Until 1968 the Lord Chamberlain was required to license plays and theatres under the Theatres Act of 1843. A very affable and engaging man, Colonel Johnston clearly regarded the whole business of censorship as a faintly exasperating farce. I interviewed him in his grace-and-favour house in Windsor Great Park.

What were the responsibilities of the Lord Chamberlain?

The Lord Chamberlain is responsible for all the departments of the Queen's household and is involved with the ceremonial aspect of the Queen's work—investitures, garden parties, state visits, royal weddings, royal funerals, those sorts of things.

Royal swans?

Yes, still swans, yes. Swan Upping. The Queen's Swan Keeper is a member of the Lord Chamberlain's office.

How did it come about that the Lord Chamberlain became involved in censoring plays?

313

Well, in Tudor times the only entertainments were those provided at Court for the King, and a man called the Master of the Revels was appointed who was an officer of the Lord Chamberlain. It was his responsibility to get playwrights to produce plays and for them to be performed in front of the King, so the Lord Chamberlain had to be sure that what the King was going to see was all right.

And so gradually the job of the Master of the Revels—wonderful title—

Isn't it!

—was absorbed into the Lord Chamberlain's job?

Well, no, the Lord Chamberlain was above that, but it became political when Walpole brought in this Act in 1737 to prevent him and other politicians being lampooned on the stage. They said: 'Right, Lord Chamberlain, you're the man to organise all this.' The Lord Chamberlain then was a political appointment, which it isn't now, hasn't been since 1924, when the first Labour government was appointed and the Prime Minister of the day said to the King: 'I haven't got a suitable person to be your Lord Chamberlain.' So it ceased to be political and— Lord, golly, I can't remember now which Lord Chamberlain it was—but whoever it was said: 'Look, is this right that the Lord Chamberlain should go on being the censor of plays when he's no longer a political appointment?'

So it became an anomaly in 1924?

Yes, from 1924 onwards it was really a total anomaly, except nobody else wanted to do it, so whenever a Lord Chamberlain approached the Home Secretary and said: 'Look, what about this?' they said: 'No, old boy, you carry on, you're doing a very good job.' They didn't want to know.

But what about successive monarchs, what did they feel about it?

I think they felt rather sorry for him, certainly the Queen did. The Lord Chamberlain wasn't, as it were, wearing his royal hat when he was censoring plays, and he didn't have to refer anything to the Queen. He was the censor.

What happened: I'm a playwright and I send a play to the Lord Chamberlain's office?

You sent a play with a fee which the Act said you had to do—I think it was something like one guinea for a one-acter, two guineas for a two- or three-act play—and it went straight to one of the play readers: they were called 'Examiners of Plays'. They would read the play, write a synopsis of the play and would draw the Lord Chamberlain's attention to anything they thought might not be allowed. I mean, ninety per cent had nothing—just said: 'Recommended for Licence'.

Then it went straight to the Lord Chamberlain to initial it and a licence was given. Or a letter would go back to the writer saying you will get a licence, but I'm afraid you've got to take this word out or that little bit of business has got to be changed.

And would there be a discussion between you as the Assistant Comptroller and the Lord Chamberlain?

Yes, it was the Reader to the Assistant Comptroller to the Lord Chamberlain, and there could be discussions between those three. And then they would write and say: 'Can you come and talk about it?'

This must have had a considerable potential for high comedy?

Yes, particularly if you've got someone like Bernard Miles, who would draw up a settee and say: 'I will now give you a demonstration of what I intend to do.'

But would you sit and talk about smutty words and whether one word was smuttier than another?

Yes. Well, the yardstick that Lord Cobbold [Lord Chamberlain] suggested to me was: if you see in a script a word that you would not expect to hear in someone's drawing room, well, they ought to think again about it. But then, of course, if the play was set in a coalmine or in a pub, or somewhere like that where drawing-room language is not used, you get into difficulty.

Did you ever have discussions where people proposed euphemisms to you?

We bent over backwards to try and give way where we could but had to hold the line somewhere, because otherwise if we said: 'Well, it's fine in this play, it's absolutely right that this word should be used, or that piece of business,' then we'd be quoted, and some other author would come along and say: 'But you allowed this in so-and-so's play.'

Was 'bloody' allowed?

One said 'bloody' wasn't allowed, and then it obviously was. I don't think the familiar four-letter word beginning with 'F' was ever allowed. I can't remember about 'bugger', I think it might have been towards the end in certain circumstances. You get into difficulty over words like 'bugger'. It's a term of endearment in Yorkshire. If the play was set in Yorkshire, a Yorkshireman would refer to the Pope as 'a dear old bugger', in a nice, friendly, loving way. There was another one—I can't remember the name of the play—but the inevitable four-letter word kept on appearing. It was being spoken in a Worcestershire accent, so the author said: if it was written in the script as 'firk', would that be allowed?

Yes, we said. But language didn't create so much of a problem as some of the other things.

Religion?

Well, that did—representations of the deity. Before my time it was very straightforward, the Church were against it except, of course, for morality plays and miracle plays, and so we had the support of the Church. Then there came occasions when maybe it was a bit less than total—what's the word—prohibition. So it became much more flexible. Indecency was never really a great problem because nudes were allowed in the Windmill, and the nudes were okay if they were static and didn't move. But a girl taking off her clothes in a play was not allowed because she obviously couldn't take off her clothes and remain static.

What about homosexuality?

Yes, well, until the Wolfenden Report that was a total ban, that's the word I've been trying to think of: ban, total ban. Then when Wolfenden said it was okay, as it were, it was no great problem.

Wolfenden was '57, wasn't it? After that it would just be under the general prohibition of indecency?

Yes, exactly, you could refer to it, whereas before you couldn't say that A and B were homosexuals or there was a homosexual relationship or whatever.

What about divorce and adultery?

No problem.

Royalty?

Royalty, well, representation of royalty and living persons was not allowed. I think that plays about Queen Victoria in the thirties were allowed because it was a hundred years since her birth. We had problems with *Crown Matrimonial*, but that was eventually allowed.

Because it was completely uncritical of the Royal Family.

That's right. There were various guidelines that the Lord Chamberlain followed, but he didn't invent these guidelines. There was a government committee in 1909 which made various recommendations.

Including a prohibition against showing living persons on stage. But probably some of that was driven by politicians wishing to protect their reputations.

Well, it included politicians, of course, but I don't think it was necessarily directed at politicians.

But there was a perfectly good libel law, so why did it need the belt and braces of the Chamberlain?

Good question. I've no idea. I suppose he was just trying to do the protection before it got to the point of a libel action. I mean, if it was you who was represented on the stage, it was in your interest, he said. Otherwise you'd have to go the course of the law, through the courts, to protect yourself. I think he was trying to protect you.

Very generous of him. I rather suspect that this was a legacy of Walpole's 1737 Act.

Well, you might be right. I wouldn't come down on one side or the other there.

Did you ever have to consider not granting a licence to a play on grounds of representation of living people?

Yes. What was the play called where Churchill—

Oh, Soldiers [*by Rolf Hochhuth*].

Soldiers. Ah yes. Sikorski and Churchill. That wasn't given a licence as far as I can recall.

It was going to be done at the National Theatre by Laurence Olivier but the board stepped in to stop it. Of course, the fact that it didn't get a licence made their case for them. [It was eventually presented in the West End by Kenneth Tynan.] What about diplomacy?

Yes, offending foreign countries. Again, sometimes we'd take advice from the Foreign Office. Reading back through the old papers there was much more of that in the earlier days. They were terribly afraid of upsetting the Emperor of Japan or whatever if something... Gilbert and Sullivan, *The Mikado,* I'm thinking of.

And what about what we'd now call 'political correctness'? Did you ever encounter something where you thought: well, this doesn't actually use words that are on our proscribed list but on the other hand it displays people in an unacceptable light? I'm thinking of racial prejudice?

No, I don't think so, no.

Or class prejudice? When Noël Coward's play The Vortex *was passed in front of the Lord Chamberlain in 1924, the Lord Chamberlain objected that it was portraying the upper class in a bad light. Were you ever conscious of that in your time?*

No, probably not. I was only involved from 1964 to 1968, when it all ended. Though admittedly there were quite a few controversial plays in that time, and there were prosecutions when the Royal Court were taken to court.

Over Early Morning? *What happened then?*

They were found guilty, and they were fined fifty guineas or something. It was a bit of a storm in a teacup, I think, but in a way, looking back, occasions like that were quite helpful because it brought into the public eye how rather silly it was that we were going on censoring plays in the way we were—or had to because we were merely carrying out the law—and so it made it easier to bring on the end.

Index

Index

Bold numbers indicate interviews with the subjects